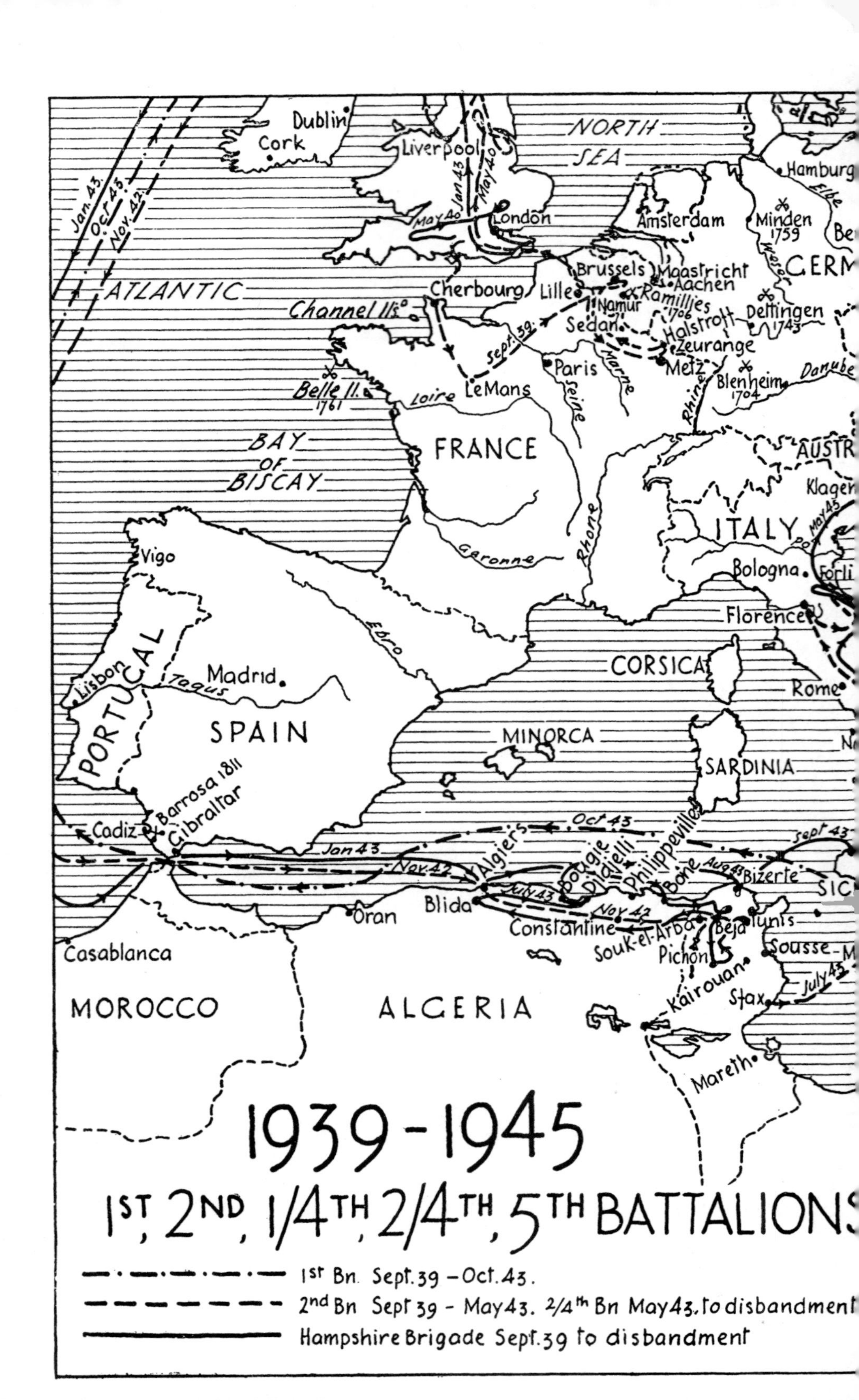

Dublin
Cork
Liverpool
NORTH SEA
Hamburg
London
Amsterdam
Minden 1759
ATLANTIC
Jan. 43
Oct. 43
Nov. 42
May 40
Jan 43
Brussels
Maastricht
Aachen
Cherbourg
Lille
Ramillies 1706
Namur
Sedan
Halstrott
Dettingen 1743
Channel Is.
Sept. 39
Zeurange
Metz
Paris
Seine
Marne
Rhine
Blenheim 1704
Danube
Belle Il. 1761
Loire
LeMans
FRANCE
BAY OF BISCAY
Klagen
ITALY
Po
May 45
Garonne
Rhone
Vigo
Bologna
Forli
Ebro
Florence
PORTUGAL
Lisbon
Madrid
Tagus
CORSICA
Rome
SPAIN
MINORCA
SARDINIA
Barrosa 1811
Gibraltar
Cadiz
Oct 43
Sept 43
Jan 43
Nov. 42
Algiers
Bougie
Djidjelli
Philippeville
Bone
Aug 43
Bizerte
July 43
Blida
Oran
Nov 42
Constantine
Souk-el-Arba
Beja
Tunis
Casablanca
Pichon
Sousse
Kairouan
Sfax
July 43
MOROCCO
ALGERIA
Mareth
1939-1945
1ST, 2ND, 1/4TH, 2/4TH, 5TH BATTALIONS
1st Bn. Sept. 39 – Oct. 43.
2nd Bn Sept 39 - May 43. 2/4th Bn May 43. to disbandment
Hampshire Brigade Sept. 39 to disbandment

U.S.S.R
Kharkov
Stalingrad
Volga
Don
Kiev
Dnieper
Vistula
Warsaw
POLAND
Bug
Dniester
OVAKIA
Budapest
NGARY
RUMANIA
BLACK SEA
Bucharest
Belgrade
Danube
GOSLAVIA
BULGARIA
Sofia
Istanbul
Izmid
TURKEY
Brindisi
Yannina
Dec.44
Khalkis
Ionian Isles 1836
Athens
Argos
Sparta
Jan.45
May 45
Canae
CRETE
CYPRUS
SYRIA
Homs
Baalbek
Beirut
May 44
Haifa
Tel Aviv
Jerusalem
July 43
Mar. 44
Feb.41.-Mar.43
Jun 44
Alexandria
Port Said
Tobruk
Buq Buq
El Daba
Benghazi
Matruh
El Alamein
Cairo
Suez
Akaba
May 43
CYRENAICA
YA
EGYPT
DEAD SEA
Nile
SCALE MILES
100 0 100 200 300 400 500

THE ROYAL HAMPSHIRE REGIMENT

GENERAL SIR RICHARD C. B. HAKING, G.B.E., K.C.B., K.C.M.G.
Colonel of the Royal Hampshire Regiment, 1924-1945

Frontispiece

REGIMENTAL HISTORY

THE ROYAL HAMPSHIRE REGIMENT

VOLUME THREE

1918-1954

BY

DAVID SCOTT DANIELL

WITH A FOREWORD BY

LIEUTENANT-GENERAL SIR FREDERICK A. M. BROWNING, K.C.V.O., K.B.E., C.B., D.S.O.

First Published 1955

TO THE MEMORY OF

ALL MEMBERS OF THE ROYAL HAMPSHIRE REGIMENT

WHO HAVE FALLEN IN ITS SERVICE

AND OF

GENERAL SIR RICHARD C. B. HAKING

G.B.E., K.C.B., K.C.M.G.

COLONEL OF THE REGIMENT, 1924-1945

FOREWORD

BY LIEUTENANT-GENERAL SIR FREDERICK A. M. BROWNING,
K.C.V.O., K.B.E., C.B., D.S.O.

THIS is the third volume of the History of the Royal Hampshire Regiment, and it covers the period from 1918 to 1954. It is mainly concerned, therefore, with the last war, in which the Regiment put six battalions in the field and lost more than two thousand officers and men killed.

It is indeed a story of which the Regiment may be proud, for one or more of the Hampshire battalions took part in nearly all the important campaigns in North Africa, Italy and North-West Europe ; and they all served with distinction and won honour for the Regiment.

The 1st Battalion served in Malta during the historic siege, and afterwards took part in the assault landing in Sicily. A year later they made another assault landing, on the right of the British line on the Normandy beaches. The 2nd Battalion went to France with the British Expeditionary Force and came out through Dunkirk in excellent order with only one man missing. They won signal honour at the battle of Tebourba, later serving in Italy with the 128th Brigade.

The 2/4th Battalion at Cassino and in the Gothic Line, and the 7th in Normandy and Holland, matched their fellow battalions in hard fighting and high morale. But my particular interest was centred, naturally enough, on the 128th (Hampshire) Brigade, which I commanded for twelve months in England when it formed part of the 43rd (Wessex) Division. In North Africa these three Hampshire Battalions showed their quality at Sidi Nsir and Hunts Gap, at Pichon and at Bou Arada. With the 2nd Battalion in the Brigade in place of the 2/4th, which had been split for special service with Beach Groups, 128th Brigade landed on the beaches at Salerno as the assault brigade of the 46th Division. The three battalions fought at the many river crossings, and in the mountains where, on Mounts Ornito and Cerasola, the 5th Battalion greatly distinguished itself. With the 2/4th re-formed, the Brigade fought through the Gothic Line and ended up at Forli.

The record of the Royal Hampshire Regiment in the last war was most distinguished, and I cannot do better than repeat the words used by General Lord Jeffreys in his Foreword to the first volume: "I trust that this long story of good and faithful service under all conditions, and especially of gallant deeds in war, may inspire future Hampshire soldiers to emulate, and even to surpass, the achievements of their predecessors."

F. A. M. Browning

27th December, 1954 — *Lieut.-General* (*Rtd.*)

CONTENTS

Current Officer's Cap Badge

ILLUSTRATIONS

MAPS

Other Rank's Cap Badge

PREFACE

THE writing of this, the third volume of the history of The Royal Hampshire Regiment, has only been possible through the willing assistance of many members of the Regiment. So many people have helped by correcting and adding material to the draft chapters, and by sending personal narratives, letters and diaries, that it is not possible to give all their names. I would like to assure them that whatever may be good in this book is due to their painstaking help.

Two officers of the Regiment must, however, be mentioned: Major H. J. Jeffery and Major P. R. Sawyer. Major Jeffery, Secretary of the Regimental Committee, saw the first two volumes through and then, well knowing all the hard work it entailed, embarked on the task of supervising the preparation of the third. He is the most enthusiastic, thorough and patient of collaborators. Major Sawyer not only proved himself to be an expert on everything connected with the campaign of the 5th Battalion, but he undertook to draw all the maps, taking infinite pains over that exacting task.

Above all I am grateful to Brigadier Cadoux-Hudson, then the Colonel of the Regiment, and to the Regimental Committee, for entrusting me with the writing of this book. The story of the Hampshire battalions in the 1939-1945 war is so full of action and gallantry that writing it down has been a most inspiring task. It is, I suppose, impossible to write a perfect regimental history of modern times; there are inevitable inequalities in the material, and everything is too near to obtain the true perspective. Some individual acts of gallantry must have gone unrecorded in the history because they were not recorded at the time. Moreover, when a regiment, as in this case, puts as many as six battalions in the field, and when these battalions are so often selected by commanders for especially important battle-duty, the historian tends to become bewildered by the abundance of material.

The book gives most space, of course, to the years of war, and in these it deals mainly with the fighting battalions. For the peace-time periods, the Digests of Service and the Regimental Journals have been used. The principal sources of information for the war period have been the War Diaries and the Battalion News-Letters. The books which have been mainly used are: *A Short History of 21 Army Group*, by Hugh Darby and Marcus Cunliffe; *The Fourth Division*, 1939 to 1945, by Hugh Williamson; *The 43rd Wessex Division at War*, 1944-1945, by Major-General H. Essame; *The Story of the 46th Division*, 1939-1945; *Club Route, The Story of 30 Corps in the European Campaign*, by Ronald Gill and John Groves; *The Campaign in Italy*, by Eric Linklater; *Three Assault Landings*, by Lieutenant-Colonel A. E. C. Breden; *Malta Strikes Back*, by Major R. T. Gilchrist; and the Reports of the Supreme Allied Commanders.

D. S. D.

EASTER, 1954

CHAPTER I

THE HAMPSHIRE REGIMENT
1919–1924

On 1st January, 1920, the 1st Battalion The Hampshire Regiment, on parade with Drums and Colours at Portsmouth, heard the gun-fire of a Royal Salute as *Renown* steamed into the harbour. The occasion was the return of H.R.H. The Prince of Wales from Canada and America, and it is indeed a fitting beginning for our story. There were the Colours, and there was gun-fire. There was to be gun-fire in abundance in the next thirty-two years, though no one then could have imagined it, and the Colours, already heavy with Honours, were to be honoured again, in Malta, North Africa, Sicily ; in Italy, Greece; and in North-West Europe. But all that was hidden in the future on that first day of January, 1920, as the 1st Hampshire received with a Royal Salute the Prince of Wales and Prince Albert.

The period immediately after a war has always been difficult for the British Army, and after the peace of 1919 there came lean years indeed. The King's enemies had been defeated, but now the bills had to be paid. The great boom in trade which had quickly flared up was as quickly dying down, and economic difficulties were crowding on the country. The nation was grateful to her soldiers, and proud of their victory, but economy was the order of the day and, as usual, the first to suffer were the fighting Services.

The Hampshire Regiment, perhaps through its traditional virility, weathered the storms of the lean years better than many others. Equipment might be short, flags might have to represent weapons and troops on manœuvres, the "Geddes Axe" might fall savagely on officers, young and old alike, and on the men, but the battalions survived cheerfully and carried on. They trained, worked and played with a zest which stood them in very good stead. Their spirit was shown in their record in recruiting in their five Territorial battalions and in their distinctions in sport.

The war had ended on 11th November, 1918, and the 1st and 2nd Battalions were re-formed at Catterick in October, 1919, and the 1st moved to Gosport on 4th November. Ten days later the 2nd Battalion left Catterick for Ireland to keep the King's peace in the tragic and most unhappy civil troubles which were tormenting that country. In March, 1920, the 1st Battalion left Gosport to go to Turkey, on the delicate mission of attempting to implement the Treaty of Sèvres with the Black Sea Army. Twenty-three years were to pass before the 1st Hampshire returned to England, and then it was only for a training interlude between the invasion of Sicily and the invasion of Normandy.

Five Territorial battalions were re-established in the first six months of 1920: the 4th, 5th, 6th (Duke of Connaught's Own), the 7th and the 8th (Princess Beatrice's) Isle of Wight Rifles. Against the stream of public opinion, which seemed to believe in perpetual peace and constant pleasure, young men drilled and trained, marched and shot with devotion to what seemed to be an out-dated cause. It was an example of the enthusiasm and dedication which had been so often made manifest in the past two hundred years, and which was to be demonstrated again in the thirty years to come.

I—1st Battalion: Turkey and Egypt, 1920–1924

In the years between the wars, sport played a very large part in the life of the Regiment, and in shooting, boxing, football and athletics the battalions won many distinctions. As early in the post-war period as 1920, the 1st Battalion played in the final of the Army Cup at Aldershot against the R.A.M.C. It was a notable occasion. Their Majesties The King and Queen were present

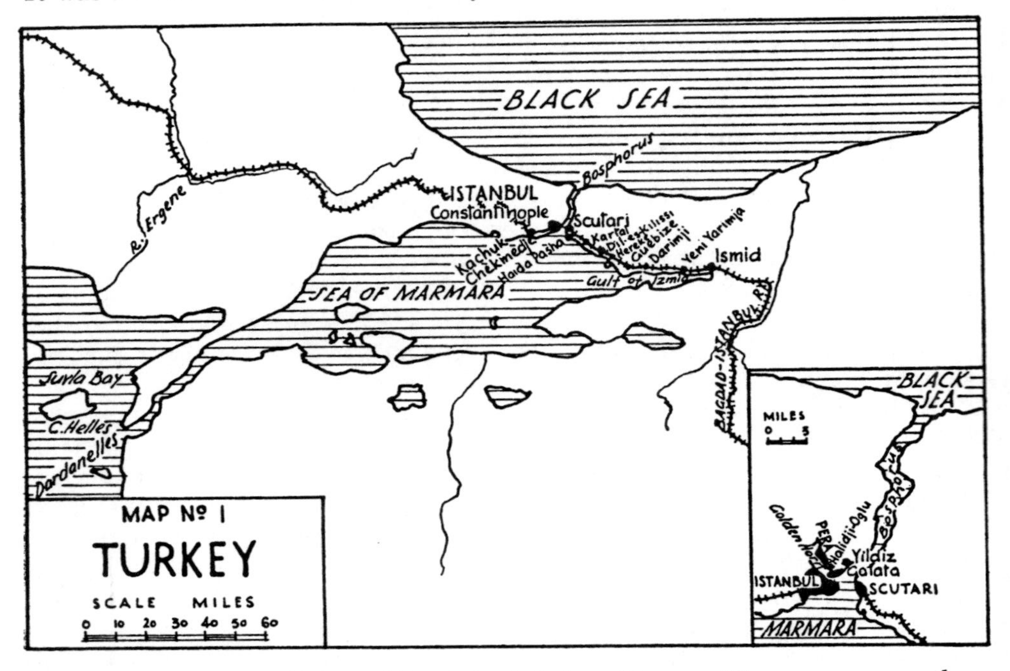

with Princess Mary, Prince Albert, and Prince Henry. There was an enthusiastic crowd of twelve thousand. The game was fast and play was of a high standard, and resulted in the R.A.M.C. winning 1—0. This was the first competition for the Army Cup since the war, and although the Hampshire Battalion lost, they had achieved the distinction of playing in the last Army Cup final before the war and in the first one afterwards.

On 30th March the 1st Battalion sailed from Devonport in H.T. *Czar* for Constantinople to join the Army of the Black Sea. Lieutenant-Colonel Andrews was promoted from the 2nd Battalion to command the 1st, in the place of Colonel Barlow, retired, with Major Wymer as his Second-in-Command. Other senior officers included Brevet Lieutenant-Colonel Earle and Major H. G. F. Frisby. Most of the officers and senior N.C.Os. were veterans of the war. Indeed, the thirty-six officers included one V.C. (Lieutenant M. S. S. Moore), five D.S.Os., eight M.Cs. and two D.C.Ms. The majority of the troops, however, were unseasoned short-service men, raw material indeed to go thus on active service. Gradually they were moulded into a really fine and happy family, and within three years the all-round reputation of the Battalion was very high.

The voyage was uneventful and at midday on 7th April the *Czar* sailed slowly past "W" Beach at Gallipoli, and the Battalion paid silent tribute to their gallant comrades of the 2nd Hampshire, so many of whom had given their lives on that historic beach in 1915. On 9th April the *Czar* arrived at Istanbul and the Battalion marched with fixed bayonets through Galata to their billets, the Turkish Artillery School at Halidji-Oglu on the Golden Horn. It was part of the 83rd Infantry Brigade, commanded by Brigadier-General Shuttleworth, in the 28th Division, commanded by Major-General Croker.

The task of the Army of the Black Sea was a difficult one. The Turks had risen in revolt under Mustapha Kemel against the peace treaty which had given the Greeks a rich share of Turkish territory. The political situation in Asia Minor was bad enough, but it was aggravated by the presence of Bolshevik Russia to the north. The thankless and, as it turned out, unsuccessful purpose of the Army of the Black Sea was to keep the peace and support the treaty. The situation was complicated by many other political cross-currents, and the soldiers were in that difficult position which always goes with other people's civil wars, of not knowing clearly who was the enemy, and of being constantly frustrated by orders and counter-orders from the political experts.

The 1st Battalion spent twenty-three months in Turkey and although they were moved about a great deal and came in for the usual duties of such work—patrols, curfew observance, the rounding-up of wanted men and even on one occasion a firing party—it was an unsatisfactory kind of soldiering. The climate was one of extremes, and there was considerable malaria.

The barracks at Halidji-Oglu were extremely dirty and smelly, and the only virtue seemed to be that real Turkish baths were available. The parade ground reached straight on to the Golden Horn. It was a noisy place and particular disturbance was caused by the steam sirens of the ferry-boats and the piercing siren of a factory. Unofficial action was taken to deal with this problem by some of the younger officers and, indeed, there is a siren, nicely polished, on view at the Depot in Winchester. High spirits were very often evident and there was one occasion when Lieutenant Moore, V.C., had to explain why he had draped a red carpet on the top of a local minaret !

Soon after the Battalion arrived at Constantinople it was decided to form a small force of mounted infantry from the British battalions in the area. The force was to be divided into two separate units, the Anatolian M.I. and the Thracean M.I. There were six platoons, and each battalion provided one of twenty-eight N.C.Os. and men, and a proportion of officers.

In June the Battalion moved to the Gulf of Izmid, with the task of protecting the Istanbul–Baghdad railway from the forces of Mustapha Kemel. This meant that the Battalion was strung along the line in company detachments from Dil-Es-Kilissi to Yeni Yarimja. The railway line was patrolled constantly and a great number of sentry posts had to be manned. The duties were so heavy, and malaria took such a toll of the companies, that the men had a very trying time. They were lucky if they had one night out of four in bed. The only consolations in a very trying situation were the plentiful fruit and the wonderful bathing. The local population was very friendly, and the Commanding Officer was embarrassed by the conciliatory presents of flowers, fruit and fish sent to him by the villagers in the gulf.

The Battalion went back to Istanbul in the autumn of 1920 and took up quarters in the Yildiz barracks overlooking the Bosphorus. Their duty now was to provide a special guard over the Sultan, whose palace was across the road from the barracks. It was at Yildiz that the first real opportunity came to start any training, and the Battalion settled down to bring its large number of recently enlisted short-service men up to standard. Detachments went to the training camp at Kachuk Chekmedjè, and the officers were able to play a little rough polo and hunted with the Mashlak hounds. There was some cricket, some athletics, and the usual round of social life.

It was from Yildiz that the Battalion saw the pitiful spectacle of the remnants of General Wrangel's White Russian Army come drifting down the Bosphorus from the Black Sea, in little ships packed with starving people. Their plight was terrible indeed, and the men all willingly gave up a day's rations and a day's pay for the refugees. A number of the refugees were later allowed into Istanbul, and before long princes and princesses were running cafés and restaurants in Pera, the fashionable part of the city and, pathetically enough, they added considerably to the gaiety of the station.

It was soon found out that a number of Bolshevik spies had also got through with the refugees, and in due course the Battalion was given the task of assisting the Allied police in the arrest of certain Bolsheviks in the city. The round-up was carried out as a military operation at dawn on 28th June, 1921, and it was completely successful. It was made more difficult by the fact that a number of the wanted people were women, and considerable tact had to be used by subalterns whose duty it was to take them to prison.

There were the usual ceremonial parades, and guards of honour were found on various occasions. The Battalion was inspected by General Sir Aylmer Hunter-Weston, and the two Minden Days were suitably celebrated. Just before the Battalion embarked for Egypt at the end of 1921 it was inspected by the Commander-in-Chief, Lieutenant-General Sir Charles H. Harington. In his address he said :

"I have watched with great interest your Battalion building itself daily, bringing back the old tone and spirit which brought success after success to your Colours. The spirit and example which Colonel Andrews instils, the spirit between the officers and sergeants—as I witnessed in your Sergeants' Mess on Armistice night last, when Sergeant-Major Jeffery and the members of the Sergeants' Mess did me the honour of asking me to dinner—the spirit existing throughout all ranks cannot fail to reach the very highest standard, the standard I remember in the opening days of the war.

"Now, men, I want to say what I think of you for the help you have given to those unfortunate Russians in this city. I have been thirty years in the Army and I have never known a more humane act of kindness and self-sacrifice than that made by the 1st Battalion Hampshire Regiment, and I am proud to bring it to the notice of the Army Council, as I intend to do. It will always be very dear to me that it was my old friends, the 1st Battalion Hampshire Regiment, which stepped out to the front to lead the way in the cause of humanity, and I thank you all for it."

The 1st Hampshire sailed for Egypt on 16th December, 1921, in H.T. *Huntsend*. "C" Company disembarked at Cyprus, where it remained on detachment for two years, and the remainder of the Battalion disembarked at Alexandria on 21st December and entrained for Sidi Bishr, a desert station some seven miles east of Alexandria, where they relieved the 1/76th Punjabis.

The Battalion was brigaded with the 2nd Sherwood Foresters in the Alexandria Brigade, 10th Divisional Field Troops. The Brigade Commander was Colonel Commandant Braithwaite, and the Divisional Commander was Major-General Gathorne-Hardy. The G.O.C.-in-C., Egyptian Expeditionary Force, at the time was Lieutenant-General Sir W. N. Congreve, V.C. The Battalion also formed part of a mobile force which was to be used in the event of disturbances in Egypt. There was indeed a serious threat of civil unrest in the country at that time, Ireland having set the example.

The Alexandria Mobile Column was commanded by Lieutenant-Colonel Andrews, and consisted of the 1st Hampshire, with one section Pack Battery, R.F.A., an Armoured Car Section, a Signal Detachment, a Wireless Section, and a Detachment Field Ambulance. The Mobile Column trained for possible service and undertook brief manœuvres, but it was, in fact, not called upon in the five months the Battalion was at Sidi Bishr.

The hutments out in the desert at Sidi Bishr were not very comfortable quarters, although the men did the best they could to make themselves at home. Training of the three companies went on apace, and they underwent three inspections in as many weeks, by the Brigade Commander, the Commander-in-Chief, and the G.O.C., Field Troops, Egypt.

At the end of 1921 infantry battalions were reorganized on a five-company basis, a Headquarter Company being added, which was composed of the Machine Gun Section, the Transport Section, the Band, the Light Trench Mortar Section, the Anti-Aircraft Lewis Gun Section, and certain authorized regimental employees.

After five months of desert hutments at Sidi Bishr the Battalion moved in May, 1922, to more comfortable quarters at Mustapha Barracks in Alexandria. Here training continued busily, and there was increased activity in shooting and sport. On 15th June the Battalion furnished a guard of honour, with the King's Colour, on the occasion of the arrival of H.E. the High Commissioner, Field Marshal Lord Allenby. Another memorable guard of honour was furnished on 3rd January, 1924, after the Battalion had moved to Cairo. The occasion was a visit by Prince Arthur of Connaught to King Fuad of Egypt.

The move from Alexandria to Cairo took place on 26th November, 1923, when the Battalion took over the Citadel. "C" Company joined them from Cyprus and the Battalion was once more complete. The only criticism which has been recorded about the quarters in Cairo is the abundance of bugs found in the Citadel, calling for a determined and only partially successful anti-bug operation. By this time the Battalion was in really good fettle ; on the parade ground, at the range, in the boxing ring and on the sports field. In his farewell address, when the Battalion left Alexandria, the Brigade Commander had said :

"There are some men in this Battalion whom I have the greatest respect for and whenever I meet them I feel inclined to take off my hat to them. I see them regularly each evening in their running shorts, training and keeping themselves fit. They do this of their own free will and without any ostentation, and I admire those men very much indeed. I hope they set the example to the others in the way of keeping fit. But you men, I know, do keep yourselves very fit and this is another sure sign of your efficiency."

There was an important event in March, 1924, when a change in command came about. Lieutenant-Colonel Andrews' tenure of command expired, and he was succeeded by Lieutenant-Colonel R. S. Allen, D.S.O. Colonel Andrews had been a very popular Commanding Officer, and his service with the Regiment had begun as long ago as 1892 when he joined the 2nd Battalion at Cork. He received a very warm send-off from the railway station when the time came for him to go. His death in 1928 at the early age of fifty-one was very much lamented.

It was while the Battalion was at Cairo that a new form of training was undertaken for officers ; an activity which was viewed with some misgiving in those days. This was aeroplane reconnaissance. At a battalion tactical exercise the men were commanded by the warrant officers and N.C.Os. under the guidance of the Commanding Officer and Adjutant, while all the other officers viewed the operations from the air. They were distributed in threes among a flight of Vickers Vimy bombing planes. The operation was quite successful and, rather to the surprise of the gentlemen concerned, there were no casualties. In November, 1924, the Battalion took part in a very sad ceremonial parade as part of the escort at the funeral of the Sirdar, Major-General Sir Lee Stack, who had been assassinated in his car in Cairo by a fanatic. This murder of a much-respected administrator shocked the Empire, and there was considerable anxiety in Cairo lest it should be the signal for an outbreak of civil disturbance. To check any such possible trouble, the Battalion made a series of demonstration marches through the streets of Cairo with band playing and bayonets fixed.

While it was in Egypt the Battalion distinguished itself in shooting, and in both 1923 and 1924 it "swept the board" at the Command Rifle Meeting, winning the Congreve Cup for the best shooting unit. On the second occasion the Cup was presented by the G.O.C.-in-C., British Troops in Egypt, Lieutenant-

General Sir Richard Haking, G.B.E., K.C.B., K.C.M.G., a very happy ceremony as he had recently been appointed Colonel of the Regiment. In April of 1924 the Battalion were the winners in the Command Athletic Meeting, by a comfortable margin of points, and this success resulted in the award to the Battalion of the Cup for the best all-round unit in the very considerable Egyptian Command, the blue riband for sport in Egypt.

The Battalion's tour of duty in Egypt drew to a close, and the first sign of the coming move was the news from Indian contractors that it was to go to Jubbulpore. The contractors were very definite in their information, and in due course it was proved to be true. On 10th January, 1925, the Battalion was inspected in line on the Citadel Square by Field-Marshal Viscount Allenby, the High Commissioner, accompanied by Lieutenant-General Sir Richard Haking.

On 17th January the Battalion left the Citadel, being played out by the pipers of the 2nd H.L.I. and the 1st Argyll and Sutherland Highlanders. The band of the 2nd Battalion The Duke of Wellington's Regiment took up in Opera Square and played the Battalion to the railway station. Here it entrained for Suez and embarked on the *City of Marseilles.* Lieutenant-Colonel Allen, D.S.O., was in command, and the strength was 24 officers, 827 other ranks, and 39 soldiers' families.

In spite of all the difficulties of soldiering in the years immediately after the war, the 1st Hampshire was in excellent condition, and it had brought itself as far as possible up to the pre-war standards. It seemed as they sailed towards Bombay that the unsettling effects of reorganizing the Battalion after the war were at last over, and that soldiering had once more settled down to the old familiar pattern.

II—2ND BATTALION: IRELAND AND BORDON, 1919–1924

The 2nd Battalion left for Ireland on 15th November, 1919, and for three years and one month they too were engaged in the most exacting and exasperating of peace-time duties, keeping the King's peace in the midst of bitter civil war. The task of the troops in Ireland was to assist the Royal Irish Constabulary in preserving order. The causes of the civil strife in Ireland were complicated, inspired by ancient resentment and prejudice which the English soldier could not be expected to understand. Moreover, the methods used by the insurgents—assassinations, ambushes and sudden murder—could not but antagonize and exasperate British troops.

The cause of the trouble was the activity of the Irish Republican Army, and the victims were in nearly every case quite innocent. A man in a raincoat skulking in an entrance to an alley-way would without warning shoot soldiers strolling together off duty on a Sunday afternoon. Bombs were thrown at lorries and cars and land mines were laid to murder troops on the march. The comrades of the victims could take no reprisals and only rarely were the murderers brought to justice. For three years the 2nd Battalion served in this tense and tragic atmosphere; it was an extremely severe test for discipline,

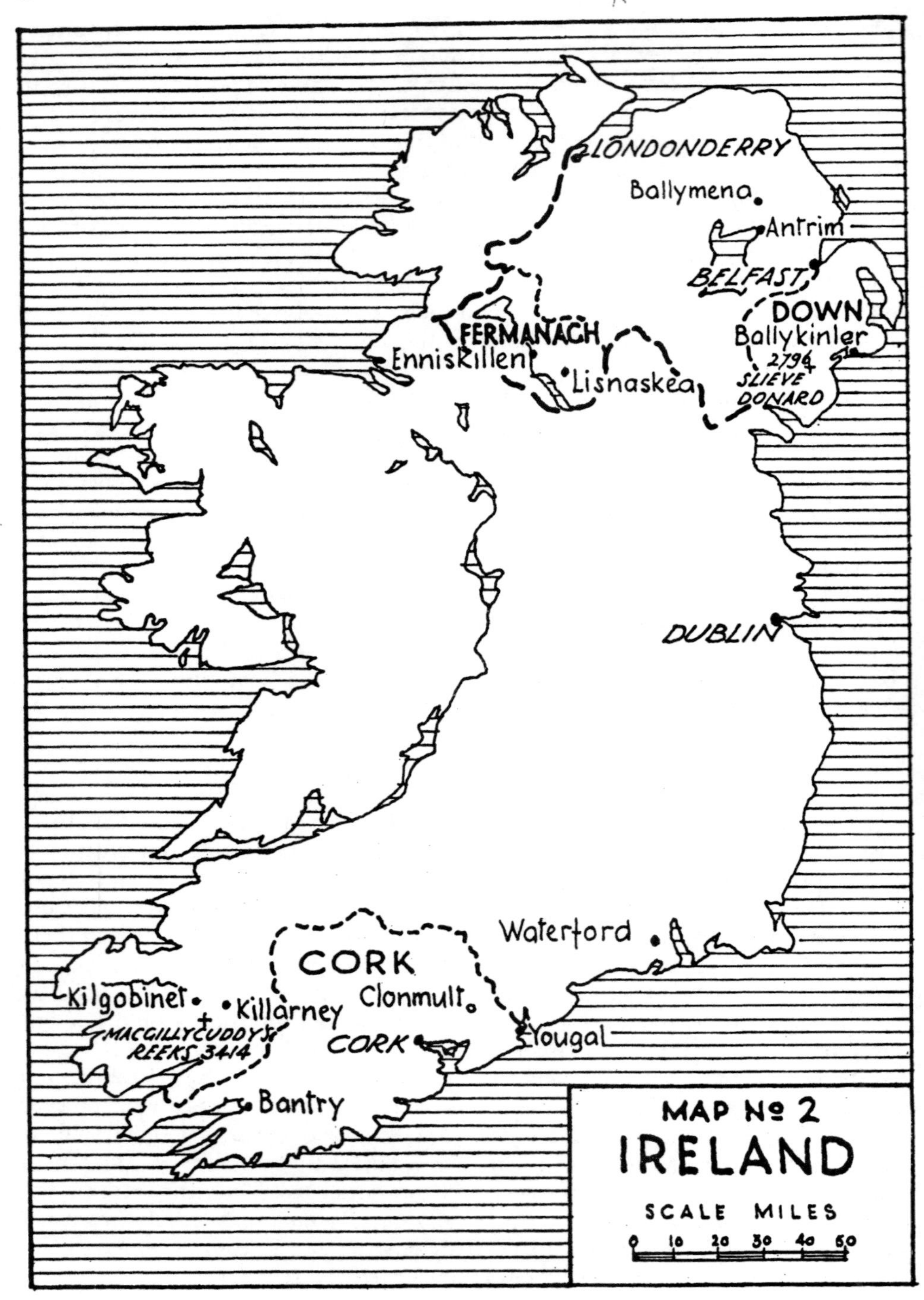
LONDONDERRY
Ballymena
Antrim
BELFAST
DOWN
Ballykinler
2796
SLIEVE
DONARD
FERMANAGH
Enniskillen
Lisnaskea
DUBLIN
Waterford
CORK
Clonmult
Kilgobinet
Killarney
MACGILLYCUDDY'S
REEKS 3414
CORK
Yougal
Bantry
MAP No 2
IRELAND
SCALE MILES
0 10 20 30 40 50

but they had the quality which could sustain them, sorely tried though they were, and the Battalion won high praise for its conduct.

The Battalion, commanded by Lieutenant-Colonel C. N. French, was stationed at Cork for the first two and a half years in Ireland, in Victoria Barracks. There was much to do ; there were escort duties, patrols after curfew, the occasional excitement of hunting for wanted men and special operations when information, sometimes accurate but often not, was received about the whereabouts of I.R.A. leaders. It was dull duty and dangerous, but every opportunity for training, sport and social functions was taken, and morale remained good.

The nervous tension was extremely wearing ; no one knew when trouble was going to break out. The Sinn Feiners burned country houses—and as a reprisal the houses of prominent Sinn Feiners were destroyed on official instructions. The peace of a country stroll would be broken by a sudden ambush. The unexpected was the normal. No one knew who was friend or who was enemy. A typical example was when a lorry carrying engineer material to a near-by fort was ambushed in a street in the middle of Cork City. The escort, commanded by a lance-corporal, fought back so vigorously, despite the disadvantage of surprise and lack of cover, that it succeeded in beating off the attackers, although only after heavy casualties.

Inquiries showed that the street had been cleared of civilians by revolver shots only a few minutes before the attack. Clearly accurate information had been obtained beforehand, but from whom? A process of elimination centred suspicion on two civilian employees, both confidential clerks and ex-service men, but their records were clean and their employers confident of their integrity. Later, other incidents occurred, such as water being found in the petrol tank of the duty armoured car when it was required urgently to go to the help of an R.I.C. patrol which had been ambushed.

Some months later an R.I.C. patrol led by men of the Battalion discovered an arms dump and the Headquarters of the 3rd Mid-Cork Brigade in a cottage. A search yielded a mass of documents, among which were copies of the orders for every sentry and every sentry group in Cork Barracks, together with a large number of signed and stamped official blank passes for entering the barracks. These were directly traceable to the confidential clerk of the Garrison Adjutant, one of the two original suspects. He was dismissed and at the same time his house searched, but nothing was found except burnt paper in all the grates. He left the barracks protesting his innocence, only to be captured within a short time by a party of the Regiment as a member of a fully armed Active Service Unit surrounded at Rahinisky House near Cork.

Often hidden stores of arms were found in unlikely places, as when an officer giving instruction to a section in a country lane not two hundred yards from the barracks discovered two fully loaded revolvers hidden in the bank. A girl of fifteen was found carrying two revolvers and a Lewis gun, and a road-mine was set off under one of the Battalion lorries by two women. The majority of the civilians were innocent and exceedingly distressed at the whole business, but some of them, innocent in appearance and charmingly vehement when questioned, were ruthless murderers. There were ever-recurring raids on houses to capture wanted men, and on one occasion a party commanded by Captain Fowle arrested, on orders, the Lord Mayor of Cork. The discipline and the success of the Battalion in these very difficult conditions owed much to the organizing ability of the Adjutant, Captain Flint, who had served for three years as Adjutant of the 1st Battalion in the war.

One trick of the I.R.A. which was effectively turned against them was the burning of broken-down British Army lorries. To counter this the Battalion improvised a "trick" lorry on the lines of the "Q" ships of the war. A lorry was fitted with an armoured space with concealed loop-holes for men, and it was then camouflaged with a load of blankets. It was taken out and pretended to break down. The I.R.A. came up, and emptied the contents of the spare petrol tin over the lorry—it was in fact water—and then the Union Jack was run up over the driver's cab, the loop-holes were disclosed and the men waiting in the lorry went into action.

So it went on, this disagreeable and exasperating duty in Ireland, with the constant round of patrolling, guards, escort duty and raids on special objectives. One raid developed into something of a set battle. On 20th February, 1921, information was received that a much-wanted I.R.A. leader and his Active Service Unit were living in a farmhouse near Clonmult, a remote village in the east of County Cork. Within two hours a party of four officers and twenty-one other ranks left Cork for Clonmult, full information being given to the Royal Irish Constabulary. The journey by lorry was uneventful and at a point about a mile away from the objective an escort was left with the lorries and the attacking party, of four officers and twelve other ranks, was divided into two patrols and approached the farmhouse, where there were twenty-one armed men of the I.R.A. After some preliminary skirmishing the house was surrounded and the occupants were called on to surrender. They answered with shots and a couple of lines of a rebel song.

It was decided to force them to surrender by firing the house, and a car was sent to get bombs and petrol from the police. Meanwhile, occasional shots were fired by both sides. After two hours the party returned with some bombs and petrol, bringing with them a number of the Royal Irish Constabulary. The final attack on the house then commenced. Fire was opened on all windows in such volume that the enemy had no chance to reply, and under cover of this an officer got close to the wall and with a tin of petrol succeeded in firing the thatch. A few bombs were dropped into the house through the hole made by the fire and the enemy surrendered.

The cease-fire was at once ordered and the Sinn Feiners were told to come out with their hands up. Half a dozen of them appeared, and our men went forward across the farmyard to meet them, and they were immediately fired on from the house. The six who had surrendered then tried to rush the soldiers to get away, but they were shot. Then the remainder of the garrison came out pell-mell, and a confused fight began in the yard and in the fields around the house. When this was brought to an end, a count revealed thirteen I.R.A. dead and eight prisoners, a total of twenty-one, which was the strength laid down by the I.R.A. for an Active Service Unit. Thus the Crown forces had succeeded in wiping out completely the Active Service Unit of the 4th Battalion Mid-Cork Brigade of the I.R.A. In the circumstances it was a necessary task, but, like all the Irish operations, it was hateful to the British troops.

The Battalion had several men murdered while they were in Cork, but the worst outrage of all was undoubtedly at Youghal, on 31st May, 1921, when "X" Company and the band had gone to Youghal for a musketry course. On this particular morning the band was playing the company down to the range, and when they were about half a mile from their destination a land mine was fired. It had been placed against a substantial stone wall at the side of the road, and the moment chosen was when the fourth or fifth section of fours of the band was opposite the mine. When the clouds of dust settled, some twenty men and boys were seen lying on the ground, and pitiful groans and cries for help were heard. Two corporals, two bandsmen and three boys were killed and nineteen of the band were wounded.

At once the men of "X" Company, led by Captain Fowle, went off as fast as they could to try to capture the men who had fired the mine, but the terrain was against them and, although two men were seen by the flankers on the left, they got away. It was found that the mine had been detonated from a point sixty yards away, where the marching troops could be seen, and it was obvious that the mine was fired intentionally when the band was opposite to it. For the two previous weeks the band had played every day for the townsfolk of Youghal and it had been very popular; it had accordingly been marked down for destruction by the I.R.A. The behaviour of the dying and injured bandsmen was admirable. One corporal, although seriously wounded, threw himself on top of a band boy immediately after the explosion to protect him from the fire if it had been an ambush. The last words of another corporal, who was mortally wounded, were: "I'm no good now—see to the rest." Colonel French, Captain Fowle and Bandmaster Orbinski all had narrow escapes.

The anger of the troops at this outrage can well be imagined, and it was thought by some that it would be a sensible precaution to confine them to barracks for the time being, but Colonel French knew his men, and he made no restrictions. There were no incidents, and the men realized that the great majority of civilians were as horrified as they themselves. An example of the men's steadiness was the behaviour of the armed plain-clothing patrols. To protect troops off duty in Cork it was the custom at times of particular tension to send out twenty soldiers in plain clothes armed with revolvers, to be ready to deal with any sudden incident in the city. These men could easily have wreaked their own vengeance and, if an explanation had been necessary, they could have pleaded a mistake, or have said that the man they shot seemed to be about to use a revolver. But for all provocation given them, nothing like this ever happened. In 1922, Lieutenant-General Sir E. P. Strickland said in his address after inspecting the Battalion:

"My great anxiety during my period of command was not in connection with the ultimate solution of the Irish problem, but lest the troops, angered beyond endurance at what they had to suffer, should take the law into their own hands. Had this happened I should have been very angry, but I admit I should not have been surprised.

"As far as this Battalion is concerned, I am glad to be able to say that this anxiety was groundless and that though, in my opinion, no battalion in Ireland was more highly tried, the discipline of the Hampshire Regiment has been beyond praise and your restraint under the great provocation has been marvellous. Your behaviour has not only greatly eased my responsibilities, but has upheld the good name and honour of the British Army."

In June, 1922, the news, hoped for for a long time, of a move from Cork was received. There was a further tragedy before the Battalion left Cork, when Lieutenant G. R. A. Dove was kidnapped and murdered during the Truce which had been signed. Lieutenant Dove was out driving with three officers of other regiments and none of them was seen again. Their bodies were found eighteen months afterwards buried in a bog at Kilgobinet. There was no particular reason why these four young officers should have been murdered ; it was part of the pattern of service in Ireland at that time.

The last act of the Battalion on leaving Victoria Barracks was to cut down the flagstaff where the Union Jack had flown, and where it had so often been lowered in tribute to men of the Battalion.

The Battalion went by sea to Belfast and then on to Lisnaskea in County Fermanagh, where they were billeted in the workhouse. From there they moved to Ballykinler in County Down, and finally, on 16th December, 1922, to the delight of all ranks, they came home to Bordon, in the Aldershot Command. Here at last they could settle down to training and to the annual cycle of exercises and manœuvres which marked the years of peace-time soldiering, for the first time since 1914.

On 1st October, 1923, Lieutenant-Colonel French retired after four years in command. He had steered the 2nd Battalion through a very difficult period of its life since 1919, when standards might well have broken down under a less sympathetic or a less capable commander. He was succeeded by Lieutenant-Colonel L. C. Morley, who had, in fact, already been commanding the Battalion while Colonel French was at the War Office on special duties. Colonel Morley was a most popular officer. He had been wounded in Gallipoli with the 10th Battalion, and at the end of the war he had shown considerable enterprise in very difficult circumstances. He was serving in Siberia with a British Mission, with Russian and Czech troops at Omsk, and a friendly disposed senior Russian official warned him that the troops were going to mutiny and that the British had better look to their own safety. Morley promptly bought a train in exchange for a number of blankets and loaded it with the members of the British Mission and other British subjects, to the number of a hundred and thirty. The train then set off for Vladivostok, a hazardous journey which called for both nerve and *savoir faire*. They reached Vladivostok safely after a journey of a month and made their way home via Japan, Canada and Liverpool.

A memorable event in 1924 was the Royal Review in the Aldershot Command by H.M. King George V in June, held on Laffan's Plain, and the Battalion was posted in the centre of the First Division, exactly opposite the royal box. It was a great day for all who were privileged to be present at the Review and, as one of them remarked, "One's attention was, of course, drawn to the Colours, the honourably faded condition of which was distinctive among all those on parade. They were well carried and, as they passed the saluting base, broke in the breeze and floated fully extended over the ranks of 'X' Company."

III—The Territorial Battalions, 1920–1925

As early as the spring of 1920 all five Territorial battalions of the Regiment had been re-formed and, starting from scratch, rapidly built themselves up to what were, for those lean years of soldiering, highly commendable strengths. The 4th Battalion, which in March, 1920, could only show a strength of one private in addition to the permanent staff, could claim by May to possess more recruits than any other in the Wessex Division. This claim was promptly challenged by the 6th Battalion, and so, with healthy rivalry and much enthusiasm, they went on from strength to strength. By the beginning of 1922, to take one example, the 4th Battalion had 25 officers and 520 other ranks, and took more than 400 to camp.

There was an alarm of serious civil disturbance in April, 1921, and the 4th, 6th, and 7th Battalions were hastily embodied, renamed as battalions of the Hampshire Regiment Defence Force, and moved to Tidworth, where they stood by. But in a few weeks the situation became normal and the battalions reverted to their proper names and status.

Despite adverse conditions, then, the Hampshire Territorial battalions flourished ; they were busy in their local drill halls, at ceremonial parades and at camp. One important change was the merging in 1922 of the 5th and 7th into the 5/7th Battalion The Hampshire Regiment. At the beginning of 1925 the Commanding Officers were: 4th Battalion, Colonel F. L. Footner ; 5/7th, Lieutenant-Colonel R. F. Gutteridge ; 6th, Lieutenant-Colonel G. R. Curtis ; and 8th Battalion, Colonel A. C. T. Veasey. In May, 1920, Lieutenant-Colonel W. B. Stilwell had retired from commanding the 4th Battalion after twenty-five years' service.

IV—The Hampshire Regiment, 1920–1924

Thus did the Regiment adjust itself to the new era of peace-time soldiering after the high endeavour of the Great War. The war-time soldiers, who had become seasoned veterans in battle, returned to civilian life, and many of the regulars were time-expired. As so often in its past history, the Regiment had to start again, that indefinable quality which is the spirit of the Regiment persisting and inspiring other men towards an unbroken continuation of the past into the future. Many of the Regular officers and senior N.C.Os. were still with the

Colours, it was true, but for the greater part the men were new and unseasoned until, swiftly and naturally, they fell into the places of their unnumbered host of predecessors.

The Regiment was grieved to learn, on 29th July, 1924, of the death of the Colonel, Major-General Sir Charles B. Knowles, K.C.B., at the age of eighty-eight. General Knowles had served in the Crimean War with the 77th Regiment, and he was first posted to the 67th Regiment in 1863, rising to command it from August, 1877, until 1882, and leading it throughout the Afghan War. He became Colonel of the Regiment in 1908. As a Battalion Commander he showed the finest qualities, and an officer who served under him wrote :

"General Knowles was the strongest Commanding Officer a Regiment could have. He allowed no slackness from anybody of any rank under his command ; and he was loved as well as respected by all ranks. The men were particularly proud and fond of him and would follow him anywhere."

Another tribute shows the manner of man General Knowles was :

"For sixteen years the grand old veteran has closely identified himself with our Regiment, whose well-being he had so much at heart. He was the *beau idéal* of a Commanding Officer. Major-General Sir Charles B. Knowles, K.C.B., Colonel of the Hampshire Regiment, stood no nonsense, and played the game fair and square with everybody. We regret his loss, but to those who knew him, his loving personality will be unforgettable."

The new Colonel was Lieutenant-General Sir Richard C. B. Haking, G.B.E., K.C.B., K.C.M.G., who was at the time of his appointment commanding British Troops in Egypt. General Sir Richard Haking had joined the 67th Foot in 1881 and he was in every way an eminently appropriate and popular successor to General Knowles.

In the years immediately following the war there were, of course, a number of ceremonies connected with the unveiling of war memorials, and the Regiment provided guards of honour and detachments at many where they were directly or indirectly concerned. The 1st and 2nd Battalions had special memorials made to their own officers killed in the 1914–1918 war, in the form of silver tiger centre-pieces for the Mess tables. Each consists of a large tiger modelled in silver, on a black plinth. At the side the names of the officers are engraved on a silver plate, and at the front is a silver Regimental badge with, beneath it, FIRST (*or* SECOND) BATTALION THE HAMPSHIRE REGIMENT—IN MEMORIAM 1914–1918. These handsome memorials were made specially and paid for by private subscription. Another memorial is displayed in the Sergeants' Mess every year on the anniversary of the Gallipoli landing. This is an exact replica of one of the lighters used by the Hampshire men at Gallipoli, made from a block of wood cut from the actual wreck. This is kept in an ebony, silver and glass case, illuminated by internal lighting.

A new idea, and one which has proved to be very successful, came into force in January, 1925, when the Regiment was allied officially with the Wellington West Coast Regiment of New Zealand. It was a happy arrangement, and it was followed later in alliances between the Regiment and other Commonwealth units.

CHAPTER II

THE 1ST BATTALION
1925–1939

I—INDIA, 1925–1938

THE 1st Battalion disembarked at Bombay on 28th January, 1925, and settled down at Jubbulpore, on the ridge about two miles from the cantonment. Thus began a tour of duty in India to last thirteen years, taking them from the optimistic days when men dreamed of universal peace to the sharp international tension of 1938 ; from the days when soldiers were considered an expensive luxury to those when the Services had once more come into their own. In the splendid training ground of India, especially in their periods of active service in the Punjab hills, and under Lieutenant-Colonel Ramsden at Rawalpindi towards the end of their tour, the Battalion won a high reputation.

Thirteen years is not, perhaps, long in the life of a regiment, but it is an important slice in the lives of the members of the battalions. The 1st Battalion had four Commanding Officers in this time, and there were many changes in officers and men, through retirements and postings. There were many promotions, too, and the Digest of Service records the posting-in of several Second-Lieutenants who were to command battalions in action in the Second World War.

Until 1935 the Battalion led the average life of a British regiment on a routine Indian tour, training hard and playing hard, with intervals of internal-security duties. The tour reached its climax in the Frontier operations of 1935 in the Mohmand country, and in those of 1936–1937 in the Khaisora valley of Waziristan against the followers of the Faqir of Ipi. The time at Razmak, when the Battalion was frequently on column in Mahsud and Wazir country, was nevertheless a period when the Waziristan tribes were quiet. It was not until the end of the Battalion's Indian tour was in sight that the much-prized opportunity of participation in a Frontier expedition arrived, with its hall-mark of a Frontier medal. From 1935 onwards opportunities for "collecting" campaign medals came thick and fast, so that the 1st Battalion could claim that from 1935 until 1945, for a period of some months in each of those ten years, it was in the field against His Majesty's enemies.

In 1935 the Battalion gained the Indian General Service Medal with clasp "N.W. Frontier 1935", and the next year the new 1936 Indian General Service Medal with clasp "N.W. Frontier 1936-1937". This gave the Battalion the distinction, rare among British units, of having the last of the famous old 1907 I.G.S. Medal and the first of its 1936 successor. Only one other British battalion achieved the two campaign medals in successive years, the 1st Argyll and Sutherland Highlanders, who served alongside the 1st Hampshire in Rawalpindi. This distinction was augmented when the Battalion went to Palestine in 1938, for its service there was recognized by the award of the British General

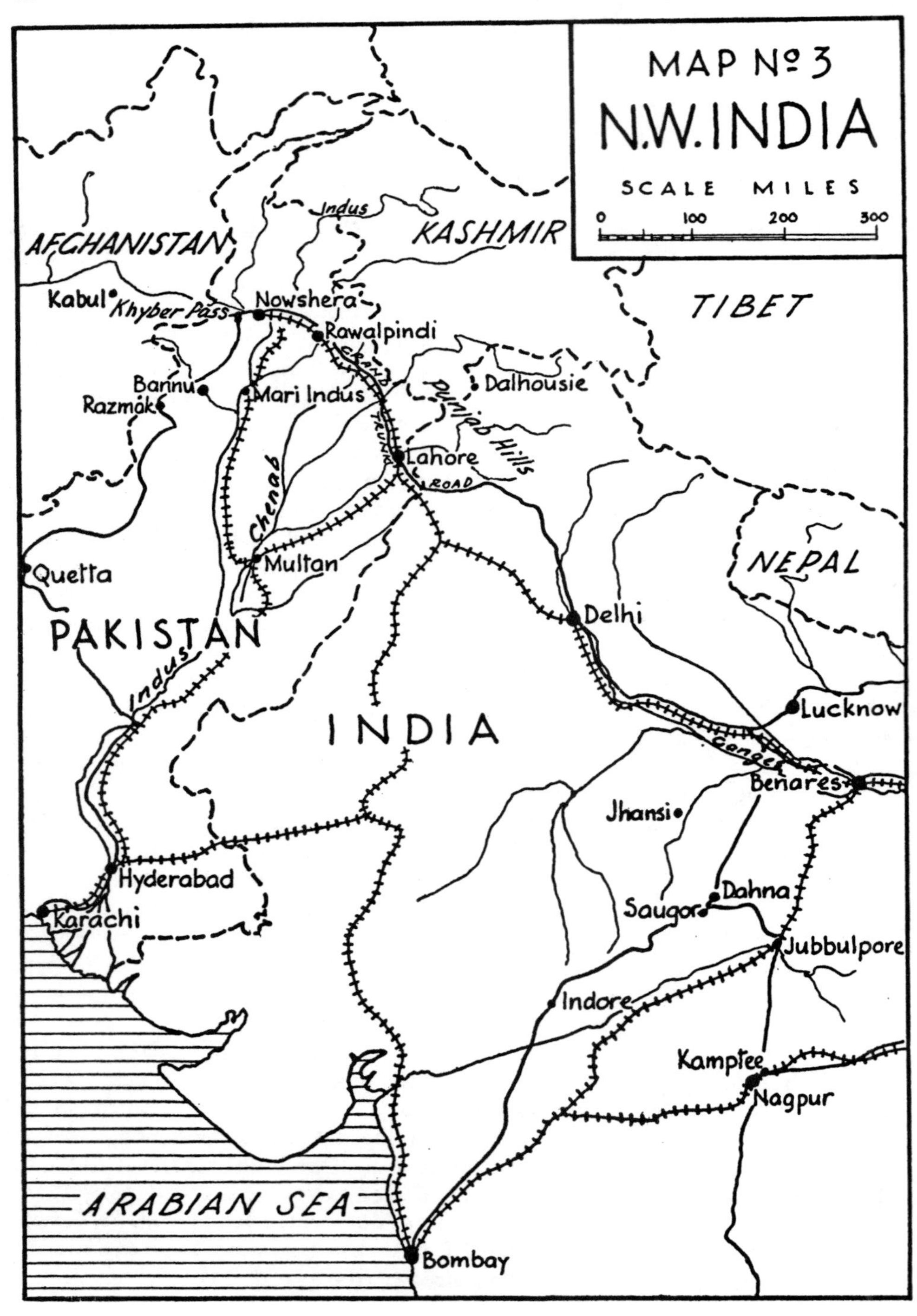
MAP No 3
N.W. INDIA
SCALE MILES
0
100
200
300
AFGHANISTAN
KASHMIR
TIBET
Indus
Kabul
Khyber Pass
Nowshera
Rawalpindi
Bannu
Razmak
Mari Indus
Dalhousie
Punjab Hills
Lahore
ROAD
Chenab
Quetta
Multan
NEPAL
PAKISTAN
Indus
Delhi
Lucknow
INDIA
Ganges
Benares
Jhansi
Hyderabad
Karachi
Dahna
Saugor
Jubbulpore
Indore
Kamptee
Nagpur
ARABIAN SEA
Bombay

Service Medal with clasp "Palestine". Thus a General Service Medal was gained in each of the three years immediately preceding the war, a unique "hat trick."

The first ten years of the Battalion's Indian tour, leading up to three very active years on the Frontier and in Palestine, were comparatively serene, and if it was later felt that full opportunity did not present itself for training, the Battalion gained considerable success in sport of every kind. There was, of course, the succession of formal parades: Proclamation Day, Armistice Day, the solemn ceremony at the death of King George V, the parades to mark the accessions of King Edward VIII and King George VI, and inspections in their seasons. On 20th September, 1925, the Colour was trooped for the first time since its presentation by H.R.H. Princess Beatrice in 1907. The occasion was the Minden Day celebration, postponed because of the monsoon, and the ceremony on the Rains Polo Ground at Jubbulpore was watched by a large crowd. The Colour was trooped again in September, 1926, and in January, 1927, as a demonstration at the special request of the District Commander. There were Minden Days, celebrations at Christmas, and, according to the amenities of the various stations, much social life. There were "married families" with the Battalion; marriages, and births. and children growing up with the Battalion. There was leave to England, leave to the hills, and tigers were shot.

A feature of service in India was, of course, the long distances covered by march route, and the first march of the Battalion on this tour was in January, 1926, when they marched from Jubbulpore to Dahna, near Saugor, to the Brigade Camp of Exercise. The distance of 115 miles was covered in eight marches, and about half-way the Battalion was seen on the line of march by H.E. the Commander-in-Chief, Field-Marshal Sir William Birdwood.

In January, 1927, the civil war in China threatened the International Settlement at Shanghai, and for a time the Battalion expected to be sent there; there was the usual spate of rumours, which were finally silenced when the 20th Indian Infantry Brigade was sent from Jhansi and a division was sent out from England. It was in 1927, too, that the athletic successes the Battalion was to win later in India were foreshadowed in the Brigade cross-country run, in which the Battalion won all the first eight places.

Jubbulpore was a healthy station, apart from the constant threat of malaria, which was kept at bay by a large anti-malaria squad. The hot season was comparatively short, as it was broken by the advent of the monsoon weather in June. Modern ideas of assisting resistance to heat by taking salt were still unknown to the army, and it was compulsory for all ranks to wear sun helmets with uniform by day all the year round, and in the summer months a spine-pad which covered shoulder blades and back to well below the waist. The efficiency of the spine-pad for preventing sun or heat stroke is doubtful, but there is no doubt that it did often cause prickly-heat rash. The spine-pad was only worn in "shirt-sleeve order," and not when the drill jacket was worn or with civilian clothes. On Thursdays and Sundays soldiers were quite comfortable in the sun wearing only singlet and shorts.

There were few amenities for the men at Jubbulpore and no welfare as we know it today. The only amusements were sports, visits to the Jubbulpore cinema, and dances at the Railway Institute. For the officers there was the Nerbudda Gymkhana Club, with a pleasant social life and tennis, rackets and polo. The small touring theatrical companies were a source of great delight, though they disappeared when sound films came to India.

Life at stations like Jubbulpore may have lacked amenities for the troops, but, as everywhere in India, the soldier had the consolation of being waited on by a horde of native servants. They pulled the ropes of the punkahs or hanging curtains which acted as fans in hot weather over the beds in barracks, and threw water on the grass screens—Khus-Khus Tatties—hanging over doors on the windward side of barrack blocks to cool the hot air. Incidents tended to occur when a soldier woke up under his mosquito net in the hot summer night and found the punkah stationary and the coolie asleep. There were nappis to shave the soldier as he lay in bed asleep, while an attendant small boy lathered the next customer, also fast asleep. There were servants to clean boots and equipment, and it was paradise for the idler.

Eventually orders had to be issued limiting the amount of valeting permitted, for there was a danger that some men would become quite incapable of looking after themselves and their own equipment. But it was all part of the traditional and, in retrospect anyhow, glamorous life of service in India.

In December, 1927, the Battalion moved from Jubbulpore to Multan, in the Punjab, where they last served from 1896 to 1898. They were given a splendid send-off from Jubbulpore, but it was saddened by having to say good-bye to their Commanding Officer, Lieutenant-Colonel R. S. Allen. Colonel Allen remained behind at Jubbulpore to take over temporary command of the 10th Jubbulpore Brigade, and as his tenure of command was due to end in March, 1928, it was most unlikely that he would see his Battalion again as its Commanding Officer. He was succeeded in command by Lieutenant-Colonel H. G. F. Frisby, of the Regiment. Colonel Frisby had first joined the Regiment in 1908 ; he had served in South Africa with the 2nd Battalion, and in France with the 2nd Welch Regiment, until he was severely wounded. He rejoined the Hampshire Regiment in July, 1919, went with the 1st Battalion to Istanbul, and remained with it until he became the Commanding Officer.

Multan was a smaller station than Jubbulpore, and with even fewer amenities as there were no other British troops there, no Eurasians and no Railway Institute. The hot weather lasted from March until September or October, and temperatures rose to 124° in the shade with minimum night temperatures of 98° at the hottest periods. On the other hand, the short winter was delightful. In the summer Headquarters moved to Dalhousie, in the Punjab hills, and the rifle companies each spent half the summer in the hills and half in Multan. One company was stationed at Multan Fort, and they were trained by the resident Master Gunner to man two twelve-pounder field guns of ancient design. Once a year the guns were taken out, drawn by magnificent commissariat bullocks of the Royal Indian Army Service Corps, and fired, the target being the River Chenab, half a mile or more wide where the firing was done. The guns, it is reported, were picturesque but not very accurate.

Two very successful race meetings were organized by the Battalion at Multan, with an unusual finishing post in the form of a white bamboo set against a shroud, obtained from the local hospital. As well as the Subalterns' Cup there was a Sergeants' Mess Race, on mules, and a race for the local Tonga ponies, with owners up. For the second meeting the entire population of the city of Multan came to watch, to the embarrassment of the organizers, but the profits on the Totalizator were wonderful.

A vivid impression of some of the consolations of service in India in the army is given by this recollection of an officer of the 1st Battalion. He was writing of a journey from Multan to the hills, where two companies were going for a spell in the hot weather :

"I have pleasant memories of riding my pony in charge of fifty bullock carts carrying our stores up the hill road in the sunset and seeing the full moon rise over the mountains, and smelling, after the dust and sweat of the Multan Plain, the cool fragrance of the first pine trees as we came over a small pass. And all the time I could hear behind me the sound of the band and drums as the half battalion left camp hundreds of feet below and two hours behind, to follow the bullock carts up the road. My object was to get the 2 m.p.h. column in and the baggage unloaded at the new camp before the 3 m.p.h. marching troops caught me up."

The Battalion distinguished itself at the Lahore District Sports Tournament in 1929 and 1930, winning the Grand Aggregate Sports Trophy on both occasions. They also won the district cross-country championship and the team boxing in both years, and they swept the board in the athletics championship. At the 1929 tournament they set up two new all-India records, for the mile and two-mile relay races, and a Far East record for the mile—by Second-Lieutenant R. C. W. Dent, in 4 minutes 39⅛ seconds. In 1930 both the 1929 relay records were broken again by the Battalion, the one-mile relay being won in 3 minutes 35 seconds, and the two-mile relay in 8 minutes 29 seconds. The Battalion excelled at boxing, too, and in 1931 won the Northern Command Boxing Tournament for the third year in succession.

There was further evidence of the Battalion's all-round excellence in the A.R.A. competitions : in 1928 the Battalion came fourth out of twenty-seven entries for the Queen Victoria Trophy, and "A" Company were runners-up out of ninety-two entries for the Company Shield. In 1929 "D" Company won the India Cup and they were runners-up the next year.

The amazing way in which information, believed to be quite secret, spread through India was shown on an occasion in May, 1930. Riots broke out in Peshawar in which an Indian regiment became disaffected, and as a result the Battalion received secret orders at four o'clock one morning to return at once from Dalhousie to Multan as a precautionary measure. The Battalion Messing Officer went to the Regimental contractor to obtain special foods for emergency haversack rations. The manager smiled broadly and produced the food, already

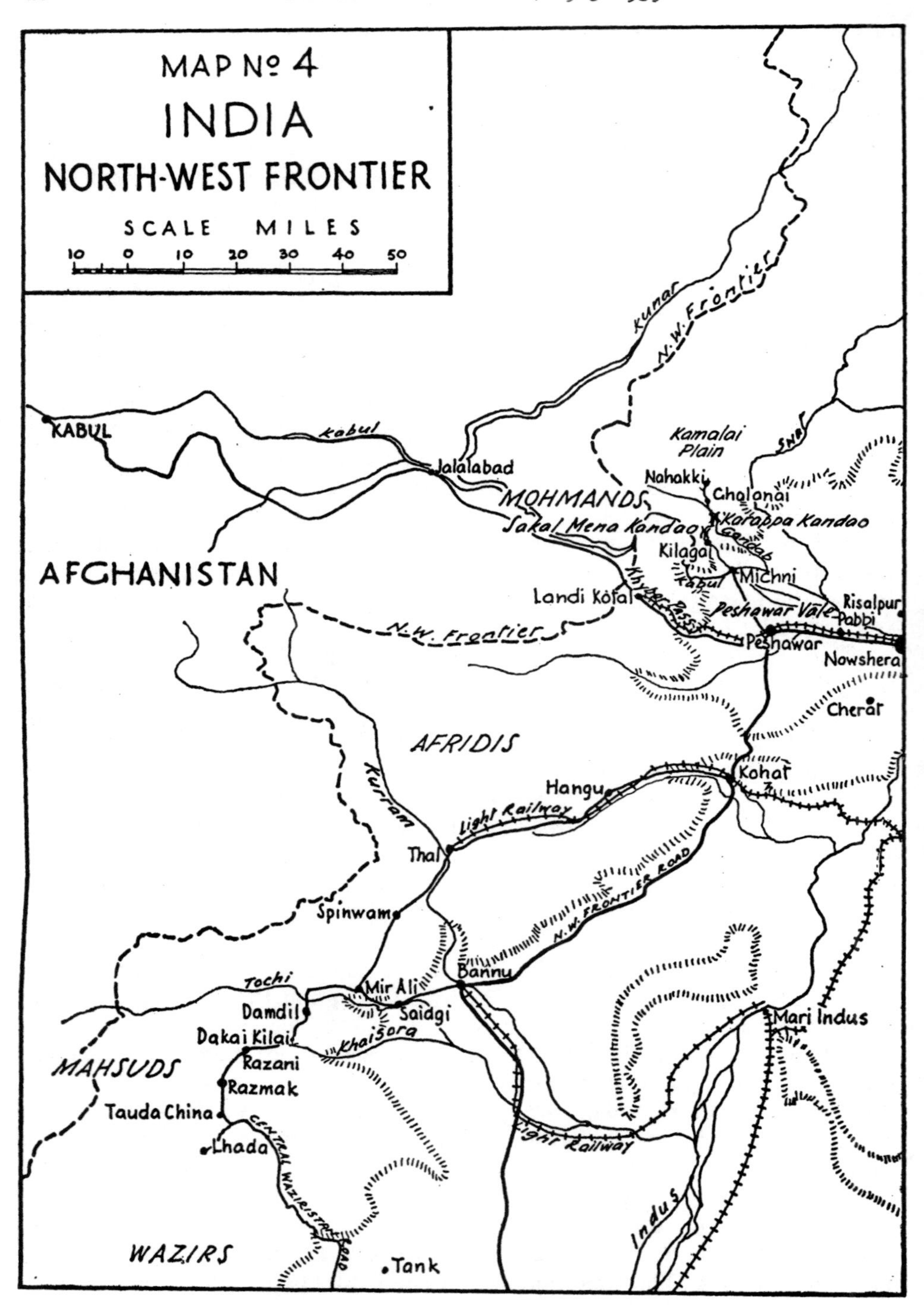
MAP No 4
INDIA
NORTH-WEST FRONTIER
SCALE MILES
10 0 10 20 30 40 50
KABUL
Kabul
Jalalabad
Kunar
N.W. Frontier
Kamalai Plain
Swat
Nahakki
Cholanai
MOHMANDS
Sakal Mena Kandao
Karappa Kandao
Kilagai
Michni
AFGHANISTAN
Landi Kotal
Khyber Pass
Peshawar Vale
Risalpur
Pabbi
Peshawar
Nowshera
Cherat
AFRIDIS
Kurram
Hangu
Kohat
Light Railway
Thal
N.W. FRONTIER ROAD
Spinwam
Tochi
Mir Ali
Bannu
Damdil
Saidgi
Dakai Kilai
Khaisora
Razani
Razmak
MAHSUDS
Tauda China
Lhada
CENTRAL WAZIRISTAN ROAD
Light Railway
Mari Indus
Indus
WAZIRS
Tank

prepared. He had received fuller details and more information than the Commanding Officer. It was just the way things were in India.

The Battalion always got on well with Indians, soldiers and civilians alike. The 5/10th Baluch Regiment was stationed at Multan at the same time as the 1st Hampshire, and when they were moved on to Razmak, the Battalion continued to play them at football, hockey and basket-ball. On one occasion the Signal Officer and two N.C.Os. came across a Dogra piquet of the 5/10th Baluch and the Jemadar in charge of the piquet asked them to have tea. In spite of being a caste Hindu, he insisted on them using the utensils of the platoon—a very great compliment. Several years later when the Battalion marched from Razmak to Nowshera the same Baluch Battalion marched the first three marches with the Battalion, and then went on to Peshawar by train. When they marched into Peshawar the senior Indian officer of the Baluch Battalion met them at the camp and, knowing the Hampshires' marching habits, had tea and cakes ready for the whole Battalion, provided on the initiative of the Indian officers and paid for by a subscription from all ranks, a splendid example of friendship between Indian and British units.

In 1930 the Battalion was due for its first spell of service on the North-West Frontier, and was to move up to Razmak in November. Two tactical advance parties went up earlier in the year to find out what would be required of the Battalion in this Frontier station. The first party was led by Major R. D. Johnston, and consisted of Lieutenant Browne, R.S.M. Oliver and two sergeants. The second party, under Lieutenant and Adjutant J. M. Lee, was Lieutenant I. M. Goff, Lieutenant (Q.M.) H. J. Jeffery, Q.M.S. H. C. Robinson and Sergeant J. Britt, D.C.M., M.M., the Provost Sergeant. This second party arrived in time to see the operations at Tauda China on the road from Razmak to Ladha in May, 1930. The story of Lieutenant Lee's advance party is best told in the words of one of the officers present :

"At Razmak we found the perimeter camp almost deserted except for essential guards and piquets. The station staff officer explained that the Brigade was out on an active service column against recalcitrant tribesmen, and suggested that we should settle down in Razmak and learn what we could.

"We raised vehement objection to this, and we were allowed to join the Razmak Brigade, commanded by Brigadier, now Major-General Sir Arthur, Mills at Tauda China. Lieutenant Lee was attached to the 4/12th Frontier Force Regiment, Lieutenant Goff to the 2/4th Gurkhas, and Lieutenant Jeffery, Q.M.S. Robinson and Sergeant Britt to the Durham Light Infantry.

"There was considerable sniping at night and, it seemed to us, too much shooting in reply from our perimeter posts. Casualties were few but sufficient to impress on us the necessity for 'digging in,' a lesson that proved to be highly valuable to the 1st Battalion during their tour of duty on the Frontier.

"Eventually a meeting was held between the Political Agent, the Brigade Commander and the tribal leaders. It was amusing to see the 'enemy' enjoying tea and cigarettes with their escort of the 10th Baluch Regiment. Bargaining went on in an affable atmosphere, but the tribal leaders' reply to our demands was considered unsatisfactory and the Brigade Column moved on to Ladha, and had the unpleasant experience of being caught by a river in full spate. At Ladha small advances were made deeper into Tribal Territory, village towers were blown up and at last the tribal leaders called a halt and made complete submission. Thus ended what was a routine affair to the tribesmen, and a very useful exercise for the British troops."

At Ladha the Adjutant of the 4/12th Frontier Force Regiment became a casualty and, as they were short of British officers, Lieutenant and Adjutant Lee took over the full duties of this fine Indian battalion until operations ended. The lessons learnt during this expedition by these advance parties were invaluable to the 1st Battalion and contributed to the very high reputation gained during their tour of duty at Razmak from November, 1930, to November, 1931. Those who took part were awarded the Indian General Service Medal with clasp "Waziristan 1930". During the active operations on 1st August all troops were amazed to see the men of the Hampshire Regiment wearing red roses in their helmets. How they were procured in the stony wastes of Waziristan only the men themselves—and the contractor—knew.

In November, 1930, the Battalion moved up to the North-West Frontier. They went by train to Mari Indus, crossed the river and went on by train to Bannu. From there they went by march route to Razmak, covering the seventy-three miles in six days, and arriving on 2nd November, 1930. The condition of the Battalion at this time is best shown perhaps by quoting an extract from the annual inspection report for the year ending 31st March, 1930 :

> The unit is well-trained and is tactically efficient and fit for Active Service. British Officers are above the average in efficiency. Drill is very good, and the men are smartly turned out. The unit is thoroughly efficient and is one that I should like to have on service with me. Discipline is excellent, crime is practically nil, and the whole tone of the unit is well above the average. The administration of the unit is excellent. The men are contented, well looked after and fit. Sports of all kinds are encouraged. Drunkenness and venereal hardly exist. The relationship of officers, N.C.Os. and men is all that could be desired. A very fine unit.
>
> (*Signed*) F. E. W. Venning,
> *Brigadier*.
>
> Multan,
> *8th April*, 1930.

The Battalion quickly settled down to Frontier conditions. They were part of the Razmak Column and, although the tribes were comparatively quiet at that time, there was plenty of column work to be done, though there were no serious engagements. There were the usual number of alarms and excursions, and the Battalion quickly learned the special art of mountain piqueting. There was some sniping by tribesmen, but the only casualty suffered by the Battalion was one mule wounded.

An interesting example of the cheerful belligerency, and of the whole atmosphere of the Frontier, was a dispute which sprang up at Razmak between Wazirs and Mahsuds. Wazir tribesmen were in the habit of grazing their flocks north of the perimeter of Razmak camp as far as a certain dry stream bed, which was the boundary of their grazing rights with the Mahsuds, who lived farther west. During the summer of 1931 a dispute in this stream bed led to sniping by each side, both quickly calling up reinforcements, while the British and Indian troops lined the camp wall as spectators. In fact little could be seen except the Political Officer driving out under a white flag to patch up a truce. Eventually an Indian Mountain Battery opened fire from within the camp and, under cover of the miniature barrage placed accurately between them, both sides withdrew with honour. It was believed that the Battery Commander fought his guns from the bar of the Razmak Club during this action.

During the Battalion's tour at Razmak, sport was not neglected and teams from the Battalion took part in the Waziristan District sports meeting at Bannu and won the trophies for association football, athletics, cross-country, and tug-of-war.

When the Commander-in-Chief in India, H.E. Sir Philip W. Chetwode, visited Razmak in April, 1931, he witnessed the beating of "Retreat" by the drums of the Battalion, and he dined with the officers. The Battalion marched past the Commander-in-Chief as part of the Razmak Column, and on 8th and 9th April furnished the Commander-in-Chief's guard. Razmak Brigade Order of 13th April contained the following passage from the C.-in-C.:

"Will you tell your troops how much impressed I was to see how very keen they all were and how obviously physically fit for the job they might have to do at any moment. They are just what Frontier troops should look like."

When the Battalion left Razmak for Nowshera on 24th November, 1931, after twelve months in Waziristan, they went by march route. The first three miles were lined by the troops of the Razmak garrison, and the bands of five units assisted in playing the Battalion out. It was a fine beginning to a march of 222 miles, which were covered in nineteen marching days. The route was Razmak, Razani, Damdil, Mir Ali, Thal in Kurram, Hangu, Kohat, Peshawar, Pabbi, Nowshera. It was a memorable march, and something of a record as no British infantry had marched from the Tochi valley about Mir Ali to Thal in Kurram. Marches averaged between fifteen and twenty miles, and band and drums played the whole way. At each night's halt where there was an Indian unit or detachment the Battalion turned out football, hockey and cross-country teams to compete with their hosts, a measure of the Battalion's physical fitness.

Nowshera, which is twenty-five miles east of Peshawar, was reached on 12th December, 1931, and the Battalion was played to Khartoum Barracks by the 2nd Battalion The Essex Regiment. The next day the Battalion returned the compliment by lining the route from the barracks to the station and playing the Essex out with band and drums. The Nowshera Brigade was then commanded by Brigadier Croft, who was succeeded by Brigadier the Hon. H. R. L. Alexander.

Christmas, 1931, at Nowshera was marred by a sudden call to action in connection with an outbreak of civil disturbance in the Pabbi area, and the manner in which the Battalion was mobilized is an excellent example of first-class security methods. On the afternoon of Christmas Eve the Adjutant, Lieutenant Goff, and the Quartermaster, Lieutenant Jeffery, were watching a football match when Colonel Frisby strolled up to them and told them to get into his car. They drove out under the Cherat hills, where the Commanding Officer told them of the whole scheme. The disturbance in the Pabbi area was caused by followers of one Abdul Gaffar Khan, who all wore, and were known as, "Red Shirts." These people were causing considerable nuisance, and the civil authorities had asked the military for assistance. For this purpose "Pabbi Column" was to be formed, consisting of a squadron of the Poona Horse and "A" and "C" Companies of the Regiment, with detachments of H.Q. Wing, under the command of Major F. A. Atchison. The Column was to be moved up to Pabbi on Christmas Day, but complete secrecy was to be observed. Preparations must be made so that no one suspected that an operation was imminent and the Christmas festivities were to go on in the normal way.

The Quartermaster solved his problem by deciding to hold a check of arms and ammunition before Christmas, and during the routine of the check he saw that sufficient ammunition was deposited in his Mobilization Stores. The troops were allowed to go into town on Christmas Eve in the normal way, sergeants and their wives gathered in the Sergeants' Mess, and the officers dressed for Christmas Eve dinner parties. At about eight o'clock, just as the two dinner parties were at the fish stage, the Commanding Officer apologized to his hostess and said that he must take all her guests away, and the same thing happened in the bungalow of the Second-in-Command. Then things moved quickly; conferences were held, the troops were rounded up in town, rations, including Christmas dinners, were packed, and by half past eleven the column moved off. Not a word had leaked out and the surprise element was complete. The remainder of the Battalion stood-to in barracks.

The task of "Pabbi Column" was to disperse the large numbers of zealous "Red Shirts" who were busy lying down on the Grand Trunk Road and wherever they could be a nuisance. The column spent four days dispersing meetings, persuading recumbent "Red Shirts" to get up and go away, removing red shirts from the backs of their wearers and rounding up prisoners. The principal difficulty was the tiresome custom of the "enemy" of lying down and refusing to move on every possible occasion. Prisoners were taken away from the scene of the disturbance, lectured on their bad manners and sent off to their villages, without their red shirts. The "rebellion" soon died down, fines levied on villages were paid promptly and pleasantly, and by 9th January all was quiet between Pabbi and Nowshera, and the troops returned to barracks, and that was the end of that expedition.

On 29th January, 1932, Lieutenant-Colonel Frisby's tenure of command expired and he was promoted Colonel and posted to command 128th (Hampshire) Infantry Brigade, succeeding Colonel E. G. St. Aubyn. Lieutenant-Colonel E. A. Corner was appointed to command the Battalion.

At Nowshera the Battalion was quartered in barracks known unofficially as "tin-town," from the temporary nature of the camp and the metal roofs. At the Officers' Club the old wine steward remembered the Battalion's visit thirty years before, and could quote names of officers. As far as social amenities were concerned, Nowshera was a disappointment to everyone. There was some hunting for the officers who kept horses, with the hounds kept by the 15th/19th Hussars at Risalpur, eight miles away beyond the Kabul river. One of the first actions of the Battalion when it arrived at Nowshera was to make themselves a football ground, with the name Fratton Park, the name, of course, of the Portsmouth Football Club's ground.

Peshawar, twenty-eight miles away, had many attractions to offer for those who could get there, but there were hazards in the journey as the activities of the "Red Shirts" made it necessary to close the road frequently at sunset. One officer, when motoring there to a dance with his partner, was robbed of all he and his partner possessed, at the point of a rifle.

In March, 1931, the Battalion was called out on internal security duty during the Indian General Elections, which the "Red Shirts" were trying to spoil. It was, as always, a difficult task. On one occasion a large crowd, trying to prevent the troops escorting voters to the polling booths, were led by men carrying copies of the Koran on their heads. The idea was to arouse religious fervour by making the troops commit sacrilege by laying their hands on the Sacred Book. However, the officer in charge was used to India and he was careful to get good Mussulman policemen to arrest the leaders, and that trick failed. After that the crowd was dispersed by the threat of fixed bayonets. Later in the day the same detachment was stoned by a crowd, and this time they charged and dispersed the crowd with their rifle butts, although the Indian Magistrate who was present had asked the officer in command to open fire.

While stationed at Nowshera the Battalion persevered with sport, even if it was felt that full advantage was not taken of opportunities for training. The Battalion won the Peshawar District Cross-Country and Hockey Championship and the Peshawar District Team Boxing Championship in 1933, and the Battalion team was 2nd, 3rd, and 1st in 1932, 1933, and 1934 in the Peshawar Point-to-Point meeting. In 1933 Lieutenant I. M. Goff won the Open Cup on "Beau Geste," a horse he had bought in the previous autumn when it was dead lame and considered a hopeless case by veterinary and cavalry experts. Lieutenant Goff received accelerated promotion to Captain in The King's Regiment in April, 1933, and died on active service in Italy in the war.

In March, 1934, it was time for the Battalion to move again, this time to Rawalpindi. The Battalion's last night at Nowshera was marred by a heavy thunderstorm. The 1st Battalion The Duke of Wellington's, who were relieving the Battalion, marched straight into Khartoum Barracks, and the Hampshire men were under canvas on the Square. During the night the weather broke and a large number of tents were washed away. The men's discomfort was quickly forgotten, however, and they were given a tremendous send-off from Nowshera by the bands of other regiments and by a large gathering of friends. The Battalion arrived at Rawalpindi early the next morning, and they were played into the Victoria Barracks by the band of Rattray's Sikhs.

Rawalpindi was in many ways the ideal Indian station. It was very large, consisting of three British infantry battalions allocated to the 1st, 2nd and 3rd Indian Infantry Brigades, a Field Artillery Brigade, two Indian infantry battalions and one cavalry regiment. The Hampshire Battalion became part of the famous 2nd (Rawalpindi) Infantry Brigade. Also serving in the station were the 2nd Argyll and Sutherland Highlanders and the South Wales Borderers. Thus for the first time in many years the Battalion had British infantry regiments to compete against in sport, with the result that the standard of the Battalion's football and hockey rose considerably.

Being such a large station, amenities were plentiful ; there was the Club for officers, with tennis, polo, golf, racing, drag hounds and shooting ; while there were cinemas, dancing and a great deal of social life for the men. The barracks were good, with electric light and electric fans, and the climate was good as well, and cool from late September to March. It would all have been most satisfactory but for one great disadvantage, which was to cause the Battalion much distress in due course.

Rawalpindi contained the Headquarters of Northern Command, of Rawalpindi District and also, of course, of the Brigade. The freedom of the Battalion was therefore very much restricted, and the Battalion was called upon to find many guards, for the arsenal, the Commander-in-Chief's house, the hospital and elsewhere. It also had to provide men for extra-regimental employment such as hospital orderlies, clerks at the several headquarters, for duty at clubs and, in short, wherever men were needed. As a result a great number of men were permanently away from the Battalion, with the result that training was almost impossible.

Major E. G. Wheeler, who was acting as Commanding Officer in the absence of Colonel Corner, on leave in England, realized the danger of this, and made strong representations to Brigade for his men to be released for training, but he received a curt refusal. Major Wheeler and his senior officers realized how sadly their Battalion, which had won so high a reputation in India, was falling away. The position was aggravated by the fact that many officers and senior N.C.Os. were posted away and their reliefs had no experience of conditions of Frontier service. Life at Rawalpindi was pleasant, but many men in the Battalion wondered what would happen if they were called upon for active service.

In September, 1935, this happened, and the Brigade was ordered to Peshawar for field service in connection with the Mohmand operations. The Mohmand clans had been troublesome for generations, indeed ever since the first Afghan War of 1838–1842. Time after time it had been necessary to send punitive expeditions to restore peace and order in their country. The trouble this time arose from an attack by the upper Mohmands on the "assured clans," six clans who had received allowances from the Government of India since 1896 to remove the "necessity for raiding."

The Battalion had stood-to to move up to the Mohmand country in 1933 while they were at Nowshera, but they had not been called upon, with the exception of Lieutenant J. H. Dyas and Second-Lieutenant T. G. Tucker, who had joined the Headquarters of the Nowshera Brigade. In September, 1935, however, the Battalion was ordered, at forty-eight hours' notice, to move to Peshawar for field service. The sequel was an event which shocked the Battalion deeply ; for it was justly proud of its reputation in India, and particularly of its marching prowess. Yet for its march up to the Frontier the Battalion received a conspicuous "black" on this occasion from the Army Commander, and its pride was cruelly wounded.

The circumstances should be considered in full. In the first place, as has been noticed, Major Wheeler had tried to get his large number of extra-regimentally employed men released for training, and his requests had been refused. Many men had not worn marching boots for six months, and for that period they had done no soldiering of any kind. There were new officers and N.C.Os. in the Battalion who had no experience of active service conditions in India. Everyone was delighted, of course, with the prospect of service on the Frontier, and hearts were full of enthusiasm and eagerness, which made the sting all the sharper when it came.

The Battalion went to Peshawar from Rawalpindi by train on 11th September, their strength being 18 officers and 650 other ranks, with Major Wheeler in command. The night of 11th September was spent in barracks and the next morning the Battalion paraded at the late hour of ten o'clock to march the fifteen miles to Michni on the banks of the Kabul river ; while the Indian battalions of the Brigade moved off in lorries. When the Battalion paraded the shade temperature was 100°, and Major Wheeler, calling his officers out, told them that it was no fault of his that they were marching at this late hour in the heat of the day ; he was so ordered. He added that the Battalion would be tried hard in the next few days, but he reminded them of the Battalion's marching reputation, and advised them not to let their minds dwell on what would be damnable, but to think instead of Hampshire green lanes and beer.

The first day's march was through the beautiful Peshawar Vale country ; it was shaded for the greater part of the day and there was a cool breeze. Yet for men who had had no training for many months it was a trying march. Only a few men fell out, but the evening's inspection showed that many men's feet were in a poor way, and the officers were very anxious about the next two days. But everyone was very thankful that evening to see the sun disappearing behind the hills in the direction of the Khyber Pass. The Brigade second-line transport, which had set out early in the morning, consisted entirely of camels and stretched for a distance of two miles. That column was commanded by Lieutenant R. G. F. Frisby.

The second day's march, to Kilagai, was much rougher going, and the last hours of the march saw many men hobbling along painfully, and again some had to fall out, and the number of men who had to be sent sick that evening was unpleasantly large. Everyone was anxious about the next and final day's march and very tired, but, of course, the Battalion had to provide a number of piquets covering the camp that night, as it was in Mohmand country.

The third day of the march, a distance of only eleven miles which took six hours, was little short of a nightmare. Many of the men had been on piquet duty and had had no sleep and only a meagre breakfast. The Battalion was not allowed to set off until long after the sun was up, and the temperature reached 118° in the shade. The road was newly built and was deep in fine white dust, and often the men had to make their way in single file along the rough ditches to allow convoys of vehicles to pass in the narrow road, convoys which set up a cloud of dust head high, which filled nose, ears and mouth, and stuck to the sweat on the men's faces. The road itself was a winding hill road, uphill for the first eight miles and at a stiff gradient, and climbed through two considerable passes, the Sakal Mena Kandao and the Karappa Kandao. That march to Ghalanai was a great test of endurance for any troops; it was certainly a challenge which the Tigers would have accepted eagerly in normal circumstances. As it was, the rear-guard, part of the company commanded by Lieutenant Langrishe, completed the march without a single man falling out. But in the main body the number of casualties was woeful, and the circumstances were such that the Battalion's failure was most conspicuous, for there were many witnesses, and thus it was that the 1st Battalion received their "black" from the Army Commander, and the hurt went deep. No one disputed that the large number of casualties on the march, and somewhat clumsy piqueting of the past two nights, deserved the reproof; but everyone felt, from the senior to the most junior, that it was not their fault, that somehow they had been let down. What was most galling was the publicity of it all.

At Ghalanai the Battalion, after a brief rest, were soon hard at it settling down in the camp. For all the failure on the march, the Battalion was perfectly fit to carry out all its tasks. Within an hour of arriving it was busy completing the defences of the perimeter camp; and before first light the following morning a rifle company supported by a M.G. platoon had moved out to open a road as far back as the Karappa Pass.

"Mohforce," the name of the column the Battalion had joined, consisted of the Peshawar, Nowshera and Rawalpindi Brigades, with their artillery, and it was commanded by Brigadier Claude Auchinleck, later to become the famous Field Marshal. The camp itself was in the Gandab valley, surrounded by numerous high hills, most of which were held by permanent piquets.

The Battalion remained out on field service for seven weeks, eager to restore its own morale and to re-establish its good name. It was not in any active operations against the insurgent tribes, but it did hard duty. One of the principal objects of the operation was the building of a road over the Nahakki Pass as far as Kamalai, which the tribesmen were trying to prevent. The

Battalion found piquets, perched precariously on sharp hilltops, and furnished patrols which soon learnt the trick of working in that most difficult country. The men became hard as nails, and when the operation ended with peace on 2nd October, 1935, the Battalion received handsome tributes. But the most welcome of all was the news that the Battalion was to march the whole way back to Rawalpindi ; it was just the restorative the men needed. The 155 miles were marched in ten marching days, and all was well.

In January, 1936, Lieutenant-Colonel Corner relinquished his command of the 1st Battalion, after thirty-one years in the Regiment, and he was succeeded by Lieutenant-Colonel W. H. C. Ramsden from the East Yorkshire Regiment. At once soldiering at Rawalpindi took on a completely new aspect. One day a week, right through the summer as well as in winter, the whole Battalion, including all employed men, went out on a field exercise. There was a weekly "mobility march" for every officer and man in the Battalion, a forced march of six miles in fifty minutes in full service order. Colonel Ramsden also insisted on one night exercise every month, and there were T.E.W.Ts. for officers. The result was the instillation into the Battalion of a tremendous zest for hard training and hard exercise.

The value of all this was shown when the Battalion was called out at short notice for active service on the Frontier in the autumn of 1936. Everything was very different from the previous year. The Battalion received its warning orders to move to Waziristan the day after it had completed two weeks' battalion training in mountain warfare—in conjunction with the R.A.F., commanded by Wing Commander Slessor—followed by ten days' brigade exercises. After a fifteen-mile march over hill-tracks the Battalion reached a bivouac fifteen miles from Rawalpindi. It was decided to have only a two-hour halt and then to march on through the night. The Battalion marched into Victoria Barracks in fine style at 1.15 in the morning, having covered thirty miles in twenty-four hours, evidence to everyone that indeed the Hampshire could march.

They moved up to Waziristan at once. On 1st December they were concentrated under canvas at Bannu, and on 4th December marched with the first echelon of the 2nd Rawalpindi Infantry Brigade to Saidgi and on the 5th to Mir Ali. The principal duties were road protection and construction, and on one occasion the destruction of a village. On 22nd December the Battalion took part in operations at Dakai Kilai.

The Brigade left camp at two in the morning of 22nd December to piquet the route of the Razmak Brigade up the Khaisora hills. After the Razmak Brigade had passed through, the 2nd Brigade started to withdraw at about midday. As the Battalion, as brigade rear-guard, began to withdraw from Hampshire Hill north of Dakai Kilai, considerable firing broke out from the left and it was clear that the tribesmen intended to follow up. However, covered by two mountain batteries and the Hampshire machine-gun company, the Battalion withdrew successfully, suffering only two casualties wounded, who were safely evacuated. These were a private and Lieutenant R. G. T. Baines, who was subsequently killed in action on the Normandy beaches in June, 1944, commanding a company of the 1st Battalion.

The 2/2nd Punjab on the Battalion's left were not so successful, and when the Battalion machine-gun company had withdrawn, tribesmen could be seen moving round to follow them up. Because of casualties in the Punjab battalion, and on account of counter-attacks necessary to extricate a Punjab company, it became clear that the Brigade would not be able to reach its camp, some five miles down the valley, before darkness fell. The Brigade Commander decided therefore to make a camp about a mile down the valley, and he ordered Colonel Ramsden to establish piquets and protection for this camp, to which the rest of the Brigade would withdraw. This was successfully done. The decision proved to be a wise one, for the last rear-guards reached camp in the fading light in a flurry of shots, which caused weary Hampshire soldiers digging-in for the night to jump to arms and man the perimeter at a speed which no one seeing them a moment before would have thought possible. Intermittent sniping went on all night, but as everyone was dug-in the only casualties were a few mules. For their share in this brisk action, Colonel Ramsden, Major Newnham, Captain G. D. Browne and four sergeants were mentioned in despatches. At the end of the operations the Battalion rounded off its good reputation with a fine flourish by marching twenty-five miles to Bannu, piqueting the route as it went, and covering ten miles of very rough country to start with.

The Battalion entrained at Bannu and arrived back at Rawalpindi on 27th January, 1937. Service at Rawalpindi continued along peaceful but vigorous lines throughout that year, against the background of the ever-increasing political tension in Europe. The sinister gestures of Hitler and Mussolini added a grim note of realism to soldiering.

The Battalion's last move in India took place on Christmas Day, 1937. Christmas Day was spent in the Rest Camp at Rawalpindi and the Battalion entrained at ten o'clock at night for Kamptee, a few miles north-east of Nagpur, where they arrived on 29th December. The journey of four days in the train was familiar enough in India in the old days, but is now a thing of the past. There was the enormously long train, with troops, wives, bearers, dogs, horses and the Sikhs of the Indian platoon. There were the wayside halts for meals and exercise, daily inspections of turn-out and weapons—all detraining and entraining done as a drill to the bugle.

Kamptee was a very small station, the complete contrast to Rawalpindi. Fifty years before Kamptee had been a large place with a brigade of infantry, two regiments of cavalry, and gunners, including an elephant battery of heavies. The two polo grounds were still there, the racecourse and the ornamental gardens with the bandstand. In the garrison church were the memorials to officers and men who died from sickness, some regiments having as many as two hundred names. All this was but an echo of other days, and when the 1st Hampshire were at Kamptee there was only one other battalion, an Indian one. The barracks were good and comparatively modern, though many of the officers' bungalows were old, with thatched roofs. The cantonment had an air of being left over from the nineteenth century.

The Battalion was not able to sit down to its Christmas dinner until 1st January, when dinner followed the Proclamation Parade. On this occasion Major Cadoux-Hudson commanded the Battalion and Lieutenant-Colonel Ramsden, as Station Commander, commanded the parade, attended by Lieutenant Langrishe as Station Officer. It was an historic occasion, as it was the last time the Battalion was commanded by a Commanding Officer mounted. Whilst the Battalion was at Kamptee one company was stationed in Fort Sitabuldi in Nagpur, standing on a hill between the Indian and European cities. This fort was equipped with old-fashioned guns, manned by the company under the orders of a Royal Artillery Warrant Officer Master Gunner.

Reorganization and revised training were very much in the air at this time, in view of the situation in Europe, and in September, 1938, the Battalion was reorganized into four rifle companies, each of three platoons of three sections, with a Headquarter Company consisting of six platoons. These were Signals, A.A. and L.M.G., Mortar, Carrier, Pioneer, and Administrative ; an establishment which was to become very familiar during the next seven years.

What was perhaps more disconcerting to old soldiers was the new method of drill, by which men had to fall in in threes instead of in two ranks as they had done for time immemorial. At the same time many of the old parade ground commands which had echoed through the lives of generations of soldiers were changed and simplified.

It was in September, 1938, that orders were unexpectedly received for the Battalion to move at very short notice to a secret destination, amplified later as a rendezvous at sea with H.M.S. *Norfolk*. These orders came in the midst of a period of more than usually dramatic news from Europe, at the time of Munich, when the latest utterances of Hitler and Chamberlain were picked up eagerly by those who had adequate wireless sets. Busy days followed ; there was, of course, the usual flurry of postings in and out, a great deal of packing up, a mountain of sudden administrative work and problems galore, such as, for example, the giving up of all the pets which British soldiers manage to acquire wherever they may be. New homes had to be found for the Battalion's dogs, cats, pigeons, and monkeys. Privately owned horses had to be sold quickly, and motor-cars and personal possessions which had accumulated in the long tour in India had to be disposed of.

At last all was ready, and on 28th and 29th September the Battalion, divided into two parts for the move, entrained for Bombay, and embarked in s.s. *Vasna* and s.s. *Strathnaver* for the Middle East. The total strength of the Battalion on leaving India was 23 officers and 689 rank and file, commanded by Lieutenant-Colonel H. C. Ramsden. The ships sailed under sealed orders and in wireless silence.

This was the first occasion on which the *Strathnaver* was used for trooping and the stewards felt very uneasy about having soldiers aboard their luxurious ship. As a precaution the stewardesses were stood off and sent home before the

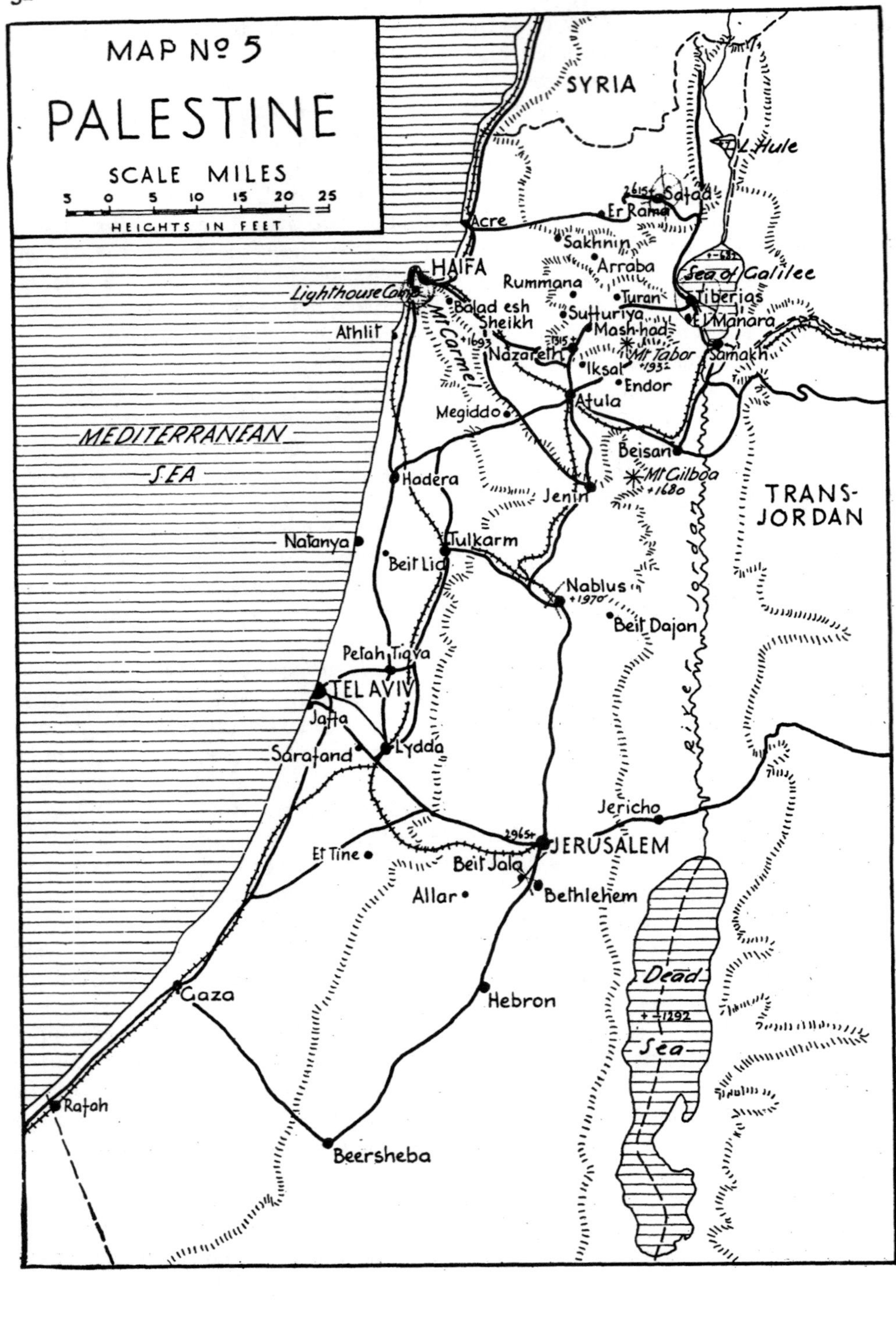
MAP No 5
PALESTINE
SCALE MILES
5 0 5 10 15 20 25
HEIGHTS IN FEET
SYRIA
L. Hule
Safad
Er Rama
Acre
Sakhnin
Arraba
Sea of Galilee
HAIFA
Lighthouse Camp
Rummana
Turan
Tiberias
Balad esh Sheikh
Sulturiya
El Manara
Athlit
Mt Carmel
Mash-had
Mt Tabor
Samakh
Nazareth
Iksal
Endor
Atula
Megiddo
MEDITERRANEAN SEA
Beisan
Mt Gilboa
+1680
Hadera
Jenin
TRANS-JORDAN
Natanya
Tulkarm
Beit Lid
Nablus
+1970
River Jordan
Beit Dajan
Petah Tiqva
TEL AVIV
Jaffa
Sarafand
Lydda
Jericho
JERUSALEM
Et Tine
Beit Jala
Allar
Bethlehem
Dead Sea
-1292
Gaza
Hebron
Rafah
Beersheba

vessel left India. Never before had the troops travelled so luxuriously. The officers had an entire deck to themselves, the warrant officers and sergeants another, and the food was superb. Long before the ship reached Palestine, the stewards were completely won over by the troops' good behaviour and they were genuinely sorry to see them disembark at Haifa.

II—PALESTINE, 1938–1939

On disembarking at Haifa on 9th and 10th October the Battalion was issued with motor transport at full scale and told to drive itself to Nazareth, Acre and Suffuriya. This was somewhat embarrassing as the only drivers the Battalion had were mule-drivers. Accordingly the staff produced Jewish civilian drivers, who spoke Yiddish and many other oriental languages, but not English. They were also gun-shy and their response to a sniper was to drive into the ditch and run for it. However, everyone arrived at their destinations: Headquarters, and "B" and "C" Companies at Nazareth and "A" and "D" at Acre and Suffuriya respectively. There was, however, a difficulty about arms as well as over the M.T. In India the Battalion had used Vickers machine guns, the property of the Indian Government. When they left India these were replaced by Lewis guns, which everyone had to re-learn. Then in Palestine the Lewis guns were replaced by the Bren gun, a completely new weapon. Six months after landing they drew their first three Bren gun carriers.

The Battalion had landed in a country profoundly disturbed by civil war, and they served there for nine months, and difficult months they were too. As always in such peace-time service, the task of the military was to assist the civil authorities to preserve law and order. At this period in the unhappy history of Palestine it was the Arabs who were in arms against the Jews, and the Battalion was fully occupied in keeping the King's peace by patrolling, providing road piquets, searching for rebel leaders, punitive expeditions, clearing road-blocks and occasionally on specific operations. Two new features of the work were the co-operation of the R.A.F. and the use of police dogs.

Searching Arab villages for arms was a wearisome duty ; but soon the men became expert in discovering caves under houses and various caches of arms. One man in the Battalion possessed a marvellous instinct for discovering hidden arms, whether several yards up a cave so small that he could only just wriggle up flat on his stomach, or in the country where his skill in following tracks could lead him to a rifle in the middle of a field of growing corn.

Never during its service in Palestine was the Battalion together in one place ; it was scattered in detachments usually of less than company strength. At first Battalion Headquarters was at Nazareth, and later at Acre. The Battalion's welcome to Palestine was typical of the months to follow, for on the very first day a bomb was thrown at the "C" Company billets in Nazareth and, like so many that were to follow it, it fortunately failed to explode. The next day a bomb did explode, and the Battalion suffered its first casualty in one corporal wounded. The early attack at Nazareth was due, according to gossip, to the fact that the Battalion was wearing Indian pattern pith helmets, and the Arabs mistook them for a Jewish battalion. Anyhow, sniping quickly ceased in Nazareth itself. It would perhaps be enlightening to quote two typical days from the Battalion Digest of Service :

> "January 24th. Two Columns from Nazareth, 'Affcol' from Affula, and a Column of R. Ulster Rifles, the whole under command Lt.-Col. W. H. C. Ramsden, raided Bolad Es Sheiksh. Many arrests were made.
>
> "One pl. 'A' Company, commanded by L./Sgt. Dimmack, escorted police dogs from the scene of an armed robbery near Tiberias. The line led to a house in the Al Manara—four arrests were made."
>
> "January 26th. 'NAZCOLB' and 'AFFCOL,' commanded by Major P. H. Cadoux-Hudson, raided IKSAL. Several rebels were detained.
>
> "A patrol from FURDET pqt., commanded by P.S.M. Moore, raided a Bedouin encampment near Rummana. Two wanted rebels were taken.
>
> "A patrol on the Tiberias road, under command Lt. F. M. Shaw, was sniped near Mashad. The patrol attempted to work round the rear of the snipers, but owing to the darkness and the difficult nature of the country no contact with the band was made.
>
> "Mashad was visited by 'NAZCOLA' on the following day and a fine of £25 was imposed on the village."

So it went on, and the good spirit, and indeed the good humour, of the troops proved to be a very valuable asset. The kind of tasks which fell to the Battalion is well shown in a letter home by one of the officers of the Battalion :

"I am afraid this letter got rather held up as I was on a search on the early morning of the 22nd. I think it was the most unpleasant show I've ever been on. We started at 12.30 a.m. in sheets and torrents of rain and walked across country without even a path to help us. I was leading platoon. It was so dark I couldn't see where I was putting my feet. I fell down at least half a dozen times and cut both my knees. While, judging by the noise, every soldier must have fallen down and dropped his rifle more than a dozen times. There was a mist over the hills and I couldn't see their outline, so I had to travel by sense of direction. At five o'clock we almost stumbled right into the village, but we had to wait until it began to get light before attempting to cordon the village. I did the southern part and there I stopped in the rain, soaked to the skin and covered in mud up to my knees—some of the rifles were so clogged they would never have fired without splitting the barrel—until 9.30, by which time all the inhabitants had been collected. Our Arab picked out twelve bad men and then I went off with him, a section, the C.O., two policemen and a patent machine called a Detector which detects any metal up to a range of two feet by making a buzzing noise. It buzzed four times ; the total bag was a piece of chain, a horse-shoe, an old tin can and a coffee pot. At 11.45 I had breakfast ; at 12.45 we left the village, and we got back soon after four."

So the difficult weeks passed, no one ever knowing what was going to happen next. As well as the throwing of bombs and laying of land mines, some of which exploded and some of which did not, the Arabs laid occasional ambushes of mobile patrols, and there was sudden sniping and the constant destruction of telegraph posts and communications. It was all in a day's work, however, and the Battalion made the best of the unpleasant circumstances. In spite of all this, sport flourished to such an extent that the Battalion hockey team reached the final of the Command competition, the Chancellor Cup.

Training was carried out in what little time could be found for it. There were constant patrols in the vehicles, to which they rapidly became accustomed, and there were visits by important persons. The most memorable of these was the tour of the C.I.G.S., Lord Gort, so soon to command the ill-fated and gallant British Expeditionary Force in the first phase of the war.

Another visitor was General Montgomery, who was inspecting piquets manned by the Battalion when a sniping attack was opened from near-by hills. The General took command of the situation and issued fire orders, and the fusillade from the piquet successfully silenced the snipers. The enemy suffered no casualties, which was just as well, since they were men of another famous British regiment. It was all arranged—to entertain the distinguished visitor.

On 28th June, 1939, Colonel Ramsden said farewell to the Battalion, on being promoted to a command in the West Lancashire area. Under Colonel Ramsden the Battalion attained a high state of tactical and physical efficiency. He was a most energetic, firm and fair commander, who set a fine example of leadership to all ranks. Colonel Ramsden had handed over the Battalion to his Second-in-Command, Major Cadoux-Hudson, in February, 1939, when he went to Haifa as acting commander of the 16th Infantry Brigade, and Major Cadoux-Hudson commanded the Battalion until 30th July, 1939, when Lieutenant-Colonel H. C. Westmorland took over command.

In July, 1939, the Battalion left Palestine for El Daba, in Egypt. The international tension which had been sustained for many anxious months was now reaching its climax. On several occasions in August "most secret" orders were received for action to be taken "in certain eventualities," and suddenly on 25th August all leave was cancelled. On 1st September news was received that Germany had invaded Poland, and on the 3rd that Great Britain was at war with Germany. The next day the long-expected signal was received from H.Q., B.T.E.:

> *"Mobilize. All regular troops under your command are to be regarded as on Active Service from today's date."*

CHAPTER III

THE 2ND BATTALION
1925–1939

THE 2nd Battalion The Hampshire Regiment returned from service in Ireland to Bordon in 1923, where they were able to settle down at last to peace-time soldiering, with Lieutenant-Colonel L. C. Morley in command. On 12th January, 1926, they moved to Plymouth, taking up quarters at Crownhill Barracks, and on 1st October of that year Lieutenant-Colonel Morley completed his period of command and was succeeded by Lieutenant-Colonel C. R. U. Saville, Royal Fusiliers. Colonel Morley was given a memorable send-off by the Battalion, all ranks taking the opportunity of showing the affection in which he was held.

The 2nd Battalion settled down to a period of undisturbed training at Plymouth and stayed there for two and a half years. They were difficult times, of course, owing to the policy of strict economy in all service matters, and there was a great deal of "making-do." It was, however, a happy period for the Battalion ; nothing of significance occurred and, like the happy nation, it had no history. Sport flourished and by shooting with distinction in the Southern Command Weapon Training Meetings the Battalion began a series of successes at the range which was to be a feature of the inter-war years.

In November, 1928, there was an important move overseas, for a spell of duty with the Army of the Rhine. This was no more than a routine change of station and the Battalion, 10 officers and 415 other ranks, took its families with it. Battalion Headquarters, H.Q. Wing and "Y" and "Z" Companies were stationed at Bingen and "X" and "W" Companies were on detachment at Schierstein. Quarters were comfortable, but the Battalion found to its dismay that it was sadly off for sport. At Bingen there was only one indifferent football ground, situated on top of a hill. As it turned out this did not matter a great deal, as the winter was extremely cold and the Rhine was frozen. They found the civilian population very friendly and their thirteen months in Germany passed peacefully and pleasantly.

In spite of the difficulties, sport of every kind got going as soon as the thaw came, and in March the Battalion defeated the Leicestershire Regiment at association football—the first time the "other Tigers" had been beaten for two and a half years. In the Rhine Army Cup the Battalion beat the Royal Welch Fusiliers, but lost to their brother Tigers in the final. The Battalion also continued their success on the range by winning the Rhine Army Weapon Training Meeting. The Battalion left Germany on 8th December, 1929, for Catterick, and, as in Cork, the last act on leaving Bingen was to cut down the barrack flagstaff on which the Regimental flag had been flown.

On 16th May, 1930, Colonel Saville relinquished command of the 2nd Battalion on being appointed to the China Command as G.S.O.1, and he was succeeded by Lieutenant-Colonel G. F. Perkins. The Battalion served at Catterick, "the Aldershot of the North," for two years until February, 1932, when on the 25th of the month it was moved south to its own county, to Parkhurst in the Isle of Wight. The citizens of Portsmouth took the opportunity to give the Battalion an enthusiastic civic reception as it passed through. The Lord Mayor of Portsmouth, accompanied by the Colonel of the Regiment, delivered an address of welcome to the Battalion, which paraded in front of the Guildhall, inspected the ranks drawn up in double companies and took the salute at the march past. The Battalion crossed to the Island and disembarked at Ryde, an historic occasion as it was the first time a Battalion of the Regiment was stationed on the Island. From Ryde it set off for Parkhurst by march route. There were two more civic welcomes, at Ryde, and again at Newport, where General Sir Richard Haking received an illuminated address of welcome. On the march from Newport to Parkhurst a large number of the inhabitants of the town accompanied the Battalion.

At Parkhurst the 2nd Battalion was quartered in the Albany Barracks which, in the words of one of the officers, "was pleasantly situated next door to Parkhurst gaol with, in the surrounding neighbourhood, a workhouse, a Borstal institution, a lunatic asylum, an infirmary, and a cemetery." In spite of these unpromising surroundings, the Battalion thoroughly enjoyed its stay on the island. In the summer the Battalion went to Salisbury Plain for exercises, and in the summer of 1933 it took part in a very interesting ceremony at Southampton. This was the laying-up in St. Mary's Church, Southampton, of the King's Colour of the 2nd Battalion The 67th Regiment, which was raised in Dundalk in 1803. This Colour had been carried by that battalion until June, 1817, when it was disbanded at Canterbury. The Colour had previously been kept in a place of honour in the old "Audit House."

Colonel Perkins relinquished command of the 2nd Battalion on 9th September, 1933, seven months before the expiration of his tenure of command, on appointment as A.Q.M.G., Southern Command, and once more a popular Commanding Officer was given a warm-hearted send-off. The new Commanding Officer was a very happy appointment, as it was a well-known officer of the Regiment, Lieutenant-Colonel B. B. von B. im Thurn. Colonel im Thurn had joined the 1st Battalion twenty-seven years before in 1906. He went to France with the B.E.F. and served with the 1st Battalion throughout the strenuous days of 1914–1915, being the last of the original officers of the 1st Battalion to survive the ordeal, and he remained until he was invalided home at the end of May, 1915. During those ten months he had won a splendid reputation for gallantry and devotion to duty. He was back in France in November, 1916, where he remained until the end of the war. Colonel im Thurn joined the 2nd Battalion at Bordon in March, 1924, and at once set about encouraging the Battalion's traditional excellence in rifle shooting with immense enthusiasm. It was almost entirely due to Colonel im Thurn's personal devotion to weapon training that from 1925 to 1936 the Battalion swept the board in rifle shooting wherever they were stationed ; he raised the reputation of the 2nd Battalion to that of the best shooting unit in the Army at home.

While the 2nd Battalion was stationed at Parkhurst it achieved a particularly fine series of results each year in the Southern Command Weapon Training Meeting. It won the Grand Aggregate Cup (the Congreve Trophy) in 1932, 1933, and 1935 (which was for the sixth time), and in 1934 it was runner-up by one point only to the 1st Battalion The Rifle Brigade. In 1932, 1933 and 1934 the Battalion also won the Infantry Aggregate Cup, and was runner-up in 1935.

At the Aldershot Command Small Arms Meeting in June, 1936, the 2nd Battalion won the Aggregate Challenge Cup by 26 clear points from the runner-up with fifteen units competing. At the same meeting it won the H.Q. Wing Match, the Anti-Aircraft Match, the Company Match, and the Platoon Match. Another notable achievement of this period was the winning of the *Portsmouth Times* Marching and Shooting Cup. The object of this competition is, of course, to obtain something of the conditions comparable to firing in an attack after an advance, and the competitors march ten miles and then immediately fire off the competition. The units competing are from the Royal Navy, the Royal Marines and the Army stationed in the Portsmouth district. The trophy has only rarely been won by Army units, and the Battalion's success in 1934 was the first occasion when the Cup had been in the hands of the Army since it was won in 1911 by the Gloucestershire Regiment.

It was at Parkhurst that the 2nd Battalion received its first motor transport, in the form of four Lloyd carriers. A mortar platoon also came into being, consisting then of four men, four bicycles and four green and white flags.

The four years on the Isle of Wight came to an end on 3rd January, 1936, when the Battalion left Parkhurst for Corunna Barracks, Aldershot, relieving the Queen's in the 1st Guards Brigade. Training was done as seriously as the continual shortage of N.C.Os. and men would permit. The Army was still struggling to attain and maintain efficiency under the extremely adverse conditions caused by the policy of the Government, and this was the 1st Division and the year was 1936. Each company of the 2nd Battalion had only two platoons, often of only fifteen men each. But everyone persevered and the very best was made of the unpromising and discouraging conditions.

At the King's Birthday Parade in 1936, Lieutenant-Colonel im Thurn, as the senior Lieutenant-Colonel, commanded the 1st Guards Brigade, and the 2nd Hampshire won most favourable comment from a large gathering of most critical spectators by their performance beside the Grenadier Guards and the Scots Guards.

It was while the Battalion was busy with brigade training at Warnham Camp in Sussex that it was suddenly recalled to Aldershot to mobilize as part of the 1st Division, for active service in Palestine. There was, of course, a great deal of administrative activity. Three hundred and sixty class "A" reservists, recalled to the Colours for the emergency, were posted to the Battalion. They came from eleven regiments, mostly from the north of England, and they did not prove to be the most malleable of material. However, as always, everything was ready on time after all, and the 2nd Battalion, 24 officers and 708 other ranks, embarked on the s.s. *California* at Southampton on 22nd September, 1936. The ship had been taken straight from the New York–Bermuda summer cruise.

The Battalion disembarked at Haifa on 1st October, and went to Jerusalem, settling at a Christian Arab village, Beit Jala, some six miles south of Jerusalem, overlooking Bethlehem (*see map on page* 32). The situation in Palestine was very much as it was when the 1st Battalion served there two years later, though the revolt was in its early stages and was not therefore so virulent. The quick action of the Government in sending the 1st Division seemed to have damped the spirits of the Arabs for the time being, and the state of emergency was sufficiently easier to permit the reservists to be sent home on 6th November. On 30th November the Battalion moved from Beit Jala to Nablus, where they stayed for three weeks. In that time they were transferred from the Guards Brigade to the 17th Infantry Brigade, the two Guards battalions returning to England. Nablus was a distinctly hostile town, but the Battalion's short time there was uneventful. They then moved to Tiberias, on the Sea of Galilee, where they spent Christmas with traditional festivity.

On 1st February, 1937, the Battalion was re-formed as the 1st Battalion had been, the machine-gun company being abolished. The change from horse to mechanized transport had been completed the year before ; with the immediate result that there were many disconsolate "horsy" soldiers with no horses to care for, and not nearly sufficient motor drivers, a situation which was adjusted in the course of time.

Another move took place in May, 1937, to Lighthouse Camp, Haifa. The camp was at the foot of Mount Carmel, close to the seashore and the ruins of a Crusader castle at Athlit. A feature of the service in Palestine was the dispersal of the Battalion in detachments, and even when the move to Haifa took place, one company remained detached at Safad, in the hills near the Syrian frontier. The Essex were also in Haifa at the time ; they were next to be with the 1st Battalion at Minden in 1951. It was at Lighthouse Camp that Lieutenant-Colonel A. E. Stokes Roberts, from the Worcestershire Regiment, took over command of the 2nd Battalion, Lieutenant-Colonel B. B. von B. im Thurn having completed his tenure of command on 9th September, 1937.

The Battalion moved again, returning to Tiberias on 22nd October, still with one company at Safad. The Arabs were giving a great deal of trouble at this time, and the Battalion was kept busy with patrolling, providing guards on the railway, searching villages for arms and ammunition, and co-operating generally with the Palestine Police, the Transjordan Frontier Force and the Royal Air Force. The Brigade was widely dispersed, with Headquarters at Haifa, and units saw very little of each other.

With the declaration of martial law in Palestine, military courts were set up. At the first trial of an Arab caught red-handed carrying arms Major

Fawkes presided. The Arab was sentenced to death and hanged, and for the rest of the Battalion's stay in Palestine Major Fawkes had to have a constant military escort.

There were numerous small engagements, quite often fruitless through the somewhat unco-ordinated information received. On one occasion the whole Battalion turned out to watch crossings of the Jordan south of Beisan as attempts to smuggle arms across the river into Palestine were suspected, and for this operation elaborate anti-malarial measures were taken. Sudden "swoops" across the plains were made and villages searched. Places which were much in the news at the time were Arraba, Sakhnin, Turan, Endor and Suffuriya.

The most elaborate action of this time occurred, as so often it seemed to do, on Christmas Day, 1937. A message was received on Christmas Eve from a Transjordan Frontier Force patrol asking for assistance, and reporting that there had been action between the T.J.F.F. and a large body of well-armed Arabs. The Battalion was turned out early on Christmas morning, and there followed three rather confused days of movement and patrolling under active-service conditions, in which one Arab sniper was killed and a C.Q.M.S. of the Battalion was wounded. The operation lasted until Boxing Day, thus depriving the Battalion of its Christmas feasting and festivity. The men were, however, able to sit down to their Christmas dinners in their billets on 3rd January.

This spell of service in Palestine was a busy one, but every opportunity was taken for sport. The hockey team played its way into the semi-final of the Army in Palestine Competition, and cross-country running, boxing and cricket all flourished as far as duty permitted. There was also some excellent small game shooting, for which Colonel Stokes Roberts was an enthusiast, and it was particularly good round Lake Hule. On 16th December the G.O.C.-in-C., General Wavell, was entertained to a shoot, appropriate protection being given to the distinguished guest and his party by providing Lewis gun sections in trucks at the head and tail of the M.T. column, and piqueting the hill near the area where the shoot was to take place. The bag was 25 snipe, 105 wild duck and 30 coot—the latter shot for the beaters.

In January, 1938, the Battalion was relieved, and embarked at Haifa on 15th January on the s.s. *California*, the ship which had taken them out to Palestine. At Southampton the Battalion was welcomed by General Sir Richard Haking, the Mayor of Southampton and many senior officers. The Battalion formed up in three sides of a square and was addressed by the Mayor, and Colonel Stokes Roberts replied.

After two months' leave the Battalion settled down again at Aldershot, once more in Corunna Barracks, and soon they were again in the 1st Guards Brigade, commanded by Brigadier Beckwith-Smith. In 1938 and 1939 soldiering was done against the background of Munich and the ever-increasing tension as Hitler and Mussolini proceeded on their fantastic courses. Training had a purpose, and there was much to do. There were new weapons to learn; the Bren gun, the anti-tank rifle and the anti-tank gun, though the last remained in fact no more than a green and white flag. Training included co-operation with tanks, and there was a brigade demonstration with a composite tank battalion. Another new task was to learn to handle and drive carriers, which were to play so important a part in the years to come. It was at this time, too, that Captain R. F. M. Humphrey became Adjutant in the place of Captain J. H. H. Robinson.

The splendid condition of the 2nd Battalion on the eve of the war was shown by their successes in sport in 1939. Boy Chaston won the Boys' Army 220 yards and was the leader of the Boys' boxing team which won the Guards Brigade Cup. The remaining horses in the Battalion won one of the few cups open to the infantry at the Aldershot Command Show. The Battalion team won the Aldershot cross-country run and came third in the Army run in Windsor Great Park. Second-Lieutenant MacKillop was the Army Javelin Champion and runner-up in the A.A.A. Championship. Two officers, Lieutenants Dewar and Purcell, played cricket and rugby football for Aldershot Command, the one playing lawn tennis and the other hockey as well. Lieutenant Gratton played for the Command at cricket, lawn tennis and squash racquets.

Certain "characters" of the 2nd Battalion of the days before the war are remembered by all who served with them. There was Lance-Corporal Beasley, with six good-conduct stripes running up his left arm to join the one N.C.O.'s stripe, who looked after the bandboys, controlled innumerable football, hockey and cricket matches, and was an admirable mentor to young soldiers in all sports. There was Lance-Corporal Budden, post corporal and sports storeman, and for many seasons goal-keeper for the hockey elevens. There was Private "Tiny" Bent, weapon training storeman and at the age of thirty-five, with but little hair on his head, ever to the fore in the rugger pack. There was Lance-Corporal Jack Huggins, later to be Provost Sergeant, who was one of a famous trio of the "3 H's"—Holmes, Haines and Huggins—who had lent so much lustre to the Regiment in the boxing world in the twenties. Sergeant "Squibs" Rule, later Major C. H. B. Rule and Second-in-Command of the 11th Battalion, was for many years associated with Battalion athletics and cross-country running. There was Lance-Corporal Jack Pointer, C.O.'s groom and an expert in horses and their ways, and also one of the best shots in the Battalion. Stalwarts of the football team were Sergeant "Totsy" Watts and Corporal Bob Truran, both of whom in due course became Quartermasters in the Regiment.

These "characters" were well known and well remembered by the men of the 2nd Battalion in the days before the war, when the Battalion, in fine fettle in work and play, was appropriately placed in the 1st Guards Brigade in the 1st Division. They were, in the main, the men who went to France in the British Expeditionary Force in the autumn of 1939, and whose performance in the spring of 1940 shed such lustre on the Regiment.

With the war clouds gathering dark over Europe, the Battalion went on 30th July by march route to Holt End Camp for brigade manœuvres. But very bad weather spoiled everything and after three days the mud was so deep that the camp had to be evacuated. The men were given five days' leave, and their training was continued in barracks until, ten days afterwards, the weather had improved sufficiently for the Brigade to return to the camp. All went well until suddenly, on 24th August, the Battalion returned to barracks. All leave was cancelled and emergency measures towards mobilization, which had been prepared previously, were put into effect. The air was full of rumours and speculation until complete mobilization was ordered on 1st September, to be followed two days later by the declaration of war.

CHAPTER IV

THE HAMPSHIRE REGIMENT, 1925–1939

I—The Territorial Battalions

In the years between 1925 and the outbreak of the Second World War the Territorial battalions maintained to the full the vigorous life they had begun in the difficult days immediately after the previous war. Led by enthusiastic officers and N.C.Os., the battalions carried out the routine of spare-time parades in their drill halls scattered about the county. From time to time there were company parades, and every summer the battalions turned out in good strength for the annual camps, where battalion and brigade exercises kept them all up to scratch. The value of their peace-time work was realized when war broke out in 1939 and the Territorial battalions were found to be fit and ready, with the minimum of adjustment, for active service. How they fared in action will be seen as their tale is unfolded in later chapters.

There were, of course, many changes in the fourteen years between 1925 and 1939; old friends went and new men came in; there were cross-postings and, from time to time, changes in command of the battalions. The 4th Battalion was commanded by Colonel F. L. Footner, D.S.O., T.D., from 1920 to 1928, when he was succeeded by Lieutenant-Colonel B. E. T. Parsons, D.S.O., T.D., who in his turn commanded the Battalion for eight very successful years. Colonel Parsons was succeeded by Lieutenant-Colonel H. J. Brooks, D.S.O., M.C., T.D., in 1936, who was in command in July, 1939, when the Battalion was divided into two, as it had been in the last war. The 1/4th, recruited from Andover, Winchester and Romsey, had its Headquarters in Winchester, and the 2/4th, recruiting from Aldershot, Alton, Basingstoke, Farnborough and Cove, had its Headquarters at Aldershot. Together with the 5th Battalion the 1/4th and 2/4th constituted the famous 128th (Hampshire) Infantry Brigade, and the newly formed battalions at once began intensive training. A great deal more will be told of the "Tigers" Brigade later in this book.

In 1926 Lieutenant-Colonel R. F. Gutteridge, T.D., was succeeded in command of the 5/7th Battalion by Lieutenant-Colonel C. W. G. Palmer, O.B.E., T.D. Colonel Palmer was succeeded in 1928 by Lieutenant-Colonel The Lord Templemore, D.S.O., O.B.E., who commanded the 5/7th until 1931, when his promotion to full Colonel was gazetted. Lieutenant-Colonel The Lord Manners took his place. In 1935 Lieutenant-Colonel C. E. Elliot, T.D., became Commanding Officer, and he was still in command in August, 1939, when the Battalion once more became the 5th Battalion, a 7th Battalion being formed under Lieutenant-Colonel A. W. Malim. One memorable occasion was the guard of honour provided by the 5/7th Battalion on 26th July, 1933, for His Majesty King George V when he opened the new Graving Dock at Southampton.

The 6th Battalion (Duke of Connaught's Own) was commanded by Colonel

G. R. Curtis, T.D., until on the completion of his tour of command he was succeeded by Lieutenant-Colonel L.W. S. Blackmore, who remained in command until war broke out again. The 6th Battalion was originally formed in 1859 as the 3rd Hampshire Volunteer Battalion. When the Territorial Army was formed in 1908 it became the 6th (Duke of Connaught's Own) Battalion, with His Royal Highness as Honorary Colonel. The Battalion had served in South Africa during the war and in the 1914–1918 war in India and Mesopotamia.

In 1938 came the startling news that this "old and bold" infantry battalion was to be converted to Royal Artillery as the 59th and 69th Anti-Tank Regiments. After the first shock everyone entered into the spirit of the change, realizing that such changes were inevitable with a new war threatening, a war which would call for different methods. If tanks were to attack infantry, there must be men to kill them, and the 6th Battalion felt confident that they could do that as well as anyone else. Moreover, though members of the Royal Regiment they would still be Tigers in spirit.

Both Regiments were in due course given ample opportunity to kill German tanks, the 59th in Normandy and Holland, the 69th in France in 1940 and later in Burma. In 1951 their title was changed again, and their Hampshire association officially recognized in their title. Their service as Gunners in the war was a continuation in every way of their previous enthusiastic and spirited record as infantry.

The remaining Territorial Battalion, the 8th (Princess Beatrice's Isle of Wight Rifles), were also to suffer a fundamental change of character from Infantry to Artillery. After the 1914–1918 war the Battalion was commanded by Colonel A. C. T. Veasey until he was succeeded in 1925 by Lieutenant-Colonel E. G. St. Aubyn, D.S.O. When in 1929 Colonel St. Aubyn was given a brigade, his place was taken by Lieutenant-Colonel G. H. Hodgkinson, followed in December, 1932, by Lieutenant-Colonel R. O. Spencer-Smith and, four years later, by Lieutenant-Colonel C. W. Brannon, M.C., T.D., a noteworthy appointment as in Colonel Brannon the Battalion was commanded for the first time by one who had risen from its ranks.

To Colonel Brannon fell the somewhat sad duty of supervising the transfer of the Battalion to the Royal Regiment of Artillery. By 1937 the War Office considered it necessary to reorganize the defences of Portsmouth and Southampton and to increase the artillery on the island. It was felt that the only people who could conveniently supply the need for more Gunners were the officers and men of the 8th Battalion The Isle of Wight Rifles, and the Battalion was asked to agree to being converted into a Brigade of Heavy Artillery, with the important task of manning some of the batteries on the Isle of Wight which were part of the vital outer defences of Portsmouth and Southampton. The War Office realized what a great sacrifice of ancient ties of loyalty and affection the change would make, and attempted to mollify this to some extent by permitting the new unit to retain its identity and distinctive title, and to remain affiliated to The Hampshire Regiment.

It can well be imagined what a shock the news was when the Commanding

Officer announced it, but realizing the hard necessity which lay behind the proposal, officers and men of the Isle of Wight Rifles agreed to the change. Thus the 8th Battalion The Hampshire Regiment became in May, 1937, The Princess Beatrice's (Isle of Wight Rifles) Heavy Brigade, Royal Artillery, T.A. In May, 1937, Her Royal Highness The Princess Beatrice, V.A., C.I., G.B.E., was reappointed Honorary Colonel. The 8th were lost to the Regiment in effect, though not in name or affection. Becoming Gunners, they were still Tigers.

II—The Hampshire Regiment, 1925–1939

We have related briefly the more significant events in the story of the battalions of the Regiment from 1925 to 1939. There were, of course, events significant to the Regiment as a whole, the most notable of which was probably an addition to the Regimental Colour. This was announced in Army Orders in July, 1935, and stated that His Majesty The King had been pleased to approve a centre badge for the Regimental Colour of The Hampshire Regiment, "a double red rose fimbriated gold," the "Tudor Rose." In October, 1932, another regimental alliance was notified in Army Orders, between The Hampshire Regiment and the Sault Ste Marie Regiment, Non-Permanent Active Militia of Canada.

Our story has reached the historic date, 3rd September, 1939, which found The Hampshire Regiment lined up for battle. In the years between the wars the Regular battalions and the Territorials had maintained their keenness and their traditional verve, often under difficult conditions, and as the portents gathered around them they had toned themselves up so that, when the time came, they were "at the ready."

CHAPTER V

THE 1ST BATTALION IN THE MIDDLE EAST AND MALTA

3RD SEPTEMBER, 1939, TO 30TH MARCH, 1943

THE outbreak of war with Germany on 3rd September, 1939, found the 1st Battalion in Egypt, commanded by Lieutenant-Colonel H. C. Westmorland. They were stationed at El Daba, about half-way between Alexandria and Matruh, out in the Western Desert which was later to be the scene of much historic fighting (*see map on page* 48). El Daba itself was a small untidy place consisting of a huddle of unprepossessing hovels, the Suk or shopping centre, the lines of the Egyptian Camel Corps, and a few official and administrative buildings. The Battalion's role was the protection of the Lines of Communication of the British and Egyptian forces stationed between Ma'aten Baggush and the Libyan border.

At this time Italy was still neutral and the Western Desert Force, the predecessor of the Eighth Army, was in a mobile role, operating up to the Sollum frontier wire. The Buffs were in Matruh—the Egyptian Army was still there as well—and the 1st Hampshire were at El Daba. The possible methods of attack against which the Battalion at El Daba made provision were by air, by airborne troops, from small forces landed from the sea, and from saboteurs. As at home, however, the war still seemed to be unreal, and the air-raid precautions, the gas-mask drill, gas-chamber experience, censorship and all the conditions of active service needed something of an act of faith.

There was, however, a great deal to be done, and the Battalion was busy and expectant, wondering where and how they would see action. To some it seemed that they were to be left out of it all, and they envied the 2nd Battalion their luck in getting out to France quickly.

Soon after war was declared the 1st Hampshire moved up to Matruh to take part in an exercise to test the defences of Matruh, where the garrison was mainly Egyptian. The mock attack succeeded and General Maitland Wilson, then G.O.C.-in-C., Egypt, held a brusque summing-up which can have left the Egyptian Army in little doubt about his views of their efficiency.

The Battalion was moved, but, it seemed, still farther away from the war, for they went back to Palestine on 12th December, 1939, to take up once more the familiar business of keeping the peace between Jews and Arabs. Battalion Headquarters, H.Q. Company, "D" Company and one platoon of "C" were at Sarafand in Talavera Barracks ; the remaining two platoons of "C" Company were at Lydda Airport in a hutted camp ; "A" was at Gaza and "B" at Gaza Airport. Thus once more the Battalion was scattered and once more everyone was busy with punitive raids after gangs had made a nuisance of themselves by cutting telegraph lines, burning houses and sniping all and sundry. One of the few incidents worthy of note was the rounding-up and "winding-up" of a notorious gang at Beit Dajan on 15th December.

Christmas Day was passed peacefully enough and everyone made merry in the true style. Early in January came the notification of decorations for distinguished service in Palestine between April and July, 1939, in which Lieutenant-Colonel Ramsden was awarded the D.S.O., Captain Frisby the M.C., and Private C. F. W. Hutchings the M.M. The Battalion made various moves in Palestine, so that at the end Battalion Headquarters, H.Q. Company and one platoon of "B" Company were at Hebron, "A" Company was at Allar—comprising "Allcol"—"C" was at Sarafand, and "D" was at Deir Shaar, in "Shalcol." One duty carried out when Battalion Headquarters moved to Gaza soon after Christmas was preparing the reception of the first Australian formation to arrive in the Middle East. This entailed the erecting of a tremendous number of tents, receiving and administering advance parties and, incidentally, the brewing of vast quantities of tea when the Australians arrived.

After six months the Battalion left Palestine, on a memorable date, 2nd June, 1940—the day when their comrades of the 2nd Battalion were making their way home across the Channel in an assortment of craft from Dunkirk. The 1st Battalion's move was one of extreme urgency; their destination was unknown and rumours were rife. Their new post turned out to be Moascar, in the Suez Canal Zone, with one company up at El Daba for railway protection. At that time the gigantic arsenal and garrison of the Middle East, which was to play such a vital part in the great pattern of victory, was taking shape. Defence duties included boat patrols in the Canal, and the shadowing of Italian and other suspect ships through the Battalion sector.

A week after the Battalion arrived at Moascar came the news that Italy had declared war on Britain and France. In accordance with a set scheme, the Battalion rounded up the Italian colony during the night and by dawn they were all interned. Italy's entry into the war changed conditions in Egypt. The enemy was on the doorstep, and Marshal Graziani crossed the Libyan border and began to establish his army for the invasion of Egypt. Air-raid alarms were frequent, but as no Italian bombers penetrated to the Canal Zone, no bombs were dropped. This was the time of the collapse of France and elements of their army in Syria concentrated in the Canal Zone. The Battalion was given the task of administering detachments of the French Foreign Legion at Moascar, and a few British Legionnaires were enlisted into the British Army. The Foreign Legionnaires, particularly some Spaniards, were rather difficult to deal with, but when a squadron of Spahi Cavalry arrived in Moascar they took over the administration of the various Foreign Legion parties.

Marshal Graziani's advance into Egypt had taken him as far as Maktila, a fortified position east of Sidi Barrani. The Italians built a hard macadamized road to support their transport, and they threw out a screen of positions to the south. They had heavy numerical superiority and their plan was to by-pass the nearest British fortress at Mersa Matruh, seventy miles nearer to Alexandria, and then to sweep along the coast to Alexandria, where they could threaten the Nile Valley. It was the plan that Rommel put into action later in the war.

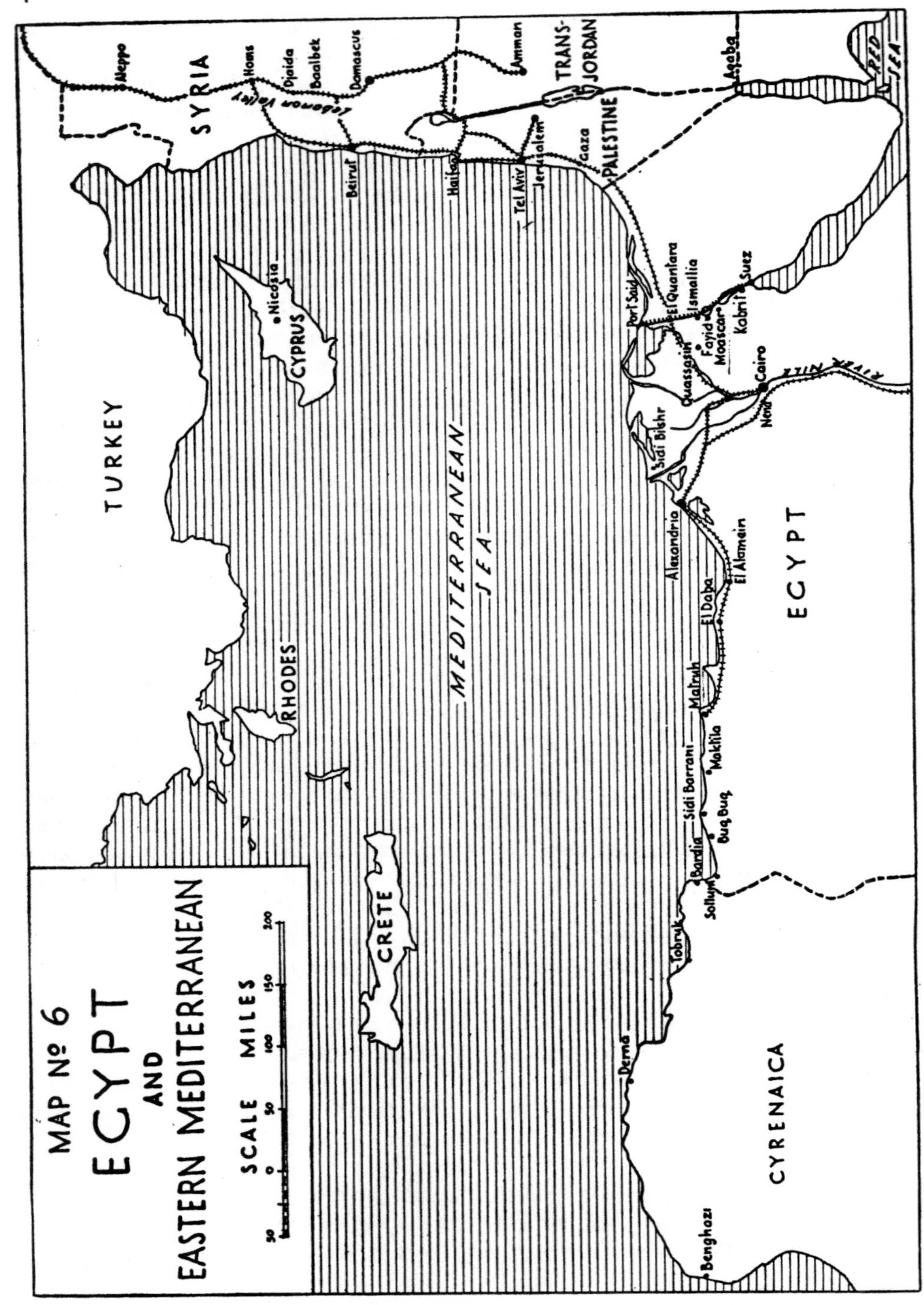
MAP No 6
EGYPT
AND
EASTERN MEDITERRANEAN
SCALE MILES
50 0 50 100 150 200
TURKEY
SYRIA
Aleppo
Homs
Djaida
Baalbek
Damascus
Lebanon Valley
Amman
TRANS-
JORDAN
Aqaba
RED
SEA
Beirut
Haifa
Tel Aviv
Jerusalem
Gaza
PALESTINE
CYPRUS
Nicosia
RHODES
CRETE
MEDITERRANEAN
SEA
Port Said
El Quantara
Ismailia
Fayid
Moascar
Kabrit
Suez
Quassasin
Cairo
Nera
RIVER NILE
Sidi Bishr
Alexandria
El Alamein
El Daba
Matruh
Maktila
Sidi Barrani
Buq Buq
Bardia
Sollum
Tobruk
Derna
Benghazi
EGYPT
CYRENAICA

On 15th September, 1940, while the Italians under Graziani were still advancing, the Battalion was ordered to move up to Mersa Matruh, once Cleopatra's bathing resort, some two hundred and fifty miles west of Alexandria. This was one of the nearest outposts in the line to the Italian defences, previously held by units of the Egyptian Army which was being replaced as quickly as possible. The Battalion's move to Matruh took place at a time of mounting tension. When they arrived they found that the tidy little villas and the two neat hotels on the very blue lagoon had been damaged by air raids. Companies were at once led to previously reconnoitred sectors and the order was to dig in at once. The Battalion was told that it might expect the enemy in front of its defences in forty-eight hours, but it was soon apparent that Graziani intended to consolidate his position at Maktila and the sense of urgency subsided.

There followed a period of very heavy raids by Italian bombers. At first the air defences of Matruh were in the hands of Egyptian gunners, whose light anti-aircraft guns had a comparatively low ceiling, so that the Italian planes could cruise round in comfort and bomb at leisure. The only British planes available were three relatively slow Gladiators, but the situation was improved in mid-October, however, when a few Hurricanes came on the scene and the Italian mass daylight raids on Matruh soon stopped. The raids were mostly directed against the railway station and the harbour buildings; companies manning the perimeter were bombed less than the installations and Headquarters in the centre. As the result of this, Battalion Headquarters was moved to a dug-out on the hillside on the outskirts of the town, and the Commanding Officer and Adjutant made themselves at home in an ancient tomb.

At that time the garrison of Matruh consisted of a battalion of Scots Guards, D.L.I., South Stafford, King's Own, a Cheshire (M.G.) battalion and the 1st Hampshire. As soon as possible the Egyptian anti-aircraft gunners were replaced and Field and Medium Artillery joined the garrison. Digging in was very difficult and required power tools, and great numbers of mines were laid, sometimes causing casualties as the mines had been locally made in Egypt. Tank ditches, mostly ineffective, and several belts of wire, with battalions deployed fairly widely but in considerable depth, formed the defence of Matruh. Some of the local place-names are worthy of record, such as Charing Cross, Pottery Mound and Doubtful Corner.

As soon as it was clear that the Italians were not going on but were staying in their positions just inside the frontier, mobile training started. At the end of October the Battalion was called upon to provide all its transport and the carrier platoon, and a number of officers to act as umpires, for big exercises by Western Desert Force. After the exercise it was reported that it had gone only moderately well and was therefore to be repeated. No one was surprised, therefore, when shortly afterwards the Battalion was again detailed to send out the carrier platoon and all its transport for another exercise.

This new exercise was, however, General Wavell's celebrated bluff covering his attack on the Italian positions at Sidi Barrani on 7th December. Even

Battalion Headquarters did not know until the night of the attack that it was not an exercise but battle. The Italians were completely hoaxed. They knew all about the exercise with live ammunition in the desert and did not suspect the second exercise until it was only too obvious to them that it was much more. To add to the security, on the morning of the attack General Wavell was seen at the races at the Gezira Club in Cairo.

The part played by the Matruh fortress in the operation was to provide a firm base on which the whole plan hinged. It also provided one column of the Scots Guards. To make this one battalion fully mobile all the other battalions of the garrison placed their carrier platoons under command and handed over their transport.

General Wavell's brilliant operation was completely successful. The Matruh fortress provided a force of 1,500 which attacked the enemy and prevented him going down the coast from Maktila. At the same time two divisions struck northwards from the desert and the R.A.F. attacked in force and the Royal Navy bombarded from the sea. Dummy tanks and guns made of canvas and wood were set up and the ruse succeeded beyond all expectation. Italian generals with their staffs were captured still in their pyjamas and confusion reigned in the enemy camp. On 11th December Sidi Barrani fell and General Wavell's force of not more than 20,000 had completely routed an enemy more than double its size. The prize was won by dash and audacity, and this first desert victory came at a time when good news was sorely needed.

The number of prisoners taken was so great it set a new problem in the desert, where water and supplies were scarce. The Matruh force of 1,500 alone counted 8,000 prisoners while the battle was still on, and when Sidi Barrani fell there were 26,000 more. The Battalion was at once heavily involved. Escorts went up to the Barrani area and took over long columns of prisoners, bringing them back to Matruh railhead. Soon the railway was congested and coasters were run into Matruh and filled with escorts and prisoners. This kept the Battalion at full stretch over many hundreds of miles. When Sollum was captured the Battalion sent a detachment there to help in opening its small port, required for moving up supplies for the forward troops then approaching Derna and Tobruk.

One other aspect of the Battalion's share in the Barrani battle was that several small parties were attached to the column for special duties. One such consisted of Lieutenant G. R. Hogan and four other ranks, who travelled hundreds of miles across the desert in car and truck on liaison duties, encountering various adventures *en route*.

On 23rd December orders were received for the Battalion to move up next day to Buq Buq to clear the battlefield. The Greeks were at this time very hard pressed and every available weapon and vehicle that could be salvaged from the Barrani area was urgently needed for immediate shipment to Greece. It was a formidable task, of which Colonel Westmorland wrote afterwards:

"The task of clearing, sorting and evacuating this mass of material is one of the thankless tasks that have to be carried out in war. After a fortnight of hard work, mountains of food, thousands of rifles, hundreds of automatic weapons and great piles of clothing and equipment appeared at the dumps.

"The troops worked from dawn to dusk so that valuable equipment could be used against the enemy here and elsewhere. Water was rationed at half a gallon per man per day, and once a sandstorm blew so hard that no cooking was possible for more than twelve hours and visibility was reduced to a few feet."

* * * * *

On 21st February, 1941, the 1st Battalion left Egypt for Malta, sailing in H.M.S. *Orion* and H.M.S. *Ajax* for "an unknown destination." Two days later the Battalion disembarked in the Grand Harbour at Valletta and found itself part of the Malta Infantry Brigade, which was also to be known as the Southern Infantry Brigade (S.I.B.), the 1st (Malta) Infantry Brigade, and more permanently as the famous 231st Infantry Brigade. Their colleagues in the Brigade were the 2nd Devons and the 1st Dorsets. These three battalions, with two other brigades and various non-brigaded units, were to undergo together the tremendous bombing of Malta, the famine and all the hardships of the siege of the George Cross Island (*see map on page* 52).

The Battalion was dispersed with Headquarters and H.Q. Company at Shelili Tower, and rifle companies at Guidia, Zurriek, Safi airstrips and Imkabba. Rifle company locations were modified to some extent from time to time, but generally they remained the same ; and although companies were rotated, "C" Company will always be associated with the Safi Strips, "D" Company with Imkabba and "A" Company with Guidia.

The role of the 1st Hampshire was the defence of the Safi airstrip and the southern dispersal areas of Luqa airfield, defence of a considerable area against airborne invasion, and finally as brigade reserve. Apart from four platoons which manned defence posts protecting the airfield, the Battalion was not committed to static positions, but it was held in mobile reserve for use in a counter-attack role, and to this end all work and training was directed.

The Brigade was responsible for the defence of an area with thirty miles of coastline, twenty miles of which was suitable for sea landings ; the brigade area also contained an aeroplane base, an aerodrome used by R.A.F. fighters and torpedo-carrying aircraft of the Fleet Air Arm, two emergency landing strips, one of which was used as a decoy, and a dispersal area for aircraft.

At first, after the bare desert, life in Malta gave the appearance of being very comfortable ; food was plentiful, everyone made themselves as comfortable as they could and there was a lively and cheerful social life. It was not altogether as it seemed, however, for air raids were frequent and violent. Everyone felt that they were there for the rest of the war, there was no way out, and the enemy was determined to "neutralize" Malta. They seemed to have all the cards, and all the aircraft. But the Malta Garrison settled down to stick it out, to hit back as hard as they could and to see that, come what may, Malta was not "neutralized."

The pattern of life in 1941 was to work hard, to train hard and to play hard. When Major-General D. M. W. Beak, V.C., D.S.O., M.C., took over the command of the Army in Malta in January, 1942, he confirmed that policy. In a lecture to officers he said, "You will do P.T. every morning before breakfast, you will cycle in full equipment for twenty miles, you will run and walk alternately for fifteen miles in full equipment!" That was the tune and everyone became proud of their task and proud of themselves.

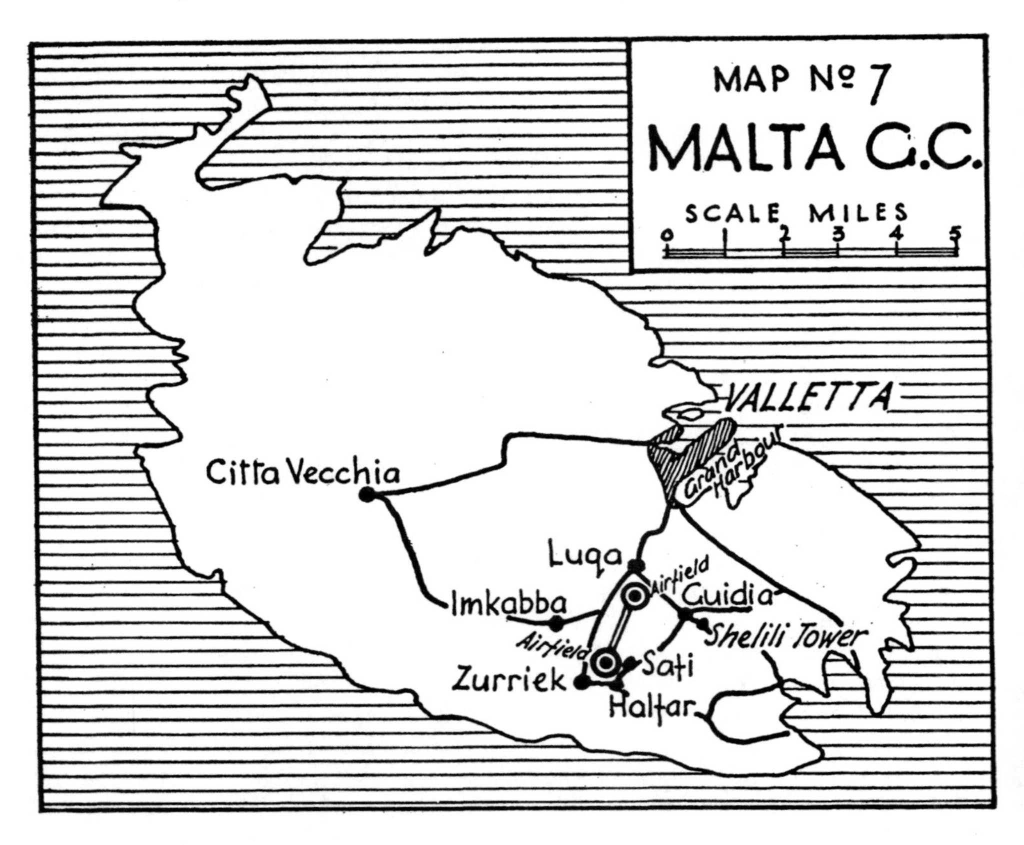

Towards the end of 1941 the Luftwaffe moved to Sicily and German aircraft began to take the place of the Italian in a carefully worked-out plan of attacks on Malta. At first bombers came over in threes or fives, often a dozen times a day, and attacked specific targets, dealing first with the airfields and the docks. Our own machines were destroyed on the ground, and the few Hurricanes on the island became casualties one by one as they gallantly fought against odds. Gradually the Germans won the mastery of the air and convoys had to run the gauntlet and fight their way through to Malta. No ships were able to get through between November, 1941, and 23rd March, 1942, when three ships of a convoy of four fought their way through. Two of these were only partly discharged when they were sunk in the Grand Harbour. The third, damaged on the voyage, was towed to another anchorage, but she was sunk there.

As the Germans had gained the mastery of the air over Malta they could choose their targets and deal with them methodically. First it was the docks and airfields, and aircraft on the ground. Then they changed to military targets. People not in the immediate vicinity of the target were reasonably safe, but troops engaged in working parties in the centre of an airfield were in a poor position. Everyone became expert in the art of dispersal and taking cover, but casualties were inevitable, especially as the Battalion was very often engaged in repairing craters in the airfield, and on such tasks as resurfacing and widening the airstrips. On one occasion the whole Battalion were employed on crater filling. They perforce made very vulnerable targets from the air and were consequently bombed and suffered casualties, but owing to the vital importance of the work at that particular period, the Battalion neither dispersed nor ceased work. Other tasks were the building of pens for aircraft when some were flown in, clearing debris after raids and putting out crop fires.

In the first part of 1942 Lieutenant-Colonel H. C. Westmorland relinquished command of the Battalion, and was succeeded by Lieutenant-Colonel J. L. Spencer, M.C. Colonel Westmorland had the unique distinction of commanding a Battalion of the Regiment both in the 1914-1918 war and in 1939 ; he had taken over command at El Daba, and had led the Battalion in the early chapters of its war story, setting the tone in Malta which, carried on by Colonel Spencer, won such a fine name for the Battalion in the Middle East. Colonel Spencer was an officer with immense drive and enthusiasm. Under his command the 1st Battalion was brought to a very high standard which won for it a magnificent reputation.

The morale of the Malta garrison was high ; and the worse things became, the better the morale. The index of the garrison's anxiety might well have been taken as the top of the chimney of the brewery. When the mass air raids began everyone's heart fell as smoke ceased to curl upwards. Eyes were often on that smoke-stack, hoping to see that wisp of smoke which would mean beer again. N.A.A.F.I. was also short of beer, and in the spring of 1942 everything began to be short. The troops tightened their belts, grumbled, and dreamed of the day when a convoy would tie up in the Grand Harbour with a sufficient load of food—and beer. In the early summer of 1942, with the Eighth Army back on the Alamein line and the Germans masters of the air, that time seemed very remote.

So the battle for Malta went on in the first half of 1942. The Gunners were magnificent, fighting their guns in the midst of the heavy raids, with little rest and against what seemed like a hopelessly unending number of enemy planes. It was a red-letter day when the first few Spitfires were flown in. They fought heroic battles against immense odds, and it was a heartening sight to see half a dozen Spitfires in the air, shining and beautiful in the sun, taking on all comers until they were shot down, but rarely without scoring successes. The raids became heavier and heavier. In April over 2,000 tons of bombs were dropped in the 231st Brigade area alone. No convoys could get through. Our fighters were finished. Only the anti-aircraft guns stood between the island and invasion—and ammunition was getting desperately low. Guns were rationed to a few rounds a day. Some guns were given twenty-four hours "stand-down" periods and could not engage targets during that time.

The plight of Malta was well known at home, and great gallantry was shown by the Royal Navy and the merchantmen to try to bring succour. Once fifty Spitfires were flown in, but most of them were soon knocked out. Then came the exhilarating battle, and the victory, of May, 1942. On 8th May sixty-five Spitfires arrived on the island from the aircraft carrier *Wasp* (U.S.A.) and H.M.S. *Eagle*. By sheer hard work and good organization twenty-three Spitfires were airborne for the first alert on 9th May. It was a grand sight and the morale of the island rose visibly that morning. Fourteen JU 88's and fifteen JU 87's came across the island on that day, and they received an unexpected welcome and were roughly handled. Seven enemy aircraft were shot down and many badly damaged. The 10th May was destined to be the great day and elaborate arrangements were made to put every serviceable Spitfire in the air, to keep the aerodrome open and put up a terrific barrage over the Grand Harbour. The Germans, as was expected, attacked the cruiser *Welshman*, which was in the harbour, having brought in some much-needed ammunition for the anti-aircraft guns. For the first time the enemy was routed over Malta; and he lost altogether sixty-three aircraft. In the words of a spectator, "Planes were dropping out of the sky in bits and pieces at all angles." H.M.S. *Welshman* was undamaged.

The 10th May, 1942, marked the end of the mass attacks over Malta, except for one tremendous but equally unsuccessful raid in October. Small formations of enemy aircraft continued to raid the island after the battle of May, but they came circumspectly and had special targets, and all the while our Spitfires continued to take a heavy toll.

There were many actions of personal courage during the battle of Malta, but they were so much part of the way of life that most of them go unrecorded. A typical example was when Lieutenant Methven, Sergeants Shave and Chinnock and Privates Blake and Kenton saw a British bomber crash and ran to it. The crew warned them to stand clear, as the plane was loaded with bombs, and had begun to burn. The soldiers helped three of the crew to safety, and then stayed to rescue the other two, who were both wounded, one of them severely. They dragged the last man out and took him to the shelter of one of the many low walls which divide Maltese fields, when the aircraft blew up. One bystander was killed.

The food situation had been difficult in the spring, but by July it became really serious. Everything was short and rations had to be cut severely. Everyone was hungry, and petrol, ammunition, cigarettes, and all the "extras" were almost non-existent, yet morale became even higher than before. Men took a pride in doing things well and quickly. Training schemes were begun and carried out with terrific enthusiasm. People tried to outdo everyone else in personal smartness and efficiency. Petrol was rationed, for example, to thirty gallons a month per battalion. The 1st Hampshire decided to do much better than that and used only nine and a half gallons. To give the Battalion some mobility as brigade reserve practically every man had a bicycle. Seventy bicycles on the war stores of each company was the cause of considerable anxiety to company commanders, particularly as at that time bicycles could be sold for three times their value in the flourishing black market. The Battalion took to soldiering on bicycles with the same enthusiasm and *élan* as they did everything else in Malta.

Another duty which fell to the Malta garrison was dockworking, and the Battalion became stevedores as well as everything else. On the great occasions when one or two ships fought their way into harbour, work began at once. At Tobruk troops had discharged 600 tons of cargo a day ; the Malta garrison decided to do better. Soldiers became winch-drivers, "top-men," stevedores and quay-labour. As a ship berthed, so the intricate organization began, with a smoke-screen, lorry drivers, dock control, dumping systems and everything. When the *Orari* and *Troilus* berthed at Valletta in June, 1942, 3,200 tons were discharged in the first twenty-four hours, 4,800 tons in the second, and in the whole operation 15,000 tons of cargo was moved from ships' holds to the dumps in 108 hours.

These two ships brought precious cargo, but not enough to make any marked difference to the situation in Malta. By August, 1942, it was clear that the island could only withstand the siege for a few weeks longer. Prodigious efforts were made by the Royal Navy and the Merchant Navy to get supplies through, and at last, after one of the most heroic voyages of the war, a tanker and four merchant ships reached harbour, battered but afloat. One of these, the *Melbourne Star*, was discharged by the 231st Brigade, and the Battalion established new records for the number of tons discharged and moved from the quays.

In October, 1942, the Germans launched their last mass raid on Malta in a final attempt to regain command of the air. But the Gunners were ready for them, and this time they had abundant ammunition. The R.A.F. were ready with their fighters, and the Germans suffered another decisive defeat. It was their last attempt. As though to mark the great victory, a trickle of smoke was discerned coming from the smoke-stack of the brewery ; there was to be beer again.

Then in November the success of the Eighth and First Armies in North Africa changed everything. Benghazi was captured and the siege of Malta was raised. There was still a great deal of work for the troops ; a succession of small convoys sailed regularly into the Grand Harbour. Men toiled as stevedores in the docks, as labourers on the airfields, and in parties clearing debris and rubble from towns. The old "nothing but the best and a bit better" mood was still there, and in dockwork the Battalion took all records, their best being the unloading of the *Robin Locksley*, when 7,785 tons of cargo was discharged between dawn on 20th November and six o'clock in the evening of 25th November.

On 23rd December, 1942, the Battalion was inspected by Lord Gort, and the Commanding Officer received the following letter the next day, dated from the Palace, Malta:

My Dear Spencer,

Coming as I do from the Isle of Wight, I felt it to be a special privilege to be given the opportunity to take the salute yesterday.

I now write to express my admiration for march discipline, the physical fitness and the obviously high *esprit de corps* of the Battalion. Having seen your battalion on the march, I am confident that, when the opportunity comes, the 1st Battalion will undoubtedly equal in gallantry the memorable fight of their sister battalion in Tunisia—more is not possible. With every good wish to you and the 1st Battalion for Christmas and a successful 1943.

Yours sincerely,

Gort.

The reference to Tunisia was, of course, to the battle of Tebourba which had been fought by the 2nd Battalion on 4th December, as is recounted in a later chapter. But in Malta there was no fighting—that was over. Instead there was a great deal of hard work and hard training—for battles to come. The Battalion took a holiday only on Christmas Day, when everyone sat down, the first time for many months, to a full meal consisting principally of half a tin of steak and kidney pie per man and Christmas pudding. The Battalion Headquarters Officers' Mess had been trying to fatten a pig for Christmas Day. This was not easy as the entire Battalion could barely supply enough swill to keep the animal alive. It was indeed a matter of doubt whether or not the poor pig would die of starvation before Christmas Day. It just made it, but the pork was very lean.

The two years spent in Malta were years of hard service. It was a long and desperate siege; at times the prospect seemed well-nigh hopeless. Ammunition, stores and rations were short and there was little relief from hard and diverse work and hard training. The Battalion could reasonably claim to have been the most bombed in the British Army, for its area was within a mile of both Luqa and Hal Far aerodromes, with the taxying strip running through the middle of its position, and these were the most popular targets for the enemy air raids. At one time or another practically every billet and administrative building in the areas of two of the companies was destroyed by direct hits. It was not so much the intensity of the bombing that they had to endure; it was the constancy of it. The men could never get away from bombing, though companies were moved round periodically so that each had a fair share of the good and bad areas. But day after day, week after week, the men just had to endure the constant bombing, and they stood up to the ordeal with wonderful fortitude.

Bearing in mind the long months of bombing, often when troops were at work, the casualties of twelve killed and twenty-seven wounded were comparatively slight. For his service in Malta commanding the Battalion, Colonel

Spencer was awarded the O.B.E. and Captain M. D. Van Lessen won the M.C. Many officers and men were mentioned in despatches. One interesting incident was the repatriation of four time-expired men in mid-1942 by submarine. Between them they had accumulated more than eighty years' continuous service overseas. They were the only men who left the Battalion while it was on the island. The Battalion itself had been overseas, of course, for twenty-two years, since March, 1920.

Before the Malta story is concluded we should record a notable dance which was held in January, 1942, during the worst weeks of the siege. The Battalion was dispersed and there was no chance for it to get together, nor had there been since it had left India in 1938. It was decided, therefore, that an opportunity should be made. Accordingly a Regimental Dance was held in the Vernon United Services Club in Valletta, and since an evening dance in those days of black-out and constant air raids was out of the question, it was held between 2.30 and 6.30. The Cheshire Regiment provided the band and a cabaret was provided by artistes of the "Command Fair." There have been many Regimental Dances, but none, surely, quite as notable as the one in Malta in January, 1942.

The Battalion left Malta with the 231st Brigade on 30th March, 1943. So many friendships had been made with the civilian population during the two years of trial mutually shared that the occasion was a sad one. As the transports sailed out of Grand Harbour, the band of the Royal West Kent Regiment played regimental marches, and the men looked back at battered but unconquered Malta, where it had been an honour indeed to serve, and where under Colonel Spencer's inspiring leadership it had become a very fine Battalion. Their destination was Egypt ; their task was to begin special training for a new role—for attack.

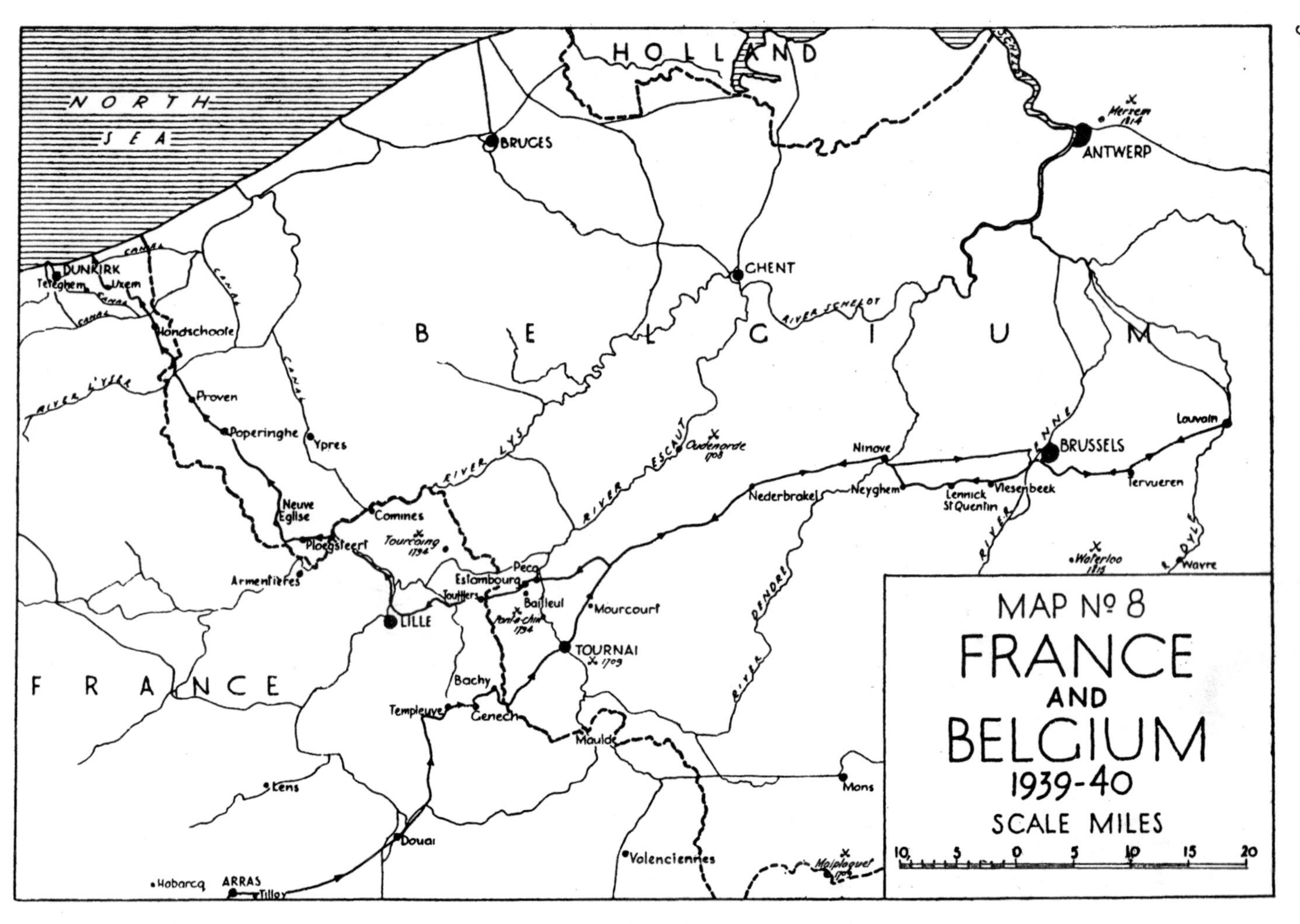
MAP No 8
FRANCE
AND
BELGIUM
1939-40
SCALE MILES
10 5 0 5 10 15 20
HOLLAND
BELGIUM
FRANCE
NORTH SEA
ANTWERP
Merxem 1814
BRUGES
GHENT
River Scheldt
BRUSSELS
Louvain
Tervueren
Wavre
Dyle
Waterloo 1815
Vlesenbeek
Lennick St Quentin
River Senne
Ninove
Neyghem
Nederbrakel
River Dendre
Oudenarde 1708
River Escaut
River Lys
Mons
Malplaquet 1709
Valenciennes
Mourcourt
TOURNAI 1709
Maulde
Bailleul
Pont-à-Chin 1794
Estambourg
Toufflers
Bachy
Genech
Templeuve
LILLE
Douai
Tourcoing 1794
Comines
Ploegsteert
Armentières
Neuve Eglise
Ypres
Poperinghe
Proven
Hondschoote
Canal
River L'Yser
DUNKIRK
Teteghem
Uxem
Lens
Habarcq
ARRAS
Tilloy

CHAPTER VI

THE 2ND BATTALION IN FRANCE

SEPTEMBER, 1939, TO JUNE, 1940

WHEN war was declared on 3rd September, 1939, the 2nd Battalion was mobilizing at Aldershot. Lieutenant-Colonel A. E. Stokes-Roberts was in command, with Major J. P. Fowler-Esson as Second-in-Command, and Captain R. F. N. Humphrey adjutant. The Battalion was in the 1st Division, brigaded in the 1st Guards Brigade with the 3rd Grenadiers and 2nd Coldstream. The 1st Division was to form part of the spearhead of the British Expeditionary Force, so the first days of September were busy and exhilarating.

Three hundred reservists reported for duty on 2nd September, bringing the Battalion up to full war establishment. Nearly all the reservists had seen active service in India on the North-West Frontier or in Palestine, and had two or three campaign medals each. Their experience was a very great asset. Weapons and equipment were delivered quickly and there was great activity in the orderly rooms, the quartermaster's stores and on the parade ground. The second-line transport was brought up to establishment by the issue of requisitioned commercial vehicles of all types, with their owners' names still on them. They had to be sprayed khaki and made as military as possible. New weapons, for so long represented at exercises by coloured flags, were unpacked, and everyone eagerly set themselves to learn all they could about the Bren gun, the anti-tank rifle and the 2-inch mortar. Gas drill was carried out, respirators were tested and all ranks passed through the gas chamber.

The advance party of the Battalion left for France on 13th September, followed by the rest of the Battalion on the 19th. The Battalion sailed from Spithead and disembarked the next day at Cherbourg, the first British battalion to be completely disembarked in France. The British Expeditionary Force was small, but it was of first-class quality, well equipped and well commanded Spirits were high.

The Battalion went by train from Cherbourg to Sille-le-Guillaume, a few kilometres north-west of Le Mans, and marched to good billets at Neuvillalais and Maison Care. On 29th September the Division began a move of two hundred and fifty miles north-west to take up its position in the Allied line.

The plan was for the British I Corps to take over the French sector on the Belgian frontier, lying between that of the French First Army and French XVI Corps. This line was lengthened to a total distance of fifty-five miles ten days later when II Corps came up ; this was the Gort line, named after the Commander-in-Chief, General Lord Gort, V.C. I Corps was commanded by General Sir John Dill, and II Corps by General Sir Alan Brooke. The 1st Division was commanded by Major-General the Hon. H. R. L. G. Alexander, and the 3rd Division of II Corps also had a distinguished commander in Major-General B. L. Montgomery.

I Corps took up its position in the line on 3rd October, the 1st Division on the left and the 2nd on the right. The complicated move of two hundred and fifty miles from the Divisional Assembly Area near Le Mans to Arras went smoothly, and the 2nd Hampshire was settled into billets at Tilloy on 29th September. From here they marched by easy stages to the Belgian frontier, arriving at Genech on 10th October. Battalion Headquarters was established with Brigade Headquarters in the Château, and Companies were billeted in the village of Bachy. This was to be the home of the Battalion throughout the very severe winter. There were a number of Channel Islanders in the Battalion's ranks, who proved to be of great help in making contact with the local people and in getting billets.

There was a great deal to be done, mainly in the construction of elaborate defensive work to protect the frontier of France from the northern end of the Maginot Line to the North Sea. Owing to Belgium's insistence on strict neutrality, the Maginot Line, which ran north from the Swiss border along the German frontier to Luxembourg, ended abruptly at the beginning of the Belgian frontier. Here the only defences were scattered pill-boxes and an anti-tank ditch.

When the Battalion arrived they found only a few half-finished concrete pill-boxes. They were very large and completely uncamouflaged, and their loopholes were sited to fire down a large tank trap which was not yet completed. One of the tasks of the Battalion was to improve these defences by building a system of trenches sited to give cross fire covering the approach to the anti-tank ditch. While the soldiers toiled at their trench construction, the Royal Engineers built new pill-boxes and improved the old ones. Trench digging was not easy, for water lay from six inches to a foot below the surface; it was, however, a problem which had to be solved and everyone worked hard. The French people were friendly and the only notable drawback to the situation was the weather, for it was an unusually cold winter with deep snow everywhere and very low temperatures.

The Battalion received many distinguished visitors at Bachy. The first was the Duke of Gloucester, and on 5th December His Majesty King George VI, accompanied by General Ironside, the C.I.G.S., inspected the Battalion's blockhouses and defences. On 10th December the Prime Minister, Mr. Neville Chamberlain, came to see the defences, and when the men waved their shovels in greeting he replied by waving his umbrella. On 24th December, 1939, Lieutenant-Colonel Stokes Roberts was appointed G.S.O.1, 61st Division, and the command of the Battalion was given to Lieutenant-Colonel P. H. Cadoux-Hudson, who arrived at Bachy to take up his command on 8th January, 1940.

When the B.E.F. had been in France for three months, employed almost entirely in manual work many miles from the area of possible hostilities, it was decided that British troops should be transferred, a brigade at a time, for a three weeks' tour of duty on the Saar front. They were to man a section of the defences of the Maginot Line, and gain experience in patrol work. Accordingly on 4th February the Guards Brigade moved westwards to Metz, near to the Maginot Line.

At last it seemed that war was getting nearer, for although few or no Germans were seen, the troops in the *ligne de contact* could hear the intermittent roll of gun-fire day and night. The "No man's land" which lay before the Battalion was a very ill-defined area, as the enemy positions were well concealed and little movement was seen by day. The positions the companies had to hold were mostly breastworks—platoon posts. A memorandum was circulated describing the modern slit-trenches used by the Germans. But the deep snow and the very short tours in the line of battalions prevented a change from breastworks to slit-trenches. There was, however, still nothing very urgent about the situation because on 7th February there was a full R.S.M.'s parade and saluting drill. On 13th February the Battalion moved, still in the *ligne de contact*, to Halstroff.

During this time the Battalion patrol group, commanded by Second-Lieutenant C. L. Thomas, gained valuable experience out in "No man's land." They felt particularly uncomfortable on their first patrol because they were dangerously conspicuous in their battledress against the virgin snow which mantled "No man's land." After that they wore white overalls or pyjamas over their uniforms, white cloths over their heads, and they powdered their faces and bandaged their weapons.

On the night of the 23rd/24th February the patrol of the Grenadiers and of the Hampshire joined forces for a night raid on the village of Zeurange, a deserted village on the German side of the valley opposite our sector. On several mornings a party of Germans had been seen leaving the village, and the plan was for the patrols to search the village in the dark and remain there until midday to capture any Germans who came near it. The operation was eerie and exciting and there were many alarms, such as when they surrounded a house in the upstairs room of which they heard people moving about, raided it and found that the occupants were two elderly sows. The adventure was made all the more difficult by the fact that the village road was covered by an inch of polished ice. The patrols returned across "No man's land" at midday with, unfortunately, no Germans.

The Brigade's tour in the Maginot Line completed, the Battalion returned to Metz on 28th February, and life seemed to settle down to the same strange non-belligerent conditions as before. From Metz the Battalion went back to Templeuve, and with the improvement in the weather a full training programme was begun and carried out vigorously. Life was still very pleasant, and there was regular leave to England. It was at Templeuve that the Commanding Officer decided to train the Battalion in defensive night withdrawals, and a series of exercises were carried out which were to be of incalculable value in a few weeks' time.

With the coming of spring the "twilight" war began to draw to an end. On 9th April Germany invaded Denmark and Norway, and Allied Intelligence showed that considerable troop movement by the enemy indicated that an attack on the Allied positions was soon to take place. The Belgian neutrality was naturally a great danger point in the Allied strategy, and it had been arranged that if the Germans invaded Belgium the Allied armies would immediately enter Belgium to give her support. The most complete plans were made for this eventuality, though they were of course only on paper, as no actual reconnaissance or troop movements could be made across the Belgian frontier.

Behind the positions presumably to be occupied by the Belgian Army were three rivers, roughly parallel with each other, the Dyle, the Dendre and the Escaut, forming a valuable series of natural tank obstacles. Two plans were made. Plan "E" was for the Allies to advance into Belgium and secure and hold the line of the Escaut from the point where it crosses the frontier at Maulde northward to Ghent, where it was intended to make junction with the Belgian forces extending to the sea-coast. Plan "D" was for an advance much farther into Belgium, to hold the Dyle from Wavre to Louvain. The British front was to be occupied by I Corps on a two-division front on the right and II Corps on the left on a front of one division, the Divisions being the 2nd, 1st and 3rd, in that order.

On 10th May, 1940, the strange somnolence of the Western Front ended, and battle of an unexpected fury blazed up. The prelude was the bombing of targets in the British zone by the German Air Force, and at seven o'clock in the morning came the news, so long expected, that the Germans had invaded Belgium. They attacked from Aachen in Germany into Maastricht in Holland, and thence into Belgium, striking towards the junction of the French and British position on the right of the B.E.F., and then the whole attack with 126 divisions and 10 panzer divisions was launched. The new war, bewildering in its speed and fury, had begun.*

Orders to put Plan "D" into operation were immediately issued by General Gamelin, the Allied Commander-in-Chief, and on 11th May the British 1st Division crossed into Belgium. The 2nd Hampshire moved from Templeuve to Mourcourt and thence by bus through Brussels, which looked neat and prosperous in brilliant moonlight, and civilians waved enthusiastically to the troops from windows and street corners. The Battalion drove on to Tervueren, where it was posted as the centre battalion of the Brigade, in divisional reserve. Already the roads were full of refugees.

On 14th May the Battalion moved forward to take up defensive positions near Louvain and began to dig in. There was a great deal of enemy air activity, but no bombing in the Battalion area. Companies worked desperately hard to prepare their positions, and awaited the enemy attack; at last, it seemed, everything would be put to the test.

The civilian population fled from the area, and there was the usual tragic sight of families loaded with cherished possessions riding or trudging along the roads westwards, away from the German threat. There was a convent school near the Battalion's positions, whose Mother Superior was at her wits' end. The Battalion *agent de liaison*, M. du Puy, got to know of her distress and the

* See map on page 240.

Battalion was able to help her. After considerable persuasion by du Puy and the Commanding Officer the inmates of the convent were induced to leave, and what was for those days a fairly reasonable evacuation was managed. M. du Puy was subsequently quite sure that the blessing of the Battalion by the Mother Superior was the cause of the comparatively few casualties in the Battalion in the withdrawal to Dunkirk.

But the attack on the 1st Division's positions never came. For the German army had struck elsewhere with a ferocity and a speed which was throwing the Allied line into tragic confusion. To the north the Dutch were falling back before violent attacks, furiously dive-bombed by Stukas, and infested by parachutists and saboteurs. To the south of the B.E.F. two panzer divisions had driven back the French Ninth Army and were forcing their way through the Ardennes to cross the River Meuse south of Namur and at Sedan. All attacks on the British positions were repulsed. By 16th May, however, the right flank of the B.E.F. was completely turned and orders were given for the French First Army and the B.E.F. to withdraw in three stages to the Escaut.

Accordingly, on 16th May, the Battalion was ordered to withdraw and it marched back through Brussels again. It was beginning to get light as they marched through the echoing and deserted streets, and there was no sign now of life nor any jubilant civilians. The Battalion took up a new position to hold the River Senne, with the Coldstream on their right and the Grenadiers in reserve. Once again everyone worked furiously preparing the new positions, while the Sappers blew the bridges over the Senne.

Then came more bad news—that the Dutch army had laid down its arms, so that the Allied left flank had gone. To the south the French Ninth Army was rapidly disintegrating before the tremendous thrusts of the panzer divisions, while the French First Army on the immediate right of the B.E.F. was in serious trouble, and was falling back rapidly. The success of the German attacks, and the appearance of saboteurs everywhere, was affecting the morale of the French and Belgians badly. Disasters fell in quick succession and the German armour was roaring through France and swinging northwards towards the Channel ports, led by a dashing German commander, General Rommel.

But still no serious attack was made against the positions of the B.E.F. The British soldiers wanted to stand and fight, and the recurrent orders to withdraw exasperated them. The fatigue and disorganization of continued withdrawal were beginning to tell. It was a time when first-class command, clear orders and some experience in the problems of withdrawal stood a unit in good stead, and here the 2nd Hampshire were very fortunate.

In the withdrawal from the Senne everything seemed to go wrong. An accident to a despatch rider prevented the attendance of the left forward company commander at the Commanding Officer's conference. Another accident delayed the withdrawal order reaching the same company commander until only a quarter of an hour before his company was due to fall back. In a miraculous way the company did pull out in time. In one village on the Battalion's way back the main road, as marked on the map, suddenly shrunk to a narrow alley-way between houses. It happened to be ten minutes to the clock hour when the Battalion got there, so it was halted while the Intelligence Officer penetrated the alley and climbed a sign-post and was able to confirm that the Battalion was on the right road. A little later the Battalion was halted by a long column of stationary vehicles; investigation showed that the driver of a vehicle at the head of the column had fallen asleep with fatigue over his wheel. He was awakened and the convoy and the Battalion moved on.

Shortly after this a small convoy was seen coming towards the front of the Battalion. It was pulled up and found to be their own Brigade Headquarters, which had made a complete circle and was driving towards the enemy. Soon after this convoy was put on the right road another approached; and this turned out to be the previous convoy which had held them up; they too had made the circle and were heading for the Germans. It was at this time that the only unwounded man of the Battalion to become missing during the withdrawal was lost.

There was no chance to make a stand on the River Dendre and at midnight on 17th May the positions were finally abandoned, and with the Carrier Platoon holding the cross-roads, the Battalion marched back via Vlessenbeek, Quentin and Neyghem to Ninove, some twenty miles west of Brussels. At Ninove the Battalion took up a position again on the west bank of the canal which runs through the town. Here the enemy made signs of staging an attack on the battalion position, for suddenly there was a violent action by mortars and machine guns from the east side of the canal. But no attack materialized, and at ten o'clock the next morning, 19th May, the position was abandoned, and with the carriers again holding the position to give the companies cover, the Battalion marched for two hours to Nederbrakel, and there embussed. The transport took them back for two hours, and then once more the tired troops formed up and marched for three hours until the River Escaut was crossed.

The night was spent at Pecq, in a large school building with a big glass roof, and headquarters was established in an unusually luxurious château, with valuable pictures and rare furniture, all deserted. There was a lake in the grounds, and some enterprising spirits took out a rowing boat and fished with grenades and came back with a bucketful of small fish, a much appreciated addition to the irregular and spartan fare of those bewildering days. The battalion area, and the château, were heavily shelled, and in the afternoon a figure with a blackened face and torn uniform reported to Battalion Headquarters. He was one of the Intelligence section who had been manning an observation post in the attic of a near-by house, which had been hit. He had come to the Headquarters to ask the Intelligence Officer to give him another observation post.

That night the Battalion moved back to Estambourg, where for three days they formed a defensive bastion round the village to link up with the reserve company of the Grenadiers at Bailleul. "Z" Company was under command the Grenadiers holding Bailleul, "Y" was under command the Coldstream in Pecq, and "W" and "X" were holding Estambourg. The positions were heavily shelled, as was the road in the rear, and there were air attacks. The employed platoon of H.Q. Company was formed up and took its place in the line. There was a considerable amount of patrolling and movements of companies to co-ordinate with the two Guards battalions.

Carriers were detached and sent off to help a dangerous situation when the enemy managed to establish a pocket on the west of the river. At another time the enemy made a determined attack at the junction of the two Guards battalions. There was no rest for the tired troops, but they did have the satisfaction of being at last in action. At this time the 5th and 50th British Divisions and the 1st Army Tank Brigade were fighting their gallant battle to hold Arras.

By 22nd May the general situation before the British 1st Division was stabilized, and the Battalion War Diary notes "quiet night, situation normal—very quiet day." There was, however, renewed and heavy enemy shelling the evening of the 22nd and orders were received to withdraw again, and at dawn on 23rd May the Battalion crossed the frontier into France. They were now only seven miles from Bachy, holding the positions the Army had held before advancing into Belgium.

Once more the Battalion toiled at taking up defensive positions, but only slight enemy movements were observed, with a little sniping. In the afternoon of the 24th increasing enemy infantry movement was observed all along the battalion front and an enemy patrol approached "Y" Company, but was stopped by their fire. Late at night on 24th May positions were changed so that the Brigade held the sector with three battalions up; the Grenadiers on the right, the Hampshire in the centre and the Coldstream on the left. The 25th May was a quiet day with patrolling activity by the Brigade. On the evening of the 26th there was a bombing attack on Battalion Headquarters, an event which had occurred several times before. Fortunately the Commanding Officer seemed to possess a sixth sense about these things and he had moved his Headquarters just in time.

Meanwhile the German plan for overrunning France was proving so successful that it was reported that even Hitler was incredulous. Fortunately Hitler was more concerned with the capture of Paris than the encircling of the B.E.F. On the Belgian frontier the Guards Brigade waited grimly in their positions, but little happened. But on the evening of 28th May there was a sudden increase in enemy activity on the Brigade front, and at a Brigade conference held at three o'clock in the next afternoon it was announced that the Brigade was to fall back on Dunkirk. At ten o'clock at night the position was abandoned by the infantry while the Carrier Platoon held on till midnight.

By this time everybody realized how wise their Commanding Officer had been in exercising them in a night withdrawal. Everywhere was chaos; the roads were filled with refugees and disorganized and unarmed groups of French and Belgian soldiers. Some British units, more roughly treated by the fortunes of war than those of the 1st Division, were bewildered and lost. The swift withdrawal following the high expectations of the past nine months was damaging to morale; but in spite of fatigue, despite the air and artillery attack, and despite the disorder all about them, the Battalion continued to withdraw in good order and under perfect control. Good leadership was bringing a valuable reward indeed.

The 28th May was the crisis of the operation, the vital day when everything hung in the balance. General Brooke with II Corps was fighting magnificently. The 5th Division had held on with desperate valour, and the 50th Division, the 4th and the 3rd Divisions plugged the gap in the vital corridor to Dunkirk. The Germans had orders to fire off all their ammunition, and they did. To all this furious battle the 1st Division stood in reserve.

Through the night of 28th/29th May the Battalion marched back into Belgium, through the northern outskirts of Lille, through Ploegsteert and on to Neuve Eglise. They took two hours' rest in a field while a battle was being fought not far away, so that shells were falling close to them. A check of the men's feet was made and a number of men were allotted seats in the carriers and ambulance. The Officers' Mess truck was emptied to provide further accommodation in case of need. It was a sad sight to see the kit jettisoned and bottles of wine being broken on the roadside. A number of civilian bicycles were commandeered and divided among the companies so that one platoon in each was mounted. These platoons cycled to the next halt and awaited the arrival of their company, when another platoon took over the bicycles, and the process was repeated. Progress was difficult as French troops were withdrawing along the same road, and west of Poperinghe the route was blocked by bombing.

The Battalion reached Proven at 4 p.m. on 29th May. In the two days they had travelled more than forty-five miles—under very difficult conditions. But the Battalion was together and in complete good order. At Proven they were taken on in vehicles until stopped by a very intricate traffic jam. Eventually they got to Hondschoote and took up positions to defend the canal. It was while they were there that the order came for all vehicles, except the carriers and the Commanding Officer's car, to be destroyed on the south bank of the canal. There was much evidence already of jettisoned lorries and equipment, and also the horse transport abandoned by the French who had turned their horses loose. The Battalion caught enough horses to provide one Mounted Infantry Platoon for the last stages of the retreat.

A few hours later the Battalion moved to occupy new positions, the last defensive ones in the operation. These were at Uxem and companies were posted at road junctions with one platoon of "Y" Company with the carriers holding the bridge at Teteghem to close a temporary gap. The road running along the far side of the canal was so thick with abandoned vehicles that there was no field of fire at all. In spite of this, "Y" Company platoon and the carriers had some shooting at Germans coming up the canal. On 30th May Uxem was shelled heavily and the Battalion held the position throughout the 31st under continuous and very heavy shelling. In the evening "Z" Company was moved up to assist the Coldstream on the right. Enemy shelling continued all night and with renewed vigour on the morning of 1st June. Once again Battalion Headquarters was moved just in time. Among the casualties on that day was Captain R. E. M. Humphrey, the Adjutant, who was wounded and taken back to the casualty clearing station. But as he was not a "walking wounded" he could not be evacuated from Dunkirk, and he subsequently died from his wounds at Enghien. Captain P. A. T. Halliday became Adjutant. Another officer was wounded at Uxem after the casualty clearing station had closed down. The Liaison Officer, M. du Puy, tried to get him in a French hospital, but as he was British their regulations forbade them to accept him. So du Puy then commandeered a French ambulance, dressed the wounded officer in a French uniform and drove the ambulance to the hospital again, when this time the casualty was accepted. Unfortunately, the officer died later.

This Liaison Officer, Mareschal-des-Logis-chef, Comte du Puy, was a very good friend of the Battalion. He went back with the Battalion to England, changed his name to Pitt, joined the Essex Regiment and eventually got a commission. In 1941 he was parachuted into France and worked with the French Resistance in his home area. After six months of this dangerous duty he was taken by the Germans and put in prison. After nine months of solitary confinement he was sent to a British prisoner-of-war camp.

On 1st June the Commanding Officer issued his final withdrawal order. The "intention" was that "2 Hamps. will withdraw to the Mole at Dunkerque for embarkation." Paragraph 9 of this order read: "Coys will embark fully equipped and carrying all Brens and A/Tk rifles." The order also stated that "Embarkation will carry on in spite of bombing or shelling, and the flow to the boats will on no account be stopped."

The withdrawal of companies began at half past five in the afternoon of 1st June and the position was abandoned by ten o'clock. It is worthy of note that all companies marched past the Commanding Officer closed up in threes, marching as well as ever they had done, and complete with all equipment. The Carrier Platoon held out at Uxem until midnight.

So the 2nd Battalion marched along the crowded roads towards the beaches of Dunkirk. The perimeter which held the B.E.F., and those French and Belgian units which had managed to get through to it, was shrinking rapidly. The enemy was thrusting desperately north-west to cut off the B.E.F. from Dunkirk, its one remaining chance of escape. Scattered units on the perimeter fought with the utmost gallantry to hold the enemy at bay. In Britain the nation waited anxiously, not daring to hope that the miracle would take place. Mr. Churchill had expressed his fear that, at the best, only 30,000 men of the B.E.F. could be rescued. From every possible port, ships, big and small, made their way across the calm summer sea on their errand of rescue. The Luftwaffe wrought havoc on the beaches, and, unknown to the soldiers waiting there so patiently, fighters of the R.A.F. fought against fantastic odds behind the perimeter. The miracle of Dunkirk did take place. From the battered beaches men found their way to the friendly ships and home, and not 30,000 but 330,000 British troops escaped.

The companies of the 2nd Battalion reached the beach at Dunkirk and took their places in the long and orderly queues. They went home in ships of all kinds, and were landed at scattered ports up and down the coast. Many and varied were their adventures. One group of ten men put to sea in a gig and pulled out to a motor lifeboat, which transferred them to a minesweeper. Another party, who spent the night of 1st June on the beach, waited throughout 2nd June until at last in the evening the long-awaited order came to fall in, and they marched off in threes, under the German shelling and bombing, into the sea and embarked on a destroyer.

One party of a sergeant, a corporal and a driver of the Carrier Platoon stopped behind to make sure that the carriers were destroyed and then had to make their own way to the beach. They fell in with a Sapper officer, who took them into his party. Exploring the beach they found a small motor-boat, and on examining it and testing the engine it seemed that it might be sound. The party settled down to sleep until the tide should come in and, they hoped, float her. At eleven o'clock the next morning the boat was afloat, the motor was started and they put to sea. They came across several abandoned boats and took on supplies of petrol and oil, and they took on tow as many small boats as possible. They also picked up a couple of wounded soldiers from a sinking French destroyer and then they set the course for home. At four o'clock, fifteen miles from Dunkirk, they were picked up by a submarine chaser, which was just as well because they then found that the course they were on was taking them back to France. After an adventurous voyage in which the ship rescued some wounded survivors from another chaser and went off after a U-boat, the ship arrived off Ramsgate at 9 p.m.

Some men of "X" Company were taken on board a paddle-steamer, which was crowded with troops, so that every corner and corridor was packed with sleeping soldiers. At dawn the steamer set off for England, and a little way out they were able to pick up Colonel Cadoux-Hudson from a flat-bottomed boat, which owing to a strange accident to its compass was cruising steadily in circles. In the words of one of the soldiers, "The C.O. was anxious for our safety and he was pleased to hear that so many of us had remained together. In the afternoon white cliffs appeared and later a peaceful sunbathed town replaced the war-scarred ruin, with its black mantle of smoke, which we had so recently left."

One private who had been given the task of remaining at a cross-roads to act as a road guide until half past two in the morning of 2nd June began to make his own way to the beach and, as he put it, "I tacked on to a mixed crowd, after having watched all companies of the Hampshires march through in perfect order." Eventually he boarded a small sailing boat and a sergeant volunteered to take command. They began a very slow journey out to sea and in the evening a naval pinnace came alongside and took off a couple of their wounded and left a naval officer on board. He put them on the correct course and the men slept as best they could until, in the morning, a British tug took them in tow and put them ashore in Dover.

"Y" Company, commanded by Major Lee, came home together. The Company was detailed by the Commanding Officer to remain behind as escort to "certain important people" still in Dunkirk. The Company, 170 strong, passed a quiet night on the beach and in the morning of 2nd June a message was received that the Company could go, but there seemed to be no ships available. They decided to wade out to two Thames sailing barges lying off shore, and although all but the tallest had to swim they reached them safely. The idea was to signal to other ships. They found that the barges were well equipped with food and water, and being joined by a Sapper Major and a Captain of the Coldstream, both of whom had sailing experience, they decided to hoist the sails and make their own way home. Their crossing was slow and uneventful, except for the sight of an unsuccessful bombing attack on a hospital ship. At five in the afternoon they were hailed by a trawler who gave them the good news that they were only eight miles from Dover. They were quickly transhipped to the trawler and landed at seven o'clock. At Aldershot it was found that the Hampshire party were 100 per cent. complete in equipment, with all rifles, Bren guns, anti-tank rifles and 2-inch mortars. They were congratulated on this by the Minister of War, Mr. Anthony Eden.

So the 2nd Hampshire came home, complete with arms and equipment. The Battalion had perhaps been more fortunate than many, but their return with so few casualties and complete with equipment and arms after the grim adventure of the retreat to Dunkirk was not all luck; it was the result of brilliant leadership and fine morale.

The 2nd Battalion met together at Wakefield in Yorkshire on 5th June and quickly re-formed and made themselves ready for an immediate return to France. There was great eagerness to do this, but it was not to be. They were to be privileged to take their revenge earlier than most units, but the first task was the defence of Great Britain, now alone against the new Master of Europe.

The Battalion moved into Lincolnshire on 18th June, to billets at Mablethorpe. The 1st Division was entrusted with the defence of the coast from the Wash to the Humber, and the orders for the 2nd Hampshire were "to prevent the enemy landing on the beaches from Anderby Creek to Saltfleet Haven"—a distance of twelve miles. With such splendidly English names in the order, with the North Sea before them and their own country behind them, the Battalion prepared to receive the enemy. This time there would be no retreat.

MAP No 9
HOME
STATIONS
1939-45
SCALE MILES
10 5 0 10 20 30 40 50 60 70 80 90 100
Forfar
Inverary
Gourock
GLASGOW
EDINBURGH
Falkirk
Duns
NEWCASTLE
Consett
Bellaghy
BELFAST
Banbridge
Dundalk
Catterick
Helmsley
YORK
LEEDS
Wakefield
HULL
Hessle
Patrington
Withernsea
Easington
Grimsby
Cuxwold
Usselby
Tealby
Market Rasen
Louth
Mablethorpe
Anderby Creek
LIVERPOOL
Wash
NORTHAMPTON
Bury St. Edmunds
Southwold
Cambridge
Long Melford
Sudbury
Royston
Saffron Walden
Hitchin
Dovercourt
Colchester
Harpenden
Hertford
OXFORD
Chingford
Chigwell
Wanstead
LONDON
Hartley Wintney
Fleet
Aldershot
Basingstoke
Tidworth
Andover
Alton
Bordon
Winchester
Romsey
SOUTHAMPTON
PORTSMOUTH
Bognor
Shepton Mallet
Frome
Castle Cary
Wincanton
Blandford
Lyndhurst
Beaulieu
Bournemouth
Bridport
Freshwater
Newport
Ryde
Sandown
Shanklin
Gosport
Newton Abbot
Devonport
PLYMOUTH
Milstead
Faversham
Herne Bay
Birchington
Margate
Broadstairs
Ramsgate
Deal
Dover
Folkestone
Hythe
Crowborough
Warnham
Bolney
Hayward's Heath
Lewes
Eastbourne

CHAPTER VII

THE HAMPSHIRE BATTALIONS IN THE UNITED KINGDOM 1939–1945

WHEN France fell in June, 1940, Great Britain became a fortress, and the Army's task beautifully simple : to stand by to repel invasion. The first phase of the defence of Britain against the elaborate German Operation "Sealion" was, in the words of Sir Winston Churchill, "to man the entrenched crust of the possible invasion beaches on the coast, where defenders would fight where they stood, supported by mobile reserves for invasion counter-attack." Inland a line of anti-tank obstacles ran down the east centre of the country manned by the Home Guard, and behind that line were the reserves for counter-offence. Great Britain and Northern Ireland were divided into seven Commands, then into Corps and Divisional Commands, and the whole defensive belt was about a hundred miles deep.

In July General Sir Alan Brooke became Commander-in-Chief, Home Forces, in succession to General Ironside, and the first consignment of half a million .300 rifles and three hundred thousand .303, with ammunition, came from America. While the Royal Navy went confidently about its business, attending to its many commitments, and while the Royal Air Force fought its great battles in the skies, the soldiers waited on the coast, ready to "fight where they stood."

The Hampshire Regiment had ten battalions actively engaged in the defence of Britain. These were the 2nd Battalion ; the four Territorial battalions, the 1/4th, 2/4th and 5th, serving together in the 128th (Hampshire) Brigade, and the 7th ; and also five newly raised battalions, the 8th, afterwards the 30th Battalion, the 9th, 10th, 11th (Royal Militia, Island of Jersey) and the 50th, which became the 12th Battalion. In the main the experiences of these battalions at home were the same. First they stood on the defensive and then, quite soon and with increasing intensity, they trained and equipped themselves for the offensive role. Six of them were eventually to be called upon to fight overseas. The first to go was the 2nd Battalion, to North Africa, soon followed by the 128th Brigade. All four battalions fought in the Mediterranean theatre, where they were joined by the 1st Battalion in Sicily. The 1st returned to England after Sicily with the 231st Brigade to prepare for the invasion of Normandy, and soon after they had landed there, the 7th Battalion went over as well. Two battalions, the 9th and 10th, were subsequently converted to armoured regiments, and became the 157th and the 147th Regiments, R.A.C., and both saw active service overseas. However, our immediate concern is the activities of the Hampshire battalions in England.

I—THE 2ND BATTALION

As has already been noted, the 2nd Hampshire were stationed on the Lincolnshire coast, and companies toiled at making defensive positions, and served long hours of duty manning them standing by for the codeword "Cromwell" which was to signify that the Germans had landed. There was a tragic incident in September, 1940, when Major H. C. Phillips and his driver were killed when they drove accidentally into a minefield while the Major was inspecting his defences at Mablethorpe.

There were many changes in the officers in 1940 and 1941. Major Fowler-Esson left to form the 9th Battalion, and Major Lee became Second-in-Command until December, 1940, when he left, first to command the I Corps Battle School at Lincoln and then, in February, 1941, to command the 7th Battalion. It was in February, 1941, too, that Major Lindley left to command the 11th; and in March, 1941, the Chaplain, Captain Blackburne, was posted away on promotion. Captain Blackburne had joined the Battalion just before the advance into Belgium and he was very popular with all ranks. With Captain Finer as Medical Officer and Captain Blackburne as Padre, "body and soul" of the 2nd Battalion had been wonderfully cared for. Captain Blackburne's father was Padre to the 2nd Mounted Infantry in South Africa, in which "F" Company came from the 2nd Hampshire Regiment.

The 2nd Hampshire was still, of course, in the 1st Guards Brigade, and they received visits from many distinguished persons while they were in Lincolnshire, among them H.R.H. The Duke of Kent and Mr. Winston Churchill. Battle training had already begun in August, 1940, on lines which were to occupy the Brigade with ever-increasing intensity for the next two and a half years.

There were various moves in Lincolnshire until in October Battalion Headquarters was established at Tealby, with H.Q. Company at Market Rasen, two companies at Louth, and the other two at Cuxwold and Grimsby. In January, 1941, the Battalion made its first of many visits to the training grounds in Scotland for combined-operation training at Inverary, returning to the Brigade winter training area at Usselby. In February they entrained at Louth for Inverary again for a week of landing practice and hard route marches. Back at Usselby there were brigade, division and command exercises.

A serious loss was sustained by the Battalion in April, 1941, when Lieutenant-Colonel Cadoux-Hudson was promoted to command the 164th Infantry Brigade. Colonel Cadoux-Hudson's tireless efficiency had maintained the Battalion at a very high standard, which their subsequent campaigns in North Africa and Italy were to show. He was succeeded as Commanding Officer by Lieutenant-Colonel Lee, brought back from the 7th Battalion. Colonel Lee was to command the Battalion for the next eighteen months, and to lead it into action in North Africa.

In July, 1941, the Battalion received a warning order to go overseas, and mobilization at once took place. Once again, however, nothing came of it, and in August the Battalion went to Duns for a brigade exercise, practising assault landings. At this time it was attached to the Royal Marines Brigade, but returned to the 1st Guards Brigade on 10th September. The advanced stage of training the Battalion had reached is shown by the number of times it was called upon to give battle demonstrations. On one occasion many senior officers in its Division watched a demonstration by a platoon of an attack on a pill-box, using live ammunition, while Major Wilson, the Second-in-Command, gave a running commentary through a loud-speaker. The Battalion was in Loch Fyne on board H.T. *Ettrick* at the end of September, 1941, when the Commander-in-Chief, General Sir Alan Brooke, visited them, accompanied by Admiral of the Fleet Sir Roger Keyes, then Chief of Combined Operations. Three companies demonstrated modern battle tactics before the distinguished visitors.

So the months passed ; strenuous months of vigorous training, in which the Battalion became very fit and ready for battle. In April, 1942, the Battalion moved to Forfar and found itself stationed in a town of some size for the first time since it had come back from France, and from here it took part in Exercise "Bulldog." Suddenly, on 2nd May, orders came to move at once to an unknown destination, and the Battalion was taken right down England to the Isle of Wight. At Shanklin they were at once set to practising loading, embarking and disembarking from landing craft, and there were strong rumours of a raid on Dieppe, which was indeed the intention, and the Battalion embarked on s.s. *Empress Astrid* and *Prince Charles*, and undertook strenuous practice at assault landings. But exceptionally rough weather caused the raid to be cancelled and the 1st Guards Brigade left the Isle of Wight, being replaced by the Canadians for rehearsals for the Dieppe raid. So the planned raid did not take place and the Battalion went back to Forfar.

There were more exercises in Scotland, and in the last of these the Battalion marched eighty-five miles, considerably more than any other in the exercise, and no one fell out. One of the "enemy" commanders was Brigadier Cadoux-Hudson. The Battalion suffered a sad loss on 21st August when Major Wilson died as the result of an accident on a course of instruction ; he was an officer who had contributed a great deal towards the hard efficiency which made the 2nd Hampshire such a fine battalion.

There was one more exercise in which the Battalion worked with tanks, and then quite unexpectedly the prolonged period of preparation came to an end. On 15th October Part I Orders announced that the Battalion would be inspected by "a Senior General," and on the next day the Battalion paraded on the football ground at Forfar for inspection by His Majesty The King, who wished them "Good luck, a victorious campaign, and a safe return." This time it was the real thing, and on 11th November the 2nd Hampshire sailed from Liverpool for the Clyde, and then for North Africa—and Tebourba.

II—The 1/4th, 2/4th, 5th and 7th Battalions in England : 1939 and After

Throughout the spring and summer of 1939 volunteers had come to the drill halls of the Hampshire Territorial battalions in great numbers, so that in August it was possible to double the battalions, to form the 1/4th and 2/4th from the 4th, and the 5th and 7th from the 5/7th. The first three of these, with headquarters at Winchester, Aldershot and Southampton, formed the 128th Brigade of the 43rd (Wessex) Division, commanded by Brigadier E. D. H. Tollemache, D.S.O., M.C., and then by Brigadier C. H. Woodhouse, M.C.

In the first months of the war the Brigade was responsible for the security of the many vulnerable points in the Southampton area, including, of course, Southampton docks. Stationed at Southampton and Romsey, the three battalions manned a great number of posts, provided guards for the docks and undertook a great many tasks preparing defensive works and making camps, in addition to training. They dealt also with a flow of recruits from civilian life and generally adapted themselves speedily to war-time conditions of service. They watched the B.E.F. go to France, their own 2nd Battalion among them, and envied them their equipment and their opportunity. There were difficult moments, especially at the docks when angry neutrals, not able to take the war at all seriously, resented not being allowed ashore in Southampton. There were "teething troubles" of all kinds, but all problems were overcome by the zest and good humour of the men.

In the early months the 1/4th was commanded by Lieutenant-Colonel H. J. Brooks, the 2/4th by Lieutenant-Colonel A. L. Scaife, and the 5th by Lieutenant-Colonel C. E. Elliott. Christmas, 1939, was made memorable for the 2/4th by the Commanding Officer visiting all his men on duty at the docks with gifts of cigarettes and sweets, dressed as Father Christmas and riding in a coach and four, heralded by a post-horn.

In January, 1940, the Brigade, less the 1/4th Battalion, moved to Somerset to join the rest of the 43rd Division for a period of training, and with the 2/4th at Wincanton and the 5th at Shepton Mallet, some hard and profitable work was done. The 1/4th moved from Romsey to Castle Carey in March. In February changes in command took place in the 1/4th and 5th Battalions, when Lieutenant-Colonel Brooks, who had commanded the 4th since 1936, was succeeded by Lieutenant-Colonel C. C. Smythe, and Lieutenant-Colonel Elliott, who had commanded the 5/7th since 1931, was succeeded by Lieutenant-Colonel H. C. C. Newnham. Both these officers remained in command to take their battalions into action three years later. It was while the Brigade was in Somerset that Brigadier F. A. M. Browning was appointed to command, an appointment that was to have a long-lasting effect on the Hampshire Brigade. A commander who was to win a resounding reputation in the war, Brigadier Browning's vigorous command and infectious enthusiasm laid the foundations of the Brigade's subsequent fine record in battle.

It was Brigadier Browning who proposed that the Hampshire battalions should wear black and amber shoulder titles, of the type then worn only by the Grenadier Guards. This was done and the battalions became the first outside the Brigade of Guards to have the drabness of their khaki brightened with colour. Eventually the other battalions of the Regiment sewed on their shoulder titles, and the excellent fashion spread. Official sanction was given, but not until 1952.

All hopes of the 43rd Division going to France were dashed with the news of

May, 1940, and instead the Division was moved at short notice to Hertfordshire as part of G.H.Q. Mobile Reserve in the event of a German invasion. The two 4th Battalions were stationed at Hitchin and the 5th at Royston, where they were kept busy preparing road-blocks and guarding vulnerable points. The Division was in Hertfordshire for six months, and then it moved to the Kentish coast, travelling in transport through the middle of London at speed, escorted by the Metropolitan Police.

The 1/4th at Ramsgate, the 2/4th at Margate and the 5th at St. Nicholas-at-Wade settled down to the duties of coastal defence. They had each a long stretch of the coast to guard, the 1/4th, for example, having ten miles from Bloody Point to the west of Ramsgate to, and including, Broadstairs. There was also the important R.A.F. aerodrome at Manston for which the Brigade was responsible. In each battalion all four rifle companies manned and maintained their positions, and in the bitterly cold winter of 1940–1941 sentry duty was a cold business on the exposed, windswept shore. There was, of course, a great deal of enemy air activity, but in spite of the difficulties, individual, section and platoon training was carried out, and much time and effort was given to instructing and helping the Home Guard. There were many distinguished visitors to the sector, including the Duke of Gloucester, the Duke of Kent, and General Lord Gort.

When Brigadier Browning left in February, 1941, to command a Guards Brigade, 128th Brigade was a highly trained fighting unit with a splendid confidence and morale, ready indeed for action. The next commander, Brigadier M. A. James, V.C., was a leader well suited to so spirited and keen a unit, and Brigadier James remained to lead the Brigade into action in North Africa, and until he was wounded at Salerno.

At the end of May the Brigade handed over its coastal defences and moved a little inland to Faversham, with the three battalions stationed at Faversham, Milstead and Painters Forstal. Here a period of intensive training was begun, with platoon field firing schemes, company and battalion exercises, and monthly brigade, divisional and corps manœuvres. At the end of September there was an elaborate G.H.Q. manœuvre in the east of England, Exercise "Bumper."

In February, 1942, the Brigade went back to the coast, with the battalions again at Ramsgate, Margate and St. Nicholas-at-Wade, and here they were kept busy with more training exercises. There were now four Hampshire battalions in line along the coast, as the 7th, in 130th Brigade, were next to the other three. During this month Lieutenant-Colonel Scaife was posted to H.Q., XII Corps, and was succeeded by Lieutenant-Colonel J. H. H. Robinson.

In June, 1942, the reorganization of the army made it necessary for 128th Brigade to leave the 43rd Division, to make place for an armoured brigade, and the battalions marched the eighty-odd miles to London, leaving the 7th to keep the county's colours flying in the Wessex Division.

For a month or so the Brigade was under command London District, with the battalions at Chingford, Chigwell and Wanstead. Among their other duties they spent a great deal of time with the City, North-East London and Essex

Home Guard battalions, staging demonstrations and helping with their training. Two Home Guard battalions were allotted to each company, and the enthusiasm of the Home Guard was an ample reward for the hard work everyone put in.

The Brigade left London District in August, 1942, and went back to Kent, to join the 46th Division, with 138th and 139th Infantry Brigades. The Division was mobilizing and it was apparent to everyone that the long period of preparation and training was at last drawing to an end. With the three Hampshire battalions at Shorncliffe and Folkestone, mobilization was completed and the battalions were brought up to full strength in men and equipment. As a grand finale to the three years' training, a divisional field firing exercise was held on Lewes Down, and among the many important spectators was General Eisenhower. It was during this exercise that the 2/4th Battalion lost a valuable and enthusiastic officer when Captain Lord Woolmer was killed. The Brigade was demonstrating an attack under a barrage laid by the whole Divisional artillery.

The final move of the Brigade was to their own county on 2nd December, with the 1/4th at Hartley Wintney, near Basingstoke, the 2/4th at Runfold, near Farnham, and the 5th at Fleet. Short leave was granted, inoculations were given, and motor vehicles were prepared for the journey, and stores were packed up. There was a final flurry of Battalion Orders, and sufficient training was maintained to keep everyone at the peak of fitness. Finally the Division was inspected by His Majesty King George VI, who was accompanied by the Colonel of the Regiment, General Sir Richard Haking, who afterwards visited all three battalions, the last visit to 128th Brigade before his death. After the inspection the King wished the Brigade good luck, victory and a safe return. On 6th January, 1943, the Brigade embarked at Gourock for North Africa.

* * * * *

The 5/7th Battalion was divided to form the 5th and the 7th Battalions in the summer of 1939, and the 7th, commanded by Lieutenant-Colonel A. W. Malim, was mobilized with the rest of the 43rd Wessex Division at the end of August, 1939. On 1st September the 7th Battalion went to its war station in the Portsmouth area. Battalion Headquarters and one company were established at Fort Fareham, one company was on an island in Fareham Harbour, another at Sandown and the fourth at Gosport. The Battalion was in 130th Infantry Brigade of the 43rd Division, with Brigade Headquarters somewhat inconveniently distant from the Battalion at Frome in Somerset.

In the first few months of the war companies were busy with training and organization, in most cases under considerable administrative difficulties. The Battalion had some twenty vulnerable points in its charge. Equipment was slow in coming in, and there was necessarily much improvisation and "making do." The first move of the Battalion was to Marstom House, near

Frome, in January, 1940. Here the Battalion was together for the first time since the general mobilization. It was an unusually severe winter and living conditions in the large mansion were very uncomfortable as there was neither heat, light nor water. However, equipment improved and vehicles began to be delivered, so that more realistic training could be undertaken. The intention at that time was for the Division to go to France in May or June, and spirits were high—and a great deal of hard work was cheerfully undertaken. But in the event the Battalion did not go to France for another four years, the disastrous turn of fortune in France in May, 1940, changing the whole situation. Instead, the Battalion went with the Division to Hertfordshire, as we have already seen, as G.H.Q. Mobile Reserve, and the 7th Hampshire was stationed in Hertford. Training continued, and when not training the Battalion constructed a very large number of road-blocks, Hertford being a nodal point in the general defence scheme.

The Battalion was able to have a holiday on Minden Day, 1940, and a ceremonial parade was followed by sports in Ball's Park. The Brigade Commander was startled to find that the Battalion paraded with its Corps of Drums. The Commanding Officer had tactfully kept existence of the drums from authority. Once produced it was very popular, and on the Sunday after Minden Day the Battalion marched to church with its drums, to the delight of the people of Hertford.

It was while the 7th Battalion was at Hertford that it was selected for an airborne exercise, and after considerable preparation it was transported by air at a strength of 730 from Hatfield aerodrome to Linton-on-Ouse in Yorkshire. It is believed that this was the first occasion on which a Battalion was transported by air at home. The emplaning and deplaning were watched by the Corps and Divisional Commanders, and subsequently a letter was received from Brigade saying how favourably impressed both Commanders had been by the efficiency, turn-out and soldierly bearing of the Battalion.

In September, 1940, the 43rd Division joined XII Corps, with which it eventually went to Normandy. The 7th Battalion moved to Harpenden, but almost immediately it went to Dover, the "front line" indeed. With the other two battalions of the 130th Brigade, the 4th and 5th Dorsets, they became the garrison of the Fortress. Battalion Headquarters was in the Citadel with companies out on the perimeter, and they came under enemy fire in the form of long-range shelling and a very large number of air attacks, which caused some casualties. In spite, however, of the active-service conditions, training was carried on. Rugby football also flourished, as the Battalion's Padre was an ex-Welsh international. At this time the 43rd was the only fully equipped Division in the Army, and it was for this reason that it was placed in the forefront of the country's defences.

After three months at Dover the 7th was moved to Herne Bay, where it remained through 1941. Being in line with the other two battalions in their Brigade, the 4th and 5th Dorsets, the opportunity was taken to construct anti-invasion obstacles along the whole of their coastal zone. In March, 1941, a change of station in the same area put the 7th next to the 128th Brigade, so that the four Hampshire Territorial battalions served in line, providing excellent opportunities for social and sporting engagements.

In February, 1941, Colonel Malim was succeeded in command by Lieutenant-Colonel Lee, who came from the 2nd Battalion, Colonel Malim having been given a special appointment in the Northern Ireland District. After three months Colonel Lee went back to command his old battalion and Lieutenant-Colonel Bradshaw, previously Second-in-Command of the 7th, took his place.

During 1941 the Home Guard, in whose training the Battalion had helped, was able to take over more and more of the duties of manning the defensive positions, leaving more time for training. The 7th took part in the same divisional and corps exercises as the 128th Brigade, and General Montgomery's four-day corps exercise in East Anglia, in which the Battalion marched more than a hundred miles, ending with a thirty-mile march in ten hours. Another memorable event of 1941 was the hundred-a-side tug-of-war in the Minden Day sports.

In March, 1942, the 7th moved to Deal, in July to St. Nicholas-at-Wade, and in October to Birchington : 1942 followed the pattern of 1941—constant training, realistic and strenuous. There were exercises and schemes, sometimes with tanks, sometimes with the Royal Air Force. There were, of course, many changes in officers. Lieutenant-Colonel G. D. Browne succeeded Colonel Bradshaw in September, 1942, and remained in command until August, 1943, when he was appointed G.S.O.1, 3rd Division, 21st Army Group. When Colonel Browne left his place was taken by Lieutenant-Colonel D. W. G. Ray, who remained in command and eventually took the 7th Battalion into action. Unlike their companions in the 128th Brigade, the 7th were not destined to go to North Africa ; their duty was still at home for another two years. But life was anything but dull, and the Battalion remained steadily at the peak of condition, fully equipped and ready for the day when it was to embark for Normandy.

* * * * *

The old 6th (Duke of Connaught's Own) Battalion had been changed to Gunners as the 59th and 69th Anti-Tank Regiments, R.A., and swiftly learnt their new trade. The 59th were in the 43rd (Wessex) Division, and with the 7th Battalion trained most thoroughly for the great adventure of the invasion of Normandy, where they won laurels as Gunners as their comrades still in the infantry won theirs. The 69th Regiment came back from France after helping to cover the withdrawal of the B.E.F. through Dunkirk and then sailed away to the Far East, representing the Hampshire Regiment in Burma, while the other battalions fought in Italy and North-West Europe.

III—The Eight Service Battalions

The 8th Battalion (Princess Beatrice's Own Isle of Wight Rifles) had become Royal Artillery in 1937, and had been thereby lost to the Regiment. In August, 1939, however, a new battalion was formed with headquarters in Southampton, as part of the South Hampshire Group, and in December, 1939, this became the 8th (Home Defence) Battalion The Hampshire Regiment. Lieutenant-Colonel St. Aubyn, who had a long association with the old 8th Battalion, became Commanding Officer. The Battalion formed two companies of young volunteer soldiers, who left the Battalion in September, 1940, to join the newly raised 70th Battalion. At the same time the 8th (H.D.) Battalion was duplicated, forming the 1/8th, commanded by Lieutenant-Colonel St. Aubyn, and the 2/8th, commanded by Lieutenant-Colonel Gutteridge.

In the next twelve months various changes in the organization of the Army brought about a somewhat bewildering change in these battalions. The 2/8th became, within a few weeks, the 13th Battalion, and led a separate existence as such until September, 1941, when it amalgamated again with the 1/8th to form, first the 8th (H.D.) Battalion and then, a month later, the 30th Battalion, which was commanded first by Lieutenant-Colonel im Thurn, D.S.O., M.C., and then by Lieutenant-Colonel Taylor. As the 30th Battalion the role of Home Defence was changed and it became partly operational as a counter-attack battalion and began a course of strenuous training. The Battalion, with its six companies, was still committed to guarding many vulnerable points in Hampshire. In September, 1942, however, orders were received to disband the 30th Battalion. There were two farewell parades in October: at the first the Secretary of State for War inspected the Battalion and explained that, with the Allied change from the defensive to the offensive role, the disbandment of many Home Defence battalions was unavoidable. At the second parade the Battalion marched past the Colonel of the Regiment, with Band and Drums, and in the evening of 28th October the Band and Drums beat "Retreat" outside the Winchester Guild Hall.

This brought to an end the brief life of the 8th, 13th and 30th Battalion, which had suffered many changes in its three years of existence. In that time, however, good service had been done. The 8th had, in June, 1940, worked hard at receiving and disposing of many thousands of British and Allied troops after the evacuation from Dunkirk. The Battalion had manned coastal defences, guarded vulnerable points, trained very many recruits, and had helped considerably to train the Home Guard. In the later stages the 30th Battalion had become a highly trained fighting unit, and when it was disbanded most of the officers and men were posted to other battalions of the Regiment.

* * * * *

The 9th and 10th Battalions were formed on 4th July, 1940; the 9th, commanded by Lieutenant-Colonel Fowler-Esson, at Parkhurst, Isle of Wight, and the 10th, under canvas at Aldershot, commanded by Lieutenant-Colonel

Koe, with Major K. A. Johnston, D.S.O., as Second-in-Command. With the 13th and 14th Queen's, the 9th and 10th Hampshires constituted 201st Brigade. After an intermediate move by the 9th to Cowshot camp, the two Battalions took up quarters at Bognor Regis in October, 1940, and for three months they did duty on coastal defence, and trained as much as duty would permit. Both Battalions were visited by His Majesty The King, who watched them on duty. In February, 1941, the Brigade moved to the East Riding of Yorkshire, joining the 2nd Yorkshire Division, the 9th Battalion being stationed at Burton Pidsea and the 10th in Hull itself. Here they were again occupied with coastal defence, being responsible for longer stretches than they had had in Sussex. Training was carried out strenuously, and they also suffered intense air raids, toiling long in clearing up the wreckage after the particularly heavy raids on Hull. In one raid civilian casualties were more than four hundred killed and three hundred seriously injured, and, as may well be imagined, there was a great deal of grim and desperate work to be done.

In June, July and August, 1941, both Battalions took part in elaborate exercises and battle training. On one occasion they marched eighty-five miles in full equipment, fighting "battles" *en route*, including a river crossing and an assault landing on an island. At this time H.R.H. The Duke of Gloucester visited the Battalions, and lunched at the Headquarters of the 10th Battalion. Both Battalions were moved about in the East Riding, but always on the coast ; they were at Withernsea, Easington, Hessale, Patrington, Roos and Hedon among other places.

The Battalions consisted mainly of men in their late twenties and their quality was high. There were all sorts, and, for example, one Company Headquarters of the 9th Battalion contained a batman whose father was a Belfast clothing manufacturer, and whose brother was a captain in the Royal Corps of Signals, a company cook who was second cook at a big Liverpool hotel, a mess waiter who was second butler to the Duke of Norfolk, and a sergeant who was the wine steward at Ciro's. In both Battalions there was an excellent spirit, and with strenuous training and enthusiastic leadership by officers and N.C.Os. they became very good indeed ; it was felt that when their turn came to go to war they would acquit themselves really well. But fate had a surprise in store for them, and in November, 1941, they were told that both Battalions were to be converted to tank regiments ; another effect of the Allied policy in changing from the defensive to the offensive. Both Battalions moved south again, to Bury St. Edmunds in Suffolk, and here the 9th was converted to the 157th, and the 10th to the 147th, Regiment, R.A.C. There was, of course, a considerable shuffle of personnel, and many officers and N.C.Os. were posted to other battalions. Specialists were posted in, and officers and N.C.Os. were sent to conversion courses, where they learnt the new tactics and way of life of tank men. There were many regrets, of course, at the change, but everyone realized that it was a splendid sign of the times, and only the inveterate infantryman considered it a change for the worse.

Both Regiments retained their association with the Hampshire Regiment, and though they had changed their forage caps for berets, the new Regiments had an unmistakable "Tiger" look to them. Lieutenant-Colonel Fowler-Esson commanded the 157th Regiment, with Major Smith as Second-in-Command, Captain Jehu as Adjutant and Majors Westropp, Tobin and Holbrook and Captain Bain as the Squadron Leaders. The 147th Regiment was commanded by Lieutenant-Colonel Koe, with Major K. A. Johnston, D.S.O., Second-in-Command, Captain Pitts Adjutant, and Majors Hounslow, Williams, Eldridge and Dransfield the Squadron Leaders.

On the second anniversary of the formation of the 9th and 10th Battalions, both the 157th and 147th Regiments, R.A.C., held christening ceremonies. For the first Mrs. K. Livesey named the Commanding Officer's tank "Haking," and others "Horatius," "Heedless," "Hannibal," and "Hallidon." For the 147th Regiment Mrs. Koe named her husband's tank "Minden" and all the others after Battle Honours of the Hampshire Regiment. Thus it came about that tanks wore roses on Minden Day.

The 157th Regiment trained for two years until in August, 1943, when it was stationed at Lismore Park, near Bury St. Edmunds, its career came to an end and the Regiment was disbanded. The 147th Regiment, however, the original 10th Battalion of the Regiment, was destined to serve in XXX Corps with considerable distinction. It crossed to Normandy at the beginning of July, 1944, commanded by Lieutenant-Colonel A. W. Brown, M.C., and fought through Belgium and Holland, where it often found itself alongside the 1st and 7th Hampshire Battalions.

* * * * *

In the afternoon of 19th June, 1940, Lieutenant-Colonel Vatcher, M.C., addressed the Royal Militia of Jersey on their parade ground in Jersey. There were ten officers and a hundred and ninety-three men on parade, and the news they received from their Commanding Officer was serious. The Germans had overrun France and the question had been, would the little island and its neighbours put themselves into a state of defence and resist the inevitable arrival of the enemy, or would the islands be left open? The decision had been made; the hopeless resistance was not to be attempted and the Channel Islands were to be demilitarized. The Jersey Militia existed solely for the defence of the island, and Colonel Vatcher explained the position. He then invited any men who wished to leave Jersey with him at once to fight from England to take one pace forward. The whole parade stepped forward and took up their dressing.

The next evening the Royal Militia of Jersey marched through the streets of Southampton, impressing all who saw them with their smart and soldierly bearing. From the transit camp they were posted to the 50th (Holding) Battalion The Hampshire Regiment, in the Isle of Wight, and a special company was to be formed of them. But Colonel Vatcher naturally protested to the War Office that his command was an old-established unit and accordingly they became the nucleus of a new battalion, the 11th (Royal Militia Island of Jersey) Battalion The Hampshire Regiment. They retained their own cap-badges and Lieutenant-Colonel Vatcher remained in command.

It was an interesting and historic association, by which a battalion of the Hampshire Regiment was formed embodying the Royal Militia of Jersey unit. As such the Battalion did not have a very adventurous life, but many officers and men were posted away to the Hampshire battalions on active service, and indeed to other units, including Commandos. The number of Jerseymen in the 11th Battalion dwindled as the war years passed, through the men volunteering for active service battalions.

In the Isle of Wight they literally dug themselves in, and took over the task of defending all the high ground which runs like a backbone through the Island. Battalion Headquarters were first a farm and later Rafter's holiday camp. Quite naturally other Channel Islanders gravitated to their ranks, as well as new English intake. Thus came into being a very fine battalion with, quite naturally, a special *esprit de corps* of its own.

Later in 1940 the 11th Battalion became a Field Force unit, and in February, 1941, it moved to Gosport and began training in earnest, quickly making itself a first-class fighting unit. When they were trained it was felt at the War Office that now the Battalion had become operational, drastic consequences might ensue from a single fighting unit being recruited from one comparatively small community, and accordingly no more Channel Islanders were posted in, and some of those already on the battalion strength left to join other battalions, in most cases remaining in the Regiment.

In March, 1941, Lieutenant-Colonel Vatcher was promoted Colonel and appointed Aide-de-Camp to the King, and Lieutenant-Colonel Lindley took over the Battalion, commanding it with notable success for the next two and a half years. In November, 1941, the Battalion returned to the Isle of Wight, joining the 214th Brigade, and being stationed at Freshwater. In the same month the Colours of the Royal Militia Island of Jersey were laid up in the Bishop's Chapel at Wolvesey Castle, Winchester. Ex-Lieutenant-Governors of Jersey and Guernsey were present at the very impressive ceremony.

The Battalion was fully trained, fully equipped and ready for action, and it was everyone's hope and belief that before long they would be used operationally. But, as with so many other excellent battalions, they had to continue to serve at home. In September, 1942, the Battalion joined the 77th Division and moved to Newton Abbot, where it undertook and carried out with great *élan* a new and important task. This was to absorb intakes of men who had finished their initial training, and to subject them to a course of further training to fit them for active service. The intakes were given hard physical training followed by battle training, and then, when they were toned up and fully prepared, they were passed on to other units.

This task the 11th Battalion performed for the next three years at Newton Abbot, Withernsea, Consett and Fenham Barracks, Newcastle. The Battalion itself was a happy one ; enthusiastic and well manned. When gaps appeared in their ranks through postings out, they filled them with the best of the men they had trained, and so they maintained a high standard themselves. Always, too, there remained a nucleus of Channel Islanders.

In August, 1944, the duties of the Battalion were changed. Their new task was not the training of new intakes ; instead they had to sort, test and grade the men according to their attainment, capacity and medical category, for direct disposal to other units or for discharge from the Army. The 77th Division was disbanded and the 45th Division took its place.

In September, 1944, Captain H. Le Brocq and twenty-two other volunteers from the Jerseymen still remaining with the Battalion left Newcastle for Plymouth, to accompany the force which carried out the reoccupation of Jersey in May, 1945. Captain Le Brocq had the pleasant duty of rehoisting the Union Flag at Fort Regent on 9th May, on the official flag-post where he had last seen it flying when he marched out on 20th June, 1940.

In October, 1944, Lieutenant-Colonel Lindley relinquished his long and very useful command, and his place was taken by Lieutenant-Colonel Marriott, and in November the Battalion moved south again to Wotton Underwood, in Buckinghamshire. Here their work continued, though as the war neared its end the tempo changed. For a time, in April, 1945, the Battalion adopted a new role, becoming temporarily a transit camp for returning Dominion, Colonial and Allied prisoners of war.

In August, 1945, Lieutenant-Colonel Parker succeeded Colonel Marriott, and in December the Battalion moved for the last time, to Blandford in Dorset. Here in April, 1946, the 11th (R.M.I.J.) Battalion The Hampshire Regiment was disbanded. The two hundred officers and men who had left their homes and families in Jersey in 1940 had formed a new battalion which, although not given the opportunity of showing its quality in battle, served nevertheless with considerable success ; cheerful, efficient and deservedly proud of themselves.

* * * * *

The 50th (Holding) Battalion was formed at Golden Hill Fort, Freshwater, Isle of Wight, on 4th June, 1940, under the command of Lieutenant-Colonel Wheeler, O.B.E., M.C. The main function of the Battalion was, of course, to hold trained officers, N.C.Os. and men for posting as required to the other battalions of the Regiment, but it had the additional responsibility of taking part in the defence of the West Wight coast-line. Large intakes from the Infantry Training Centres and from civilian life were received as soon as the unit was formed, and very soon the average strength was fifty officers and twelve hundred other ranks. In a few weeks the command was changed, when Lieutenant-Colonel Clegg took over.

The Battalion was changed to a Field Force unit in early October, 1940, and it was accordingly reclassified as the 12th Battalion The Hampshire Regiment, serving as such for the next four years. It had many moves in that time, and on several occasions it seemed that its wishes to become an active-service battalion were to be realized, but always those hopes were dashed. Instead the 12th Hampshire served in the less exciting but very necessary role of taking and training a large number of men who passed on to other battalions and served in North Africa, Italy and Normandy.

The first move of the Battalion was to Bournemouth in November, 1940, where it undertook anti-invasion duties and spent many wearisome hours erecting scaffolding on the beach. The first opportunity the Battalion had to get together for serious soldiering was in March, 1941, when it marched to Lyndhurst for six weeks' concentrated training in the forest and in the country around. The Battalion responded excellently to the opportunity it had been given, and then returned to Bournemouth, with its friendly local population and the everlasting erection of beach scaffolding. In August however, the men found themselves vastly outnumbered by the masses of holiday-makers who were then admitted to the beaches.

The Battalion went to the Isle of Wight in November, 1941, joining with the 11th (R.M.I.J.) Battalion in the 214th Independent Brigade. They were stationed at Parkhurst, in Albany Barracks, until January, 1942, when they moved to Sandown and were split up for beach defence duties. Training continued as far as duties permitted, and the presence in the vicinity of a Royal Marine Commando unit provided the opportunity for some interesting training exercises with them. The 12th were at Sandown when the 1st Battalion came down from Scotland for their short but strenuous visit, and many acquaintanceships with old friends were renewed. In August Lieutenant-Colonel Mason, O.B.E., took over command of the Battalion. The Battalion's next move was to Dovercourt in Essex in September, 1942, where they joined the 136th Infantry Brigade of the 45th Division.

At Dovercourt orders were received to mobilize and it was announced that the Battalion was to become a Field Force unit in a Reserve Division, and for this they were to have moved to Colchester. But suddenly all that was changed, and the Battalion was sent to Ireland, first at Bellaghy, County Derry, and then at Banbridge, County Down, where large-scale divisional exercises were carried out. In September, 1943, Lieutenant-Colonel Innes, of the West Yorkshire Regiment, took over the Battalion. The programme was as before, training and continuous drafting out of men to other battalions, and in December, 1943, the Battalion returned to England, to Wykhurst Park, Bolney, near Haywards Heath. In June, 1944, they were moved to the marshalling areas near Portsmouth, to provide staff for the invasion of Normandy, and in July came the sad news that the 12th Hampshire was to be disbanded, its duty done. Battalion Headquarters moved to Eastbourne and there, on 9th September, 1944, the Battalion was finally closed down.

* * * * *

The 70th Battalion was formed at Southampton on 26th September, 1940, from the two "Young Soldier" companies of the 8th Battalion, under the command of Lieutenant-Colonel R. S. Lambert, M.C. Two weeks after formation Battalion Headquarters moved, with one company, to Oakridge Farm Camp, Basingstoke, where it remained for most of its existence. The remaining companies were formed in November and December and the Battalion was quickly brought up to strength. The Battalion's task was the defence of airfields in the Hampshire Divisional Area, and companies took over an airfield each, Middle Wallop, Worthy Down, Chilbolton and Ibsley, which last was changed for Eastleigh. Two additional companies were formed, one for training and the other for administration, and both were stationed at Basingstoke. The necessary if monotonous duties of guarding airfields were performed until the summer of 1942, when the Royal Air Force Regiment was able to take over the duty.

The Battalion was then changed to a counter-attack battalion, with the appropriate establishment, and on 1st October, 1942, the Battalion went to Bridport, where they were engaged on beach defence for a few weeks, until they moved first to Cambridge and then to Saffron Walden. Here they were able to train in their proper role. Training was undertaken with zest, but it was marred somewhat by the large number of recruits who were posted in for training. The winter of 1942-1943 was an exceedingly busy time for the Army, and pressure on Training Centres made it necessary to call on the 70th and similar battalions to train recruits.

At Saffron Walden Lieutenant-Colonel Taylor became Commanding Officer of the 70th Battalion, and there was another change when it was announced that they were to become a Field Force unit ; hopes rose that there might be active service when they went by march route to Colchester. But soon demands came to post away large drafts to other battalions ; it was the writing on the wall, which was confirmed on 23rd May, 1943, with the news that the 70th Battalion was to be disbanded. The final parade was held on 1st July, 1943, when General Templer took the salute, and the 70th Battalion The Hampshire Regiment ceased to exist.

Like the 12th Battalion, the 70th had carried out its duties with a fine spirit ; it had trained a large number of men who had been passed on to active service battalions ; it had sent a constant supply of volunteers to the Commando units and to the Parachute battalions, and it had passed a hundred and forty men successfully to Officer Cadet Training units.

* * * * *

The Regimental Depot had resumed its normal function in August, 1919, and throughout the inter-war years it continued to train and draft recruits to the Home Battalion. In those twenty years it was commanded successively by :

Lieutenant-Colonel W. H. Middleton, D.S.O.
Lieutenant-Colonel F. W. Earle, D.S.O.
Major T. C. Spring, D.S.O.
Major D. Mills.

Lieutenant-Colonel H. H. Gribbon, D.S.O.
Major P. H. Cadoux-Hudson, M.C.
Major C. C. Smythe, M.C.

There were various preparations in case of war during 1938, and billets, and even horse-lines and forage barns, had to be earmarked ; visits from senior officers included a memorable one from General Sir Archibald Wavell. This visit resulted in several vital structural alterations in the Depot barracks which proved to be of great advantage when the eventual mobilization took place. In 1937 the issue of a new War Establishment based on mechanical instead of horse transport made it possible to prepare a new and modern mobilization scheme.

About that time a popular innovation was the formation of a Regimental Company of the Auxiliary Territorial Service. The young ladies who had volunteered spent a week in barracks training with the departments with which they were to serve in the event of mobilization. Later many of them performed very valuable whole-time duties at the Depot before they were officially embodied.

In 1939 further preparations had to be made, and considerable heart-burning was occasioned by the orders that in the event of war the Depot would leave Winchester. It was also learned that the role of the Depot was to be changed, and in June, 1939, billets were listed in the Isle of Wight for at least a thousand recruits.

In the summer of 1939 the Militia were posted to the Depot for training, and then, on 3rd September, within two hours of the declaration of war, the reservists began to arrive. By 5th September both the officers' and sergeants' messes were filled to overflowing, and twelve hundred or more men had the barrack square as their dining hall. On 9th September the advance party, with Major H. J. Jeffery in command, left for Parkhurst, Isle of Wight. The Depot was merged with the Hampshire Regiment Infantry Training Centre with Lieutenant-Colonel B. im Thurn, in command. It is interesting to note that at this time the Hampshire Company of the A.T.S. was commanded by Junior Commander Joan im Thurn, and when Colonel im Thurn led the column from Winchester Barracks on 16th September for Albany Barracks, Parkhurst, his daughter marched in the rear commanding her company of the A.T.S.

As with everyone else, the first phase of organization for war had been difficult, and the fact that the mobilization of fifteen hundred reservists, their equipment and dispatch to their units, and the intricate arrangements for the complete move to the Isle of Wight went without any hitch reflects considerable credit on Major Smythe, Major Jeffery, the Quartermaster, and Lieutenant A. H. T. Hogge, the Adjutant.

It was while the Depot was on the Island with the I.T.C. that the Regiment became the foster-parent of a live tiger. This was Blang, who lived in the London Zoo. War conditions presented the authorities of the Zoo with a serious catering problem, so the Regiment adopted Blang to help them out.

Every battalion sent subscriptions to Colonel im Thurn, and Blang was fed and maintained in the manner to which he was accustomed. Thus it was that, in a manner of speaking, to the various tiger skins adorning the Regimental Mess was added a live tiger ; altogether a very appropriate arrangement.

In June, 1940, came warning orders to prepare to receive at least five thousand troops from the Expeditionary Force, and to have ready for immediate issue everything that a man might require after such a retreat and evacuation. The urgency of the situation set those responsible gloriously free of regulations and normal systems of indenting ; common sense and imagination had to take their place. Firms on the Island and on the mainland were raided, marquees sprang up on the sports ground, and everything conceivably necessary was ready—and then the orders were cancelled. Cancelled, too, was the freedom from accounting, and everything obtained had to be systematically "taken on charge" and accounted for, including perishable rations for three days for five thousand troops. The arrangements had been made in desperate haste, the weather was unusually hot and there was no cold storage, yet not one pennyworth was lost.

After Dunkirk, Colonel im Thurn, as Officer Commanding Isle of Wight Garrison, was ordered to prepare the Island defences against invasion, and a great deal of activity ensued. Colonel im Thurn continued in command until December, 1940, when the garrison was reinforced by a freshly formed brigade under Brigadier M. Prower, who became Garrison Commander. Brigadier Prower had begun his service in the Regiment before the 1914 war. The I.T.C. received many notable visitors while on the Island, among them Generals Paget, Auchinleck, Alan Brooke and Montgomery, and His Royal Highness The Duke of Gloucester.

In July, 1941, the I.T.C. was moved to Oxford, and the Depot came into being again as a Depot Party of two officers, Major C. D. Fawkes and Major Jeffery, and twelve other ranks, with the duty of safeguarding regimental property. The officer establishment was later reduced to one, and Major Jeffery was in command when the Depot party returned to their old quarters in Winchester in November, 1942. As well as safeguarding regimental property, its duties included liaison with all the battalions of the Regiment, and also with the American troops in the Rifle Depot and surrounding district. Major Jeffery remained in command of the Regimental Depot until September, 1947, when he retired after over forty-two years' continuous service with the Regiment.

The I.T.C. performed most vigorous service throughout the war, training an enormous number of officers and men. As an example of the flexibility in administration of which the I.T.C. was ever capable, just before Christmas, 1940, six hundred men were drafted in, and so large a batch of new officers that there were ninety in mess on Christmas Day. At its peak at Parkhurst the unit was over 3,000 strong. The fundamental purpose of the I.T.C., to provide the Hampshire battalions with well-trained, good-quality reinforcements, was accepted as a challenge by the permanent staff, and the invigorating spirit of the unit was infectious.

In July, 1941, the I.T.C. as such was temporarily disbanded and opened up again in Cowley Barracks and Slade Camp, Oxford, with the Oxfordshire and Buckinghamshire Light Infantry as No. 16 Combined Infantry Training Centre, with training staff found equally by the two regiments. The whole was commanded by Colonel im Thurn, and the most friendly relations were established between the two regiments. Recruits were given a vigorous training at Oxford, including a rather alarming assault course and a "blitz" course.

The I.T.C. moved next to Colchester, where more courses were established to turn the recruits into soldiers fully prepared for conditions of modern battle. From Colchester the I.T.C. was moved, in November, 1943, to Northampton, becoming No. 14 I.T.C. and sharing quarters in Talavera Barracks with the Devons and the Northamptonshire Regiment. Here it remained for two years, until the changing conditions of the war made it necessary to make Talavera Barracks a Military Dispersal Centre, and the I.T.C. moved into the Old Barracks, Northampton, commanded by Lieutenant-Colonel Cadoux-Hudson. Here the I.T.C. continued its very active and useful existence, until it was disbanded at the end of the war.

CHAPTER VIII

THE 2ND BATTALION IN NORTH AFRICA

TEBOURBA, DECEMBER, 1942

THE 2nd Battalion sailed for North Africa on 11th November, 1942. Their departure from Forfar for Liverpool was very inconspicuous; the troops marched from their billets to the railway station in small parties, wearing gym shoes, and security measures were very thorough.

The Battalion was commanded by Lieutenant-Colonel J. M. Lee, with Major D. E. G. Chamberlain Second-in-Command, Captain M. J. Barton Adjutant, and Lieutenant C. A. Northmore Quartermaster. From Liverpool the ship went to the Clyde, where it anchored while the convoy formed up. The voyage was uneventful; the ship, commanded by a fiery Norwegian skipper, was small, and quarters were restricted. The convoy arrived at Algiers on the afternoon of 21st November, and the Battalion marched at once, heavily laden, to a bivouac area near Maison Blanche, where it was soon tucked away safe from air attack.

The first orders received were that the Battalion was to take over aerodrome defence at Bone. But when the train to Bone had reached Constantine, new orders were received from General Anderson, commanding First Army, directing the Battalion to report to 78th Division at railhead. This was good news, as the Battalion considered itself too good to be used for aerodrome defence. At Souk-el-Arba the Battalion was met by a staff officer of the 78th Division. One platoon of "W" Company was left to guard baggage and a prisoner-of-war camp and the Battalion moved to a bivouac. The Commanding Officer reported to the Divisional Commander who was full of confidence and most anxious to get to Tunis before V Corps could become operational.

The initial Allied landings in North-West Africa had taken place a week before the Battalion landed at Algiers. At first the situation had been very confusing, but the political attitude of the French was quickly cleared up and the French forces in North Africa ceased their resistance and became available for operations against Germany and Italy. Thus Morocco and Algeria were secured, and Tunisia alone remained to be taken. It was to this problem that General Eisenhower turned his attention. The capture of Tunis was to prove to be a much tougher proposition than was expected. The enemy were reinforcing themselves rapidly, and it was estimated that towards the end of November they had 20,000 men and some armour in position to defend Tunis.

The British First Army, commanded by General Anderson and consisting then of little more than the 78th Division, had begun a general advance from Bone towards Tunis on 24th November. The advance went well at first; first Medjez-el-Bab was captured and then Tebourba. But on 29th November it was slowed down and on the next day violent counter-attacks by the enemy

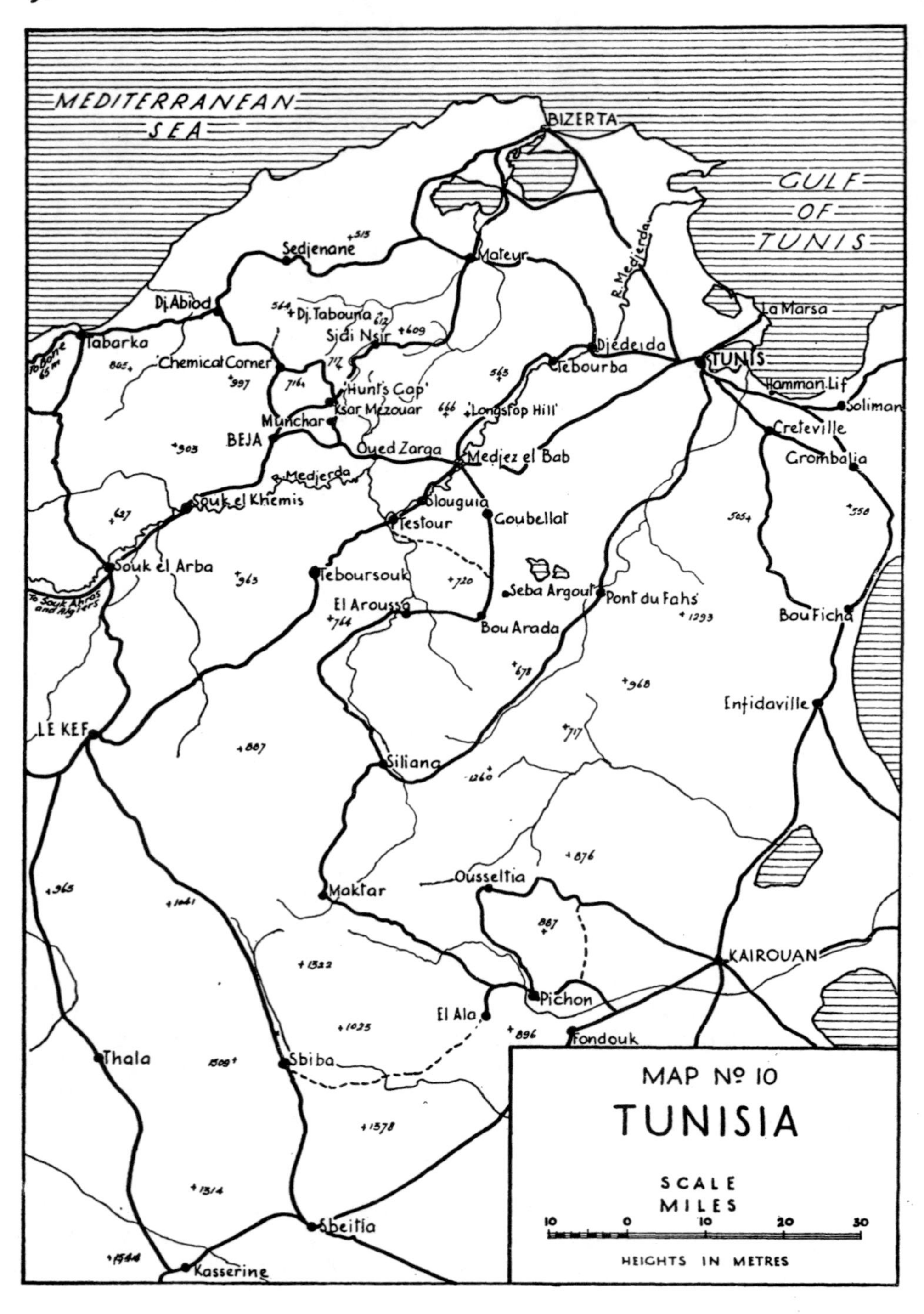
MEDITERRANEAN SEA
BIZERTA
GULF OF TUNIS
Sedjenane
Mateur
R. Medjerda
Dj. Abiod
Dj. Tabouna
Sidi Nsir
La Marsa
Tabarka
Chemical Corner
Djedeida
Tebourba
TUNIS
'Hunt's Gap'
Hamman Lif
Ksar Mezouar
'Longstop Hill'
Soliman
Munchar
Creteville
BEJA
Oued Zarga
Medjez el Bab
Grombalia
R. Medjerda
Souk el Khemis
Slouguia
Testour
Goubellat
Souk el Arba
Teboursouk
Seba Argout
Pont du Fahs
El Aroussa
Bou Ficha
Bou Arada
Infidaville
LE KEF
Siliana
Maktar
Ousseltia
KAIROUAN
Pichon
El Ala
Fondouk
Thala
Sbiba
Sbeitla
Kasserine
MAP No 10
TUNISIA
SCALE
MILES
10 0 10 20 30
HEIGHTS IN METRES

brought it to a halt, with the British positions some twenty miles from Tunis. The First Army was resisting these determined counter-attacks as best it could with battle-weary troops at the time the 2nd Battalion moved into the area, coming under command of the 11th Brigade. The Brigade Commander told Colonel Lee that the plan was for him to replace the 2nd Lancashire Fusiliers, and to move up to Medjez-el-Bab (*see map on page* 90). The next afternoon General Allfrey, commanding V Corps, visited the Battalion; he said quite bluntly that the situation was most unpromising and that the Division was in for a sticky time, which proved to be a very true prophecy.

New orders were received from Brigade on the evening of 29th November that the Battalion was to move at once to relieve the 6th Northamptons east of Tebourba, posting one company in Djedeida, a town a mile and a half in front. Colonel Lee had already been up to see the situation and he knew that Djedeida was strongly held by the enemy; he therefore decided to take the whole Battalion to Tebourba and to send "Z" Company on to Djedeida only if the situation had improved. The move forward to Tebourba was made in troop carriers that evening. On the way up one carrier overturned and put a platoon of "W" Company out of action. One platoon of this company had already been detached for duty at Souk-el-Arba, so that "W" Company was short of two platoons during the following four days of battle.

Shortly before the Battalion reached Tebourba a message was brought up from Brigade saying that a company was not to be sent forward to Djedeida; a comforting endorsement of the Battalion Commander's own appreciation of the situation. The take-over from the Northamptons was completed by midnight and platoons immediately dug themselves in. The Battalion was disposed with "X" Company forward on the right and "Y" Company forward on the left, Battalion Headquarters in the wood twenty yards to the rear of "X" Company, and "W" Company (less two platoons) immediately to the rear of Battalion Headquarters; "Z" Company, in reserve, was situated in the rear of "W" Company. The remainder of the Battalion—H.Q. Company, Mortars, Carriers, Pioneers, the transport and the regimental aid post—were in another wood about a mile and a half to the rear of "Z" Company. "B" Echelon were some two miles to the west of Tebourba. Artillery in support of the Battalion consisted of one troop of 25-pounders and one troop of 6-pounders in anti-tank role, sited in depth down the wood, and a troop of 25-pounders with its observation post with "Y" Company on the high ground to the left of the battalion front. "Y," "X" and "Z" Companies each had a detachment of 3-inch mortars under command.

That, then, was the position the Battalion took up on the night of 29th/30th November, 1942. The battle of Tebourba was to last four days. It was a desperate and an heroic fight, essentially a junior leaders' battle, and a most severe test for men who had landed only a week before. The Germans outnumbered the Battalion by four to one; they had modern tanks and complete air supremacy. Before the battle the Battalion strength was 689 all ranks; afterwards it was 194. The positions the Battalion took up were bequeathed to

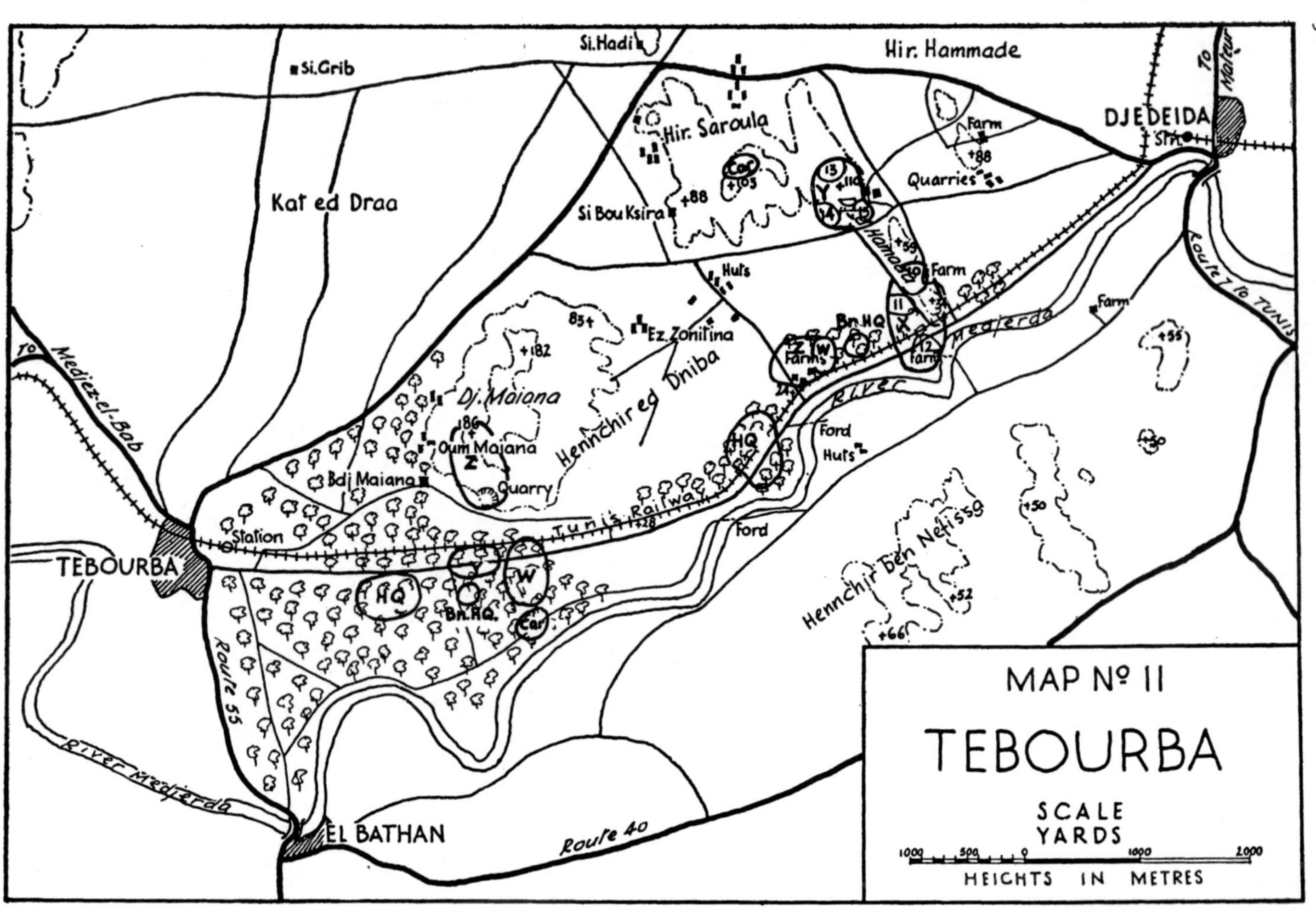
MAP No. 11
TEBOURBA
SCALE
YARDS
1000 500 0 1000 2000
HEIGHTS IN METRES
Si. Grib
Si. Hadi
Hir. Hammade
To Mateur
DJEDEIDA
Stn.
Farm
+88
Quarries
Hir. Saroula
+103
+88
Si Bou Ksira
+110
Kat ed Draa
Hamada
+55
Farm
Route 7 to TUNIS
Huts
Ez. Zonitina
Henchir ed Dniba
Bn. HQ
Farms
Farm
Medjerda
River
+55
+30
83+
+182
Dj. Maiana
186
Oum Maiana
Quarry
Bdj Maiana
To Medjez-el-Bab
HQ
Ford
Huts
Tunis Railway
+28
Station
Ford
+50
Henchir Ben Nefissa
+52
+66
TEBOURBA
HQ
W
Bn. HQ.
Car
Route 55
River Medjerda
EL BATHAN
Route 40

them, and they were ill-suited to defence, being overlooked by high ground to the right and to the front. Yet the Battalion denied passage to the enemy to Tebourba for four days, a feat of the utmost importance to the Division, and the news of this dogged and resolute fighting came as a most valuable tonic to everyone at home at a time when such a tonic was of the greatest value.

Colonel Lee had made a reconnaissance of the position and at once saw the danger of the situation. He asked to be allowed either to attack Djedeida immediately and take up positions based there, or else to form a strong defensive position with his right on the Medjerda river and his left in contact with the East Surreys, where he would be able to present a formidable front ; but neither plan was permitted. Ironically enough on the fourth morning the Battalion fell back and took up the precise position Colonel Lee had advocated, but with a greatly depleted battalion.

On the first day of the battle, Monday, 30th November, the Battalion was subjected to heavy shelling by infantry guns and mortars, and there was considerable air activity. The Brigade Commander came up and said that the Battalion must hold the ground it stood on. During the day Captain Page, commanding the Carrier Platoon, established a standing patrol on the high ground behind "Y" Company with one of his sections to observe any enemy movement to the rear and north of the position. The mortar detachment with "X" Company scored a direct hit on a lorry-load of enemy infantry approaching the railway on the right of the company's position. Fighting patrols probing the vicinity of the positions after dark made no contact with the enemy, except one which went forward to the outskirts of Djedeida, where contact was made with enemy machine guns on fixed lines. So the first day was passed.

During the morning of Tuesday, 1st December, considerable enemy activity was observed on the battalion front, and in the early afternoon the enemy attacked along the fronts of both forward companies, using infantry supported by mortars and machine guns. In front of "X" Company they advanced into the wood, but they were resolutely driven back, so that the Company Commander was able to report the situation under control and casualties slight. The attack on the left of the Battalion was also held off by the fire of "Y" Company.

Towards the evening the enemy made an attempt to get some men and machine guns established in a small farm in front of the right-hand platoon of "Y" Company. "Z" Company was accordingly ordered to counter-attack the farm with a platoon, and Lieutenant Griffith, attached to the Battalion from the Welsh Guards, led his platoon in a spirited attack, supported by artillery and mortars. It happened that the approach to the farm was down an exposed forward slope, and the platoon suffered heavy casualties, among them the platoon commander himself. The attack was pressed home, however, and some men reached the farm, which was set alight by enemy fire. Later the platoon was ordered to withdraw to the company as the position was considered to be untenable with so few men. The withdrawal was completed at dusk, with the exception of some badly wounded, and seven men who were missing. After dark Lieutenant Wright, second-in-command of "Z" Company, although himself wounded in the ankle, went out with stretcher-bearers. The wounded platoon commander, eight badly wounded soldiers and the seven men previously reported missing were brought in. For this action Lieutenant Wright was awarded the M.C.

The second night, 1st December, was again fairly quiet and patrols reported no enemy on the Battalion's immediate front, but soon after daylight on 2nd December the enemy got snipers and machine guns on the high ground on the Battalion's right, across the river. These machine guns opened fire on the whole front and the enemy advanced in strength, supported by tanks. There were also tanks advancing on the right of "Y" Company's position, one of which was able to fire direct into the right-hand platoon, commanded by Lieutenant Seth-Smith, from a range of only twenty yards, and nothing more was seen or heard of this platoon.

Meanwhile both 6-pounders and 2-pounder anti-tank guns were actively engaging the enemy, and two tanks and an infantry gun towed by a lorry were set on fire, while one other was stopped and put out of action. One tank got into a position where it was able to fire into Battalion Headquarters, causing many casualties, which included Lieutenant Pritchard, the Signal Officer, and five signallers. Headquarters was then heavily mortared, and withdrew to a position behind "W" Company, leaving the Anti-Aircraft Platoon and the Pioneers to strengthen the "W" Company position.

At the same time very heavy fighting had been going on in "X" Company positions. The Company had been attacked heavily all the morning, but time after time Captain Thomas, the Company Commander, and Lieutenant Hart drove the enemy back with bayonet charges. At one stage the western end of the wood was defended only by Captain Thomas and five men ; he gathered his few men together and, firing a Bren gun from the hip, led a most gallant bayonet charge clean through the enemy tanks to the infantry beyond and drove them back. But at last the enemy's recurrent attacks with tanks and infantry overran the position. The anti-tank guns were put out of action, and all who remained of "X" Company were one officer, one sergeant and five men. For this very gallant fighting Captain Thomas was awarded the D.S.O.

"W" Company, with three anti-aircraft detachments and some Pioneers, were moved up to the position previously held by Battalion Headquarters and became the right forward company. The Second-in-Command, Major Chamberlain, was killed endeavouring to locate enemy mortar and machine-gun positions. An enemy tank, approaching over a ridge about three hundred yards to the left front of Battalion Headquarters, was stopped and set on fire by a 25-pounder gun. "W" Company then reported by wireless that enemy infantry were advancing in strength down the wood and were close to his position. Colonel Lee ordered "Z" Company to send a platoon down the wood to drive the enemy off with the bayonet, and Lieutenant Freemantle, leading his own platoon, carried this order out most successfully ; he drove the enemy off, killed or wounded some forty of them and took six prisoners. Lieutenant

Freemantle himself, his platoon sergeant and four men were wounded. The platoon went back to its original position in very high spirits.

The situation on "Y" Company's front was obscure, and enemy infantry and machine guns could be plainly seen on the hills to their left and rear. As Colonel Lee had not been able to get in touch with them since midday he feared that they had been overrun. At about four o'clock, however, two runners, one the company clerk, the other the N.C.O. in charge of transport, got into Battalion Headquarters with a report on the situation. To get back they had crossed very open ground swept by machine-gun fire, after they had already seen one runner seriously wounded in attempting to get across.

The message from "Y" Company Commander, Captain Brehaut, showed that the situation was indeed desperate. Casualties had been very heavy, they were out of ammunition and water, and they were cut off from the rest of the Battalion ; they were, however, still holding on to their position. Captain Wingfield and a few men at once set off with a carrier loaded with ammunition and water, and succeeded in fighting their way through to the beleaguered company.

Shortly before dusk the liaison officer with Brigade, Lieutenant Symes, got through to the Battalion to get the situation, as communication between Battalion and Brigade had broken down before midday. Colonel Lee reported that he was still preventing the enemy from reaching Tebourba, but in view of the heavy casualties he had suffered he did not think he would be able to withstand another full-scale attack by infantry supported by tanks.

The enemy attacks died down after dark and the Battalion set about finding and bringing in its wounded. Just before midnight Lieutenant Symes returned from Brigade with the order for the Battalion to take up another position about a mile and a half in the rear, with its right on the river and its left holding a high feature, Point 186.

The Battalion had been in violent battle for three days, harassed constantly by a most desperate enemy. Yet when the troops passed Colonel Lee as he stood in the clearing between the two woods, discipline and morale were perfect. Everyone was alert, silent and most orderly ; it was an exemplary retreat.

The Battalion withdrew to its new position at 1.30 in the morning of 3rd December. The depleted companies were disposed with "W" on the right, "Z" Company on the left, including Point 186, and "Y" astride the railway line slightly to the rear of the other two, covering the gap between them. By dawn Colonel Lee had been round the new positions and had arranged his artillery support. He ordered two sections of the Carrier Platoon to cover the right flank of "W" Company, which was very thin on the ground for the area it was holding. In these positions the Battalion awaited the fourth day of the battle.

At first light on 3rd December the enemy began a very heavy artillery and mortar attack along the whole front. This was maintained until ten o'clock, when he launched a general and very determined advance, paying most attention to the Battalion's left flank, held by "Z" Company. An hour later Major H. W. Le Patourel, commanding this company, reported that the enemy had gained possession of some high ground on his immediate left, which they had captured from a company of another unit after a furious battle. The Germans were establishing themselves there and were bringing heavy machine-gun and mortar fire on his left-hand section at Point 186. The fighting at this stage was extremely heavy and confused.

It was in a desperate attempt to clear the enemy from the high ground on the Battalion's left that Major Le Patourel led a party of four volunteers in a most gallant action, for which he was awarded the Victoria Cross. To quote from the citation :

> On the afternoon of 3rd December, 1942, the enemy had occupied an important high feature on the left of the company commanded by Major Le Patourel. . . . This officer then personally led four volunteers under very heavy fire to the top in a last attempt to dislodge several enemy machine guns.
>
> The party was heavily engaged by the machine-gun fire and Major Le Patourel rallied his men several times and engaged the enemy, silencing several machine-gun posts. Finally, when the remainder of his party were killed or wounded, he went forward alone with a pistol and some grenades to attack the enemy machine-guns at close quarters, and from this action he did not return. . . . Major Le Patourel's most gallant conduct and self-sacrifice, his brilliant leadership and tenacious devotion to duty in the face of a determined enemy were beyond praise.*

With Major Le Patourel in this very brave attack was Lieutenant Lister, who was killed.

Meanwhile the battle continued with unremitting fury. All the morning the enemy were held off ; often they were driven back by bayonet charges by small parties of men. At last, however, enemy infantry, supported by tanks, succeeded in breaking through on the extreme right and got round behind "W" Company's position. Captain Waldron drove them off with a bayonet charge, in which Captain Pearce-Serocold of the Welsh Guards was killed. After the charge enemy were dispersed at the rear of the company's position with small-arms fire. Captain Waldron was awarded the M.C. for this action. At the same time a party of "Y" Company, under Captain Brehaut, cleared Germans who had got close to the front of his position. "Z" Company, by now reduced to only one weak platoon, grimly held the enemy off in the main position. All day the Gunners had been fighting magnificently. They had knocked out five tanks with 25-pounders, and all targets had been taken on over open sights. By five o'clock in the evening only one gun remained in action.

Colonel Lee's intention, when the enemy began to get round to his rear, was to hold the position until dark, and then to break out, recapture Point 186 on

* It was believed that Major Le Patourel was killed and, indeed, his Victoria Cross was awarded posthumously. It was discovered later that he had been seriously wounded and taken prisoner.

MAJOR H. W. LE PATOUREL, V.C.

Face page 96

his left and hold it until further orders. For this purpose he ordered all his remaining troops to form a square round Battalion Headquarters, with the remnants of "Y" Company on the left, "Z" Company under command forward, "W" Company to the right and Battalion Headquarters and the remainder of H.Q. Company in the rear.

At dusk it was obvious, however, that the position was untenable. The enemy was still attacking with unflagging determination and had worked round both flanks so that he reached the railway from both sides. The Battalion was now reduced to ten officers and two hundred men. Short of ammunition and water, the only result of continuing to hold the position would be the complete annihilation or capture of them all. Colonel Lee therefore ordered everyone to arm himself with as many automatic weapons and rifles, grenades and ammunition as could be found or taken from casualties and the dead. He ordered everyone to fix bayonets and form a line in extended order, to move with its right on the railway.

On the Commanding Officer's word the line charged, with automatic weapons firing. Very confused fighting took place with casualties on both sides, including Captain Page, killed, and Major Tathem, who was severely wounded. But the line remained unbroken, and fought back to the outskirts of Tebourba. Here the remnants of the Battalion formed up and marched into the eastern end of the village to report to Brigade Headquarters.

It was then found that all troops had been withdrawn from Tebourba to Medjez-el-Bab. The main road back from Tebourba was cut by the enemy, who had machine guns placed there on fixed lines and tanks in position on the road. A reconnaissance was made to try to find a way back to Medjez-el-Bab either by the road or by crossing the River Medjerda, where Lieutenant Roche was drowned trying to save one of his men. After the reconnaissance the Commanding Officer decided the only solution was for all troops to make their own way back to Medjez-el-Bab in small groups, getting through the enemy positions as best they could. Water and rations were taken from stranded vehicles and the order to disperse was given. Thus ended the battle of Tebourba, of which the King said to cadets at Aldershot : "I recommend you to read the story of the 2nd Battalion of The Hampshire Regiment in Tunisia in 1942. That was a triumph of individual leadership and corporate discipline."

A Gunner officer who fought with the Battalion in the battle wrote :

"As the Artillery F.O.O. who was with the Hampshires on 3rd December, 1942, I should like to add a personal tribute to the most gallant and determined conduct of the officers and men of the Battalion during this action. In spite of enormous casualties on the previous day, and to a lesser extent during this engagement, and in spite of the enemy's great superiority, the Hampshires never ceased to fight with the greatest bravery and determination. The fact that even during the final phases of the enemy's assault the Commanding Officer was personally controlling all fire of the unit, and that their final break-out from the position was carried out in perfect order, are in themselves sufficient tribute to the unit's magnificent discipline and *esprit de corps*. It is impossible to assess the effect of their resistance on the enemy, but it is certain that they inflicted tremendous casualties upon them."

Tebourba was indeed a stern battle, a vital four days' rear-guard action which covered a general withdrawal in the face of the enemy's determined attack. This attack was made with at least three battalions of infantry and thirty-five tanks, supported by heavy dive-bombing. The 2nd Hampshire Battalion bore the brunt of this, and by denying Tebourba to the enemy made it possible for Medjez-el-Bab to be held as the jumping-off ground for future attacks against Tunis. The Battalion was severely cut up, but the casualties it inflicted on the enemy and the tactical benefits of its stand were of very great value. As well as the Victoria Cross won by Major Le Patourel, Lieutenant-Colonel Lee and Major Thomas were awarded the D.S.O., Captains Brehaut, Barton, Wingfield and Waldron and Lieutenant Wright the M.C., and the M.M. was awarded to Sergeants Cockram, Wilton and Wiggins and Lance-Corporal Harris. Among the other awards were the M.B.E. to Lieutenant (Q.M.) Northmore, and a number of Mentions in Despatches.

Tebourba was a memorable battle, a most gallant stand, in which the 2nd Battalion, to all intents and purposes unaided, enabled the Medjez position to be held against the most desperate attacks. It is not too much to say that without this four-day stand at Tebourba the Allies might well have been driven out of Tunisia. The spirit of the men who fought this battle was graphically described by a correspondent of *The Times* :

"Yesterday, I found resting in a wood the heroes of this astonishing feat of arms which had inspired the First Army. They were grimed but their fighting spirit was as high as ever, and they have begged to be allowed to return to the hills to search for the Colonel and Adjutant. And one man, when I said that they had earned a rest, replied : 'We have no business to be here. We ought to be back in the hills as guerillas fighting those bastards.' They are filled with contempt for the enemy, whom they have repeatedly put to flight with the bayonet, and are genuinely eager to get at him again as soon as possible. They are savagely angry with the enemy, too, after seeing mortar shells dropping among their helpless wounded. All were filled with admiration for their doctor and Padre, who brought in and attended to the wounded for four days and nights without rest.

"Out of their matter-of-fact talk, lurid glimpses of the fighting emerge. There was the Corporal who was last seen in the middle of a ring of Germans (Corporal Wiggins) swinging round and spraying them with a tommy-gun. There was an officer (Captain Page) and party who found a 25-pounder with the crew killed and, though infantrymen, managed to make it work and knocked out a German tank with the first shot. There were hints of fantastic bayonet charges—one mild looking private (Private Cuckson) had charged with ten others and bayoneted thirty Germans and all eleven of our men returned safely. There were many stories of German invitations to them to surrender, all of them refused. One was very persuasive ; the Germans promised safety and good treatment and so on, and the Battalion answered as one man, with one derisive word."*

There were many stories to be told, and much gallantry went unrecorded, but it was a Battalion affair and the credit was collective. As they made their way back towards Medjez-el-Bab many, including the Commanding Officer, were taken prisoner. The remnants of the Battalion gathered in a wood near Medjez-el-Bab on 5th December under the command of Captain Brehaut. There were six officers, including the Padre and the Medical Officer, and one hundred and ninety-four other ranks, which included those whose duties had kept them in the rear and out of the battle. On the following day the Battalion took up a defensive position round the railway station, to the north of the town. Here, on 8th December, a Thanksgiving Service was held by the Padre.

The situation in Tunisia was very tense ; the enemy had the initiative and were thrusting determinedly to drive the Allies back. Medjez-el-Bab was one of the vital positions, as it was the perfect jumping-off ground for subsequent attacks against Tunis. For four months there was to be desperate fighting in Tunisia, while the Eighth Army fought its way rapidly westwards over the desert. But it so happened for the first few weeks after the battle of Tebourba that the Battalion was afforded a much needed respite in the Medjez-el-Bab area. In the middle of December first- and second-line reinforcements came up to the number of nine officers and two hundred and sixty other ranks, and the Battalion was able to reorganize and re-equip. On 24th December the Battalion moved up to the Munchar area, under command of the newly formed "Gap Force," and on Christmas Day, 1942, it was digging into new positions. There was, however, a free issue of beer and cigarettes and a sing-song was held in the evening.

The Battalion was still at Munchar on 15th January, 1943, when General Anderson inspected it and decorated officers and men who had won awards at Tebourba. The General congratulated the Battalion on its feat at Tebourba, and also on its drill and turn-out on that parade. A week later, on 22nd January, the Battalion was visited by Brigadier James, V.C., commanding the 128th Brigade, which had landed at Algiers the week before. With the Brigadier were three Hampshire Battalion Commanders, Lieutenant-Colonels Smythe, Robinson and Newnham, commanding the 1/4th, 2/4th and the 5th Battalion. On 30th January Lieutenant-Colonel Martin, who had been Second-in-Command of the 5th Battalion, took over command of the 2nd, with Major Stern, of the Grenadier Guards, as Second-in-Command, and, later, Captain Symes as Adjutant. Thus it was that at the end of January, 1943, the 2nd Battalion awaited further action in Tunisia, reorganized and ready, the wounds of Tebourba healed.

---

* Extract reproduced by permission of *The Times*.

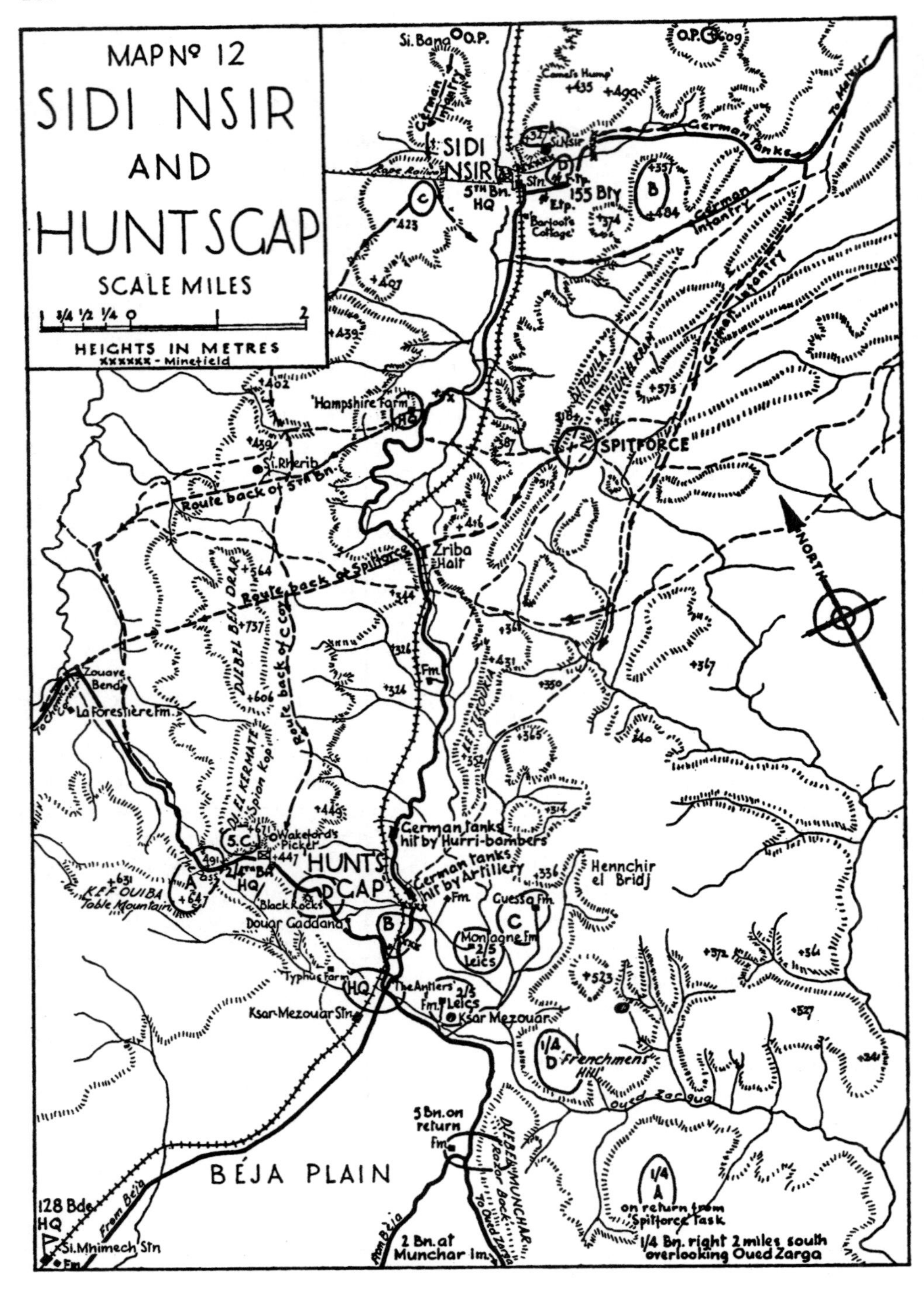
MAP No 12
SIDI NSIR
AND
HUNTSCAP
SCALE MILES
HEIGHTS IN METRES
xxxxxx - Minefield
SIDI NSIR
5TH Bn. HQ
155 Bty
Hampshire Farm
SPITFORCE
Route back of 5TH Bn.
Route back of Spitforce
Route back of C Coy
Zriba Halt
German tanks
German Infantry
DJEBEL BEN DRAA
Zouave Bend
La Forestière Fm.
Spion Kop
Wakeford's Picket
German tanks hit by Hurri-bombers
German tanks hit by Artillery
HUNTS CAP
2/4TH Bn HQ
Black Rocks
Douar Gaddana
KEF OUIBA
Table Mountain
Hennchir el Bridj
Guessa Fm.
Montagne Fm.
2/5 Leics
Typhus Farm
The Antlers
Ksar Mezouar Stn
Ksar Mezouar
Frenchmen's Hill
Oued Zarga
5 Bn. on return
BÉJA PLAIN
128 Bde HQ
Si. Mhimech Stn
From Béja
2 Bn. at Munchar Im.
To Oued Zarga
DJEBEL MUNCHAR
on return from Spitforce Task
1/4 Bn. right 2 miles south overlooking Oued Zarga
NORTH
To Mateur

CHAPTER IX

THE HAMPSHIRE BRIGADE IN NORTH AFRICA

January to July, 1943

(*See map on page* 90)

The 1/4th, 2/4th, and 5th Battalions

The 128th Brigade left for North Africa on 6th January, 1943, sailing from Gourock, the 1/4th and the 5th Battalions, with Brigade Headquarters, in the *Leopoldville* and the 2/4th in the *Orbita*. The 138th Brigade went in the same convoy and the 139th Brigade, the remaining one of the 46th Division, was already in North Africa. The voyage was uneventful, save for a severe buffeting the convoy suffered in the Atlantic, but in the Mediterranean one vehicle transport was torpedoed, fortunately with but little loss of life.

Thus three of the four Hampshire Territorial battalions were at last serving overseas after three and a half years at home, and now only the 7th Battalion remained in England, to continue training until their turn was to come in the following year to take part in the invasion of Normandy.

The 46th Division was sent to North Africa to reinforce the meagre and tired First Army, which at that time consisted only of the 78th Division, part of the 6th Armoured Division, two Commandos, Numbers 1 and 6, and some parachute troops. Since the failure of the ambitious dash to capture Tunis at the beginning of December, the First Army had been hard put to it to hold its positions in Tunisia against very determined enemy counter-attacks.

At this time the enemy was estimated to have 35,000 troops contained somewhat precariously by the Allies in the east of Tunisia. All but 3,000 of these were German, and there was a constant daily build-up by air to Tunis airport. The enemy also had some 300 tanks and a sufficiency of fighters and light bombers operating from airfields within easy distance of the front, and they had something like a thousand long-range bombers based on Sicily, Sardinia and Southern Italy.

The convoy with the two Brigades of the 46th Division sailed into Algiers on the morning of 17th January and the troops disembarked immediately. The 138th Brigade marched off for Maison-Carre, but the 128th Brigade were immediately transhipped into small vessels and were taken with a destroyer escort along the coast to Bone, arriving just before sunset. There the three battalions hastily disembarked, for Bone was a frequent target for enemy aircraft, and indeed an air attack began before disembarkation was finished. The Brigade marched to a new and uncompleted transit camp among the sand-dunes some five miles east of the town. Here it remained until the end of January, being subject to frequent enemy air attacks which were, to a great extent, kept off by the protective barrage.

While the Brigade awaited further orders in the transit camp the losses in vehicles and equipment sustained when the transport was sunk were made good. Senior officers of the Brigade took the opportunity to visit the positions beyond Beja to which the Brigade was destined to move. They also visited the 2nd Battalion, which was at Munchar holding part of the line. On 25th January the Brigade sent detachments to take part in the Victory Parade in Bone to celebrate the Eighth Army's capture of Tripoli.

At the end of January the 128th Brigade moved forward and took over the defensive positions in the hills in front of Beja, holding an extensive position astride Hunts Gap. This was a particularly vulnerable part of the British positions, as Hunts Gap was the only tank run into the area.

The 1/4th Battalion, commanded by Lieutenant-Colonel Smythe, took over the sector at Ksar Mezouar and the 2/4th, commanded by Lieutenant-Colonel Robinson, took up defensive positions astride the Beja–Mateur road and in the hills to the left. Later the 1/4th moved farther south with their left holding "Frenchman's Hill" and their right at Oued Zarga, while the 2/4th extended their positions to include Ksar Mezouar and Guessa Farm, a frontage of some seven thousand yards. These two positions were some miles from the enemy, but vital for the defence of the key position of Beja if the enemy attacked through Hunts Gap.

The 5th Battalion, commanded by Lieutenant-Colonel Newnham, was "out in the blue" some twelve miles in advance of the other battalions, where it had taken over from the 1st East Surreys at the village of Sidi Nsir. Its task was to serve as a buffer in front of the main position, with the duty of delaying the enemy to allow time for the main position at Hunts Gap to be reinforced if he attacked. Sidi Nsir was no more than a cluster of stone hovels inhabited by a few Arabs, some twenty-five miles north-east of Beja, with a small railway station on the line from Beja to Mateur. The road from Beja follows a broad valley as far as Sidi Nsir, where it leaves the railway and turns east through the hills.

During the three weeks before the battle each battalion provided patrols forward from Sidi Nsir, often making contact with the enemy. Major Chandler, Second-in-Command of the 5th Battalion, organized this patrolling and received the reports. It was a tense period, for it was apparent to all that a major enemy offensive was being prepared.

Von Arnim was now in command of the enemy forces, and he planned to launch a major offensive to break through the Allies' encircling positions, to join Rommel's army, hard pressed by the British Eighth Army in south-eastern Tunisia. The 5th Battalion had received very full reports from the East Surreys about the enemy's strength and positions, and worked hard improving its defensive positions against the expected assault.

The Battle of Sidi Nsir

Von Arnim's great attack began on 26th February, taking the form of eight different thrusts, westwards and south-westwards, with more than half his total strength put into the offensive. One of these thrusts was launched south-westwards from Mateur directly at Sidi Nsir, in a violent attempt to smash through to Beja. It was precisely to check such an attack that the 5th Hampshire had been put out at Sidi Nsir, and the Battalion had to bear the full force of the attack. The enemy used tough young parachute troops of the Barenthin Regiment, supported generously by elements of the 10th Panzer Division and Mark VI tanks of the 501st Heavy Tank Battalion.

The 5th Battalion was disposed on the circle of hills round the railway station, with "E" and "F" Troops of 155 Battery, R.A., echeloned on either side of the Mateur road. Headquarters was in the station buildings with part of H.Q. Company in the station yard. "C" Company was on high ground across the valley, "A" forward to the right, near "Camel's Hump," "D" on the immediate right of the station, and "B" farther to the right on slightly higher ground to the right of the Mateur road. There were outlying platoons two miles out in the mud village of Sidi Bana and on Hill 609. A forward administration post was housed in "Hampshire Farm," three miles back from the station down the road to Hunts Gap. "A" Company of 1/4th Battalion, known as "Spitforce," commanded by Captain Norwood, was under command 5th Battalion and took up a position to the south of "B" Company, though with a gap of over two miles between the two. The task of this company was to engage any enemy who might outflank the 5th Battalion, and to watch the valley to their south-east. It was in these positions that the 5th Battalion fought its great battle of Sidi Nsir.

The first sign of enemy activity came on 22nd February, three days before the main battle began. This preliminary clash occurred during patrolling, when a platoon of "B" Company, commanded by Lieutenant Moody, ran into three companies of the crack Barenthin Regiment, a strong reconnaissance in force to discover our dispositions and strength. There was no cover on the rocky djebels or in the open valleys, and the enemy could see the patrol approaching. They were surrounded, but the fight went on for a considerable time until, inevitably, the patrol was wiped out. Soon afterwards machine-gun and mortar fire was opened on "B" Company's front and right, and Germans in considerable numbers were observed about three thousand yards away. Fire was exchanged at long range throughout the day, though the Germans made no move forward.

The weather had been cold and wet, and the tracks which passed for roads around Sidi Nsir were muddy and difficult, but 25th February was a fine day of sunshine. Both the Divisional Commander and the C.R.A. came up and had a view of the enemy territory from Hill 609. During the night 25th/26th February the enemy showed abnormal activity. Many flares were seen both forward of Hill 609 and to the north of Sidi Bana. The enemy indulged in prolonged bursts of machine-gun fire, and aircraft were often overhead. It seemed probable that the noise made by the enemy was to cover the sound of tanks and vehicles moving up. In fact the enemy were getting ready for an all-out attack to get through to Hunts Gap.

At six in the morning of 26th February Lieutenant Heath, the platoon commander on Hill 609, reported intense mortar fire on his position. At 6.30 firing was heard from the right where the enemy was mortaring "B" Company and "F" Troop heavily. Shortly afterwards "B" Company reported that enemy tanks were approaching down the road from Mateur, and soon a long line of German tanks was moving down the Tunis road. The leading tank went up on a mine and they were temporarily held up on the minefield and hotly engaged by the guns of "F" Troop, which knocked out three. Reports were then received that infantry were debussing from lorries behind the tanks. In spite of heavy machine-gun fire and mortar fire from "B" Company, the German infantry were soon deployed and had mortars and heavy machine guns in action against "B" Company and against the gun positions.

At ten o'clock Lieutenant Heath's platoon on Point 609 was attacked and overrun and nothing more was heard of it. The loss of communication with Point 609 was serious, as it was the Battalion's only observation point on the Mateur road, which had been reported to be full of enemy tanks and vehicles.

The other outlying point, up the railway line at Sidi Bana, was attacked by two companies of infantry, and again stood to its post and fought back until the platoon commander, Lieutenant V. C. Amos, spoke to Battalion Headquarters on his wireless—"*Self and three men left. It can't be much longer. Good-bye and cheerio.*" After that there was silence.

The infantry attack developed all round the company positions and all were under almost constant air attack by fighters, two of which were shot down. "B" and "D" Companies were under heavy mortar fire. At "Camel's Hump" "A" Company was being attacked in strength, and the enemy had seized the hill but showed no disposition to go on towards "A" Company's main positions. The only company not yet under very severe pressure was "C" Company, commanded by Major Darling, to the left of the railway line.

The infantry battle continued throughout the afternoon, and all the while the confusion was increased by enemy dive-bombing. Mortars and infantry guns were being brought up to engage the railway station, though as yet the enemy had no observation post on the station. It began to seem that the enemy's object of a break-through on to Beja would succeed, but stubborn fighting still held him off.

Throughout the day 155 Battery fought an epic battle. When the German tanks first appeared driving down the road from Mateur, they were halted by the accurate fire of the field guns. Throughout the morning the guns engaged every tank which came within sight, and whenever possible turned their attention to other targets to relieve the constant pressure on the company and platoon positions. Soon the observation post, telephone lines and wireless transmitter of the Battery were smashed. Messerschmitts continually dive-bombed the guns and ammunition vehicles, raking them with machine-gun and cannon fire. Supply vehicles with reserve ammunition were set on fire, and ammunition had to be salvaged from the flames. The loss of men at the guns became serious, but the survivors fought on. Their job was to protect the Hampshire Battalion, and they meant to do it. By midday thirty German tanks had worked well down the road accompanied by self-propelled guns and lorried infantry. At 3 p.m. the road to the rear was cut by infantry. This was particularly serious as the road had been used by the Battalion carriers to bring up 25-pounder ammunition to the guns, and it was on the straight stretch running up to Sidi Nsir station that one carrier was hit in an air attack, Lieutenant Ashton being killed. With the road cut by the enemy it meant that no more ammunition could be brought up. Every shell had to be man-handled to the guns.

At 3.30 p.m. the German commander tried to deal the death blow, and a column of tanks raced down the road to the heart of the battery position while other tanks gave covering fire from hull-down positions. The gunners fought back magnificently, firing over open sights. They knocked out three tanks and checked the attack. But the tanks stood and concentrated on the two troops, dealing with one gun at a time.

The dying 155 Battery continued to fight. At four o'clock the German tanks advanced again, against "F" Troop. No. 1 gun smashed the leading tank and then a direct hit killed every survivor of the gun's crew. The three guns still in action engaged the enemy at very short range until all were killed or wounded. Thus died "F" Troop.

The Germans then turned on "E" Troop. At about half past six, as it grew dark, the tanks smothered the gun positions with machine-gun fire and gun-fire, using tracer ammunition, until only one 25-pounder and one Bren gun were still firing, engaging the enemy at ten and twenty yards range. Then came the last message from the gunners—"*Tanks are on us*"—followed by the "V" sign in Morse. When the battle began there were nine officers and one hundred and twenty-one other ranks on the gun positions, command posts and observation posts. Nine survived, two of whom were wounded.

There was a comparative lull in the general battle in the later afternoon, though enemy fire was kept up on company positions and the railway station. After five o'clock, however, when the battle between the tanks and 155 Battery was at its height, a new attack was thrown against "B" Company, whose strength was now no more than thirty. The enemy closed in on the front and right flank. Reporting this the Company Commander, Captain J. H. Lytle, ended his message by saying that he considered the situation "serious, but not yet critical." That was the last message from "B" Company; no further report was received, for soon they were overrun.

Dusk was now falling and it was obvious that little more could possibly be done from the position the Battalion was holding so desperately. Tanks were getting into position to attack the station and it was under constant fire front and back. The C.O. was no longer in touch with "A," "B" or "D" Companies, so he ordered "C" Company to withdraw and make for "Hampshire Farm." The railway station, containing the now useless telephone exchange, wireless and all documents, was prepared for burning. As many men as could be found in the growing darkness were ordered to move west to "C" Company patrol position and then south to "Hampshire Farm." The Commanding Officer intended to make a further stand astride the road, using "Spitforce," "A" Company of the 1/4th Battalion, who as far as he knew were still intact, and "C" Company and such others of H.Q. and Support Companies as could be withdrawn.

While these preparations were being made, enemy tanks were still firing bursts of tracer bullets along each side of the station building, and they could be heard rumbling by in the darkness to take up new positions. The order was given for the station and all material there to be burned. Small parties were sent off independently to make their way as best they could through the enemy to "Hampshire Farm." Most of these parties got through, though some were killed or captured on the way.

The headquarters party arrived at "Hampshire Farm" at half past nine, to be met by Major P. R. Sawyer, commanding H.Q. Company, and Lieutenant Cowland-Cooper, Second-in-Command of "Spitforce." Colonel Newnham outlined his plan for forming a new defensive position and tried to get through to Brigade, to find to his disgust that the line had gone. His Brigade wireless set had been destroyed at Sidi Nsir station. Similarly no contact could be made with "A" Company of 1/4th Battalion, "Spitforce," though a code of signals by Very light had been previously arranged. All was quiet at "Hampshire Farm," and down the valley could be seen the glow of the fire at Sidi Nsir. Lieutenant Cowland-Cooper reported that his company had not been engaged; to their chagrin they had been helpless spectators of "B" Company's destruction. He also told the Commanding Officer of German movement during the day to the east and south of their position, from which it seemed probable that the enemy were between "Hampshire Farm" and Hunts Gap. Of "C" Company there was no sign or news, but it was evident that they were not expected at "Hampshire Farm," since they would have reached it earlier if headed that way.

The position was now considered. They were out of touch with Brigade, but had carried out orders and imposed delay on the enemy, though at great cost. The enemy would no doubt continue his advance towards Hunts Gap as soon as he had reorganized, but he had some way to go and could not reach Hunts Gap in strength and with his armour before 10 o'clock next morning. Could the small force at "Hampshire Farm" impose further worth-while delay, even though the enemy were already behind them, or should they make use of the darkness to try to reach Hunts Gap and there be available to strengthen its garrison? It was finally decided to wait till midnight. If by then the enemy came on, they would fight where they stood in the dark. If not, they would withdraw to the west and then south, with the knowledge that the enemy tanks at any rate would not reach Hunts Gap for some hours. To remain in unfavourable positions in daylight and lacking heavy support weapons would have been useless.

No further enemy movement being apparent, at midnight the Commanding Officer gave the order to move. "Hampshire Farm" was set on fire, and the agreed Very light signal for withdrawal was made to "Spitforce." In darkness and in pouring rain the party made its way westward into the hills, and then southwards. The column consisted of about a hundred men, including the nine survivors of 155 Battery. At eight o'clock in the morning of 27th February, cold, wet, hungry and tired, they reached the command post of the 2/4th Hampshire in Hunts Gap. The survivors of "C" Company had got back to Hunts Gap an hour before. "Spitforce" got back to "Chemical Corner" intact, having been most skilfully led by Captain Norwood in single file out of the hills in the dark. Occasionally small parties of the 5th Battalion filtered in during the day. Of the four companies, however, there remained at the final count only "C" Company less one platoon, and Lieutenant Pemberton and twenty-nine men of "D" Company, who had made their way back through the enemy's line in the darkness.

The infantry strength of the enemy and their casualties at Sidi Nsir are not known, but their strength has been assessed at upwards of three battalions with full tank support. They had been desperately determined to break right through to Hunts Gap and only the magnificent fighting of the 5th Battalion and 155 Battery stopped them. By the time they could mount a co-ordinated attack on Hunts Gap, further infantry and artillery reinforcements, and some tanks, had been brought up to strengthen the main defensive line. The gallantry of the 5th Battalion and 155 Field Battery was, therefore, by no means in vain.

Of his men at the battle of Sidi Nsir, Colonel Newnham wrote to the Colonel of the Regiment:

"I remember in the last war, when I was with our 1st Battalion in the 'Stone Wall' Brigade, I thought they were tough, but these lads were tougher than anything I have ever served with or hope to serve with. There was no suggestion of a waver; every man stood to his rifle, his Bren, his mortar, until the end. We are more than fortunate to have so many survivors and great credit is due to them for their providential escape.

"The way back was long and arduous, but nobody lost heart and they were soon back in battle helping another battalion in the Brigade."

Colonel Newnham had commanded the 5th Battalion in a most difficult and violent defensive battle against heavy odds with great skill and doggedness, and his fine action was recognized by the award of the D.S.O. and the American D.S.C. Lieutenant Pemberton was awarded the M.C., and Private Minnigin received the M.M. for his gallantry in taking up ammunition under fire.

The Battle of Hunts Gap

(*See map on page* 100)

While the 5th Battalion was so desperately delaying the enemy at Sidi Nsir, the 1/4th and 2/4th Battalions remained in positions on either side of Hunts Gap, positions they had occupied for three weeks. Hunts Gap was the immediate objective of the enemy in his violent thrust southwards from Sidi Nsir towards the vital road and railway junction at Beja; it was in fact the doorway to the Beja Plain, and therefore the focus of the attack. The Beja

Plain narrows to a valley about three and a half miles wide at Hunts Gap, running north-east to Sidi Nsir between the foothills of the Hennchir El Bridj and the Djebel El Kermate. The valley is flat except for low undulations and knolls. Hunts Gap was guarded by the 2/4th Battalion on a three-mile front, with the 1/4th and the 2nd Battalions in support.

Battalion Headquarters of the 2/4th was near Point 447, on the left of the Gap. "B" and "C" Companies, commanded by Major R. J. Sawyer and Captain J. Butler, were in the valley, "B" astride the road and "C" on their right at Guessa Farm. "D" Company, Captain Denne-Bolton, occupied a low ridge to the left of "B" Company and "A" Company covered "The Pass," with one platoon on Point 647 and the rest of the Company under Captain Wallace at Point 491. "A" and "C" Companies were supported by mortar sections, and the 6-pounders and the solitary 17-pounder of 231 Anti-Tank Battery helped the battalion 2-pounders to cover the minefield which had been laid in front of "B" Company's positions. When the battle started these guns proved to be no match for the German tanks. The only reserves available to the 2/4th were the Headquarters Company and two carrier sections under Captain Way which were held at "The Antlers," to the rear of the "B" Company positions. No one could be spared to hold Djebel El Kermate, so an observation post was established on Point 671, supported by a platoon of "D" Company and a machine-gun section, commanded by Lieutenant Wakeford, at "Wakeford's Picket."

The German offensive had begun on 14th February when Rommel's 21 Panzer Division and Von Arnim's 10 Panzer Division broke through the Americans in the Fayid Pass towards Tebessa. At this time Colonel Smythe and Colonel Robinson were preparing plans with 139th Brigade for the 1/4th and the 2/4th Battalions to attack on "Green Hill" and "Baldy Hill" on the Sedjenane front to the north. Not only had this offensive to be cancelled, but reinforcements had to be sent south, so that the 1/4th were side-stepped to the right. The gap which this made between the 2/4th and the 1/4th Battalions was filled by the 2/5th Leicesters, who had been reduced to two-company strength by their fighting at Sedjenane and Kasserine just before the battle for Hunts Gap started.

When Von Arnim's offensive began all the Allied positions were subjected to heavy dive-bombing, but for the first two days nothing was seen of the enemy on the ground at Hunts Gap. The Germans would probably have advanced on Hunts Gap immediately Sidi Nsir was overrun, but the night of 26th February brought heavy rain and the enemy tanks were bogged down ; thus bad weather added a further breathing-space to that won by the 5th Battalion in their stand at Sidi Nsir.

As has been stated, the 2nd Battalion was in support to 128th Brigade in the Munchar area to the rear. This Battalion had been moved about considerably since Tebourba. Lieutenant-Colonel S. J. Martin had taken over command at Munchar, the Battalion being considerably reduced in strength and very short of equipment. More than five hundred reinforcements were sent up, new equipment was provided, and the Battalion was in the middle of training when Colonel Martin received orders for the Battalion to report to the 1st Guards Brigade at Shiba. Here the Battalion occupied a defensive position in support of the Grenadier and Coldstream Guards, sending out long-distance patrols over the surrounding country. The next move was to the Kasserine Pass, where it came under command of the 6th Armoured Division in a critical situation. The 2/5th Leicesters had been overrun the day before and our tanks had been badly shot up. Only two companies of the Rifle Brigade and a few tanks remained to meet the heavy enemy attack which was expected the following morning. The 2nd Battalion was ordered to take up a position on a low ridge forward of the position then held, but by the time the Battalion could get up, being dive-bombed on the way, the position had been taken by the enemy. An alternative position was chosen and, after suffering further bombing attacks, the Battalion occupied it.

Fortunately the expected enemy attack did not materialize, and a few days later the 2nd Battalion was ordered to report to the 38th (Irish) Brigade at El Aroussa. It was moving there when it was redirected to the Beja–Munchar area, finally moving up to the left of the 1/4th Battalion in a support role at the battle of Hunts Gap.

Thus it was that the vital passage to the Beja Plain at Hunts Gap was held by the 2/4th Hampshire, supported by the 1/4th two miles to the south, with the 2nd Battalion next to it. The two hundred survivors of the 5th Battalion and "C" Company, consisting of two platoons which had come through the Sidi Nsir battle practically unscathed commanded by Major Darling, were under command of the 2/4th, in a position on the spur north of the 2/4th Battalion Headquarters.

In many ways the battle for Hunts Gap resembled the battle of Sidi Nsir. Enemy tanks had only one approach, down the road between the hills, and it was astride this approach that the 2/4th Battalion had its positions, and there it was to bear the brunt of the fight. There was little in the way of anti-tank defence; only two batteries of 25-pounders, 153 and 154, the 5th Medium Regiment, 231 Anti-Tank Battery, and 457 Light Anti-Aircraft Battery. The enemy could call on as many tanks as we had guns. Artillery reinforcement was being brought up as fast as possible from sixty miles away, and the Churchill tanks of the North Irish Horse were making a desperate two-hundred-mile forced march to Beja. We had one great advantage: the enemy had only one road for his tanks.

About midday on 27th February a strong force of enemy tanks advanced down the road in an attempt to achieve an immediate break-through. They came on until they ran foul of the minefields in front of "B" Company's positions, then accurate shooting by the gunners and some splendid dive-bombing by the R.A.F. stopped the attack completely. The dive-bombers knocked out two tanks and two more were halted by the anti-tank guns. One Tiger tank crossed the minefield safely and advanced right up to "B" Company's position. The Company's 6-pounder anti-tank guns engaged the Tiger and halted it. But the tank's 88-mm. gun quickly put both guns out of action. Nevertheless the Tiger put about and withdrew, but without its commander. This officer had scrambled out of the tank when it was hit, and he was prevented from getting back to his tank by excellent small-arms fire. The Tiger made its way back and, as luck would have it, lost a track on a mine. The enemy then called off their tank attack.

While the tank versus guns and aircraft duel was going on in front of "B" Company's positions, the 2/4th Battalion O.P. on "Spion Kop," which was manned by the Intelligence section, reported German infantry debussing from vehicles in the road and deploying through the hills. They were obviously building up for a co-ordinated attack on the defences at Hunts Gap, an attack which in fact took place the next day. In the absence of a F.O.O., the observation post relayed artillery fire orders and corrections through Battalion Headquarters to the guns for the rest of the day, so that the German infantry positions were very effectively shelled. The German guns were busy, too, and our positions were very heavily shelled, "B" and "D" Companies getting the most attention. Two companies of German infantry attempted an enveloping movement over the high ground east of "C" Company's positions, but without success.

It rained very hard during the night on 27th February, so that the slit trenches were soon partly full of water. In the darkness a party of Royal Engineers, assisted by patrols from "B" Company, took loads of explosives forward and immobilized the Tiger tank and two others, and repaired the minefield. The battle flared up to its full intensity on 28th February with a general attack of great determination and violence, the enemy using units of the 7th Panzer Regiment and the 1/86th Panzer Grenadiers.

The battle began before dawn when tanks advanced in strength down the road, forced the minefield, and penetrated into "B" Company's positions before they were halted by our Churchills, firing in hull-down positions. At the same time infantry came down the railway line and overran the platoon commanded by Lieutenant Vicary, who was killed. Thus the enemy gained a position on "B" Company's left. However, this company, pinned down in their water-logged slit trenches, put up a magnificent resistance and most stubbornly held the enemy at bay until late in the evening, when their positions were at last overrun. Survivors of one platoon, commanded by Sergeant Tinkler, and Company Headquarters, Captain Cock, got back to H.Q. Company at "The Antlers" after dark, and Lieutenant Knight skilfully extricated his platoon and led it back to Montaigne Farm, which was held by the Leicesters. The rest of the company were either killed or taken prisoner, among them Major R. Sawyer, who was wounded and captured.

While the battle was raging round "B" Company, enemy infantry, supported by mortars, attacked "D" Company in the afternoon, but a well-timed counter-attack by the reserve platoon of "A" Company with "C" of the 5th Battalion drove them back, badly mauled. "C" Company's isolated position at Guessa was heavily dive-bombed, shelled and mortared throughout the day, and in the evening the enemy followed this up with a most determined infantry attack and overran the position. Captain J. Butler was wounded and died later. Thirty men under Lieutenant Horne managed to get back to H.Q. Company, but the rest of "C" Company were killed or captured.

Thus throughout 28th February the 2/4th held off the enemy's desperate attacks on Hunts Gap; they lost many men and two of their positions, but the gap was still denied to the enemy, while in the rear the time thus won was being used to establish stronger defences to protect Beja. The enemy attacked again in strength at half past four in the morning of 1st March, this time against the ridge held by the two platoons of "D" Company. The attack came in under cover of a thick morning mist, and when it cleared it was seen that the enemy were in occupation of most of the ridge. A counter-attack by two platoons of "C" Company of the 5th Battalion, and two carrier sections, was unsuccessful.

Meanwhile, enemy machine guns managed to work round to the rear of Battalion Headquarters, bringing it under close fire, so Colonel Robinson moved his headquarters, and the remnants of the forward companies and the support company, into a perimeter between "A" Company, which was still intact, and "Wakeford's Picket." The enemy now held Djebel El Kermate in force and overlooked the 2/4th's positions. His mortar fire was continuous, and movement out of the sangars by day was very difficult. The Battalion was cut off except for a narrow approach by a wet and slippery track skirting "Table Mountain," up which a limited amount of supplies could be manhandled forward by night.

H.Q. Company and the survivors of "B" and "C," under Captain Way and Lieutenants Becquet and James, still held "The Antlers." On one occasion two tanks which had penetrated the "B" Company positions were put out of action on the road bend by two 2-pounder guns manned by Sergeant Dillon, the Armourer Sergeant, Lance-Corporal Hammond, the Mess Corporal, and others. This "David and Goliath" success delighted the men holding "The Antlers."

Successive attacks made by the supporting battalions to regain Black Rocks and Douar Gaddana were unsuccessful, but the 2/4th, mauled as they had been by three days of violent battle, held on to their positions on Point 491 and "Table Mountain" in spite of repeated enemy attempts to dislodge them and Hunts Gap remained closed to the enemy. Fortunately wireless communication with Brigade held and mortar and defensive artillery fire was called to break up the attacks. Inevitably there was much close-quarter fighting amongst the rocks. On one occasion Lieutenant Wakeford and two men crawled out from the "Picket" in daylight and captured a machine gun and one prisoner. Major F. Mitchell, the Second-in-Command, had received a bad leg injury on the first day of the battle, but he refused to be sent back and commanded "Wakeford's Picket" throughout the whole battle, until the Battalion was relieved.

The first evidence of the success of the defence of Hunts Gap came on 2nd March, when the enemy tanks were seen withdrawing towards Sidi Nsir, pounded by our artillery and aircraft and pursued by the Churchill tanks, which had now got up. The Germans' thrust towards Beja had failed; and they had lost thirty out of their original tank force of sixty. But their infantry still held Guessa, Douar Gaddana and Djebel El Kermate, and they stayed on those positions for the next month until, in fact, the stalemate was broken with the start of the Allied offensive on 7th April.

General Alexander visited 128th Brigade Headquarters on 2nd March, and in the evening the 9th Argyll and Sutherland Highlanders, veterans of the campaign, came under command of the Brigade. The next morning they made a counter-attack against the Douar Gaddana feature, which, though not completely successful, did enable one company to get through to the 2/4th position.

On the night of 4th/5th March the 2/4th were relieved by the Argylls, and the Battalion was ordered to move back across country to Beja. The relief was carried out under harassing artillery fire, and as the enemy was active the men in some posts had to be extricated by making local counter-attacks. All the Battalion transport except essential tracked vehicles had been moved back to "The Antlers" the day before the battle started, but in spite of strenuous efforts it was found impossible to move back the remaining vehicles. Some were rushed down the road towards "Chemical Corner," but they were ambushed on mines and had to turn back. Some were bogged down in the dark on the slippery track. When later in the month the 2/4th Battalion took over the positions again from the Argylls, all the vehicles except one were successfully evacuated, to the great credit of the M.T. section and the battalion fitters.

By 5th March the weary 2/4th Battalion had concentrated in "B" Echelon at Beja and received their first-line reinforcements to replace the seven officers and sixteen other ranks killed and the two hundred and twenty men missing in the battle. The stubborn manner in which the 2/4th Battalion had fought at Hunts Gap, most obstinately denying the enemy the vital pass to Beja, was recognized by the award of the D.S.O. to Colonel Robinson, who had commanded his Battalion so magnificently.

Although it was the 2/4th Battalion which had borne the full force of the attack on Hunts Gap, the 1/4th, the 2nd and the very depleted 5th Battalion had all held extended forward positions throughout the battle, and they all suffered casualties from shelling and persistent dive-bombing. They were also fully occupied with constant patrolling and observation duties. When the main assault on the Gap was called off by the enemy, it was only a change in intensity, for he remained in the positions he had won.

The defensive positions of the Brigade had been rearranged, so that the 1/4th was at Ksar Mezouar, with the 2/4th on their left and the 2nd on their right. Here the Battalions remained throughout March, subject to a good deal of mortaring and shelling, and in weather conditions which started "trench feet" until dry socks were sent up each evening with the rations for a nightly change. Little movement was possible by day, but intense patrolling took place each night and frequent contact was made with the enemy. In this month, for example, the 1/4th Battalion suffered some hundred casualties, mostly in "B" and "C" Companies, including Lieutenant N. F. Brown killed, Lieutenant Cross missing, and the Second-in-Command, Major Portsmouth, wounded.

The 2/4th held the high ground around Typhus Farm overlooking "The Antlers" with "A" Company, Captain Tinniswood, and "C" Company, Captain Gilmore, forward on Point 491 and the lower spurs of Point 647. Fighting patrols operated nightly against the enemy on Black Rocks, but the most successful venture was carried out by Captain Cock, Lieutenant Dive and two men, in daylight. They entered the enemy position, woke up three Germans manning an anti-tank gun, blew up the gun with the Germans' own mines, and brought back the crew as prisoners, after noting various other enemy posts. This earned the M.C. for Captain Cock.

The 5th Battalion, at first reorganized on a two-company basis, and reinforced on 10th March by five officers and one hundred and fifty men, were similarly occupied throughout March. There was a great deal of patrolling and many skirmishes from their position near the vital road junction known as "Chemical Corner," and occasional minor operations to clear up pockets of enemy resistance. On 26th March the 5th Battalion was given the task of demonstrating in strength against the enemy, as a diversion for another operation elsewhere. This was carried out with great dash and verve and was completely successful. Among those who distinguished themselves was Lieutenant Conder, who won the M.C.

Lieutenant Conder was a young officer of enterprise and great courage, known to all as "Boy Conder" because of his youth. On one occasion during the fighting for "Chemical Corner" he was sent on a patrol. Taking one man with him, he climbed the forward slope of the enemy's position and found a combined look-out and machine-gun post temporarily unmanned, as the enemy section were inside their dug-out in the side of the hill. Conder pulled aside the blanket covering the doorway and called upon the enemy to come out, throwing in a grenade to hurry them up. Two came out and were promptly shot dead. He then collected some valuable equipment and returned. It was on one of the many patrols sent out by the 5th Battalion at the time that Captain Bennett was killed.

After the battle for Hunts Gap the 2nd Battalion was put under command the 38th (Irish) Brigade, as had been intended before it was diverted to Munchar and was given a part in an attack made by the 78th Division. The objective given to the 2nd Battalion was a height on the extreme left of the attack, and although there was considerable opposition in certain parts of the divisional front the 2nd Battalion's objective was taken without difficulty.

There followed an attack with the Inniskilling Fusiliers against a ridge on which stood the village of Zatriah. The leading companies of the Battalion made good progress until they came under enfilade fire on the ridge, while the Inniskillings were meeting stiff opposition on the right. Zatriah was eventually captured, but the Battalion was then pinned down by heavy mortar fire so that it could make no further progress to the next objective. It was withdrawn after dark, having suffered casualties. For the remainder of the campaign until the fall of Tunis the Battalion carried out several more moves until, finally, it joined 128th Brigade in the place of the 2/4th Battalion.

By the end of March Von Arnim's great effort to penetrate the Allied positions in northern Tunisia was brought to a standstill. He had had many successes, but nowhere was success complete. The key positions of Beja, Medjez-el-Bab and, to the south, Bou Arada remained in our hands, though in each case it meant some desperate clinging to the positions, and the enemy had pressed uncomfortably close, especially to the Beja–Medjez road. In view of the fact that the final attack on Tunis would have to be mounted and launched from the area of Medjez-el-Bab it was necessary that the enemy be driven out of the commanding positions he had acquired north and north-east of the town. To do this the 46th Division, using the 138th Brigade and a Parachute Brigade, attacked towards Sedjenane on 28th March, captured it and drove the enemy back to a more comfortable distance.

At the same time the Mareth Line, the narrow neck of land which was the gateway to southern Tunisia, was forced by the Eighth Army. The frontal assault on the line at Mareth was unsuccessful, but a great outflanking movement across desert tracks, a "left hook," to the El Hamma Gap, forty-five miles behind the Mareth Line, took the Germans in the rear. They had to race back to a new line, and the Eighth Army was inside Tunisia in strength. On 8th April United States patrols working south and Eighth Army patrols moving north met, and the great junction of the First and Eighth Armies had taken place. At last the stage was set for the full Allied offensive in Tunisia.

Pichon, Bou Arada—and Tunis

The first effect of the new phase in the campaign on the 128th Brigade was a sudden move on 5th April a hundred miles south to El Ala. They handed over their positions before Beja, positions only too familiar to them, and after a day's rest moved south ; they were depleted in numbers but well seasoned by battle. The operation they were to carry out was a pleasant contrast to their experience so far in North Africa ; it was an advance as part of a IX Corps plan to take Pichon and Fondouk, and to capture the Fondouk Gap, so that 6th Armoured Division could pass through and into the Kairouan Plain to intercept the retreating Afrika Korps. The whole plan was a most encouraging sign of the change in the fortunes of the campaign.

The 128th Brigade arrived in El Ala just before daylight on 7th April after a two-day journey by truck, followed by a wet march to the assembly area in a cactus grove. The plan was for the 1/4th to capture Pichon and the high ground a thousand yards to the south-east, and for the 2/4th first to capture a wadi and then to take high ground above Pichon. When these objectives were achieved the 5th were to pass through and secure the northern side of the Fondouk Gap.

At dusk the 1/4th and 2/4th Battalions marched as silently as possible for six miles and waited until 4.30 a.m., when a river was crossed with only slight opposition. While a crossing-place for the tanks was being found—no easy task as it happened—the assault companies of the two battalions formed up on the far bank and advanced against their objectives. Each battalion had one squadron of tanks under command, and one Field Regiment and one section of Medium Artillery in immediate support.

Advancing on the village of Pichon, the leading companies of the 1/4th, "A" commanded by Captain Norwood and "B" commanded by Captain Hodges, became pinned down by heavy fire from machine guns, mortars and artillery. "D" Company, under Captain Pryce, was accordingly ordered to carry out a left flanking movement into the village. This solved the problem. There followed some classic street fighting by 17 Platoon under Sergeant Wood and 18 Platoon under Lieutenant Elwin, with 16 Platoon, under Lieutenant Sole, in reserve. By midday the village was taken. The battle was fought in a howling gale which covered everyone and everything with thick dust. After a short pause the Battalion pushed on quickly to the final objective, the high ground beyond Pichon. Opposition was now slight, and the final objective was quickly taken, though the companies came under very accurate mortar fire and had to dig in on the reverse slopes.

The 5th Battalion had meanwhile come up and advanced through Pichon with tanks and captured the high ground of the Fondouk Gap. Here they came under heavy mortar fire, causing some casualties, but withdrew slightly to the reverse slope of the hill, and the vital positions were held. The next day the Brigade had a splendid view of the British armour moving through the Fondouk Gap and into the Plain. It had been a swift and successful attack, with every objective taken exactly according to plan. Our casualties were comparatively slight, but they included Captain Gilmore and Lieutenants Dive and Tillbrook of the 2/4th, and Major Rothery and Lieutenant Hawker of the 5th, all killed. Lieutenant Duncan of the 1/4th, who fought splendidly with his platoon, was severely wounded. The enemy suffered heavily and lost more than a hundred and fifty men taken prisoner.

On the morning of 11th April the Brigade began a very difficult march of sixteen miles over rough country bordering the Kairouan Plain, to cut the enemy's escape route from the Djebel Ousselat area. It was a most trying march ; it was very hot, the going was rough, and at times precipitous, and the columns were attacked from the air. Everyone suffered considerably from thirst. Apart from some skirmishing at the end of the day's march by the leading company of the 2/4th, there was no fighting on the march, but everybody was very thankful when their destination was reached. A miserable night was passed with no food and with only a pullover as extra clothing against the severe cold. On 12th April transport came up and the Brigade was moved back to El Aroussa, where it joined the rest of the Division, which was then preparing for a major attack north of Bou Arada. At El Aroussa the Brigade was able to rest for ten days.

The campaign in North Africa was rapidly approaching its climax. The First Army had been fully built up. On the 128th Brigade's arrival there had been only the battalions of the 78th Division strung out along the hills ; now there were whole divisions preparing for the knock-out blow. The Eighth Army was pressing triumphantly forward as well. The enemy was packed closely with more than a quarter of a million men in his reduced perimeter.

A general divisional assault on the enemy's positions was planned for 22nd April, and in this the 128th Brigade was to attack Bou Arada, a scrub-covered rocky feature, while the 138th Brigade attacked another feature three miles to the north. This time the Brigade was to have ample artillery support, including a hundred and twenty 25-pounders, and their operation was part of a closely knit plan. The enemy was the Hermann Goering Division, a fine fighting force of young and ardent Nazis, who were expecting the attack and had their positions carefully prepared.

The divisional attack commenced at two o'clock in the morning of 22nd April, and the battalions of the 128th Brigade, with the 16th Durham Light Infantry under command, crossed their start line an hour and a half later, with 1/4th on the right, 2/4th in the centre and the 5th on the left. The 16th Durham Light Infantry were in line on the extreme right. Five Field Regiments and two Medium Batteries supported the brigade advance, giving concentration of fire on known enemy localities on a timed programme. Soon the valley was filled with smoke, which hung about for some hours.

The enemy were firmly entrenched below a ridge of low hills. The objective of the 1/4th Battalion was a high feature, Mehalla, and some Roman ruins beyond it. As they advanced they met very heavy fire, but Mehalla was captured successfully. "C" and "D" then went forward to capture the ruins, but suddenly the morning mist cleared and "D" Company were caught in a gully by strong machine-gun fire from both flanks and were pinned to the ground, suffering heavy casualties. Meanwhile "C" Company were caught in the open too, and stopped by withering machine-gun fire, suffering many casualties, among them the Company Commander, Captain Hall, who was killed. To make the situation worse, a tank had been put out of action in a narrow gap and was holding the others up. No progress could be made and eventually "C" Company and the remnants of "D" withdrew to their first objective just west of Mehalla. Lieutenant-Colonel Smythe was wounded and all four Company Commanders were killed or wounded. For the time being the Adjutant, Captain Cowland-Cooper, commanded the 1/4th.

The 2/4th also achieved their first objective, "Plough Top," successfully, but the leading companies were unable to reach the far edge of the hill as the ground was swept by machine-gun fire. The support group was ordered up and "B" Company was given the task of capturing the remaining part of the hill by a right flanking movement. As "B" Company moved forward with "A" Company on the right for flank protection, both companies were exposed to heavy machine-gun fire when the mist lifted. "A" Company was able to take up a position in a small wadi, but "B" was on the open ground and could not manœuvre. It suffered some thirty casualties, including the Company Commander, Captain Cock, who was killed within a few yards of an enemy post. Both companies withdrew two hours later and took up defensive positions near "Plough Top." The sudden clearing of the mist caught "C" Company in an exposed position, too, and they were heavily mortared and shelled and suffered some twenty casualties before they were dug in.

The objective of the 5th Battalion was a hill, Ber Rabal, which they had named "Brer Rabbit." There were two other hills to be taken before the final objective and these were captured with no difficulty. "C" and "D" Companies had been assigned the task of capturing Ber Rabal and they moved forward and took what they believed in the mist to be their objective. But they found that Ber Rabal was still ahead of them when the mist cleared and further advance in the teeth of the very heavy fire laid down from the enemy defences was not possible. All they could do was to hold tight for the rest of the day where they were, being subject, as were the other battalions, to considerable mortaring and shelling.

Thus it was that all along their front the 128th Brigade were held up short of their final objectives, pinned down by heavy and accurate fire. During the night the battalions held on grimly, consolidating as far as possible against the counter-attacks they expected. These, however, did not take place. By splendid fighting the 138th Brigade had been successful and the positions they had won were a menace to the rear of the obstinate forces holding up 128th Brigade. Accordingly when the three battalions advanced just before dawn on 23rd April to their final objectives they found that the enemy had gone. The main infantry battle of Bou Arada was over ; it was planned to last five hours, but it had taken in fact thirty-three.

The 1/4th Battalion had suffered many casualties. In addition to those already mentioned, the casualties included Captain Hodges, Lieutenants Sayce and Hyam, wounded ; Captains Norwood and Pryce wounded and missing ; Captain S. W. Brown and Lieutenant Elwin missing. The last three were able to escape two weeks later in the final Allied advance. The rifle companies were reduced to three officers and eighty men. Major Coombes, who had been with the battle reserve, came up and took over command of the Battalion, but he was wounded that evening by a mine when he was going forward with his Intelligence Officer, Lieutenant Hallett, who was killed. On 24th April Major Chandler, Second-in-Command of the 5th Battalion, took over command of the 1/4th. At first the Battalion was reorganized as two companies until a draft of reinforcements, mainly from the Royal Warwickshire and the Leicestershire Regiments, made it possible to muster three companies. Captain Matthews, Royal Scots of Canada, who was attached to the 1/4th, and Captain Hodges, were awarded the M.C. for their gallantry in the action.

The 2/4th Battalion had already been depleted before the battle, and it had lost one officer, Captain Cock, and eighteen other ranks killed and two officers and thirty-six other ranks wounded. Here again reorganization, on a three-company basis, was necessary.

The Brigade was now in divisional reserve and the three battalions remained in their positions until 27th April, when the Brigade moved in transport to the Medjez-el-Bab sector to take over ground just won after hard fighting by the 38th (Irish) Brigade. Here there were minor operations to be carried out, and from the hilltops they had a magnificent view of the final battle for Tunis. From time to time there were warning orders to stand by for action, but the days were comparatively undisturbed except for the R.A.F. and the flies. Finally, on 7th May came the expected news of the fall of Tunis and the end of the North African campaign. On 13th May General Alexander telegraphed to the Prime Minister : *"Sir, It is my duty to report that the Tunisian Campaign is over. All enemy resistance has ceased. We are masters of the North African shores."*

The 128th Brigade was put under command 1st Division for mopping-up operations. There were other changes in the Brigade, too, for the 2/4th left it for special service and the 2nd Battalion replaced it. Thus, though it meant a parting of friends, it was still to be the Hampshire Brigade, and it was satisfactory for the 2nd Battalion to find a permanent home, and a Hampshire home at that, after its many moves. For since the 2nd had left the 128th Brigade in March it had moved from command to command. It had taken part in actions with the 38th, 12th, 2nd, and 10th Infantry Brigades, finishing up with the battle of Goubellat Gap on 4th May.

The 2/4th moved to Bougie, where it was reorganized as part of 20 and 21 Beach Groups. The Battalion was divided into two : "A" and "B" Companies and half of H.Q. and Support Companies became the Defence Unit of 20 Beach Group, commanded by Lieutenant-Colonel Robinson, while the other two companies and the remainder of the Battalion, commanded by Major Mitchell, became the Defence Unit of 21 Beach Group. The purpose of the Defence Units was to defend the maintenance area of the Beach Group when it made a landing where no port was available. Both units began a very thorough training in their new duties, 20 Beach Group at Oued Marsa and 21 at Bougie.

There was much work for the 128th Brigade clearing up the battlefields. Moved to the area just south of Tunis, the Brigade helped in the gigantic task of taking prisoner the thousands of still-martial Germans and the very non-belligerent Italians. These prisoners had to be organized, caged, fed and guarded. There was the Victory Parade in Tunis at which every unit in the First Army was represented, and each battalion in the Brigade sent a party of a hundred and fifty officers and men. At this time three officers, Captain Pryce, Captain S. W. Brown and Lieutenant Elwin, with Sergeant Dicks and twenty-five men, rejoined their battalion. They had been taken prisoner at Bou Arada and had escaped from their captors. There was another parade on 3rd June when 128th Brigade provided a party of two hundred to line the route to welcome Mr. Churchill, and then the 5th Battalion left for Blida, south of Algiers, on a four-hundred-and-fifty-mile train journey in cattle trucks.

The other two battalions joined the 5th at Blida and there the Brigade trained hard until 23rd June. At the same time they were all brought up to full

War Establishment, and in doing this the 5th Battalion found itself with an entire platoon of Welshmen in "C" Company; a Hampshire sergeant was added for liaison purposes, as it were. At Blida the Brigade took part in Exercise "Conqueror," to afford training for the 1st U.S. Division in making an opposed landing.

The next move was east again, to Djidjelli, and here the Brigade began intense training for combined operations. There were exercises with landing craft and exercises among the hills overlooking the little harbour. There was incessant disembarkation practice followed by assaults up the beach. It was obvious that the 128th was to be the Assault Brigade of the Division. In July came the news of the invasion of Sicily, in which the 1st Battalion in 231st Brigade and half of the 2/4th in 20 Beach Group took part, and an added zest was given to the hard training 128th Brigade were undergoing.

In the second week in August the Brigade moved by transport to Bougie and thence by sea to Bizerta, where training was intensified, vehicles were water-proofed and senior officers began to take a share in operational planning. Exercise "Jennifer Dryshod" provided a full-dress rehearsal for an assault landing, including the off-loading of vehicles and stores, the making and extension of a beach-head and, in fact, the whole intricate business of invasion—for Operation "Avalanche."

On 1st September Headquarters, 46th Division, was established on board U.S.S. *Biscayne* and the loading of vehicles, guns and stores began. There was a fatal accident while men of the 5th Battalion were loading mines on to a truck; fifteen men were killed and thirty injured, including "C" Company Commander, Captain Foster-Moore. By 5th September the embarkation of the Division was complete and the next day the convoy began to form up in the Bizerta roadsteads. That night there was a hundred-plane raid on Bizerta and the town was heavily bombed. But the convoy remained untouched, and at dawn on 7th September, 1943, it sailed for Salerno.

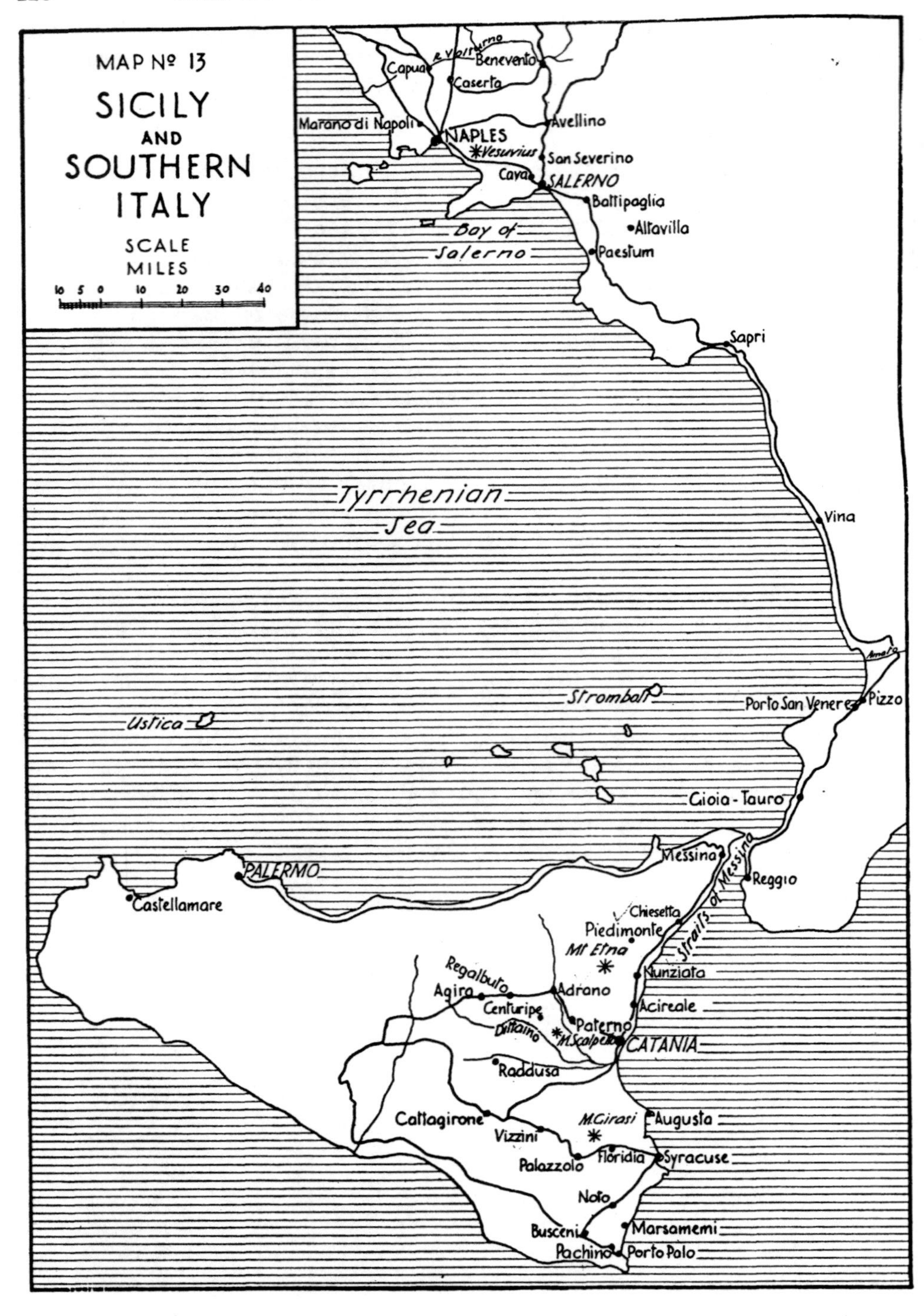

MAP No 13
SICILY
AND
SOUTHERN
ITALY
SCALE
MILES
10 5 0 10 20 30 40
R. Volturno
Capua
Benevento
Caserta
Marano di Napoli
NAPLES
Vesuvius
Avellino
San Severino
Cava
SALERNO
Battipaglia
Altavilla
Paestum
Bay of Salerno
Sapri
Tyrrhenian Sea
Vina
Stromboli
Porto San Venere
Pizzo
Ustica
Gioia - Tauro
Messina
Reggio
PALERMO
Castellamare
Chiesetta
Piedimonte
Straits of Messina
Mt Etna
Nunziata
Regalbuto
Agira
Adrano
Centuripe
Acireale
Dittaino
Paterno
M. Scalpello
CATANIA
Raddusa
Augusta
Caltagirone
M. Cirasi
Vizzini
Palazzolo
Floridia
Syracuse
Noto
Marsamemi
Busceni
Pachino
Porto Palo

CHAPTER X

THE 1ST BATTALION IN SICILY AND ITALY

July to October, 1943

The 1st Battalion landed at Alexandria from Malta on 3rd April, 1943, after two years' service in the famous siege. The "Malta" Brigade, now called 231st Brigade, consisted of the same three battalions, the 2nd Devons, the 1st Hampshire and the 1st Dorsets. The 1st Hampshire Battalion was commanded by Lieutenant-Colonel Spencer, with Major Nelson Smith Second-in-Command, Captain Methven Adjutant, and Captain Stone Quartermaster. Major Van Lessen and Captains King, Guest, Boyd and Greenaway commanded the companies. On landing in Egypt the Battalion strength was 30 officers and 600 other ranks.

At first the 231st Brigade was quartered at Sidi Bishr, for re-equipment, reorganization and some much-needed recuperation. After the short commons of the long months of siege the abundance of rations was delightful ; for some it even proved to be too much. After two weeks' rest at Sidi Bishr the Brigade moved to Mena Camp, just on the outskirts of Cairo and very close to the Pyramids. Here the many rumours that the Brigade was going home were scotched once and for all by the beginning of strenuous training in combined operations. It was learnt that the Brigade was to become an independent Brigade Group. This meant the addition to the Brigade of a complete set of supporting and service units, including a squadron of a tank regiment, a regiment of field artillery, a battery of anti-tank guns, a battery of light anti-aircraft guns, a field company R.E., a field ambulance, and also such additional units as provost, postal and R.A.S.C., and even a "nomad" pigeon loft. Moreover, it was to become an Assault Brigade Group, and a Beach Brick was to be added ; it was quite apparent that 231st Brigade was intended for action of the more interesting kind.

After an extensive course of "dry-shod" training under a special War Office team, the Battalion moved on 5th May, with the Brigade, to Kabrit on the Suez Canal for more comprehensive training in combined operations. Substantial drafts were received to bring the Battalion up to full war establishment, many men of long overseas service having been flown home. Lieutenant-General Leese paid a visit to the Brigade and announced that it was now part of Eighth Army's XXX Corps, made up of the 51st Highland and the 1st Canadian Divisions. A select few also learnt the exciting news that the objective towards which their training was directed was the invasion of Sicily, "the soft underbelly of Europe."

At Kabrit, 231st Brigade lost its commander, Brigadier K. P. Smith, who left for an appointment in England, and he was succeeded by Brigadier R. E. Urquhart. Brigadier Smith had commanded the Malta Brigade since 1941 and by his particular genius had turned it into a famous fighting force. His successor was to lead it in Sicily and Italy with the cheerful and dashing efficiency the Brigade required. Throughout the training at Mena camp and at Kabrit the Battalion was without its Commanding Officer, as Colonel Spencer had been wounded in the leg, gaining battle experience with Eighth Army in the final stages of the Tunisian campaign. Fortunately, he was able to return to the Battalion just in time for the invasion of Sicily.

The preliminary training was followed by a series of exercises in combined operations, ending with Exercise "Brightling," for which the Battalion embarked at Suez on the *Otranto*. The exercise was to take place in the Red Sea and very detailed preparations had been made. Complications brought about by bad weather and other factors made this impossible and instead the exercise took place at Aqaba. Thanks to the arduous training the Battalion had already undergone, the exercise went smoothly and gave everyone concerned valuable self-confidence. The Brigade went back to Fayid on 17th June, and for the next ten days the Battalion was very busy with all the final preparations for the invasion of Sicily—Operation "Husky." The very complicated planning was brought to its final stages, equipment and stores were checked, and General Montgomery and General Leese visited the Brigade. At last, on 28th June, the Battalion embarked once more on s.s. *Otranto* at Suez, this time for action ; here was the opportunity to hit back after the long and bitter siege of Malta.

The voyage was uneventful, though when the ship passed Kabrit on the Canal, and the combined operations instructors waved farewell to the troops, the nature of the comments shouted from ship to shore can be imagined. The Gulf of Suez was packed with shipping of all kinds, all lining up for Operation "Husky," and the troops began to realize how vast was the venture they were on. In addition there were huge convoys preparing in North Africa and others were bringing the Canadian Division from home. It was all very exciting. At Port Said the Battalion disembarked for a route march and a bathe, and when the ship left all ranks were most thoroughly briefed about the operation, with models, aerial photographs and large-scale maps, until there was no man who did not know precisely the task which lay ahead and his part in it.

The initial landings were planned to be made at 1.30 a.m. on 10th July, and 231st Brigade was to establish a beach-head by an assault landing near the village of Marsamemi, on the east coast of the Pachino Peninsula. The Hampshire were to land on the left and the Dorset on the right, each to turn inward and attack the enemy's flanks. Immediately the success signals were seen the Devons were to land mortars and machine guns on both beaches. The next phase was the main landing of the Brigade Group on these captured beaches, and the infantry battalions were to move inland to capture three further objectives until an area of some two and a half miles in depth was consolidated. The password was "Desert Rats" with the answer "Kill Italians."

On 9th July a signal was received from Lord Gort from Malta : "The 1st Malta Brigade—the title by which we will always remember you—is very much in our thoughts on the eve of the date of battles to come, which are sure to discomfort the enemy on his own soil. Never shall good fortune desert the fighting men of Devonshire, Hampshire and Dorsetshire. This constitutes our fervent prayer. May victory be yours."

The weather throughout the voyage had been perfect, but on the evening of 9th July it deteriorated; the wind rose and a heavy swell set up. This continued throughout the night, but fortunately it eased a little before midnight when the troops took their places in the landing-craft; even so lowering the craft from ships' davits was very difficult, and when they were safely launched they pitched violently and shipped water. It was soon after midnight when the men in the first flights of the assault set off on the dramatic and most unpleasant trip of seven miles to the beaches, through a heaving sea with a strong cross-current. More than half the men were violently seasick, and many of the officers were none the better for having had a "Christmas dinner" the evening before, with turkey and Christmas pudding. Everyone's clothes were soaked. The frail landing-craft set off in carefully ordered flights, but the bad weather and the cross-current soon scattered them and many had to navigate as best they could. This meant that there was a certain amount of confusion on the beaches at first, but, most fortunately, the enemy were caught napping, being convinced that no landing could be made in a sea so rough. Thus the difficult and precious element of surprise was achieved.

It was soon found that the opposition consisted only of a coastal defence battery, a mortar post, and a few pill-boxes manned with machine guns. In spite, then, of the unpropitious start, the Battalion achieved its first objectives by 4 a.m. and was able to fire success signals. Thereafter all went smoothly, though there were exciting episodes. Captain Boyd and Corporal Higgins, for example, found the section of beach on which they landed swept by fire from an enemy pill-box, surrounded by a double-apron wire fence. They ignored the possibility of mines, rushed at the wire and threw themselves on it to make a path for the troops following them. Lieutenant Le Brecht attacked some buildings with three men, killed several enemy and captured two officers and thirty-five men. Sergeant Parris stalked an enemy pill-box single-handed, attacked it with grenades and killed the occupants.

The Dorsets had been equally successful on the right and very quickly the Brigade's beaches were securely in our hands. The Devons were able to push through and exploit farther inland. Dawn showed the sea filled with a great armada of ships of all kinds. Battleships, cruisers and destroyers prowled watchfully up and down, while landing-craft of many sorts and Dukws plied busily from ships to beaches with guns, vehicles, petrol, ammunition and stores. Enemy resistance varied on different beaches in this area of the invasion, but nowhere was it formidable, and it was obvious at an early hour that Operation "Husky," in the opening stages at least, was successful. By noon the Brigade's third objective was reached, and the Battalion settled down to hold its sector. At eight o'clock in the evening it assembled and marched off inland, not halting until 1.30 on the morning of 11th July. It was a very trying march. The troops had been on board ship for ten days with very limited opportunities for exercise. The day had been long and exciting, and it had begun with the exceedingly disagreeable trip in the landing-craft through a heavy sea. Everyone was very tired and suffered the reaction from the excitements of the day. The march of seventeen miles was memorably unpleasant.

At half past six in the morning of 11th July the Battalion marched off again along the main road through Noto, where the civilians received them joyously; it was the first of many such experiences our men were to have during the fighting in Sicily and Italy. There were still few traces of the enemy, although it was known that German troops were being hurried south towards them and that resistance was stiffening farther inland.

The initial landings being successfully completed, a swift advance inland was made, to gain appropriate positions for withstanding enemy counter-attacks and to relieve the congestion in the area of the Pachino Peninsula. The plan for XXX Corps was to advance rapidly north-west as far as Caltagirone and then north to Agira, on the south-western outskirts of Etna, to cover XIII Corps for its attacks successively on Syracuse, Augusta and Catania. The 231st Brigade had come under command of the 51st (Highland) Division when the landing was successfully completed, losing for the time its independent role.

For the first two days the advance of the Brigade was unexpectedly easy. The battalions pressed forward, using all available transport on the ferry principle, and the only sign of the enemy was the Italians surrendering in increasing numbers. Palazzolo was passed triumphantly and it was not until the afternoon of 13th July, near the town of Vizzini, that resistance was first encountered. Here the advance was firmly checked by accurate and steady artillery fire from hills ahead. It was the Hampshire Battalion's turn to lead and shortly before midnight the enemy positions were attacked, "A" Company being given the task of clearing the obstruction.

As was to be discovered, the position was more strongly held than was believed, and in the event it proved to have been unfortunate that only one company was used. The ground over which the attack had to be made was very difficult and platoons got dispersed. Nevertheless two platoons penetrated to the enemy positions and there was some spirited if scattered fighting before the Company Commander, realizing that the odds were too heavy, ordered a withdrawal. It was later discovered that the enemy was a unit of the Hermann Goering Armoured Division, holding not one position but four, sited in depth and each perfectly placed to give covering fire to the others. "A" Company lost many men at Vizzini, among them Lieutenant Le Brecht, who was killed leading his platoon in a very gallant attack on the German positions. There was one amusing incident when two men of the company got completely lost in the dark and found themselves in Vizzini. They explored and came across forty-five Italian soldiers and an officer, took them all prisoner and escorted them back to the Battalion.

The next day a full battalion attack was made by the Devons, but even this was unsuccessful, and it was not until Vizzini itself was attacked in force by the 153rd Brigade that the Germans' resistance was finally overcome and the road was open for the advance to continue. The Battalion spent a day of comparative rest at Vizzini and formed a mobile column of "C" and "D" Companies with a section of carriers, 3-inch mortars and machine guns, all mounted in transport, commanded by Colonel Spencer. Known as "Shelleli Force" after the village in Malta occupied by the Battalion Headquarters for two years, this column patrolled for two days from Vizzini, but only came into contact with the enemy on one occasion. Once more the Brigade became independent under the command of XXX Corps.

The advance continued to Caltagirone without check until the River Dittaino beyond Raddusa was reached. The river was defended in strength by Italians and the task of forcing a crossing was given to the Battalion. Colonel Spencer decided to make a surprise attack on two hills overlooking the river on our side, which were to be taken by "B" and "C" Companies. Then the other two companies were to pass through, cross the river at separate points, above and below the road bridge, and capture two other hills about half a mile beyond. When the crossing was secure the Devons and Dorsets were to pass through and on. The bridge, which, like so many in Sicily, had not been demolished, was to be captured by "C" Company as its second objective. As it was to be a surprise attack there was no preliminary artillery support, though supporting fire was held in readiness.

"B" and "C" Companies took their first objectives without opposition, crossing the start line half an hour before midnight in moonlight. Three-quarters of an hour later "A" and "D" Companies advanced to the river. Major King was the first to cross with "A" Company, and then he led them against a succession of objectives on a series of steep heights. The difficult task of reorganizing the company in darkness and under enemy mortar and machine-gun fire was carried out without a hitch. At first light the company attacked again and cut off the enemy in their reserve position. Meanwhile "D" Company, commanded by Captain Edkins, crossed the river exactly on time and advanced, firing light machine guns and tommy-guns from the hip. Here again there was a series of positions to be taken on steeply rising ground, but the company's battle drill was perfect and, with the accurate artillery support which had been called up as soon as the strength of the opposition was realized, the company's objective was successfully achieved earlier than had been expected.

The crossing of the Dittaino was, in fact, a model operation. Accurate enemy shelling had delayed the Battalion's approach to the river line sufficiently to prevent a daylight reconnaissance, so that everything had to be planned "off the map." The enemy had fought back with more spirit than had been found with Italian troops so far in the campaign and their positions had been good. For a few of the Battalion wounded, many of the enemy were killed and 20 officers and 864 men were taken prisoner.

On 20th July a fighting patrol consisting of one platoon of "C" Company with a section of carriers came across a German tank with the crew taking their ease alongside it. The patrol immediately attacked, but enough of the crew got back to their tank to withdraw it. Almost at once the enemy counter-attacked with several tanks and infantry and surrounded the patrol. The patrol commander, Captain A. K. Guest, most gallantly attacked the enemy tanks with a handful of men and made it possible for the rest of the patrol to get away. Captain Guest was wounded and taken prisoner, and was later awarded the Military Cross for his brave and spirited action.

In nine days 231st Brigade had advanced a hundred and forty miles and, although opposition had been slight, except at Vizzini and on the Dittaino, they had been fighting all the way. After the Dittaino, however, the first really serious opposition was encountered at Agira, which was to be the scene of a grim and costly battle. The Brigade, now under command of the 1st Canadian Division, was given the task of harassing the enemy's rear while a Canadian brigade attacked the town.

Agira itself was a medieval town perched on the top of a very high hill amid wild and mountainous country in the shadow of Mount Etna. It was held by Italians, strongly reinforced by elements of the Hermann Goering Division and the 29th Panzer Grenadier Regiment in particularly well-sited positions. The 231st Brigade was to harass the enemy by attacking from the south while the Canadian brigade launched a full assault from the west. This meant that the Brigade had to attack and overcome in turn a series of substantially defended high points.

Just before midnight on 22nd July the attack on the Agira position was put into operation. The plan was for the Devons and the Dorsets to attack two important positions on either side of the road while the 1st Hampshire stood ready either to advance up the main road if no resistance was met or, alternatively, to work round the right flank of the brigade area. Unfortunately, the main operation did not go as planned. The Canadian attack on the town from the west failed and for two days of intermittent fighting and almost continuous shelling and mortaring by the enemy, no progress was made. The other two battalions of 231st Brigade had achieved their objectives, had consolidated them and were holding them under great difficulties.

It was not until the night of 24th July that the Hampshire Battalion was ordered forward in accordance with a general plan made by the Canadian commander. The plan for the Battalion was for "C" Company to move forward to a twin-topped hill called the Pyramids and to hold it as a secure base. Next "D" Company was to take up a position in front of the Pyramids, "A" Company to get into positions astride the main road still farther in front, and finally "B" Company was to send two platoons forward to take a very prominent feature known as Campanelli. These positions were along a south-to-north line due west of Agira and about a mile and a half from the town, and provided good positions from which to assault the steep sides of the hill to the town when the Canadians attacked.

The companies moved forward, beginning at eight o'clock in the evening of 25th July. By two o'clock the next morning all four had taken up their positions, but news came that the Canadians had again failed in their attack, but were proposing to make another immediately. Some alteration in the company positions was made by Colonel Spencer and everyone waited for the word to go in to attack. But unfortunately the Canadian attack failed yet again. There was nothing else for the Battalion to do, therefore, but settle down to wait in its uncomfortably exposed and extended positions. "A" and "B" Companies were both forward on the exposed Campanelli feature, which they were ordered to hold.

These two companies were in a difficult situation indeed. Their positions were entirely overlooked by the dominating height of Agira, with its extremely steep eastern slopes. Any movement was at once detected and drew vicious fire. The feature was of considerable tactical value, as it commanded the roads leading north and east from Agira, which were now the only means of escape for the Germans, as the Canadian brigade six miles to the west of the town completely closed all others. The companies had no supporting fire of any kind—neither artillery, 3-inch mortars nor heavy arms—nor could any be got to them, and it was tantalizing to see the Germans using the road, though several light vehicles were successfully attacked by small-arms fire by "A" Company, and others were forced to turn back. A limited amount of artillery support became available later in the day, but as any firing by our guns or mortars was invariably answered by very heavy gun-fire it was an unprofitable bargain.

At about four o'clock in the afternoon the Germans attacked the Campanelli feature with guns and mortars, followed by an infantry attack on the north end. In the very fierce close fighting "B" Company suffered heavy casualties before it was driven off the top of the hill and back along the feature. Major Nelson Smith, who was commanding the two companies, was unable to call up artillery support, the enemy's attack was increasing all the while, and machine-gun fire enfilading the position from Agira made it obvious that further resistance could only end in complete disaster. Accordingly he gave the order for the Campanelli feature to be abandoned. The retreat was a difficult one, but it was very skilfully carried out. The remnants of "B" Company fell back, covered by "A," and took up new positions at the Pyramids. "A" then fell back to a position south of the road.

It was discovered later that the Germans' order for their eventual withdrawal from Agira was signed while "A" and "B" Company were holding the Campanelli feature, which may have meant that the desperate holding of the tactically unsound position had after all been worth while. It was also discovered that the German opposition were units of the Hermann Goering Division and S.S. Paratroopers, some of the most resolute troops in the German army.

Still no news came of Canadian success against Agira, and the Battalion continued to hold its position under almost constant shelling, driving off many counter-attacks. In the evening of 26th July "D" Company's position south of the Agira road was resolutely attacked by German infantry with tanks. The company withdrew a little and then counter-attacked with such determination that it regained the position.

It was not until 29th July, three days later, that Agira was finally taken, and then it was found that most of the Germans had got away. The main operation had taken much longer than had been expected, but the Battalion had carried out its difficult task of harassing the enemy in their rear. Through no fault of the 231st Brigade, Agira was an untidy and costly action for the Battalion, which was at the end reduced to the strength of three rifle companies.

The Brigade now faced the task of advancing due east from Agira to Regalbuto, and progress could only be made by hard fighting in the most difficult type of country. A succession of ridges ran at right angles to the road, providing excellent defensive positions which the Germans used to the full. Only some of the ridges were defended, but the enemy was clever at lying low until the right moment, and each ridge had to be attacked as though it was defended. Sometimes there was no enemy, at others he was there in strength. This was the case on the Regalbuto Ridge itself, which the Battalion attacked on the evening of 29th July.

"A" Company crossed the starting-point first, followed by "C," and both were at once caught in cross-fire from six-barrelled *Nebelwerfers*, which caused very heavy casualties at the very beginning of the assault. Nevertheless the companies pushed forward stoutly, only to be caught again in the cross-fire from unsuspected machine-gun positions. Casualties were so high and the ground gained was so small that the attack was called off.

At dawn it was possible to make a more careful examination of the enemy positions, and it was realized that the Germans were using the Regalbuto Ridge for their main defensive position. Accordingly a brigade attack was launched, and only after some very tough fighting was the Ridge taken.

The hard fighting of the past few days had been matched elsewhere as the Germans fought their determined rear-guard action, while away to the north they were withdrawing as fast as they could to the mainland of Italy. The Sicily campaign was over. It was one of considerable historical importance, though it had lasted but three weeks. In that time the Battalion's casualties were eighteen officers and two hundred and eighty-six men killed and wounded. The Battalion's awards included the D.S.O. to Lieutenant-Colonel J. L. Spencer, M.C., and the M.C. to Major H. D. Nelson Smith, Captains A. P. Boyd and A. K. Guest, and Lieutenant C. Y. Williamson and Captains I. Joseph, R.A.M.C. There was also the award of six M.Ms. and one D.C.M.

Between 1st and 6th August the Battalion remained in its positions near Regalbuto, training and resting and requisitioning mules for mountain operations in case they were necessary. On 7th August it marched to new positions at Adrano, where a week was spent re-forming, re-equipping and training. On the 14th the Battalion moved by transport to Nunziata and marched to Piedemonte, which was entered in the early hours of the morning with no opposition at all. Training continued, and once more combined operations were the order of the day, carrying their own implications. At Piedemonte an other ranks' club was opened, with the homely name of "The Swede Bashers' Arms." General Montgomery visited the Brigade at Piedemonte on 1st September and presented medal ribbons to those who had received awards. In his speech "Monty" complimented the Brigade on its fine record in the Sicily campaign, and added as a compliment that he hoped to take the Brigade with him wherever he went. As 231st Brigade had been overseas longer than nearly everyone else in Eighth Army, the reaction to this remark was not very good, until the General added, "Of course, I might go to England!" This was greeted with loud cheers.

All ranks were briefed for the new assault landing on 3rd September, the day the 5th Division began to cross from Messina into Italy. The landing was to be at Gioia, about half-way up the west coast of the "toe" of Italy, to get behind the German positions. The Battalion embarked in landing-craft at Chiesetta at noon on 5th September and moved, in convoy, up the coast and through the Straits of Messina, which were filled with shipping ferrying troops and stores across to Italy. At five o'clock they disembarked on the north-east corner of Sicily, ready to take off for Gioia just before midnight. The voyage, with fighter aircraft for cover, was uneventful. Everyone slept on the beach near their craft. Unfortunately, a violent storm broke and a heavy swell set up. The Navy decided that a voyage of twenty-five miles in landing-craft in the dark was not possible with the heavy sea running, and at the last moment the operation for landing the Brigade Group at Gioia was cancelled. Instead the battalions embarked in their landing-craft for a further combined operations exercise while the staff tackled the problem of their next move.

Their decision was quickly made, and on the same day a new destination for the landing was announced, at Porto San Venere near to Pizzo, some twenty-five miles farther north. The 5th Division were making such splendid progress in Italy that if the Brigade Group was to land behind the enemy a more northerly point had to be found. The new landing at Porto San Venere meant a sea journey of fifty miles, and the Brigade's task was to hold a bridgehead near Pizzo until the 5th Division made contact, coming up from the south; this was expected to take three or four days.

This sudden change of plan gave no opportunity for the careful planning necessary for an assault landing. The new plan had to be drawn up in a few hours, and much had to be left to improvisation by commanders on the spot. The officers and N.C.Os. were briefed on the morning of 7th September, and at five o'clock in the evening the convoy sailed.

It was soon very apparent that a delicate operation such as an assault landing needs much more than twenty-four hours' preparation. The naval officers commanding the landing-craft had been insufficiently briefed, and there was much uncertainty as to both the times and the places where they were to land the troops they carried. The flotillas quickly lost formation in the dark and it soon became obvious that the operation was going to depend almost entirely on good fortune and that most valuable military gift—improvisation.

Fortunately, the three infantry battalions of the Brigade Group were seasoned soldiers and had excellent understanding of each other, for in the initial stages of the landing at Porto San Venere everything went wrong.

Quite contrary to all intentions, it was the Battalion Headquarters of the 1st Hampshire which landed first, at four o'clock in the morning of 8th September. They were put ashore on the wrong beach, some six hundred yards out of position, and they were well in advance of the Commando units who were supposed to have been the first ashore. Fortunately, there was but little opposition and Colonel Spencer was able to call in his rifle companies for a dryshod landing at the jetty, although "C" Company had already landed at a beach selected by the Company Commander. By five o'clock, however, when the Battalion was ashore, artillery fire opened up from enemy defensive batteries, both on shipping and on the beaches. Improvisation continued to rule as companies of the other battalions were put ashore under fire, in daylight, and on incorrect beaches. The first representative of the Dorsets to land was a Major of Rear Headquarters carrying a sack of mail.

An assault landing made according to plan in darkness would have achieved complete surprise; there was, however, no surprise on this occasion—but there was fortunately much to be thankful for. The beaches were neither mined nor wired, and the 231st Brigade, comrades in adversity on so many occasions, quickly sorted themselves out and took up positions to protect the beach-head, acting on an emergency plan of their own previously worked out and rehearsed by Brigadier Urquhart. The discipline and training of the infantry battalions saved the Brigade Group from what might well have been disaster.

The Hampshire Battalion was the first to go into action. While getting into position on the high land behind the beach, "B" and "C" Companies suddenly came across enemy vehicles on the main road. Captain D. J. Warren, who had led the advance up the difficult hill country behind the beach with surprising speed, attacked the enemy immediately, destroyed the vehicles and killed most of the enemy, and gained and consolidated the positions he wanted. During the morning the beach was heavily dive-bombed and at 2.30 German troops and armoured fighting vehicles were observed assembling near the Pizzo cemetery. It was not possible to call up fire from the 25-pounders which had been landed, as the Commandos were thought to be in Pizzo village. In the afternoon the Germans attacked the battalion positions with tanks and infantry and a running fight continued until dusk. It was a very confused and difficult situation, but the issue was simple on our side: to keep the enemy from the bridgehead while supplies, vehicles and guns were being landed. "B" Company were attacked by a strong enemy force and were unable to keep their position, but only withdrew after one platoon was lost to a man. "D" Company suffered casualties and were driven back. But the Battalion still presented an unbroken front to the enemy. There were many incidents of special gallantry. C.S.M. Bowers and Corporal Touzel led attacks against an A.F.V., under heavy fire with hand grenades, knocked it out and killed all the crew. They then went on to put three other vehicles out of action, killing and wounding many of the crews.

So the Brigade's first day on the mainland of Italy ended, with the beach-head securely held. And during the night the enemy withdrew from Pizzo. The next morning, 9th September, the Battalion marched along the road to new positions on the left flank of the Brigade. Positions were taken up and everyone was ready for a heavy counter-attack ; but none came, and during the night of the 9th the enemy withdrew again. The fact was that the opposition in the Pizzo area had ceased. The 5th Infantry Division's lightning advance northwards and the reinforcements which came quickly through the Pizzo beach-head decided the Germans to fall back to a line farther north. For several days the Battalion acted as leading troops to the 5th Infantry Division, which involved heavy marching and occasional clashes with enemy rear-guards. Advancing by march route and up the coast in landing-craft, 231st Brigade covered a hundred miles in under a week.

But the campaign on the mainland of Italy was virtually over for 231st Brigade, for a total cost of thirty-two casualties to the Battalion. On 10th September the Battalion moved to Vina for five days, then it was moved from place to place, until on 23rd September it embarked in landing-craft at Sapri Beach for Sicily, *en route* for home. It was now known that General Montgomery had meant what he said when he had hinted that he might be taking the Malta Brigade home with him.

Before leaving Italy the Battalion lost its Commanding Officer. Colonel Spencer, promoted Brigadier, took over command of the 128th (Hampshire) Brigade, and the Second-in-Command succeeded. Thus when the 1st Battalion went back to Sicily it was commanded by Lieutenant-Colonel H. D. Nelson Smith.

The great moment came on 18th October, 1943, when the Battalion embarked at Augusta on the *Durban Castle*. One officer, a prejudiced witness of course, wrote that it was "the best organized non-operational move in my experience." Accommodation on the ship was exceedingly crowded, but no one minded. The Battalion had left England twenty-three years before ; Captain Stone, for instance, had joined the 1st Battalion in Constantinople twenty-two years before and had been with them ever since, with only two leaves at home in the years before the war.

The Battalion had served in Turkey and Egypt ; it had put in a long spell of peace-time soldiering in India. It had fought in the 231st Brigade through the historic siege of Malta and had been one of the spearhead units for the invasion of Sicily. It had crowned all this by setting foot in Italy, and now, at long last, the *Durban Castle* took it home. They were, however, marked men ; they had shown their qualities to such effect that they were to undergo long and strenuous training so that they could have the honour of leading the great invasion into Hitler's "Fortress Europe" itself.

CHAPTER XI

THE 2/4TH BATTALION IN SICILY AND ITALY

JULY TO DECEMBER, 1943

(*See map on page* 120)

WHEN the 2/4th Battalion was withdrawn from the 128th Brigade for special service in May, 1943, the Battalion was reorganized at Bougie to form two Beach Group Defence Units. Lieutenant-Colonel Robinson, the Commanding Officer of the Battalion, became the Commander of the Defence Unit of 20 Beach Group, and the Battalion Second-in-Command, Major Mitchell, became Officer Commanding the Defence Unit of 21 Beach Group. The units were thoroughly reorganized for their new duties and underwent special training in North Africa, until 20 Beach Group left to take part in the invasion of Sicily on 10th July, 1943, and 21 Beach Group in the landings at Salerno on 9th September.

It is convenient, therefore, to take the adventures of the two halves of the 2/4th Battalion in their new role one by one. 20 Beach Group completed its final training for combined operations at Sousse, from where it went to the assembly area at Sfax on 4th July. From Sfax, "A" Company, under command 51st (Highland) Division for the landing, sailed in L.C.Is. and landed with the assault troops to cover the landing points, while Headquarters and "B" and "S" Companies embarked in L.C.Ts. with 20 Beach Group. The convoy sailed for Sicily with a strong naval escort on 8th July for Porto Palo, on the extreme south-easterly tip of Sicily near to Pachino, some five miles south of the beaches where the 1st Battalion were to land on the same day.

The foul weather on the night 9th/10th July gave the troops in the L.C.Is. an extremely rough buffeting, and it was feared that the men would be unfit to fight when they were put ashore in the morning. Fortunately, the heavy seas eased considerably at the last and the assault troops landed according to plan. H.Q. and "B" Companies landed with the leading units of the Beach Group later in the day, and the work of unloading stores and vehicles began at once and went on until 12th July, when they moved up to Pachino. The whole purpose of a Beach Group is, of course, to land stores and supplies on to beaches whilst the Defence Unit keep the enemy at bay until a port is captured. The complete success of the landings in this part of Sicily and the absence of resistance meant that there was no such work for the Defence Unit, and Command seemed to be at a loss as to what to do with it. As a result the two companies of the 2/4th Battalion were moved about from Pachino to Busceni, to Noto, to Palazzolo and to Mount Girasi behind the swiftly advancing infantry, until on 20th July the 2/4th companies came under command of the 51st (Highland) Division.

The half-battalion went into the line as infantry on 22nd July, and advanced overnight a distance of five miles to capture a razor-backed hill, Mount Scalpello, which dominated a road vital to the enemy. "A" Company reached the feature before dawn and occupied the western half, "B" went along the top of the eastern end and there came across the Hermann Goering's Artillery O.P. A short but sharp engagement ensued with casualties on both sides, among them Lieutenant-Colonel Robinson, who was wounded in the arm. The two companies held Mount Scalpello for five days under continuous attacks from mortars and artillery, suffering some fourteen casualties wounded.

When Colonel Robinson was wounded, Major G. E. Morgan assumed command of the half-battalion. Coming under command of the 13th Brigade, the unit took over positions from the 2nd Inniskillings on 29th July, at Patterno, where they underwent some shelling but saw but little of the enemy. On 4th August they moved with the 157th Brigade into the plain of Catania, for the hard fighting for Catania was approaching its end. On the 5th the German rear-guard surrendered the city and the Brigade moved in for the clearing-up. They were kept busy street patrolling, preventing civilians from looting, and providing guards for the railway and port.

When the clearing-up was completed the half-battalion found, somewhat to its dismay, that it was to continue on garrison duty. There was much free time, and two requisitioned Italian trucks were used for "recreational transport." Etna was climbed and there was wonderful bathing. It was all very pleasant but, the Battalion felt, it was not what it had trained for, and not appropriate for a unit which had such a good fighting record in North Africa. On 13th August Lieutenant-Colonel Fowler-Esson took over command, but ten days later he was posted to command the other two companies of the Battalion with 21 Beach Group, preparing in North Africa for the landings at Salerno. Major Morgan continued to command the unit in 20 Beach Group.

The unit was still kept out of the war. It moved in September to Acireale for traffic control duties, and in the beginning of October to Floridia near Syracuse, where it remained engaged on peaceful duties.

21 Beach Group at Salerno

"C" and "D" Companies of the 2/4th Battalion, the Defence Unit of 21 Beach Group, remained training at Tripoli after 20 Beach Group left for the invasion of Sicily. Until the end of August Major F. Mitchell was in command, when Colonel Fowler-Esson came from 20 Beach Group to take over command. 21 Beach Group was attached to 56th Division, for Operation "Avalanche."

The unit embarked in L.C.Is. on 4th September and sailed from Tripoli in an enormous convoy. D Day was 9th September, and two days were spent hidden off the coast of Sicily, bathing and resting. Through the Sicilian narrows the otherwise calm and peacefully blue Mediterranean was uncomfortably rough, and a heavy swell persisted. On 8th September the assault convoy set course in the early evening for Salerno, and at half past six in the evening the B.B.C. introduced General Eisenhower, who broadcast the astonishing news that an armistice had been signed between the Allies and Italy. This pronouncement was so timed to make it impossible for the Germans to take over the defensive positions the Italians would vacate, or so it was hoped. There was a great deal of excitement in the ships, and some perplexity as to what effect this would have on the landing.

For this assault behind the main German positions, which the Eighth Army were assailing from the south, General Mark Clark commanded the British X Corps and the American VI Corps. X Corps consisted of two Divisions, the 46th and the 56th. The 46th Division was to land on a one-brigade front on the left, with the 128th (Hampshire) Brigade, and the 56th Division, to which 21 Beach Group was attached, was to land two brigades on the right.

The purpose of the operation was the capture of Naples, the only port adequate to supply an army strong enough to fight its way north to Rome. The immediate objectives were the mountain passes north of Salerno, the airfield at Montecorvino and the road and rail centre of Battipaglia. The twenty-mile stretch of beaches round the Bay of Salerno was chosen for many reasons; they were suitable for a combined operation, they were near to Naples and they were just within fighter range for planes based on Sicily. The chief drawback was the encircling ring of mountains enclosing the narrow stretch of beaches; these were most suitable for defence by the enemy. Great care had been taken over the planning of Operation "Avalanche," for the venture was hazardous and was certain to call for stern fighting.

So the great and ambitious assault convoy steamed towards the Bay of Salerno. There were vicious air attacks, powerfully fought off by the very strong naval escort. It was to be a surprise landing, so there had been no preliminary bombardment. But news had leaked out, and as the ships dropped anchor well out to sea German searchlights swept the foreshore, and their batteries opened fire. As the first flights of landing-craft approached the beaches, having left the anchorage at three o'clock in the morning of 9th September, the British battleships, cruisers and destroyers opened fire on the beaches with salvo after salvo, which whistled over the heads of the men in the craft. Through the noisy and garishly illuminated darkness the men of "C" and "D" Companies of the 2/4th approached the beaches alongside their comrades of the 2nd, 1/4th and 5th Battalions, on an audacious adventure which was to have a very important effect on the campaign in Italy.

The two companies of the 2/4th Battalion landed on their beaches at 3.30, "C" Company under command of the 2/5th Queen's on the right, and "D" under command 2/7th Queen's on the left. At four o'clock the Command Post personnel landed behind "C" Company, which was soon discovered to be on the wrong sector of the beach, so that the first phase of the assault was not possible until it was light. The beach was thickly mined and wired, though the Royal Engineers were hard at work clearing it. It was also unhealthily congested through various units landing on the wrong sectors. It was under artillery fire and in parts heavy machine guns were firing on fixed lines across the beach. "D" Company of the 2/4th had under command for the time being one officer and seventy other ranks of the 5th Hampshire, who had been put ashore on the wrong beach, until they were able to join their own battalion the next day. However, the briefing for the operation had been very thorough, and the confusion was not so serious as it seemed to the men on the beaches. Many defensive posts were taken by assault, and soon after dawn a firm defensive line was established. The defences were based upon several strong points, supported by self-propelled and divisional armour working in groups of tanks and armoured cars.

The Beach Group was not called upon to operate as in theory it was designed to do, and the two companies of the 2/4th were moved into the line. The first night was comparatively quiet in their sector, except for air attacks on the beaches and on the shipping in the bay. The 10th September brought little action to the companies of the 2/4th, although there was plenty in other parts of the beach-head. The unit then came under command of 167th Brigade and at midnight, and without any previous reconnaissance, took over the defence of a vital cross-roads on the road to Battipaglia on the right of the 56th Divisional line. The second night ashore was marked by increased attack from the air. On 12th September the companies moved forward, sweeping the area before them, and they made good progress until they were halted by very heavy mortar fire. They fell back to the cross-roads, regrouped and remained there for the next four days, in which there were several skirmishes with enemy patrols and occasional attacks by troop-carrying vehicles.

At midnight on 13th-14th September vigorous attacks against the cross-roads positions were made by motorized infantry on both flanks of the detachment, though principally against "D" Company. This developed into a brisk battle, but after much confused and resolute fighting all attacks were beaten off and the position was maintained. The 14th September passed quietly at the cross-roads, though it was lively elsewhere and Battipaglia was heavily bombed. On the evening of 15th September the unit's positions were attacked in a most determined manner by motorized infantry in half-tracked A.F.Vs. "D" Company, astride the main Battipaglia road, was overrun by ten of these vehicles, which penetrated so effectively that they were driving over the company's slit trenches. They were men of the crack Hermann Goering and Panzer Division. "D" Company fell back and re-formed, while our 6-pounder anti-tank guns picked the vehicles off one by one. "D" Company surrounded the bewildered infantry and dealt with them most effectively. Then, using every available man, including cooks and drivers, the old "D" Company position was counter-attacked, recaptured and held. The next day the enemy attacked with a full battalion, supported by tanks, but on the principle that "Holdfast is the best dog" the two companies of the 2/4th held their position and drove the enemy off. It was during this battle that Lieutenant Heald won the M.C. for his gallantry and Sergeant Hopgood was awarded the D.C.M. for commanding his platoon in the absence of his officer with conspicuous gallantry and success.

The two companies hung on to their position grimly and desperately for six days, suffering many casualties, and when at last the battle-weary troops were relieved on 17th September they moved back to reserve at Pasmara. Their respite was, however, very brief, for the next day they went forward again and reoccupied their only too familiar positions at the cross-roads.

By this time Battipaglia had been taken, though there was still considerable danger from a counter-attack by the enemy. On 19th September the companies advanced with 131st Brigade to Battipaglia and took over positions captured by the 6th Queen's the day before. It seemed that for all their specialized training in a Beach Group, "C" and "D" Companies of the 2/4th were to continue with proper infantry soldiering. This, however, was not to be.

For the first ten days the situation around the Salerno beach-head had been very uncertain, but hard fighting and the rapid increase of men and supplies through the later convoys had eased the tension. The town of Salerno itself had fallen and the ring of mountains which surround the Salerno area was in our hands. On 23rd September the Beach Group was moved back to the 131st Brigade marshalling area on the beaches, and working parties were formed to carry out twelve-hour shifts handling stores and cargo. The companies provided five labour parties and, as was the custom, shirtless and deeply bronzed under the hot sun, the men toiled, and whenever possible swam in the warm blue sea.

As soon as it was clear that the destiny of the Hampshire companies in 21 Beach Group was no longer to fight Germans but to provide working parties, Colonel Fowler-Esson sent a signal to X Corps asking where the rest of 2/4th Battalion were. When he received the information that it was still with 20 Beach Group at Catania in Sicily, he asked Corps to reunite the two halves of the Battalion to serve as infantry in accordance with an undertaking given previously by A.F.H.Q. to Colonel Robinson. As no satisfactory answer was received, Colonel Fowler-Esson flew to Sicily to see the rest of the Battalion. From this point onwards, while the companies with 21 Beach Group worked in labour parties at Salerno and the companies with 20 Beach Group performed garrison duties in Sicily, the Commanding Officers of both halves of the Battalion began a persistent campaign to get the Battalion united again. At last, on 8th October, they wrung from Headquarters, 15 Army Group, an assurance that the Battalion would be reunited. On 15th October this was received in writing and working parties, instead of humping supplies to the dumps, began the much more pleasant task of building a camp for the other half of the Battalion at Pontecagnano. On 18th November the half-battalion which had been with 20 Beach Group landed at Naples from Sicily, and the 2/4th was together again at Pontecagnano, under Colonel Fowler-Esson. But all was not yet well, and a great deal more persistent worrying of command was necessary by the Commanding Officer before the Battalion was treated as it wished.

The first news was that the 2/4th Battalion would be under command X Corps for operational employment as necessary, and that was highly satisfactory. But then the Battalion was startled to receive an order to dispatch five officers and a hundred men to each of the three battalions in 128th

Brigade, out of a total strength of 28 officers and 568 other ranks. The next day Colonel Fowler-Esson hastened to see the Commander of X Corps and protested somewhat indignantly against this order and asked that his Battalion, which was strong, fresh and well equipped, should be put into the line as a whole and not dismembered to fill gaps in units which had been fighting almost continuously since the landing at Salerno. He won his case again and X Corps issued a standfast order on the postings.

The next shock was when X Corps informed the Commanding Officer that he was required to start a cadre for the specialized training of reinforcements, prior to their posting out to Battalions. Accordingly, on 7th December the Battalion moved to Pugliano, as the "2/4th Hampshire Training Centre," organized with a staff of six officers and seventy-seven other ranks, with Major Morgan as chief instructor. The employment of the rest of the Battalion was not yet specified.

Undaunted by the continued difficulty in getting his own way, Colonel Fowler-Esson made repeated visits to X Corps, where he never ceased to protest. Matters were made worse when orders were received to form a detachment of three officers and one hundred and eighty-eight other ranks for porterage and labour duties. Another detachment of fifty men were to be posted to the Provost Corps for traffic duties. These orders were carried out, but not without further very definite protests by the Commanding Officer to X Corps.

There seemed to be no sign of any relenting by Corps and the Battalion was still dispersed, and to its own way of thinking quite inappropriately employed, when Christmas Day, 1943, came round. The fare was good and there was much singing, and on Boxing Day the Battalion received a handsome Christmas present in the form of a teleprint :

> "SECRET. (1) FOLLOWING FROM 5 ARMY STOP QUOTE STOP 2/4 HAMPS REQUIRED SHORTLY FOR 11 IND INF BDE AND WITH EFFECT FROM TODAY UNDER YOUR COMMAND FOR ADMINISTRATION AND TRAINING ONLY STOP NO EXISTING PERSONNEL WILL BE POSTED AWAY FROM THE BATTALION STOP FLAMBO WILL POST PERSONNEL EARLY TO COMPLETE UNIT TO WAR ESTABLISHMENT STOP (2) 58 MEN AT PRESENT ON TRAFFIC DUTY WITH 40 DIV ARE RETURNING TO PUGLIANO BY 2000 HOURS 30 DECEMBER."

Perseverance had triumphed. The 2/4th Battalion had won its battle with authority. It was to be a fighting battalion once again, and as such was to win other battles in Italy as long as the hard campaign lasted.

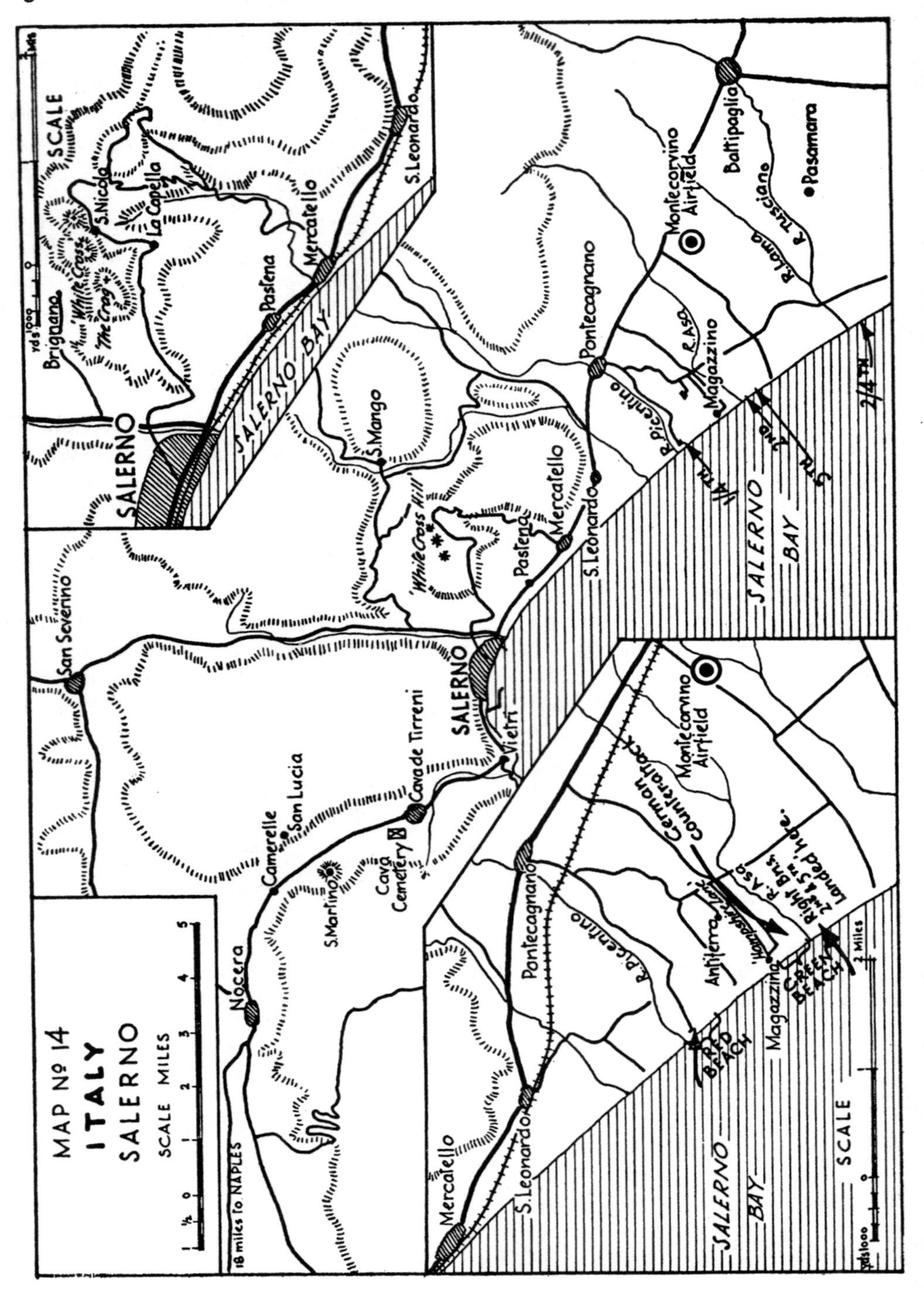
MAP Nº 14
ITALY
SALERNO
SCALE MILES
18 miles to NAPLES
Nocera
Camerelle
San Lucia
S.Martino
Cava Cemetery
Cava de Tirreni
Vietri
SALERNO
San Severino
S.Mango
'White Cross Hill'
Pastena
Mercatello
S.Leonardo
Pontecagnano
R.Picentino
Magazzino
R.Asa
Montecorvino Airfield
Battipaglia
Pasamara
R.Tusciano
R.Loma
SALERNO BAY
SALERNO
Brignano
'White Cross'
'The Crag'
S.Nicola
La Copella
Pastena
Mercatello
S.Leonardo
SALERNO BAY
SCALE
yds 1000
Mercatello
S.Leonardo
Pontecagnano
R.Picentino
German Counterattack
Montecorvino Airfield
Antiferra
Magazzino
RED BEACH
GREEN BEACH
Landed here.
SALERNO BAY
SCALE
yds 1000
2 Miles

CHAPTER XII

THE HAMPSHIRE BRIGADE AT SALERNO

SEPTEMBER, 1943

As we have already seen, the 128th (Hampshire) Brigade had been selected as one of the three assault brigades of X Corps at Salerno. The British X Corps was to assault the left sector of the beaches and the United States VI Corps the right. Two divisions were selected for the assault in the X Corps seven-mile sector, the 46th on a one-brigade front on the left, nearest to Salerno itself, and the 56th on a two-brigade front on the right. The one brigade to make the initial assault on the left was the 128th, while at the same time part of the 2/4th Battalion landed with the assault troops of the 56th Division, as has been related in the last chapter.

The plan for the 128th Brigade was to force a landing between the Rivers Picentino and Asa, on a front of about one mile, and to destroy enemy local defences. That done, the Brigade was to capture the hills overlooking the Salerno road. The 138th Brigade was to follow up over the same beach and capture the town of Salerno itself. Then both Brigades were to advance and make good the defiles leading north, to Cava and San Severino. The plan for 128th Brigade was for the 2nd Hampshire to land on the right and the 1/4th on the left, with the 5th coming in immediately behind the 2nd Battalion. The Battalion Commanders were Lieutenant-Colonel S. J. Martin, the 2nd Battalion, Lieutenant-Colonel R. Chandler, the 1/4th, and Lieutenant-Colonel D. Colville, the 5th. The password for the operation was "Mailed Fist," with the answer, "Hearts of Oak."

The assault convoy anchored some five and a half miles from the beaches at 1.30 on the morning of 9th September. Immediately violent fire was opened from the coastal batteries, with shrapnel. The guns of our battleships, cruisers and destroyers opened in reply. Most of the troops had heard General Eisenhower's broadcast the evening before and knew that Italy was out of the war. But this heavy and accurate gun-fire implied that the sensational news was to make little difference to the Salerno operation.

Exactly on time at three o'clock the first wave of landing-craft left the convoy and moved shorewards in steady lines. There was the crash of gun-fire from ships and shore, the whine of shells overhead, and bursting shrapnel; the overture to Salerno was indeed impressive. The moonlight was too faint to recognize the landmarks which had been so carefully studied in the very thorough briefing which had been given to all ranks. The 1/4th landed on time on their correct beach, but the rocket ship at the head of the 2nd fired its terrific barrage five minutes before the landing half a mile south of its proper target, so that the Battalion leapt ashore at 3.30 at that point and on the wrong side of the Asa. Fifty minutes later "A" Company of the 5th landed, followed half an hour after by the remainder of the Battalion, all on time but also on the wrong side of the river. Thus the three Hampshire battalions assaulting the left flank of the twenty-mile sector were ashore and in action.

The 2nd Battalion landed on a beach raked by machine-gun fire from defensive posts, and shells tore up the sand. In the darkness, without the expected landmarks, the companies could do little beyond attacking immediate targets, which they proceeded to do with the greatest determination. When light came the Battalion advanced against strong opposition towards its planned objectives. It was, of course, a somewhat confusing scene, against a background of much noise of gun-fire, friendly and enemy, with the approaches to the beaches thick with landing-craft of all kinds as second flights of troops came ashore. Some craft were burning, others, when the ramps were dropped, met violent machine-gun fire. Already there was a certain amount of congestion on the beach.

But occupied solely with its own task, the 2nd Battalion fought its way forward, suffering casualties in the process, and by eleven o'clock, with the sun hot and the whole drama of the invasion spread out behind them, Battalion Headquarters was established at the pre-arranged point and companies were in position, having gained their first objectives on the high ground behind the main road to Salerno. One company actually fought their way into Pontecagnano itself. They consolidated their positions and stood by for enemy counter-attacks. Among the casualties in the first hours were Major D. D. Crofts, killed, Captain Stewart and Lieutenant H. R. Smith, missing, and Lieutenants G. H. Brown, Brister, Phillips and White, wounded.

The 1/4th Battalion made good progress too. The assault Companies, "A" and "B," commanded by Majors Salmond and Cowland-Cooper respectively, stormed ashore on time and pressed forward with determination over the sand and shingle. Here, on the extreme left, the beaches were not as heavily defended as those on the 2nd Battalion's front ; the enemy had relied mainly on mines and artillery fire, but casualties were fairly heavy and progress was slow. Major Cowland-Cooper and Lieutenant Roberts were wounded and evacuated immediately to the hospital ship in the bay. Major Portsmouth, the Second-in-Command, was also wounded on the beach, but he was able to remain at duty. "C" and "D" Companies landed behind "A" and "B," and the whole Battalion fought its way across the main Salerno road and started the ascent to the first objectives.

"B" Company, now commanded by Captain Perkins, reached its objectives by ten o'clock. Behind "B" Company, "D" Company fanned out northwards along the hinterland towards Mercatello, clearing all opposition and thereby securing the northern flank of the flimsy bridgehead. On the right "A" Company thrust forward on to their objective while the Commanding Officer, Lieutenant-Colonel R. Chandler, joined "C" Company to try to make contact with his forward companies. In this first phase of the landing six Germans and over one hundred Italians were taken prisoner.

During the day companies remained in their positions, with the exception of "D," which was moved in the afternoon to cover a bend in the road to Salerno, down which enemy transport had been seen moving. It was not until the afternoon that the 1/4th Battalion learned of the Italian Armistice. The next day Captain Cresswell and Lieutenant Querée were blown up on mines attempting to rescue the pilot of one of our aircraft after it had made a forced landing on the beach. Lieutenant Querée recovered from his wounds, but Captain Cresswell died almost immediately, and the 1/4th Battalion lost a very gallant officer.

The 5th Battalion, although brigade reserve, were in trouble early. "A" Company suffered casualties from shelling when their L.C.As. were being lowered from the mother ship, and Second-Lieutenant Hayter was killed and Second-Lieutenant Darrock wounded among more casualties on the beach, while the three L.S.Is. with the remainder of the Battalion were under machine-gun and mortar fire as they went in. As they landed enemy machine guns were still firing tracer bullets from the back of the beach. The starboard ramp of the Battalion Headquarters ship jammed and the American crew showed great coolness and efficiency in off-loading all the troops down the port ramp. The shelling on the beach was considerable. Troops dug in with their hands and stuck it out until, before dawn, the last enemy machine gun was silenced and the Battalion had reached the top of the beach.

When dawn came it was immediately realized that the Battalion was on the wrong side of the River Asa. Battalion Headquarters was out of touch with all companies by wireless, so verbal orders were sent to "B," "C" and "S" Companies to move over the Asa to the arranged concentration area. Neither "A" nor "D" could be contacted. It was later discovered that "A" Company had got to Antiferro and "D" had advanced straight inland for a mile, east of the Asa, and had taken some German prisoners before being held up.

After crossing the river, "B" Company advanced up the main road from the beach, while H.Q., "C" and "S" Companies got to a building known as the Magazzino and advanced up a narrow lane, a track with stone walls on either side, subsequently known as "Hampshire Lane." When they were some six hundred yards inland "B" and "C" were met by a strong German counter-attack with tanks. Their situation was desperate indeed. They were caught in the open without support and overrun. The attack swept over "A" Company and Battalion Headquarters too, and a tragic number of men were lost, including nine officers taken prisoner. These included Major Wallis, commanding "B" Company, Captain Simpson, commanding "C," Captain Christopherson, second-in-command of "A" and the only surviving officer with that company by that time, Major Hogge, Second-in-Command of the Battalion, and the Adjutant, Captain Balch.

Battalion Headquarters were trapped between the walls of the narrow "Hampshire Lane" when one tank advanced straight down the lane, firing as it came and running over dead and wounded. A direct hit from a shell killed three officers—Captain Kirkup, commanding "A" Company, who had been called in for orders ; Lieutenant Sharples, the mortar officer ; and Lieutenant Barker, the Signal Officer—as well as the signallers on the wireless sets, which were destroyed. Colonel Colville had a narrow escape with a bullet through his helmet. The attack was halted short of the Magazzino, where elements of the Battalion collected by Major P. R. Sawyer held out until at last the enemy withdrew and fighting died down. During the night "D" Company came in and a few stragglers from the others, and the Battalion, sadly depleted so soon after the landings, sorted itself out. It had lost in all five officers and thirty-five other ranks killed, and more than three hundred of all ranks wounded and taken prisoner. The next day the Battalion concentrated in Pontecagnano, where it was joined by those of its vehicles and heavy weapons which had survived the landing.

After the first long day at Salerno the three Hampshire battalions stood to in their positions through a quiet night, holding a seven-thousand-yard front. The only activity was from German aircraft, who were busy raiding the beaches and the shipping in the bay. The Assault Brigade had done its job ; the Fifth Army was ashore and holding the beach-head from which the vital attack on Naples could be made. The town of Salerno itself was taken, and units of the 46th Division were in positions beyond it. There was still violent fighting on the long stretch of the landing beaches, particularly in the American sector around Paestum, but in the British sector there was a lull, and troops, tanks, guns and stores were coming ashore fast, though through artillery fire. For the next two weeks there was to be grim fighting to hold the beach-head, for the Germans wanted desperately to drive the invaders back into the sea, not only for the obvious reason but for the immense propaganda value.

Holding The Bridgehead

On 12th September the enemy launched a general offensive against the Salerno beach-head. He had brought crack troops down from the north of Italy and nearly all his troops from the south, leaving only rear-guards to oppose the Eighth Army's advance northwards. His onslaught on the beach-head was furious. The 56th Division were driven out of Battipaglia and the Americans were forced back from Altavilla. The situation became even more critical when the left flank of the U.S. VI Corps were all but driven into the sea. The enemy was menacing our tenuous hold on the passes from the plain of Salerno into the plain of Naples. On the 46th Division front the situation was so critical on 13th September that sappers and administrative groups were brought into the line, and reinforcements went straight into action as they landed. Our positions were under constant shell and mortar fire and attacks with tanks and infantry were pressed home with a kind of fanatical zeal. The gallant share of the two companies of the 2/4th Battalion in this fighting has already been recounted in the previous chapter.

During 11th September the Hampshire Brigade had moved forward into the foothills above Salerno. The 2nd Battalion was put temporarily under command 139th Brigade and moved to the Pastena area, where a congratulatory letter on their action on D Day was received from the Corps Commander. On 13th September the Battalion moved forward and had some successful skirmishes with the enemy, in one of which Major Phillips was killed. On the night of the 14th/15th one company was detached to assist the 5th Battalion in the battles for White Cross Hill. Patrol activity continued until the 20th, when reinforcements were received and the Battalion was relieved and moved to a rest area. From 15th September until the 20th Colonel Martin assumed command of the 128th Brigade, his place as Commanding Officer of the 2nd Battalion being taken by Major Miller.

The 1/4th had little to report for the first four days after the landing. The Battalion moved to positions in the hills above the beach during the second day, but apart from skirmishing and patrol activity, nothing happened. They moved again, taking up a position on a hill given the name of "The Crag," and on the 13th and 14th the enemy began mortaring their positions, and minor patrol attacks developed. Both the mortaring and enemy movements increased as it became evident that the enemy were preparing to attack the hills held by the 1/4th and the positions held by the 5th half a mile to their west. The battle suddenly flared up on the night of 14th September, and for the next six days there was violent fighting for these hills, fighting which is perhaps best considered from the position of the 5th Battalion.

The 5th Battalion had been reorganized after its rough handling on the day of the landing into two companies, "D" and a composite company of the survivors of the other rifle companies, the latter under Captain Rowland, while Captain Ayles commanded the carriers. The Battalion moved forward into the foothills above Salerno with Headquarters at San Nicola, "D" Company on the hill to the north, and the composite company some seven hundred yards east of "D," on White Cross Hill, which was to be the focus of the battles to come.

At dawn on 12th September while a mortar O.P. was being established on the top of White Cross Hill, a strong enemy patrol was seen coming up into the saddle between White Cross Hill and The Crag. The signallers arrived just in time with the line, and Sergeant Strugnell of the Mortar Platoon was able to fire his mortars on the German patrol with great effect. The enemy suffered heavy losses and withdrew, and this first success since the landing acted as an excellent tonic for our troops.

The 13th was a quiet day, but there were ominous enemy troop movements in the roads behind the hills and suddenly, just before midnight on 14th September, very strong attacks were launched in silence against The Crag and White Cross Hill. On The Crag the surprise attack came as "A" Company of the 1/4th had just been relieved and were preparing to move out of their positions, and they were quickly overrun. Fortunately most of the company were able to slip away across country towards White Cross Hill to join the 5th Battalion, who were themselves being strongly attacked. Here too the enemy achieved surprise with its midnight attack, and the composite company of the 5th Battalion was pushed off White Cross Hill, and "D" Company was overrun on the adjacent hill. Among the casualties were Lieutenant W. G. Reed, killed, and Major Roebuck, Lieutenant Lunn and C.S.M. Stares, who were taken prisoner.

An immediate counter-attack was made against White Cross Hill from the left by "W" Company of the 2nd Battalion, with two platoons of the 5th. They gained the top, suffering casualties in the process, but had to withdraw before first light. When dawn came it was seen that the enemy commanded all the high ground previously held by "D" Company of the 5th Battalion, and White Cross Hill itself.

During 15th September and on the days following there were many unsuccessful counter-attacks against White Cross Hill. On one occasion "A" Company of the 1/4th, under command of the 5th, made a spirited attack which nearly succeeded. Colonel Chandler put in a battalion attack with three of his companies and the remnants of "D" Company of the 5th, but although a very violent and confused battle was fought the enemy could not be dislodged. So confusing was this fighting for White Cross Hill that at one time Colonel Chandler found himself commanding seven companies of various units. Among the casualties at this time was Captain Follitt, of the 5th Battalion, who was killed, and Lieutenant Hillman, of the same Battalion, who gave his life most gallantly attacking an enemy machine-gun position.

There were many acts of gallantry in the fighting for White Cross Hill. Notable among them was the conduct of Sergeant Minnigin, who had won the M.M. in North Africa. On one occasion he had gone with a section of carriers from Headquarters at La Capella to San Nicola village to delay any enemy attempts to penetrate round the right flank of the Battalion. Throughout the day the section was under continual machine-gun and mortar fire from the Germans on White Cross Hill. By his fine example and leadership the Sergeant kept the section together in the village until dark. On several other occasions Sergeant Minnigin went up the slopes of the hill and brought back wounded. He rescued a wounded Commando from the church in San Nicola village, and on three nights he volunteered to lead his Carrier Platoon on patrol.

On 20th September the German withdrawal northwards began, and White Cross Hill was at last left clear of the enemy. The three Hampshire battalions were relieved and went back to the beach for a short respite. They were able to rest and swim in the sea. They cleaned themselves up and, with reinforcements, including complete companies of really splendid men from the 51st Highland Division, sorted themselves out. Spirits were high, for the battles to hold the beach-head were over, and now advance was the order of the day.

The line of the advance for the 46th Division was the road through Cava, which struck north-west and west, skirting the mountains of the Sorrento peninsula. Having taken the lead in the landings, 128th Brigade was in reserve while 139th Brigade probed northwards on either side of the Cava road. It was difficult country, and the enemy sustained a strong rear-guard action to cover their heavy demolition in Naples, and it was not until dawn on 25th September that 128th Brigade began to pass through Cava. The Brigade found that the mountainous country with its narrow gorges had not been thoroughly cleared, and outposts of determined troops still remained. As a result Cava was still under gun-fire, and the 2nd Battalion were held up at the cemetery on the left of their road, and the 1/4th were slowed up by constant sniping beyond the town. With the 5th Battalion on the right of the road, the three battalions advanced slowly against awkward opposition, suffering casualties from constant sniping, until they succeeded in reaching the village of San Lucia at nightfall. In this advance Major Blackburn and Lieutenant Goodrich were killed, and Captain Paterson was wounded, all of the 5th Battalion. On the left enemy resistance hardened round the terraced hill of San Martino and there was a considerable battle for the church perched on the top.

It was difficult fighting ; there were many isolated enemy posts from which our companies were being sniped, and each one had to be dealt with systematically. The story of Sergeant Bremner of the 5th Battalion shows the way of it. On the evening of 5th September Sergeant Bremner's company was held up by heavy machine-gun fire and sniping. He was leading his section on the right of the company and, in spite of heavy fire, he went on, killed two snipers with his tommy-gun and located a machine gun. He shot the gunners, and when a German section tried to stop him by throwing grenades he turned and chased them for a hundred yards and, aided by his men, wiped them out with grenades and tommy-guns. He then searched a neighbouring farm and returned to his company, bringing with him a considerable amount of German equipment. For this fine spirited action Sergeant Bremner was awarded the M.M.

The companies consolidated their positions to hold the ground gained and patrolled the immediate vicinity. The main problem was Martino Hill, and under a heavy barrage the 2nd Battalion put in a successful attack. The next day the 7th Armoured Division, whose arrival at Salerno had turned the tide, was sent forward through the infantry positions. The armour swept northwards, and on 1st October the 1st King's Dragoon Guards entered Naples. Thus the first great objective of the assault landing at Salerno was achieved. The three battalions of the 128th Brigade had fought hard for three weeks. They had made the landing on their sector of the beaches ; they had held their positions, and then they had fought on White Cross Hill. Through Cava to Santa Lucia and the Martino Hill they had advanced against strong rear-guard action in most difficult country. Now they were to enjoy a few days of well-earned rest at Marano di Napoli near Naples, to recuperate, reorganize, and take in reinforcements for the battles to come. Some of the officers and men who had joined the Brigade after the battles for White Cross Hill returned to the Highland Division, but many chose to stay, and few survived the campaign which followed. The Hampshire men and the Scotsmen were most excellent comrades-in-arms.

All three battalions had suffered heavy casualties. The 2nd had lost two officers and forty-three other ranks killed, six and seventy-six wounded and two and one hundred and seventy-five missing. The 1/4th had lost in all nine officers and one hundred and fifty other ranks. The 5th had suffered the heaviest casualties of the three battalions—twenty-nine officers, nine killed, nine wounded and eleven missing, and more than four hundred other ranks. As many as eight company commanders of the 5th Battalion became casualties in the first two weeks.

There had been changes in the command of both the 1/4th and the 5th Battalions. While the fighting for White Cross Hill was going on, Colonel Chandler was sent back sick ; he had been suffering from jaundice since before the Battalion left Bizerta. Major Portsmouth, Second-in-Command, took over the command of the Battalion. Colonel Colville left the 5th Battalion on 25th September and Major Ward assumed command until the 30th, when he went to hospital and Major Miller came from the 2nd Battalion to command the 5th. When Brigadier M. A. James, V.C., was wounded on 15th September, Colonel Martin commanded the 128th Brigade until Brigadier J. L. Spencer became the Brigade Commander on 20th September. Thus the Hampshire Brigade was commanded by a Hampshire officer.

The three Hampshire battalions of the 128th Brigade had enhanced their reputation in the fighting at Salerno, and their gallantry was recognized by a number of awards. Among them was the D.S.O. to Colonel Chandler, the bar to his M.C. for Major Brehaut, and the M.C. to Majors Doughty-Wylie, Tinniswood and Rotherham. The D.C.M. was won by Sergeant Minnigin, M.M., and Private Towler ; and the M.M. by Sergeants Bremner, D. Carter, Hughes, Wise and Wynne, Corporals Etheridge, Scott and Touzel, and Privates Lee and Pook.

CHAPTER XIII

THE HAMPSHIRE BRIGADE IN ITALY—1

October, 1943, to March, 1944

The Crossing of the Volturno

After the fall of Naples the Germans withdrew behind the River Volturno, a natural barrier running with sudden irregularities of course from the centre of Italy westwards to the sea. The crossing of this river was the next task for the Fifth Army. It was a considerable obstacle and of great value to the enemy for delaying our advance up the western side of Italy. Strong rear-guards had been left, and these, coupled with the thorough demolitions and the muddy tracks due to the wet weather in early October, made our progress slow. The 128th Brigade waited in billets at Marano di Napoli while the move forward to the river was made.

By 8th October the Fifth Army was in position south of the Volturno, from the sea to Capua and thence across to Benevento, with the British X Corps on the left, or seaward, side and the U.S. VI Corps inland. The crossing of the river presented a problem. It was most adequately defended ; all the obvious crossing-places were heavily covered, and from Capua to the sea the German 15th Panzer Grenadier Division manned the north bank in the X Corps area in a continuous line of company positions, supported by artillery with excellent observation, especially from Mondragone.

The general attack on the Volturno was planned for 12th October, and while the principal thrust was to be made inland by VI Corps, X Corps was charged with establishing bridgeheads across the river and securing the ridges north and east of Mondragone. X Corps was to cross on a six-mile front, in several places simultaneously, with the 128th Brigade crossing on the extreme left, near the mouth of the river, where it was fully three hundred yards wide. Opposition was expected here, but the Navy was in contact to give supporting fire and to land tanks on a beach to be found by the 128th Brigade north of the river.

On the evening of 10th October the 1/4th attacked and occupied the little town of Castel Volturno, to secure the crossing-places preliminary to the attack. The next night, 11th October, the enemy tried to cross the river in a dozen boats, but "D" Company under Captain Perkins dealt with the situation most effectively. All the boats were sunk and many casualties inflicted ; the number was never known as most of the bodies were swept away by the current. The enemy made no further attempts.

The plan for the Hampshire Brigade was for the 1/4th to start crossing the river in assault boats at nine o'clock in the evening of 12th October, to establish a bridgehead by making good the lateral road on the far side, and then to clear the mouth of the river and find a beach for the naval landing-craft to bring in

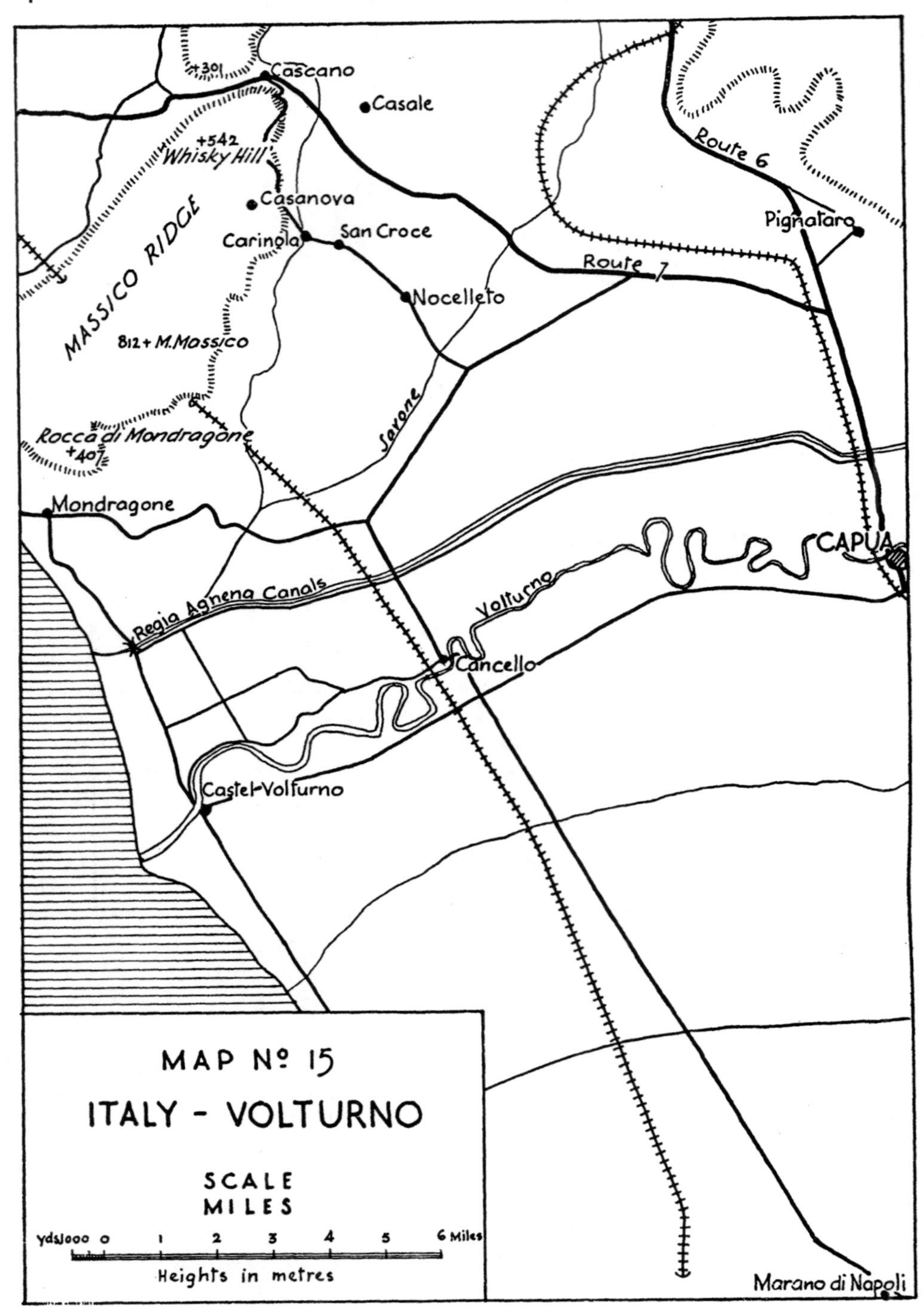
+301
Cascano
Casale
+542
Whisky Hill
Casanova
MASSICO RIDGE
Carinola
San Croce
Nocelleto
812 + M. Mossico
Rocca di Mondragone
+407
Mondragone
Savone
Route 6
Pignataro
Route 7
CAPUA
Volturno
Regia Agnena Canals
Cancello
Castel Volturno
Marano di Napoli
MAP No. 15
ITALY - VOLTURNO
SCALE
MILES
Yds 1000 0 1 2 3 4 5 6 Miles
Heights in metres

the tanks. At first light the 2nd Battalion was to cross and advance to the Regia Agnena canal, followed by the 5th, who had provided carrying parties and rowers for the crossing, which was to advance to the canals on the right of the 2nd Battalion. There were four canals to cross, all close together.

The crossings west of Capua were all silent, with no barrage, to gain what little surprise was possible in this open and flat country. When the 1/4th set off the stars were shining. There was no sound from the far bank, but considerable difficulty was experienced with the boats. The river flowed swiftly and there were strong currents. Indeed one boat capsized and the eight men in it were drowned. However, in three-quarters of an hour two companies were across and a small bridgehead was established. The rest of the Battalion was over by midnight, and leading sections had reached the first objective, the road just over the river. When this road was crossed machine-gun posts were encountered, and the advance was seriously slowed down. The country was laced with dykes and ditches and none of the objectives could be recognized. The enemy, now fully alert, moved round the flank of "A" Company, who were leading, and some fierce close-quarter fighting took place. The companies dug in and probed forward as best they could.

The other two battalions crossed and came up against the same problems; very difficult country and strong enemy positions. A beach had been found by the 1/4th and L.C.Ts. came in with their tanks, though for some time these were held up by thick minefields. Companies had to advance over open fields and they consequently suffered considerable casualties, especially when the enemy tanks came up with daylight. The 2nd Battalion crossed the river at dawn on 13th October and moved through the 1/4th towards the Regia Agnena canals, meeting considerable opposition in very difficult country. However, they gained and held a position some 2,500 yards beyond the river. In the 2nd Battalion both Sergeant E. Carter and Sergeant A. Hawes distinguished themselves greatly and for their fine fighting were awarded the D.C.M. and M.M. respectively.

The 5th Battalion crossed, moved well over to the right, and although they also met determined resistance they reached the canal that day. "B" Company, commanded by Captain Mordaunt, reached and crossed the first canal, but came under heavy fire on the intervening bank. The company dug in and held its position most obstinately for some considerable time, but it was eventually withdrawn. Captain Mordaunt received an immediate award of the Military Cross. "A" and "C"[1] were pressing forward against very strong and determined resistance, and "A" made three separate attacks on a strong-post before capturing it. The company pushed forward again until it encountered tanks and was forced to withdraw. All companies dug in under heavy fire on the flat approach to the canals. The Commanding Officer's jeep was hit by fire from a tank as it went forward, and Lieutenant-Colonel Ward was seriously wounded. Sergeant York, the stretcher-bearer sergeant, drove forward in another jeep under fire for more than a mile up the dead straight flat road towards the enemy, found Colonel Ward in the ditch beside the road, dragged him out of his jeep

1. OC 'C' Company: Captain N. S. Flower - K.I.A. 13 October 1943.
Joined 5th Bn - Salerno Bridgehead. - 16 Sep. 1943

and returned safely to the R.A.P. Sergeant York was later awarded the D.C.M. for this very gallant act.

All the next day the three battalions held their positions against frequent counter-attacks, and suffered considerable air attacks, shelling and mortaring. The low-lying swampy ground, well observed by enemy artillery and mortar positions, made progress difficult. The Brigade was across the Volturno, but it was stuck for several days in a position of stalemate. Matters were made worse by the weather breaking, turning the tracks into mud so that it was often over the axles of the jeeps, and much ironical comment was made by the troops about "sunny Italy." The flat fields between the Volturno and the Regia Agnena canals offered little cover ; our own tanks and anti-tank guns were across the river and there was little likelihood of the bridgehead being driven in, but the advance was reduced to a series of probing patrols with platoon and company attacks.

Captain Ayles, commanding a composite company of the 5th Battalion, established an O.P. in a house overlooking the canals, and with the assistance of the F.O.O. he was able to harass enemy movement on the far side. He also succeeded in taking a patrol over the canals, but being late in returning his patrol had to take cover from the shells fired by our own artillery to cover his withdrawal.

It was while the Brigade was on the Volturno that the 5th Battalion had special reason to be grateful to their R.S.M. R.S.M. "Bismarck" Barnett was always unfailingly alert for the welfare of the Battalion, and in the dreary days on the Volturno everyone lived entirely on tinned rations. R.S.M. Barnett altered that. He organized the capture and slaughter of a heifer and some pigs, set up an establishment and happily became the battalion butcher. The Battalion fed handsomely. This was typical of R.S.M. Barnett, and his outstanding services to the 5th throughout the campaign were recognized by the subsequent award of the M.B.E.

While the Brigade was in these positions the battalions relieved each other in turn for a two-day spell at the rear. It was an unusual situation because the enemy positions were so close that both sides looked at each other over the triple canals, and frequent clashes occurred. From Rocca di Mondragone the enemy had observation of the open approaches to the canals and his mortars were very active. On 20th October German officers appeared with a white flag on the bridge opposite the 2nd Battalion. They had come to discuss the return of medical prisoners, and they set up a table with wines and cigarettes to make the parley pleasant. While the discussion was being held German troops strolled along the canal banks.

On one occasion three stretcher-bearers of the 5th Battalion were out searching for a wounded man who was believed to be in the abandoned position on the canal bank, and were taken to the Germans' Headquarters and questioned. One of them returned to his company to fetch his A.B. 64 to justify his stretcher-bearer armlet. This man was not seen again, but another was later returned with a list of prisoners taken, and bearing a letter from the

Regimental Commander to General Hawkesworth thanking him for the chivalrous way his Division had fought, and saying that he looked forward to their next encounter.

At this period in the campaign there were changes in command of the 1/4th and 5th Battalions. Lieutenant-Colonel R. E. H. Ward had returned to the 5th, and Major Miller was sent to command the 1/4th in place of Major Portsmouth, who had gone to hospital. When Colonel Ward was himself wounded, Major J. L. Watson took his place. On 20th October Colonel Chandler returned to the 1/4th from hospital, and on the 26th Lieutenant-Colonel J. H. H. Robinson took over command of the 5th. Colonel Robinson was still recovering from the wounds he sustained leading the 2/4th Battalion in Sicily.

The stalemate at the canals was broken eventually by a change in the axis of the Corps attack, which was now to be made energetically along Route 7, and the 128th Brigade was taken out of the position and moved round across the Volturno at Capua. The canals had been a depressing mosquito-ridden position and everyone was glad to have them behind him.

The objective for the Brigade in the advance up Route 7 was the Massico Ridge south-west of Cascano, and little attempt was made to delay the advance. The civilians turned out in the villages to welcome the troops most exuberantly, and pressed wine and fruit on them. At one time a signal reached Major Rotherham, commanding "B" Company of the 1/4th, that the Divisional C.R.A. was offering a bottle of whisky to the first officer to bring observed fire to bear on the other side of the ridge. The advance of "B" Company at once speeded up and Major Rotherham himself, outpacing his F.O.O., was soon on the ridge calling for fire, and won the bottle of whisky. Thereafter this particular feature was known as "Whisky Hill."

The Brigade moved steadily forward with only random contact with the enemy, though there was both mortar and shell fire to contend with. The villages of Nocelleto, San Croce and Carinola were taken without great difficulty by the 1/4th and 2nd Battalions. There was a delay in front of the village of Cascano ; finally, however, two companies of the 5th Battalion moved in towards the village on each flank, while Colonel Robinson, followed by a few officers, walked up the road and entered the place, and found that the enemy had withdrawn.

At this point the three Hampshire battalions were taken out to rest, reorganize and train at Carinola, Casanova and Casale, for General Clark called a halt to rest his divisions, and to regroup and reinforce them, to establish supply routes and to build up his reserves. Ahead of the Fifth Army severe mountains presented a series of strong natural defensive positions, and the enemy now had superiority in numbers. So far the Allies had advanced by simultaneous attacks on a wide front ; now it would be necessary to attack selected points, to bring superior forces to bear with the full available artillery and air support. Established on commanding heights, the enemy would have to be dislodged from each in turn.

On 6th November the 2nd Battalion said good-bye to Colonel Martin, who

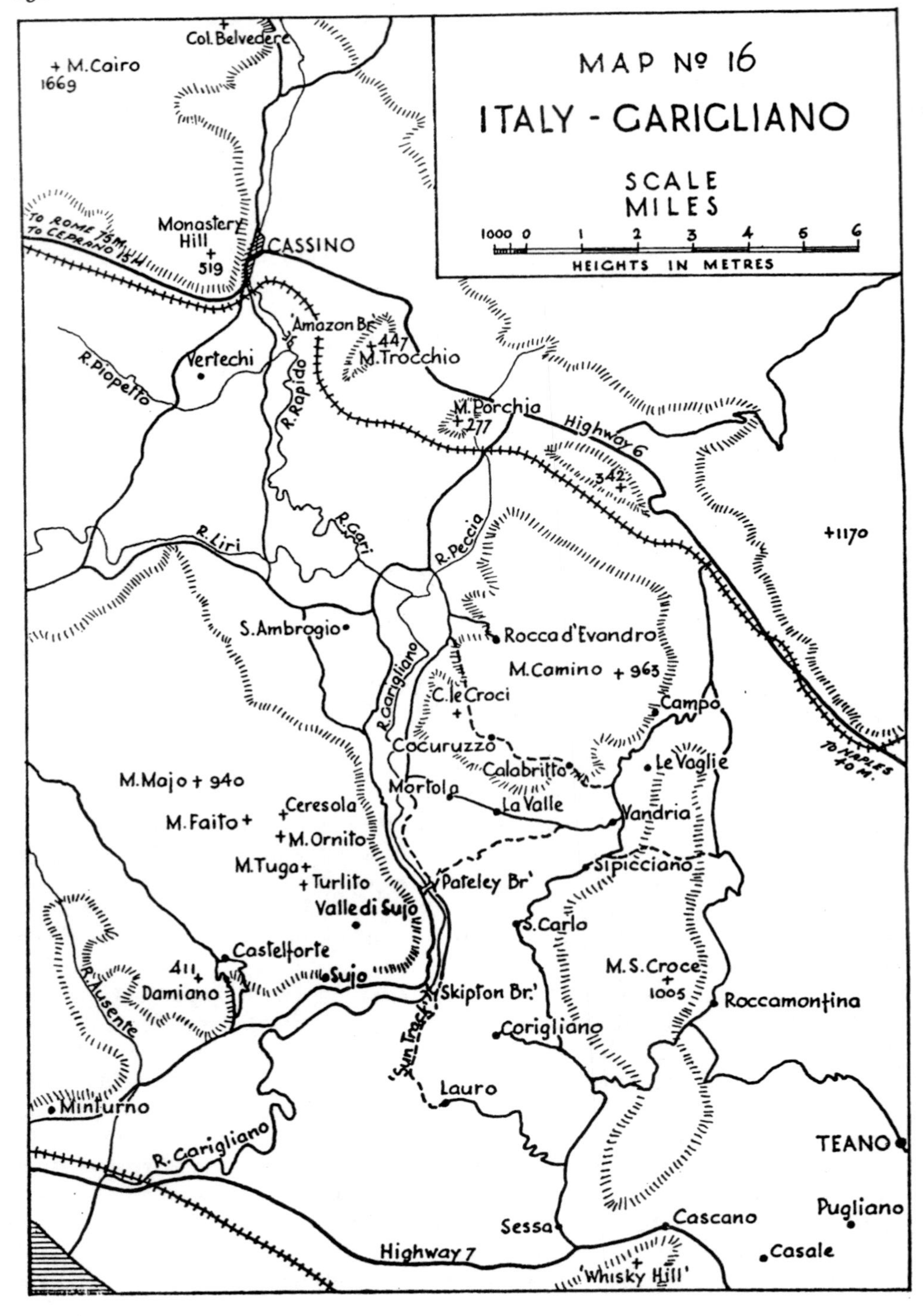
MAP No 16
ITALY - GARIGLIANO
SCALE
MILES
1000 0 1 2 3 4 5 6
HEIGHTS IN METRES
Col. Belvedere
M. Cairo
1669
Monastery Hill
519
CASSINO
TO ROME 75 M.
TO CEPRANO 15 M.
'Amazon Br'
447
M. Trocchio
Vertechi
R. Piopetto
R. Rapido
M. Porchia
277
Highway 6
342
+1170
R. Gari
R. Liri
R. Peccia
S. Ambrogio
Rocca d'Evandro
M. Camino
963
R. Garigliano
C. le Croci
Campo
Cocuruzzo
Calabritto
Le Vaglie
TO NAPLES 40 M.
M. Majo
940
Mortola
La Valle
Ceresola
M. Faito
Vandria
M. Ornito
M. Tuga
Turlito
Sipicciano
Pateley Br'
Valle di Sujo
S. Carlo
Castelforte
411
Damiano
Sujo
M. S. Croce
1005
Skipton Br.'
Roccamontina
R. Ausente
'Sun Track'
Corigliano
Lauro
Minturno
R. Garigliano
TEANO
Pugliano
Sessa
Cascano
Casale
Highway 7
'Whisky Hill'

had commanded them throughout the campaign. He was succeeded by Lieutenant-Colonel P. D. Miller, who commanded until the end of February, when Lieutenant-Colonel T. A. Rotherham took his place. The Brigade rested for three weeks, and the battalions were able to reorganize themselves again. Reinforcements arrived, some of them from the 11th, 12th and 70th Battalions of the Regiment. Among the officer reinforcements the battalions were very fortunate in having several South Africans, including Major Baillie and Lieutenants Norton and Bowles, posted to the 1/4th, and Lieutenant Roux to the 5th. Lieutenant Norton was to win the Victoria Cross in the fighting on the Gothic Line, and each of the others was to win the M.C. Reorganized and re-equipped, the battalions trained intensively for the battles to come. They had fought with but little rest for two months, and they had all suffered heavily. From 10th September to the end of October the three battalions had lost some 1,100 all ranks. These losses were quite in accordance with the losses of the other battalions in the 46th and 56th Divisions, and show the ferocity of the fighting in Italy.

The Crossing of the Garigliano: Monte Damiano and Ornito

On 27th November the Hampshire Brigade moved up to take part in the new offensive. Brigade Headquarters and the 5th Battalion went to San Carlo, the 2nd Battalion to the terraced olive groves of Corigliano, and the 1/4th to Sippiciano. Near by was the bleak Monte Camino, soon to be captured after terrific fighting by the 56th Division. During November Brigadier Spencer had left the 128th Brigade to command 36th Brigade, 78th Division, Brigadier T. P. D. Scott succeeding him.

The 5th Battalion moved forward to be ready to take part in an attack down the Mortola spur, but the attack was long delayed owing to the difficulty of taking Monte Camino. The enemy on the Mortola spur eventually withdrew, but the period spent by the Battalion was by no means without incident. The area was thickly sown with the German three-prong "S" mine; many were lifted but others took their toll, and there were casualties. Among the wounded was Lieutenant G. A. F. Minnigan, who had won the M.M. at Sidi Nsir, the D.C.M. at Salerno, and had been commissioned in the field in November. He was fortunately able to return to his battalion in time for the Ornito battle, led a notably gallant patrol to Faito, but was very seriously wounded on Mount Cerasola.

The three battalions patrolled constantly while they were in the San Carlo area, and the enemy were equally busy. On one occasion Colonel Robinson and some of his officers were caught on a reconnaissance, but the whole group escaped, though Captain Rowland was badly wounded and not found until some time later. It was a bleak, disturbing place, and the regular mists which filled the Garigliano valley created a strange uncertainty, even in daylight. The administrative problem was considerable. Supplies had to be brought by truck to roadhead and thence by jeep to "jeephead," about four miles back. Thence they were brought by troops to the company areas. Transport, including three-ton trucks, came up at night as the San Carlo road was under observed fire. The Quartermasters had most formidable problems to solve, and great credit was due to them for the way they overcame difficulties of all kinds throughout the whole period the Brigade was in the Garigliano area. The mud was terrible ; it sometimes took hours to get the brigade columns formed up for the night move. Vehicles had to be towed through deep mud by carriers, almost the only use found for them. Yet, an example of the good administration, every man had a clean pair of socks brought to him every night and there were no cases of "trench feet" and very little sickness.

On 1st December the 139th Brigade put in an attack to capture Calabritto. At the same time the 128th Brigade sent out fighting patrols, and companies of both the 2nd and 5th Battalions probed towards La Valle, and on the night of 3rd December positions were established south of the village. The attack on Calabritto had ended in a kind of stalemate, but pressure was kept up and on 6th December the two Hampshire battalions advanced on Mortola on the banks of the Garigliano without opposition. There they found guns, mines and equipment the enemy had abandoned. The 56th Division had captured Monte Camino on 7th December, winning a valuable move in attaining this commanding position.

The weather was consistently bad ; shelling, mortaring and enemy fighting patrols were frequent and all was danger, discomfort and toil. The 5th Battalion spent a spirited Christmas at Campo, behind Monte Camino, but the other two had to make the best of it in the forward positions overlooking the Garigliano, in very bad weather. It was a situation calling for the exercise of considerable patience and fortitude. The first adventurous operation was over ; it was now a question of settling down as cheerfully as possible to the drudgery of a very hard campaign. There were many stern minor engagements as battalions manœuvred for better positions for the next move, which was the crossing of the Garigliano.

Towards the end of December the Hampshire Brigade was moved to the north, with Brigade Headquarters in Rocca d'Evandro castle. Five miles to the north-west was Cassino, where five months later Captain Wakeford was to win the Victoria Cross with the 2/4th Battalion. For two weeks the battalions were kept busy patrolling towards the Garigliano ; it was bitterly cold and the New Year came in with a gale and a fall of snow. It was here, on 4th January, that the 5th Battalion's Padre, Captain the Rev. C. G. Baalam, was killed by a "S" mine going into "No man's land" to bury a dead German. The Padre had served with the Battalion since May, and was a much-loved man. On 11th January the Brigade was relieved in its forward position and moved back to the Volturno, to take a short rest, as it had been selected as the assault brigade of the 46th Division for the crossing of the Garigliano below San Ambrogio, part of the army plan for a full assault on the German "Winter Line."

After a few days back on the Volturno, practising river crossings with assault boats, the three battalions returned to Campo and Corigliano and to the forward area of Colle le Croci, for the long-awaited crossing of the Garigliano. The Hampshire Brigade was to cross west of the junction of the Gari and Liri rivers, with objectives about San Ambrogio on the hills in the north. Two hundred officers and men of the 2/4th Battalion joined the Brigade for this operation, but before it took place they were recalled to Pontecagnano, where their Battalion was being concentrated before joining the 4th Division.

The crossing of the Garigliano by the 46th Division was to be made on a two-battalion front ; the 2nd on the right, the 1/4th on the left, with the 5th in reserve. The 5th were also to provide parties to ferry the boats in which the assaulting battalions were to cross. Seeing that the river crossing was likely to be far from easy, Captain Heald was sent to Naples on a special mission, to get a supply of life-jackets for the ferrying parties. Captain Heald enterprisingly bypassed the "usual channels" and applied to the Navy, who as usual rose to the occasion. Thus it was that, despite some rather sharp notes from Army departments, the ferry parties wore life-jackets—"Mae Wests"—for the crossing of the Garigliano, and eventually the battalions had them too, and many lives were saved thereby. Captain Heald had joined the 5th Battalion at San Carlo from the 2/4th ; he had led a notable recce patrol to La Valle, and he was to distinguish himself many times throughout the campaign.

The river crossing was planned to take place at eight o'clock on the evening of 19th January, and an extensive supporting programme was to be fired by artillery and 4.2-inch mortars to cover the operation. For the sake of surprise, similar programmes were fired on preceding nights, with spectacular effect. These preliminary shoots gave the attackers the additional benefit of making the enemy disclose his defensive fire tasks, and a careful note was taken of these, and the crossing-places chosen accordingly.

The troops were very eager for the assault, to be able to get on to the hills at which they had gazed through wind and rain for two very trying months. The operation, however, was not to be fortunate. Despite several efforts, no boats or swimmers had been able to get across beforehand owing to the fast current, so that information of the far bank was limited only to that gained by observation. When it came to it considerable difficulty was experienced in getting the boats to the front. Sapper vehicles were blown up on mines and the bridge over the Peccia had been demolished. Consequently "D" Company of the 5th Battalion, who had been selected to handle the boats and row them over the river, had to off-load the boats on the far side of the Peccia and manhandle them over the river to get them into position for the crossing of the Garigliano.

The night of 19th January was calm and dark, with the moon occasionally shining through the clouds. The work of assembling the troops and moving forward to the near bank went quite smoothly, and the fire plan came down most impressively. At the appointed time the boats were launched—and then nothing went right.

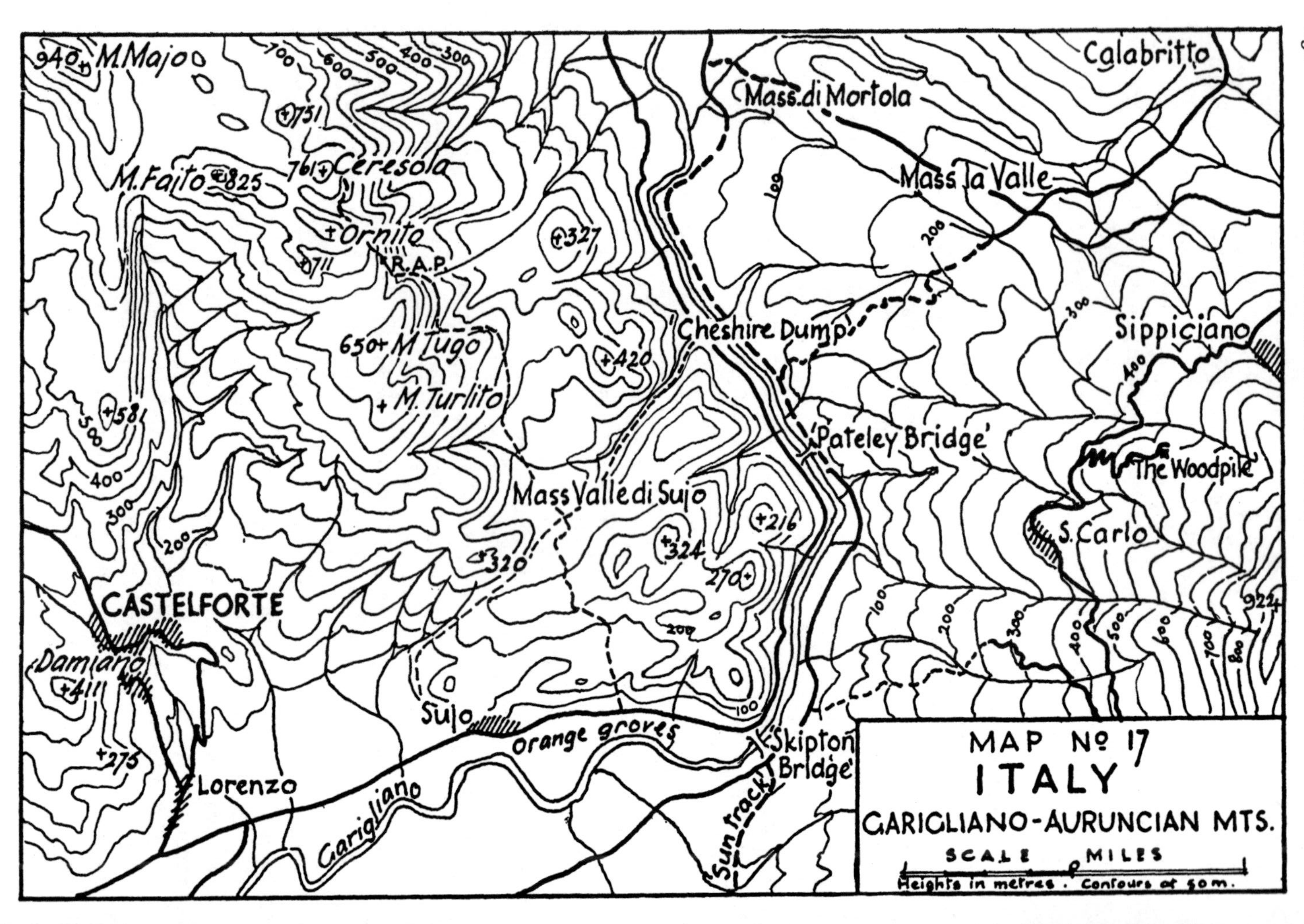
M. Majo
M. Faito
Ceresola
Ornito
R.A.P.
M. Tugo
M. Turlito
Calabritto
Mass. di Mortola
Mass. la Valle
Cheshire Dump
Sippiciano
'Pateley Bridge'
'The Woodpile'
Mass Valle di Sujo
S. Carlo
CASTELFORTE
Damiano
Sujo
Orange groves
'Skipton Bridge'
Lorenzo
Garigliano
Sun track
MAP No 17
ITALY
GARIGLIANO-AURUNCIAN MTS.
SCALE MILES
Heights in metres. Contours at 50m.

It was known that the Garigliano was flowing very fast and that there would be great difficulty in controlling the boats. It was afterwards discovered that the Germans had opened the sluice gates at San Giovanni, and the fast river flowed even faster, and was soon in flood. At the last moment it was decided to try to use the speed of the current flowing out of the Peccia to carry the boats over the Garigliano. For this one company of the 2nd Battalion embarked some fifty yards up the Peccia and succeeded in getting over. A cable control for the boats was established, but unfortunately the cables became fouled, broke and the boats were swept down-stream.

More trouble was caused by the heavy mist which settled over the river. It was impossible to see the banks when the boats were in the stream, and the speed of the current varied so quickly that the boats were swung round and the crews lost direction. A sergeant of the 5th Battalion who tried to wade across to guide a boat was swept away, and struggled ashore more than two miles down-stream.

It was the same story with the 1/4th Battalion. For all the desperate efforts of the ferrying parties no headway could be made by the 1/4th assault boats, which were launched at three points. The boats were swept back to the near bank time after time. Fourteen attempts were made by the 1/4th, including attempts by individuals in rubber boats and by swimming, to get a line across. All the time the enemy showed little sign of opposition.

The 1/4th were moved up to use the 2nd Battalion's crossing, but with no success. Try as they might, no troops were got over the river other than the one company of the 2nd Battalion. Throughout the night it was a desperate story of attempt and failure, until at last as dawn approached the project had to be abandoned. Under cover of smoke and morning fog a few of the company on the far bank got back in water-logged and leaking boats. As the Battalions returned to their former positions the enemy, so far slow to react to the attempted crossing, brought down very heavy defensive fire all along the near-side bank of the river.

Four days later, on 23rd January, the Brigade moved west towards the front held by the 56th Division, north of the Garigliano, where a crossing had been forced. Their bridgehead was, however, in little depth and there had been very heavy fighting. It was necessary to capture Monte Damiano, a bare razor-backed feature which gave the enemy excellent observation. The summit was held by the Germans, while the 2/5th Queen's were clinging like flies to a small knob some two hundred yards from the top. The rocky slopes were strewn with unburied bodies. The task of clearing Monte Damiano was given to the 1/4th Battalion, backed up by the 2nd. During a reconnaissance carried out from a flank Brigadier Scott had the misfortune to break his ankle, and command of the 128th Brigade was then assumed by Brigadier D. A. Kendrew, who remained in command until the end of the war.

The assault on Monte Damiano was made in daylight to fit in with other operations. There was no cover, and no manœuvre was possible, and it was in bright sunlight that the 1/4th attacked, having relieved the 2/5th Queen's, at half past two on 29th January. The assault was led by "D" Company, who rushed the foremost enemy posts with the greatest dash. They immediately came under very heavy mortar and machine-gun fire and lost all their officers and many men. "B" Company, who were supporting, met a similar fate, and "C" Company, assaulting the other flank, could make no progress and lost many men. One platoon, for example, was reduced to fifteen men after the attack.

The attempt failed, but it was most gallant. The losses were very heavy. The 1/4th Battalion lost four officers killed and five wounded and more than eighty N.C.Os. and men. The officers killed were Captain Wilson and Lieutenants McCreery, Reed and Dare, and Captain Mottershead, Lieutenant Perrin and three others wounded. Among the N.C.Os. killed was a very gallant old soldier, Sergeant Dicks, who died at the head of his platoon. He had been wounded twice previously, and had escaped from captivity. The D.C.M. was subsequently awarded to C.S.M. McAllister and Sergeant Fry, and the M.M. to Sergeant Rowe. Sergeant Fry, who was wounded, also received the United States Silver Star for gallantry.

On 1st February the Hampshire Brigade was moved back across the Garigliano, but twenty-four hours later they crossed the river again to their own division and took up uncomfortable positions in the inhospitable mountains. There were to be no major actions for the 2nd and 1/4th Battalions, but the 5th, put under command 138th Brigade, was to take part in the most memorable fighting for Mounts Ornito and Cerasola. These mountains, with Faito and others, were part of a bleak and desolate range which the 138th Brigade was ordered to capture.

The 5th Battalion crossed the Garigliano at the famous "Skipton Bridge" and moved up-country through Valle di Sujo to an assembly area behind Monte Tugo. In this wild mountain country all weapons and ammunition had to be manhandled. There was no time for a proper reconnaissance, and the Company Commanders were only able to take a quick look at their objectives across the mountains before nightfall. Two Commandos had already attacked the positions on the steep and bare hills, and after a day of confused and extremely difficult fighting they had captured Monte Ornito, but they had failed to take either Faito or Cerasola. When the 5th Battalion came to advance the whole situation in front was still very vague ; they did not know the positions of the Commandos or of the enemy. Add to this the absence of reconnaissance, and it will be appreciated that the successful advance on a very dark night over extremely difficult mountain country was indeed a wonderful operation on the part of "B," "C" and "D" Companies of the 5th Battalion.

The Companies moved forward quickly and without incident, though there was some shelling. "D" Company, commanded by Major P. R. Sawyer, had for its objective a small hill between Ornito and Hill 711 ; "A," led by Major Girdlestone, had Monte Ornito itself, and "C," under Major MacBeath, made for Hill 711. "B" Company, commanded by Major Job, was with Battalion Headquarters. Soon after midnight all companies were established on their objectives, the Commandos duly contacted and relieved by "A" and "C" Companies.

Strong fighting patrols soon began to come in against "C" and "D" Companies, but all were successfully beaten off. Morale was splendid, and sniping the enemy on the opposite hillside became something of a sport. The enemy, who were holding the surrounding hills, were desperately keen to recapture Ornito, which was indeed a most valuable vantage point. Five months later it was to be the spearhead position for the successful French attack on the Hitler Line.

The 5th Battalion were to spend eight days on Monte Ornito and, later, on Cerasola, and in that time they were to suffer nearly two hundred casualties from the almost incessant mortaring and shelling, and from the ever-recurrent counter-attacks. The weather was wet and bitterly cold and men lived in shelters on the sides of corries constructed from rocks and groundsheets. Men manning machine guns on the forward positions had to lie close in their sangars during the daytime, ever on the alert for any movement by the enemy. In the support positions, a few minutes' scramble below the crest of the mountain, men could move freely, but everyone had to be constantly ready for counter-attacks. As the days passed the number of German dead lying out on the rocky slopes increased, and attack after attack was driven off.

The problem of supply was even more difficult than before. It was at least a twelve-hour carry up from the vehicle point in the road in the valley. Supplies came up to the head of the "Sun Track," and then by the track over Skipton Bridge to Cheshire Dump by jeep, and up the mountain by mule and porter, a climb of from three to four hours. A constant stream of Basuto carriers was necessary to keep the troops supplied with rations, water and ammunition. On more than one occasion parties had to be sent down by the 5th Battalion to recover loads which had been hastily dumped by the porters when shells began to fall too close to them.

The R.A.P. was a stone hut down the hill, and it often took six hours to get a casualty back as far as that, and more than twenty-four to get him back to the ambulance points on the road by Skipton and Pateley Bridges. Captain David, the Medical Officer of the 5th Battalion, worked ceaselessly dealing with an endless stream of casualties. Over two hundred men passed through his hands, and his great devotion to duty and skill in dealing with them before the difficult twenty-four-hour journey down to the ambulance were rewarded with a very well-deserved M.C. He was nobly served by his team of stretcher-bearers and by a detachment of the Field Ambulance with blood plasma.

A very dangerous attack was made on Ornito in the early morning on 6th February between "A" and "D" Companies in a heavy mist. The sound of digging was heard above "D" Company, who thought it was "A" adjusting their positions, until German voices were recognized. "B" Company was sent to counter-attack at once. As they advanced up the steep side of Ornito the mist lifted and a German post was seen right above "D" Company and not more than a hundred yards away. "D" Company covered "B" Company's advance with small-arms fire and there were cheers when a "D" Company rifleman succeeded in knocking off a German's helmet and sent it clattering down the rocks. Then "B" Company started to complain noisily about "D" Company's shooting, as their bullets were ricocheting uncomfortably off the rocks round their ears. All the comfort an unfortunate wounded man could get in answer to his cries for stretcher-bearers was a general chorus of "Shut up!"

Sergeant Cooke of "B" Company had meanwhile most gallantly led his party up the open hillside, destroying a machine-gun post, and was seen standing silhouetted against the sky. Thirty yards from him stood a German N.C.O. and they were coolly firing their rifles at each other. Sergeant Cooke eventually won his duel by shooting his opponent between the eyes, and his men quickly followed him up to the crest of Ornito. Sergeant Cooke was awarded the M.M. The enemy on Ornito were overrun, and soon jack-booted Germans with hands held high were bounding down the hill to "D" Company, who greeted them with derisive cheers. There was, however, a tragic finale to this spirited and gallant counter-attack. Major Job was reorganizing his company and the collection of prisoners when an unseen German N.C.O. got up from behind a rock and shot him dead from close range.

At dawn on 7th February the 5th Battalion repulsed another determined attack on Ornito, with considerable loss to the enemy and some to themselves, and that night, as part of a general attack by the 138th Brigade, they attacked the neighbouring mountain, Cerasola, which was still in enemy hands. The Battalion crossed the gully between the two mountains some way down from the crest and swept up the spur on the eastern side, while a company of the 2nd Battalion moved forward and took the lower end of the same spur. The operation was quick and went through without a hitch, and the Germans were driven off Cerasola, though not without casualties to the Battalion ; among them Lieutenant McKerrow, who was killed gallantly storming a pill-box on the crest of Cerasola.

The rest of the operation on the other hills around was not so successful, and the Hampshire men on Ornito and Cerasola had but little respite while they were there. An officer of the 5th Battalion described it all in a letter home :

"We have been fighting in the mountains at 2,000 ft. some considerable distance from any roads, where all supplies have to come as far as possible by mule and then on by porter. For some of the time we have had to exist without greatcoats, and blankets were never even considered although the temperature was quite low. It snowed and, the nights being quite cold, the endurance test alone was quite amazing. The Battalion have put up a truly wonderful show and praises have been showered on us from all directions. One of the finest days of my life, in spite of the hell around, was on our last day. We had been due for relief the night before but had to hold on. The picture was a horseshoe-shaped hill with the Battalion all around the heights about five hundred yards across the gap. The Bosche started shelling us during the night ; at 'Stand-to' at 0530 he began in earnest and from then until 1500 hours he shelled us with everything he had, finishing off with a terrific onslaught. In spite of our casualties our morale seemed to increase, and when the shelling ceased it was marvellous to see everyone move out of their little holes up on the crest to meet him as he attacked. On top of the hill fellows were shouting, 'Come on, you dirty Bosche bastards.' It was a truly wonderful sight, and a battle which should add more laurels to the Regiment's name."

The 5th Battalion were relieved in their positions on Cerasola by the Welsh Guards on 10th February. They were shelled during the relief, and the Guards, who had many more men in their companies, were too many to take cover in the few sangars and suffered immediate casualties. "C" Company were hit by heavy shells on their way out, and suffered casualties, including Lieutenant Relph killed and Major MacBeath, the Company Commander, seriously wounded. Thus ended the grim battles of the 5th Battalion on Mounts Ornito and Cerasola. The Battalion concentrated on Valle di Sujo and moved back the next day, crossed the Garigliano by Pateley Bridge and marched back up the rough track to the road at Vandria before being picked up by transport to take them for a few days' rest at Campo, behind the Camino massif.

Colonel Robinson, who was awarded a bar to his D.S.O. for the operation, received this letter from General R. L. McCreery, commanding X Corps :

Personal 12 *Feb* 44

DEAR ROBINSON,

I want to congratulate you and your Battalion on the very fine performance you all achieved in the Ornito operations. All ranks displayed fine fighting qualities and great toughness and endurance. Well done all of you. The Battalion has every right to be proud of itself.

You captured and held those most important features and defeated many counter-attacks. I was up close to Cerasola yesterday and fully realize the difficulties of holding that feature, the bare rocky knobs and very difficult approaches. The enemy's persistent counter-attacks show what importance he attaches to that area. You have inflicted heavy losses on the enemy, and have seen him right off.

For the moment at any rate, he has had enough, and yesterday up there it was very quiet. Your take-over originally, at night, and in such an indefinite and uncertain situation, was in itself a great feat, and shows a very high standard of leadership and initiative on the parts of all concerned.

Again my heartiest congratulations.

All good luck for future successes.

Yours sincerely,
R. L. MCCREERY
(*Lieut.-General.*)

Another exceedingly well-merited award at this time was the M.C. won by Major P. R. Sawyer, who had served with the 5th Battalion since it landed in North Africa. He led the leading company of the Battalion forward in the dark across unreconnoitred ground and took over a position successfully in close contact with the enemy. Throughout the next few days Major Sawyer led his company against constant counter-attacks with great determination and coolness. It was this officer who had been mainly responsible for re-forming the Battalion at Salerno after the confused fighting on the beach, and it was he again who organized the defence and rallied the men after the tragic affair in Hampshire Lane.

On 17th February the 128th Brigade moved up again to be ready to take over the bitterly disputed and inhospitable mountains from the 1st Guards Brigade on the 20th. They were holding Ornito and Cerasola against almost constant counter-attacks, and directly they moved up the 1/4th received a message from Brigade that the Coldstream were in serious trouble on Ornito and wanted one company to go to their immediate assistance. Persistent enemy shelling and probing infantry attacks had taken their toll of this hard-pressed battalion on Ornito, and the Germans were now believed to have broken into their positions. Colonel Chandler chose "D" Company, commanded by Major Perkins, and as darkness fell the Company moved forward on foot towards Ornito.

Lieutenant-Colonel Norman, commanding the 2nd Coldstream, put "D" Company on the extreme right of his battalion's sector, withdrawing his right-hand company for what proved to be a successful counter-attack early the next morning. All through the 18th the enemy saturated Ornito with artillery and mortar fire; the 2nd Coldstream, with "D" Company of the 1/4th, were pinned to their stone sangars. For the second night in succession there was no sleep for anyone, and ration parties were unable to get up; the battalion was isolated.

An hour before first light on the 19th the shelling increased and was immediately succeeded by a determined infantry attack. The exact strength of the enemy was never established, but elements of the 1st, 2nd, and 3rd battalions of 155 Panzer Grenadier Regiment were identified. The enemy's aim was to drive a wedge between the Coldstream on Ornito and the Welsh Guards on Cerasola, away on the right. It thus fell out that almost the entire weight of the attack fell on "D" Company of the 1/4th Battalion. Large numbers of the enemy gained the crest of Ornito, but were held up at point-blank range by the determined opposition of the forward platoon, commanded by Sergeant Scott. As the early morning mist lifted, the Welsh Guards on Cerasola were able to bring fire to bear on the forward slopes of Ornito. Caught between this fire and the determined stand of the Hampshire company, the enemy collected for a final assault. "D" Company's position was critical; they were outnumbered four to one and the enemy were less than thirty yards from the forward platoons. But Captain Spencer Killick saved the situation. He was company second-in-command and he had joined the Battalion from the 11th

King's Royal Rifles only a few days before. Captain Killick led the reserve platoon with bayonets fixed straight into the enemy.

Suddenly the battle was over ; the Germans laid down their arms to a man. "D" Company took one hundred and ten prisoners, and as many again had been killed. Out of a total strength of three officers and sixty, "D" Company lost five killed and thirty-two wounded, including Captain Killick. This gallant officer was awarded the M.C., and Sergeant E. Scott and Private E. J. Smith, a stretcher-bearer, received the M.M.

On 20th February the 128th Brigade relieved the Guards Brigade. The York and Lancasters, with 128th Brigade for the time being in place of the 5th who were still with 138th Brigade, took over the position on Cerasola ; the 2nd Hampshire went on to Ornito and the 1/4th took over Tuga. The enemy became quieter, though there were occasional raids and sporadic bursts of vicious shelling. But neither side was in a position to undertake any further large-scale attacks ; a condition of dour stalemate ensued with both sides constantly on the alert. The troops settled down to suffer the hardships of a bad winter in most uncomfortable positions. Relief came at last for the 128th Brigade on 28th February, when their sector was taken over by the 10th Brigade, 4th Division. From their mountain outposts the Hampshire Brigade, with the 5th Battalion now returned to the fold, spent a final week in the line above Sujo overlooking Castelforte. It was fairly quiet, but all ranks were on tenterhooks, knowing that long relief was due, and enemy patrols caused some concern, as did the "S" mines with which the orange groves were heavily sown, and caught the inevitable wanderers.

Throughout the campaign the Division had been supported by the Desert Air Force, and the troops had often seen their planes but only very rarely the pilots. This was put right at Sujo when a party of pilots made the difficult journey up to the line to visit the 128th Brigade and, as far as conditions would permit, a very gay party ensued.

At last a brigade of the 4th Division moved up to the Suja position and 128th Brigade moved out, while a thousand-bomber raid on Cassino provided an appropriate parting salute to the men who had fought up Italy the hard way since landing at Salerno nearly six months before. At last 46th Division was to have a long rest, to re-equip and re-train. They were brought back to take part in Operation "Pitchfork," surely the most popular operation in that theatre of war to date. They moved back to Naples and on 16th March sailed for the Middle East, and by way of a final salute Vesuvius erupted. For five months they were to be away from battle with the Germans, and away from Italy. There was to be thorough reorganization and hard, continuous training in Palestine and Syria. But first there was leave in Egypt, a holiday which was surely most thoroughly deserved.

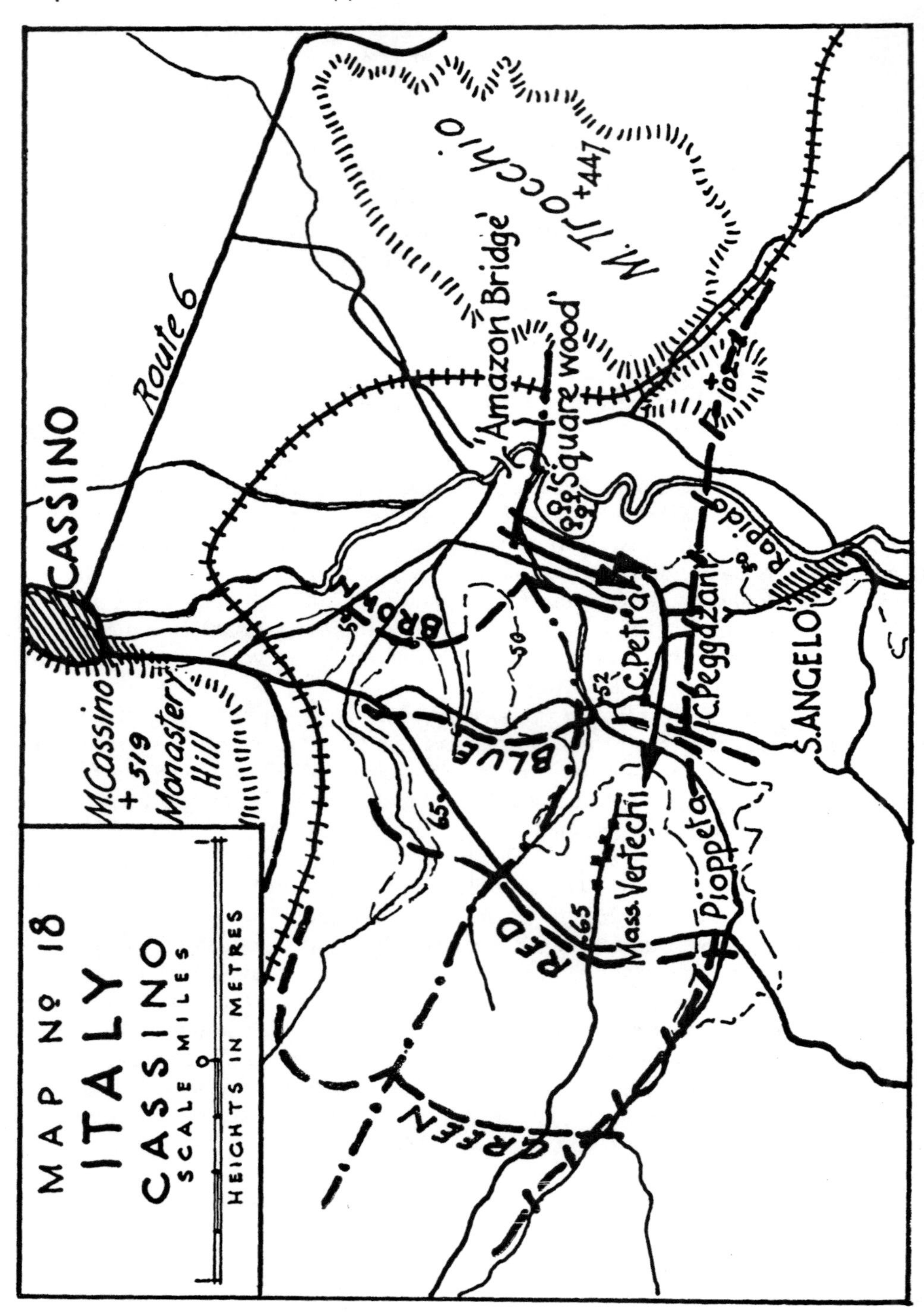

MAP No 18
ITALY
CASSINO
SCALE MILES
HEIGHTS IN METRES
CASSINO
Route 6
M.Cassino
+519
Monastery Hill
'Amazon Bridge'
'Square wood'
M.Trocchio
+447
Rapido
S.ANGELO
C.Petra
Mass. Vertechi
Pioppeta
BROWN
BLUE
RED
GREEN

CHAPTER XIV

THE 2/4TH BATTALION IN ITALY

1944–1945

The Garigliano

(*See maps on pages* 152 *and* 156)

When Lieutenant-Colonel J. P. Fowler-Esson won his determined struggle and saved the 2/4th Battalion from immolation as base troops, it was quickly reorganized and went at once into hard training. In February, 1944, the Battalion was posted to the 4th British Division, which had just landed at Naples after fighting with distinction in North Africa. A few weeks later the Battalion completed the 28th Infantry Brigade with the 2nd King's and the 2nd Somerset Light Infantry. Colonel Fowler-Esson had Major F. Mitchell as his Second-in-Command, and the Company Commanders were Majors G. E. Morgan, G. B. Blaker, W. C. T. N. Way and E. C. Henley, and Captains G. D. Knight and K. R. McK. Biggs. The Adjutant was Captain T. G. Harrison.

The Battalion went into the line on 29th February as the vanguard of the 4th Division in defensive positions along the Garigliano, opposite San Ambrogio. This was, of course, the very country in which the 128th Brigade had served through the rigours of the Italian winter, and, indeed, the 4th Division's first assignment in Italy was to relieve 46th Division at the Garigliano bridgehead. Thus it was that the 2/4th Battalion took up the way of life under which their comrades of the other Hampshire battalions had lived for so many weary weeks.

As before, all roads to the rear areas from the Battalion's positions were under constant observation by the enemy, and all supplies had to be transported at night under mortar and machine-gun fire and over difficult mountain tracks. Apart from troublesome enemy shelling, however, and one German fighting patrol, the enemy were fairly quiet and the Battalion's activity was limited to patrolling and mortaring programmes. The Battalion was relieved after ten days in the line and went back to San Martino, with the exception of "C" Company, which, as "Wayforce" under command of Major Way, went to positions beside the Guards across the Garigliano to the west. After two days "Wayforce" was relieved by "A" Company as "Morganforce."

On 17th March "A" Company rejoined the Battalion, which returned to the line to relieve the 6th Black Watch on Mount Ornito. Living on the inhospitable bare mountain was as trying as it had been for the 5th Battalion. The enemy was moderately quiet, however, but the weather continued unkind. On 18th March the enemy fired propaganda leaflets over the area, with the text taken from the Prime Minister's famous speech, "I have nothing to offer you but blood and tears."

On Mount Ornito there were occasional exchanges of rifle and machine-gun fire, but the main activity was limited to patrolling. One of the patrols went out as a direct result of a Company Commander's vigilance. Captain Knight was searching the ground with binoculars when he noticed the sun glinting on what seemed to be empty food tins thrown down by the enemy. Accordingly Lieutenant Bichard took out a patrol to confirm this position, and to inflict casualties. The patrol crept to within a few feet of the enemy post, spotted several Germans, grenaded and fired on them and returned unscathed.

During the period 19th to 24th March the Battalion had a secondary role, in conjunction with the New Zealand Corps' Operation "Spadger." This role would have sent the Battalion forward to occupy enemy positions on Mount Faito should he withdraw. In fact he maintained his positions and the Battalion was not called upon to undertake this task.

After a week on Ornito the Battalion was relieved by a French unit and moved back to the Tuga–Turlito area, and on 28th March went back to billets for a few days' rest and administration. This was followed by a strenuous training programme with particular emphasis on river crossing, in preparation for the general Allied advance against the Gustav Line, which was dominated by Monte Cassino. The Battalion was in the line again on 6th April, once more in a mountain position on the Belvedere feature above Cassino. The Battalion's position was overlooked by the enemy on six-thousand-foot Mount Cairo, and once again all supplying and movement had to be made in darkness. The Battalion were in this position for two weeks, under incessant mortar and shell fire. Patrols were active on both sides and there were numerous engagements. On one occasion an enemy patrol, using flame-throwers, automatic weapons and grenades, overran a platoon position, and the platoon commander, Lieutenant Clulow, and six men were wounded and seventeen were taken prisoner. The position was reoccupied, however, after a local counter-attack. Shortly after this incident "C" Company sent out an officer patrol with orders to capture a prisoner. It so happened that while the patrol was out an enemy patrol raided "C" Company's positions, and both patrols had arranged the same signal to call for defensive fire. This caused considerable confusion, as may well be imagined, and "C" Company's patrol had to run the gauntlet of two barrages to get back to its own lines.

After being relieved on the Belvedere feature, the Battalion underwent a further week's strenuous training, including more river crossings, night exercises, and training with tank co-operation, and drafts of reinforcements were received. On 5th May the Battalion returned to the line again, just south of Cassino, along the line of the River Rapido. The positions were overlooked by the enemy on Monastery Hill, and a continuous smoke screen was laid by a 25-pounder battery through the hours of daylight. The Battalion F.D.Ls. were about a thousand yards from the river itself. The enemy were well dug in in long-prepared positions, with their forward posts about five hundred yards from the far bank of the river. The weather was at last improving and everyone knew that the general attack on the Gustav Line and Mount Cassino was about to begin. This attack, the prelude to the great battle for Rome, was launched in the early hours of 12th May.

The outline of the plan for the crossing of the River Rapido and the capture of Cassino, as far as it concerned the 28th Brigade, was to force two crossings over the river and then to capture a succession of four report lines. These objectives were Brown Line, about a thousand yards beyond and parallel with the river, Blue Line, 1,000 to 1,500 yards farther on, Red Line, which was a bulge nearly 2,000 yards deep, and finally Green Line, some 1,500 yards farther on still. This last objective extended into a deep salient on the right and pointed towards the back of Monte Cassino. The river crossings were to be made by the 2nd King's and the 2nd Somerset L.I., who were then to continue to capture Brown Line and Blue Line. When this was done the 2/4th Hampshire were to pass through and capture Red and Green Lines. "D" Company was to act as ferry company for the Brigade.

The attack was timed to begin at eleven o'clock on the night of 11th May, half an hour before moonrise. At eleven o'clock the massed guns of Eighth Army opened fire along a front of many miles with the biggest barrage yet known. The whole horizon seemed to burst into flame. The noise was terrific and echoed and re-echoed against the mountain-sides. The sky was full of noise and the infantry waiting on the banks of the river heard the shells tearing the sky far above them and crashing down into the enemy positions.

Early on the night of the assault, "D" Company manned the control post, check points and launching points on the river. The river was about eighty feet wide, deep, and flowing at about seven knots. The enemy seemed well prepared and from the outset of the operation his fire tasks were brought to bear on the river, and "D" Company consequently bore the brunt of this shelling. A further complication arose through the assault troops of the 2nd King's arriving some thirty-five minutes late at the rendezvous. Some boats were swept away in the swift current and others received direct hits. It was a problem to know how to control the assault boats in the swift current and it was decided to ferry the boats both ways by line. The initial line was taken across by strong swimmers who volunteered from "D" Company, but the current was such that the strongest of them were carried fifty yards down-stream while making the journey across. Private Grainger swam the river three times with ropes to tow the assault boats over. Between these ventures he stood naked on the bank of the river for some four hours under intense fire guiding the assault troops into their boats. This very brave soldier was killed the next day. He had been awarded the B.E.M. for rescuing a man from drowning at Salerno. During these most difficult hours "D" Company suffered twenty-six casualties and "C" was sent down to the river to assist them. While the Company Commanders were discussing the situation, the control point in which they were gathered received a direct hit and Major Henley, Major Way and three other ranks were killed.

In spite, however, of the storm of fire from machine guns, mortars and artillery directed on both banks and along the approaches to the launching points, two companies of the King's were slowly ferried across. The bravery and daring of the men at the river were beyond praise. The Padre of the Hampshire, Captain Edwards, swam across the fast-flowing river several times during the night to succour the wounded. The troops who did manage to get across the river could make no progress and they were pinned down by the strong system of enemy posts.

By daybreak the enemy had been dislodged from none of his positions. Valiant efforts had been made by two light bridging detachments from "A" Company, under Captain Meakins, to construct rafts for ferrying carriers and anti-tank guns, but these had to be abandoned owing to the intensity of the enemy fire. It was quite impossible to continue the ferrying operations in daylight, and the Brigadier ordered the withdrawal of "D" Company, and others at the river and, together with the Sappers who had been working most gallantly under fire building Amazon, Blackwater and Congo bridges, they went back to cover.

The collection of the wounded presented a serious problem in the area of the river bank, which was constantly under very heavy fire, and there were many heroic incidents bringing the wounded in. On one occasion a jeep drove openly along the approach track down to the river and halted only when machine-gun bullets began to kick up the dust around its wheels. Captain Edwards got out, leisurely raised the Red Cross flag and unloaded dressings and a stretcher, and with the help of a stretcher-bearer he began carrying back wounded men, cheerfully disregarding the enemy's fire.

The Battle for Cassino

(*See map on page* 164)

The battalions in the bridgehead spent nearly the whole of 12th May pinned down, deafened by the constant explosion of shells and mortar bombs and by very heavy machine-gun fire. During the day it was decided that the Hampshire battalion should come under command 12th Infantry Brigade and cross the river farther up-stream by way of Amazon bridge, which had been completed after an epic night's work by the Sappers. Accordingly at three o'clock in the morning of 13th May the Battalion began to move to its new start point. The crossing was to have been made at 6.45 a.m., but owing to delays by other units they did not start until 1.30 in the afternoon. The area in which they had had to wait was under intense fire and there were some casualties.

The Battalion advanced over Amazon bridge in brilliant sunshine, but in spite of the heavy enemy barrage the casualties were light. Three hundred yards across the river the Battalion found what cover it could in shell holes and small ditches while Colonel Fowler-Esson co-ordinated his plan with O.C. Troop, 17th/21st Lancers (with Sherman tanks), and with the Gunners. The plan was for the Battalion to wheel left along the river and then to proceed towards the original objectives. Zero hour for the advance was 2.30 p.m., preceded by a fifteen-minute artillery concentration on the first objective. As the Battalion waited in the scanty cover they were under constant H.E. fire, but spirits were high. The company commanders disregarded the enemy fire and walked round encouraging their men.

At 2.30 on the afternoon of 13th May the 2/4th Battalion was ordered to advance. The companies stood up, formed into extended line, and with fixed bayonets walked grimly forward beside the river, accompanied by the Sherman tanks of the 17th/21st Lancers. At once enemy machine guns in "Square Wood" opened fire ; the tanks swung their guns round and roared in reply, and then 8 Platoon, under Lieutenant Bowers, stormed into the wood, overwhelmed the enemy and came out with seventy-three prisoners. The Battalion crossed the River Pioppeta, but the tanks were unable to cross at once as the route was blocked by an A.F.V. carrying bridging equipment. The Battalion, however, waded the river and continued the advance under covering fire from the tanks. The enemy were nonplussed by this flank attack, and daunted by the resolute advance ; finding themselves between the Hampshire Battalion and the river, they began to surrender. Soon long lines of Germans were seen doubling towards the Battalion with arms raised. The prisoners were quickly passed back, and "A" and "C" Companies on the left continued to move along the line of the river, systematically dealing with all enemy resistance, while "B" and "D" Companies on the right worked away from the river and soon began to meet stronger opposition. But they continued to press forward relentlessly, mopping up as they went.

"B" and "D" advanced up the slope beyond the Pioppeta and, having topped the ridge which had been their original objective, they pressed on. Captain Wakeford, accompanied only by an orderly and armed only with an automatic pistol, was leading "B" Company on the right. He reached the objective first, killed a number of Germans, and when his company caught up with him he handed over no fewer than twenty prisoners.

The success of the Battalion was such that there was no stopping them, and Colonel Fowler-Esson, who was with the leading companies throughout, kept them going. A strong-point in a house in the line of advance was vigorously defended, but Captain Wakeford once more led "B" Company in the assault with grenades and tommy-guns. Captain Wakeford was himself twice driven back by grenades, but with a final rush he reached a window and flung in grenades. Five Germans surrendered at once ; a sixth came out as though to surrender and suddenly shot one of "B" Company. He was immediately disposed of.

By five o'clock in the afternoon the companies had taken up positions well beyond their objectives on Brown Line. The whole operation was a fine example of a "set-piece" attack, with infantry, tanks and artillery co-operating to the finest degree. It was like a model exercise at a battle school. At the cost of comparatively slight casualties, the Battalion had cleared Brown Line across the whole front of 28th Brigade's sector and beyond. The Battalion were in the highest spirits ; they had taken some two hundred prisoners and the battlefield was scattered with German corpses. Thus ended the first phase of the attack on the Gustav Line. There had been one tragic incident when the

R.A.P. following up the advance set off an A.P. mine, and one stretcher-bearer was killed and the M.O. was so badly wounded that he died after evacuation. There were many casualties in the party.

It took the enemy some little time to get over the shock of this most successful operation, but before long the company positions came under concentrated shell fire, but fortunately casualties were only slight. The next task for the Battalion was to advance to Blue Line, a thousand yards to the west. This began at 2.45 on the morning of 14th May, a silent attack without any barrage. The Battalion advanced in extended order, keeping direction by compass and with tracer bullets to guide them along their general axis of advance. A combination of mist and cordite fumes made visibility poor, but the advance was admirably maintained and the companies made such steady progress that by seven o'clock all objectives had been reached with but little opposition. The enemy had, it appeared, straightened out his line because of a thrust that seemed to be developing on the right from the Royal Fusiliers and the Black Watch. There was confused fighting on either flank, but it did not develop on the Battalion's front, though one flanking company assisted with machine-gun fire. By midday all fighting on the battalion front had died down except for exchanges of mortar fire. By this stage of the operation the Battalion's casualties were some fifty killed, wounded and missing.

For the third phase of the attack, which was to take the Battalion to Red Line, it returned from the command of the 12th to the 28th Brigade. Their position at the end of the second phase was along the track between the Casa Petra on the right and the Casa Pagezzani on the left. In front of them an easy slope descended to the Pioppeta three hundred yards away, and five hundred yards beyond the ground rose to their objective, Massa Vertechi.

At a quarter to six on the evening of 14th May the barrage opened up, and at six o'clock the companies moved forward down the slope towards the river. The pioneers rushed down a carrier loaded with light bridging equipment, in an attempt to build a tank crossing, but the bridge sank in the soft mud beside the river so that the tanks were unable to cross. The companies advancing down the slope ran into very heavy defensive fire and lost more than a hundred men in two minutes, and as a result the attack began to lose its momentum. Then Colonel Fowler-Esson got out of the tank from which he was directing the battle, and, with Major Mitchell and R.S.M. Newsom, rallied the companies and led them forward across the stream in the teeth of fierce fire. The enemy were bringing down everything they had on the advancing troops and casualties were very heavy, including both Captain Dent, commanding "D" Company, and the Adjutant. But in spite of the inferno of fire, the advance was maintained up the slopes towards the objective.

It was at this point that Captain Wakeford came so splendidly to the fore. He was already wounded in the face and both arms, but he led "B" Company up the slope on the left of the Battalion, keeping them under perfect control through the withering fire. Half-way up the hill his company came under heavy Spandau fire ; Captain Wakeford organized and led a party which charged

CAPTAIN R. WAKEFORD, V.C.

Face page 170

and silenced the machine guns. As the company advanced again mortar bombs were bursting among the men and Captain Wakeford was wounded in both legs. But he still led on, reached the objective, organized and consolidated the remainder of his company, and reported to his Commanding Officer before submitting to any personal attention. For his extreme gallantry Captain Wakeford was awarded the Victoria Cross, and the citation ends with these words : "During the seven-hour interval before stretcher-bearers could reach him his unwavering high spirits encouraged the wounded men around him. His selfless devotion to duty, leadership, determination, courage and disregard for his own serious injuries were beyond all praise."

Captain Wakeford's batman, Private J. C. Baxter, also fought with conspicuous gallantry. In the last desperate advance up the hill, when N.C.Os. were falling, Private Baxter rallied a group of leaderless men round him and gathered up a small force of Bren gunners. He kept them together and urged them on, led them on to their objective and allotted their positions. When the enemy began to shell and mortar the area violently, he organized stretcher parties to carry away the wounded. Private Baxter was awarded the M.M.

There was indeed much gallantry on that day. Another Military Medal was won by C.S.M. Pullinger. In the final advance up the bullet-swept hillside, through exploding shells and mortar fire, C.S.M. Pullinger was a man inspired. He moved from platoon to platoon of his company, rallying the men, encouraging those who were bewildered by the fury of the opposition, himself quite careless of death and undaunted. When the hill-crest was reached the sergeant-major moved calmly from position to position, making sure that the men were digging in correctly, and only when the position was properly consolidated did he take cover himself. It was a notable example of the standards tradition has set for the British warrant officer.

The Battalion's objective was secured by 6.30, but the Battalion itself was sadly depleted. A composite company was formed from the remnants of "B" and "C" Companies. Platoons which had surged beyond the objective were withdrawn to make a firmer base. Three tanks which had managed to cross the river were brought up to make the position more secure. The casualties suffered by the 2/4th Battalion in this attack totalled one hundred and fifty killed and wounded. The night passed uneventfully, but the Battalion was shelled on the 15th and Colonel Fowler-Esson, who had led his Battalion so successfully in this very gallant operation, was wounded in the thigh. Major Mitchell, the Second-in-Command, assumed command of the Battalion and was confirmed in the appointment with the rank of Lieutenant-Colonel immediately afterwards.

In the early hours of 16th May the Battalion was withdrawn from its position and went back to a rest area. Thus ended the share of the 2/4th Hampshire Battalion in the Battle of Cassino, which was captured two days later by the Poles, and the gateway to Rome was forced open. The Commander, 28th Infantry Brigade, sent this letter to the Commanding Officer, the 2/4th Hampshire :

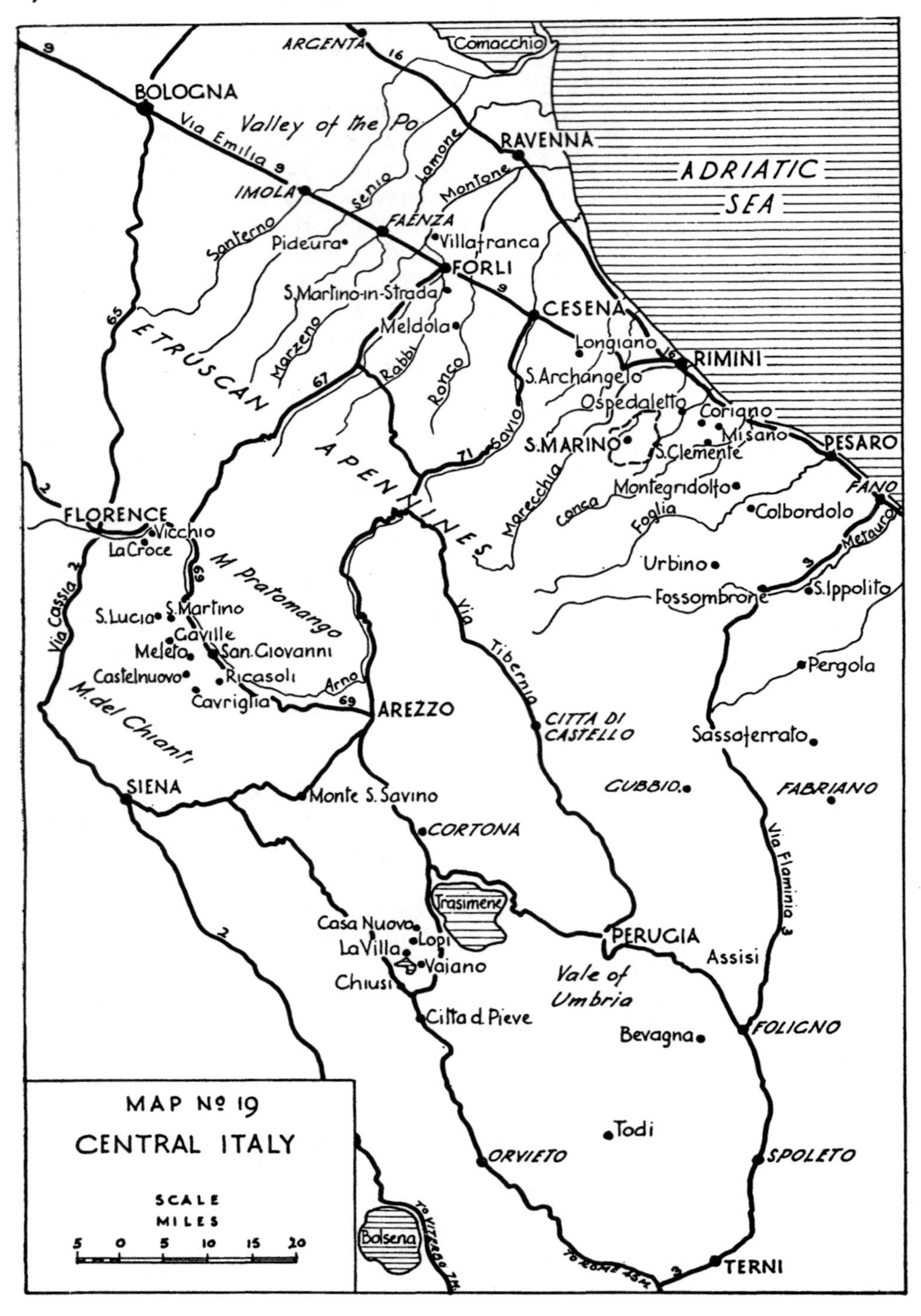
MAP No 19
CENTRAL ITALY
SCALE
MILES
5 0 5 10 15 20
ARGENTA
Comacchio
BOLOGNA
Via Emilia 9
Valley of the Po
RAVENNA
ADRIATIC
SEA
IMOLA
Senio
Lamone
Montone
Santerno
FAENZA
Pideura
Villafranca
FORLI
S. Martino-in-Strada
CESENA
Meldola
Longiano
RIMINI
ETRUSCAN
Marzeno
Rabbi
Ronco
S. Archangelo
Ospedaletto
Coriano
Misano
S. MARINO
S. Clemente
PESARO
APENNINES
Savio
Montegridolfo
FANO
Colbordolo
Marecchia
Conca
Foglia
Metauro
FLORENCE
Vicchio
La Croce
M Pratomango
Urbino
S. Ippolito
Fossombrone
Via Cassia 2
S. Lucia
S. Martino
Gaville
Meleto
San Giovanni
Castelnuovo
Ricasoli
Cavriglia
Arno
AREZZO
Via Tiberina
Pergola
CITTA DI CASTELLO
Sassoferrato
M. del Chianti
SIENA
Monte S. Savino
GUBBIO
FABRIANO
CORTONA
Via Flaminia 3
Trasimene
Casa Nuova
Lopi
La Villa
Vaiano
Chiusi
PERUGIA
Assisi
Vale of Umbria
Citta d. Pieve
FOLIGNO
Bevagna
Todi
ORVIETO
SPOLETO
Bolsena
To VITERBO 7M.
To ROME 45M.
TERNI

"I congratulate your Battalion on their extremely gallant performance during the battle. They had a really tough task, but at no time did they waver in their determination to carry it through.

"Their brave action, I fear, cost lives, but to gain supremacy of the river was essential to the whole battle, and this they achieved. Next time, with their great fighting spirit and the experience they have gained, there will be no limits to their success.

"Please thank them all for their gallant work."

The casualties suffered by the Battalion in this great battle were four officers killed—Major Henley, Major Way, Captain Jones (R.A.M.C.), and Lieutenant Mott—and eighteen other ranks; nine officers and one hundred and fifty-two other ranks were wounded. Fortunately, reinforcements of three officers and ninety-nine other ranks reached the Battalion the day after the battle. The following awards were won : V.C., Captain R. Wakeford ; D.S.O., Lieutenant-Colonel J. P. Fowler-Esson, Lieutenant J. H. Bowers, and Captain (C.F.) the Rev. R. Edwards ; M.C., Major F. Mitchell, Major R. H. Stevens, Lieutenant J. M. Godbold (U.D.F.), Lieutenant J. S. Rorich (U.D.F.), Lieutenant B. D. Fick, R.S.M. F. G. Newsom, and C.S.M. R. Bell, D.C.M. ; M.M., C.S.M. W. M. Pullinger, Corporal M. Harman, Lance-Corporal R. Hall, Privates R. V. Earl, E. J. Peters, J. C. Baxter, W. Lias and Signaller E. Shackleton (Cheshire Yeomanry, Royal Signals).

Vaiano, La Villa and Lopi

The Battalion spent nearly three weeks behind the line at Piedimonte d'Alife, where, after a short rest, a vigorous training programme was undertaken. Meanwhile heartening news came of the pursuit of the Germans as they fell back in confusion behind the broken Hitler Line towards Rome. On 5th June came the great news of the fall of Rome, and on the next day of the invasion of Normandy. They were great days, and the 2/4th Battalion, which had every reason to feel proud of its record in Italy, looked forward to the campaign to come, for it seemed the tide had definitely turned.

It was on 5th June that the Battalion was on the move again, refreshed by its three weeks of breathing-space, and went to a divisional concentration area near Ceprano, in the Liri valley, sixteen miles beyond Cassino. For the next two weeks the Battalion moved steadily northwards, for the 4th Division was following up behind XIII Corps, which was leading the pursuit of the enemy in Eighth Army's sector. It was a leisurely move, with opportunities for training and trips to Rome. The Division passed Rome some fifteen miles to the east, and through Palombara and on beyond Viterbo, fifty miles north-west of Rome. Then it was that the Germans made their first firm stand since the Hitler Line had crumbled after the fall of Cassino, and on 22nd June the 2/4th Battalion was called upon to go into action again.

The enemy were standing on a line which ran through Lake Trasimene, and 28th Brigade Group moved to a forward concentration area north of Citta di Pieve. All three battalions of the 28th Infantry Brigade were in action, the Somerset L.I. on the right, the Hampshire in the centre and the King's on the left. The 2/4th Battalion relieved the 8th A. and S. Highlanders south of Vaiano and was in position at midnight on 22nd June. For the next two days fighting patrols were sent forward to probe the situation and disposition of the enemy, and there were several clashes.

Early in the morning of 24th June a major attack was launched by the 78th and 4th Divisions. In this attack the Somerset L.I. were supported by fire from the 2/4th Hampshire Battalion, which was to follow up to attack Vaiano. The preliminary attack, however, did not go as well as expected and plans had to be changed, so that it was not until the morning of 25th June that the Battalion was ordered forward into Vaiano, which was entered and occupied without opposition. The Battalion then moved on towards La Villa, a village two miles to the north-west. They came upon machine-gun fire from a hill on the left, but Colonel Mitchell sent "D" Company with some Canadian tanks to clear it, and the hill was captured.

The next objective was a ridge running east from La Villa, and this was attacked with "C" and "D" Companies leading, with one troop of tanks, followed by "A" and "B," while the remainder of the squadron of tanks gave supporting fire from Vaiano. The enemy resisted the attack with furious machine-gun fire, and violently shelled and mortared Vaiano, where Battalion Headquarters had been set up. Both General Ward, the Divisional Commander, and Brigadier Montagu-Douglas-Scott, in a visit to the Battalion, were slightly wounded.

"A" and "C" Companies, on the right and in the centre, reached the ridge, but there was still resistance on the left. A platoon of "C" Company, sent to make a flanking attack on this position, was pinned down by machine-gun fire and lost many men, including Lieutenant Lewis, who was killed. A short but violent battle developed, but gradually opposition was overcome. In the evening the houses which "C" Company had occupied were counter-attacked by a party of some forty Germans, who were driven off after a sharp battle, during which Major Morgan, commanding "S" Company, did particularly good work with a Bren gun.

At eleven o'clock that night, as the Battalion battle patrol was going out through "C" Company's positions, German infantry crept up through the deep corn and attacked with great ferocity. The enemy opened up on the patrol with heavy machine guns and inflicted casualties, including Lieutenant W. Brown, M.M., who was killed. The farmhouse in which Company Headquarters was established was smashed in by bazooka shells and overrun by the enemy. The fighting was close and confused and ammunition began to run low. "C" Company fought back furiously, throwing grenades and firing all their weapons at the enemy, who, however, gradually worked their way round the house so that "C" Company was forced to evacuate it. They retired about thirty yards to positions in a ditch and fought back from there. Stretcher-bearers went forward under fire and brought back wounded from the perimeter of the house.

At 1.45 in the morning Captain Bichard gathered up his diminished company and launched a counter-attack, and by three in the morning he had brought his company back to its original position. Captain Bichard was the only officer left as all his platoon commanders had been hit during the day's fighting.

At dawn the next day, 26th June, patrols found La Villa empty of the enemy and the Battalion occupied the village and then advanced against only slight resistance a thousand yards farther to the neighbourhood of Lopi. From this point the 2nd King's passed through and the Battalion was withdrawn to a concentration area. In the fighting for Vaiano, La Villa and Lopi, which was against the German 1st Parachute Division, the 2/4th Battalion lost two officers killed and four wounded, and eighteen other ranks killed, sixty-four wounded and fourteen missing. Lieutenant-Colonel Mitchell was wounded in the fighting on 25th June, and the Battalion was commanded by Major Deedes for the following three weeks.

Pursuit to Meleto

In a little more than eight days the Division had fought its way through the strong German delaying divisions west of Lake Trasimene. There followed a swift pursuit which began in the first days of July as a running fight, as the Germans fell back for twenty-five miles as steadily as they could to the Arezzo Line. The Hampshire Battalion advanced rapidly from 1st to 10th July, encountering but little opposition beyond mortar and shell fire, and taking many prisoners, and so rapid was the advance that occasionally the troops rode on tanks ; not perhaps a comfortable mode of travel, but certainly preferable to marching in the dust and heat of July in Italy. The civilians *en route* received the advancing Allies enthusiastically. It seemed that the tide of battle was certainly turning at last. During this rapid advance there were some casualties, however, among them Major Blaker, who died of his wounds.

On the night of 10th July the Battalion was relieved and moved back to Badicorte, about seventeen miles east of Siena, and here Lieutenant-General Kirkman, commanding XIII Corps, decorated Captain Wakeford with the ribbon of the Victoria Cross on 14th July. Captain Wakeford had recently returned to the Battalion, having recovered from the wounds he received at Cassino. Forty representatives from each company attended the parade, and when the Corps Commander had inspected them he read the account of the action in which Captain Wakeford won the V.C.

The next day the Battalion moved up into the line again and continued the pursuit of the enemy. XIII Corps was advancing towards Florence along the valley of the Arno, with the wild mountains of the Pratomagno rising to more than five thousand feet above the river on the right, and the gentler slopes of the Monti del Chianti on the left. Progress was steady, with no more than minor engagements with light rear-guards. It was not until they were nearly half-way between Arezzo and Florence on Route 69, which follows the River Arno, that the Battalion saw action again. That was 21st July, when they cleared three miles of road of the enemy on the left of Route 69, westward from Ricasoli to Cavriglia, and went on to Castelnuovo di Sabbioni.

The next day the Battalion, with one squadron of the North Irish Horse, moved on from Castelnuovo towards Meleto, a mile and a half to the north-east and three miles west of San Giovanni on Route 69. Meleto stands in the centre of a ridge looking down on the wide shallow valley through which the Battalion had to approach. As soon as "C" Company, which was leading, was within range, machine guns all along the ridge opened fire. The company continued its advance in extended order across the bare slopes of the hills, until it came under heavy mortar fire and had to go to cover along the line of the Castelnuovo–Meleto road. When "D" Company had moved up to them, "C" Company continued its advance, in spite of continued casualties, and overran a strong enemy position below Meleto, inflicting heavy casualties and taking twenty-nine prisoners. The enemy at once counter-attacked, were driven off and counter-attacked again and again, but without success, and "C" and "D" Companies consolidated their positions ready to continue the assault of Meleto.

During this attack Private Churchill, though a small man and weighed down by a heavy Bren gun, was well up in the leading wave of the assault. When the enemy counter-attack came in it brought with it a machine gun which raked the Hampshire position from only a hundred yards away. Private Churchill crept to within thirty yards of the machine gun, then charged across the open firing his Bren gun from the hip. He silenced the gun and returned to his platoon leading four large Germans. For this spirited and gallant action Private Churchill was awarded the M.M.

The commander of 13 Platoon was wounded during the assault, and Sergeant John Savage took charge. He led the platoon with such fury up the steep hillside and through the fire of artillery and machine guns, that he overran the German defences, killing and capturing as he went. When he reached the crest he saw beyond it a Mark IV tank and an 88-mm. gun, and led his panting men on to capture both. By this time 13 Platoon and the platoon on its flank were reduced to ten men each and had no officer between them. Sergeant Savage reorganized the little force, consolidated on the ridge, and five minutes later he and his twenty men scattered twice their number of counter-attacking Germans. Sergeant Savage was later awarded the D.C.M.

Because of the strength of the enemy in Meleto and the very strong fire power from their machine-gun positions on the ridge, the attack on the village was postponed for the time being. The two companies held their positions under continued shelling and mortaring.

The next morning, 23rd July, it was found that the enemy had left Meleto and the King's passed through the 2/4th Battalion, which that same night was relieved by the Somerset L.I. In the fighting on 21st and 22nd July, the Battalion lost one officer, Lieutenant J. P. Merrett, and fifteen other ranks killed, Lieutenant R. M. Purnell and thirty-nine other ranks wounded, and two officers and two other ranks missing.

When the Battalion was relieved from its positions before Meleto it was taken back in transport to Monte San Sevino. Here it was announced that a very signal honour was to be paid to the Battalion. His Majesty The King was visiting it to confer the Victoria Cross on Captain Wakeford and on Fusilier Jefferson, of the Lancashire Fusiliers. At once everything possible was done to prepare for the great occasion, and when General Ward inspected the dress-rehearsal parade on 25th July the drill and turn-out were excellent, especially for troops just out of the line.

On 26th July the parade formed up to await the arrival of His Majesty. A dais had been erected and the Union flag flew side by side with the Battalion Colours. Captain Wakeford and Fusilier Jefferson stood before the dais and behind them the guard of honour, consisting of one hundred men under command of Major Stevens. The remainder of the Battalion was paraded in the rear in two blocks, the Guards band between them. His Majesty arrived at 9.15 and the very impressive ceremony of presenting the two Victoria Crosses was carried out, the turn-out and drill of the Battalion being faultless. The King, who was accompanied by General Alexander, inspected the guard of honour and spoke to many men. After the parade the troops lined the road as the King drove away.

Florence and Beyond

As was natural after so great an occasion, a celebration had been arranged for that evening, but it was not to be. During the day the Battalion moved back into the line, to Gaville, just north of Meleto, some fifteen miles from Florence. The British advance now ran through country completely dominated by the Chianti mountains, and although the enemy was retreating to his new Gothic Line behind Florence, he was retreating at his own speed and was always ready to give battle if he found he was being hurried. There was obviously some hard fighting ahead.

At dawn on 28th July the Battalion moved forward. As the leading company began to pass through the position held by the Somerset L.I., mortar bombs began to burst among them. The enemy fire was directed from Santa Lucia, a mile up the hillside. Colonel Mitchell sent "B" Company up to clear the hillock. The company was met by intense fire from mortar and machine guns and the Company Commander, Captain G. D. K. New, was killed, and the wrecking of the wireless set cut off the only means of communication with Battalion Headquarters. The company pressed on, now commanded by Lieutenant E. D. Evans, forced an enemy platoon back, and was only brought to a halt four hundred yards short of the objective. When Colonel Mitchell was at last able to get news of the company he sent "A" Company up, which worked round to the left of "B" Company and was closing in on the objective when machine guns suddenly opened up fiercely. "A" Company, however, broke through the defence and reached the hillock late in the afternoon, with the loss of only one man wounded.

"B" Company was reinforced by men from the carrier section and "D" Company and moved forward to cover the left flank of "A." From this position it was intended to send "D" Company against Santa Lucia itself, but this was

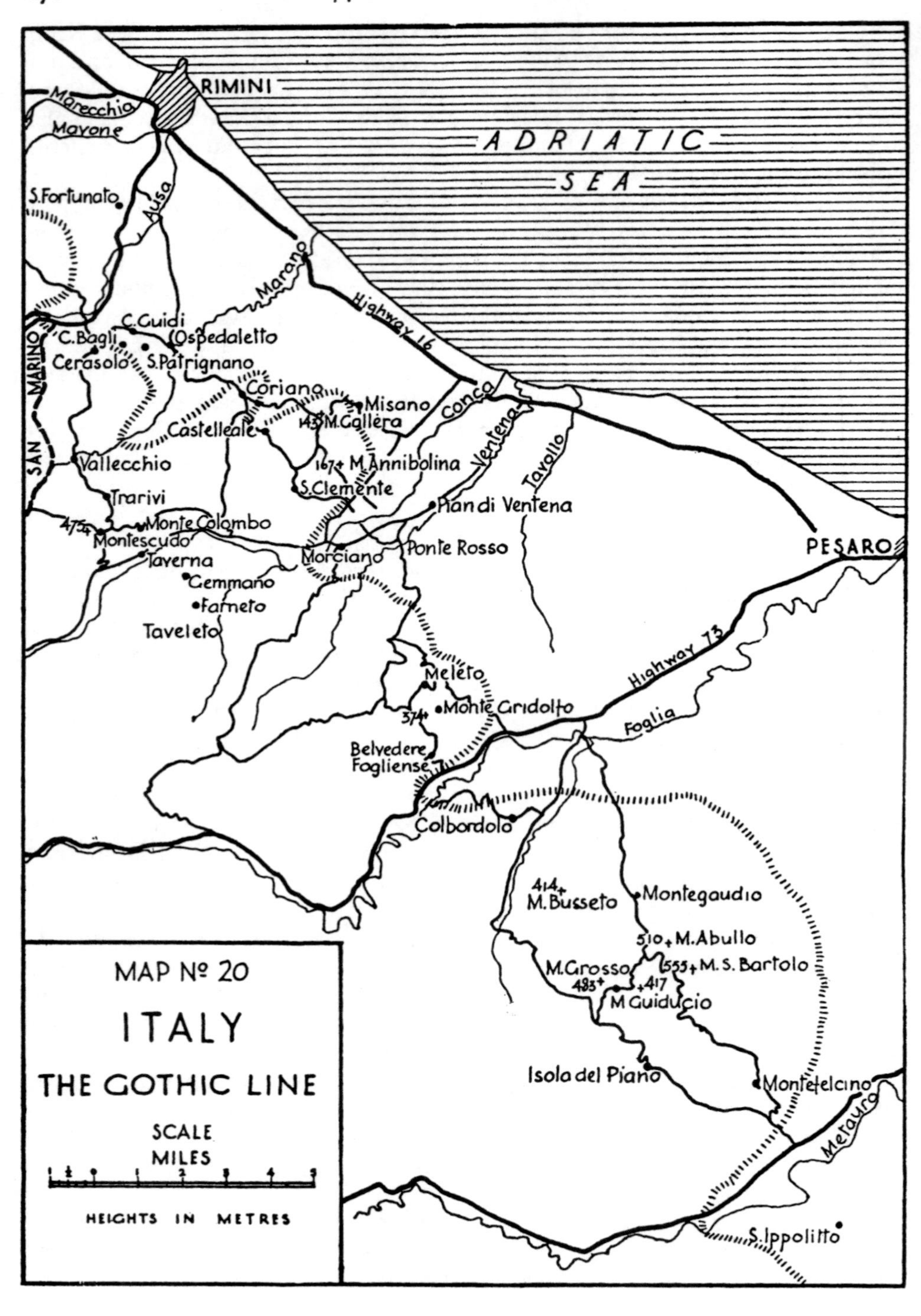

RIMINI
ADRIATIC
SEA
Marecchia
Mavone
S.Fortunato
Ausa
Marano
Highway 16
C.Guidi
C.Bagli
Ospedaletto
SAN MARINO
Cerasolo
S.Patrignano
Coriano
Misano
143 M.Gallera
Castelleale
Conca
Ventena
Tavollo
Vallecchio
167 M.Annibolina
S.Clemente
Trarivi
Pian di Ventena
475 Montescudo
Monte Colombo
Taverna
Morciano
Ponte Rosso
PESARO
Gemmano
Farneto
Taveleto
Highway 73
Meleto
374 Monte Gridolfo
Foglia
Belvedere Fogliense
Colbordolo
414 M.Busseto
Montegaudio
510 M.Abullo
M.Grosso
555 M.S.Bartolo
483 417 M Guiducio
Isola del Piano
Montefelcino
Metauro
S.Ippolitto
MAP No 20
ITALY
THE GOTHIC LINE
SCALE
MILES
HEIGHTS IN METRES

postponed until four o'clock in the morning of 30th July. The attack went in and after a brief but fierce engagement a footing was gained, and the position was taken by six o'clock in the morning and consolidated. Counter-attacks were expected, but none came during the day. In this action the Battalion lost one officer and eight other ranks killed, and forty-four other ranks wounded.

On 31st July it was found the enemy had withdrawn again, and at six o'clock that evening the Battalion marched forward to the Martino area, still on the left of Route 69, and continued to advance towards Florence. This march was very fatiguing ; it was extremely hot and the extensive demolitions in the coastal country made it difficult going. On 3rd August Florence itself could be seen quite plainly by the marching troops. Large and well-organized bands of Italian partisans had been met ; they were well armed and equipped with British equipment which had been dropped by parachute, and their leaders had most useful information. Partisans with a good knowledge of the area were sent to companies as guides. Everywhere there was a great welcome from the civilians. The march continued on 4th August, and fifteen miles over most difficult country were covered in two days with but little rest. In spite of this everyone was in the highest spirits. Florence, which had for so long been their objective, was in sight less than three miles away. It was disappointing, therefore, to find that the line of the Battalion's advance lay to the east of the city.

The advance continued northwards, to the very banks of the Arno as it turns west to enter Florence. La Croce and Vicchio were passed with but little opposition. But when "B" Company reached the river it sent back reports of enemy machine-gun fire from houses and slopes across the river. The Battalion consolidated short of the river, and on 5th August "B" Company repulsed a series of counter-attacks. The enemy followed this with so heavy a barrage that the company was withdrawn a few hundred yards to a less exposed position. For the next few days there was intermittent enemy activity and the Battalion had standing patrols in the forward positions and sent out fighting patrols, and artillery fire was exchanged. The next move was the crossing of the Arno, but it was not to be done by the 4th Division. On 10th August the British 1st Division came up and relieved the 4th, which went back for a period of well-deserved rest far to the south, to the Vale of Umbria.

The Battalion was relieved by the 2nd Foresters on 10th August, and with its Brigade went back to the divisional area near Assisi, where it was to spend the next month, the longest break since the Battalion had gone into action on the Garigliano seven months before.

The Gothic Line

During four weeks of August in the divisional concentration area near Assisi the Battalion trained hard, took in reinforcements, and repaired the ravages of the long campaign up to Florence. There was abundant entertainment, and leave to Rome, Terni and Lake Trasimene. All this came to an end in the first week of September. Eighth Army, after the fall of Florence, had switched to the Adriatic coast to assail the Gothic Line towards Rimini, and then to fight its way up the broad valley of the Po. Accordingly the Battalion left the divisional area at Assisi on 5th September for the line. The scenery was exceedingly beautiful but the weather quite dreadful, and torrential rain made many roads impassable, resulting in such serious traffic jams that all vehicles were ordered off the road on the night of 7th September. By 14th September the Battalion was in the line near Misano. The 28th Brigade was given the task of attacking across the River Marano and capturing the high ground to the west. The operation was to start at dawn on 15th September, with the 2/4th Hampshire on the left and the 2nd King's on the right. The plan for the Hampshire Battalion was to cross the river south of Ospedaletto and take San Patrignano, a cemetery beyond, Casa Guidi and Casa Bagli.

Companies moved off at eleven o'clock on the night of 14th September and after a most gruelling march over broken country desolated by war arrived in the assembly area at three in the morning. A lurid light flickered in the sky from houses the Germans had fired in their retreat, and the area was under shell fire. At 5.30 on the morning of 15th September "C" and "D" Companies crossed the start line, followed twenty minutes later by "A," with the task of passing through the other two companies and taking Casa Bagli. In spite of heavy shelling and Spandau fire as soon as the operation was discovered, all went smoothly. "D" took San Patrignano and some prisoners ; "C," temporarily held up by a tank, dealt with it and took their objective. "D" Company kept up the battalion record by capturing yet another tank complete with crew. Casualties were relatively light, but included two platoon commanders of "C" Company, Lieutenants Robins and Hart, who were both killed.

"C" and "D" Companies rapidly consolidated their positions, but they were hard pressed, beating off two strong counter-attacks. Eventually some Churchill tanks were got over the river and came up to support the companies. "A" Company was then able to pass through and captured Casa Bagli with more prisoners, bringing the total up to thirty-four. By half past eight in the morning all the objectives were taken and consolidated, and the 2nd King's, on the Battalion's right, had been equally successful. The companies held their positions throughout 16th September, under the most concentrated shelling they had ever experienced. Patrols were sent out and made contact with the enemy.

The next task for the Battalion was to attack Cerasolo, an operation of major importance as the feature enabled the enemy to dominate the left flank of the 1st Canadian Division, who were to make a major assault on San Fortunato. Accordingly "A" and "B" Companies formed up and crossed the start line at half past five in the morning of 17th September behind a very heavy barrage, in reply to which the enemy brought down a defensive artillery fire with *Nebelwerfers* and heavy machine-gun fire. Fortunately, however, most of this fell on the ridge behind the Battalion's start line. The two companies went forward in splendid style and kept close to the barrage. Their direction was excellent and they were both on their objectives half an hour later. Cerasola itself was a village built on the top of an almost sheer drop, and it was particularly hard to clear. Many prisoners were taken and the companies quickly consolidated and settled down to hold the position throughout a day of most intense shelling ; it was so intense that it seemed impossible that anyone could survive in the positions. However, the companies stuck it out resolutely until one o'clock on the morning of 18th September when they were relieved. The Battalion was then taken back behind the artillery lines in transport.

Two days later, on 20th September, the Battalion was on the move again as 28th Brigade was to pass through 10th Brigade and form a bridgehead across the River Marecchia. This business of crossing rivers was going to loom large for the Brigade for the next two months as the Eighth Army drove the enemy back up the Po valley. At 6.30 on 20th September the Battalion moved forward in transport to the concentration area through torrential rain. The rain was so heavy that the trucks only reached the area after experiencing extreme difficulties, and the Commanding Officer's car was bogged down, so that he was compelled to spend the night in a wayside house.

The rain brought about a change of plan, as the tanks were unable to move, and on an alternative plan the Battalion advanced with the intention of capturing and consolidating the Casale area and then passing through to further objectives. "D" Company led the advance and by four o'clock in the afternoon entered Casale, which was reported clear of the enemy. Although the advance was made without contacting the enemy there was much difficulty owing to the very thorough German demolitions. All bridges and culverts were blown except those left intact with charges in place. Rations had to be manhandled to forward areas.

Patrols were sent across the River Marecchia and the enemy were encountered on the other side. "A" Company was warned for a further advance across the river to hold the ground for an armoured advance. Meanwhile all units of the 4th Division received orders that on receipt of the code word "Beeswax" all traffic would clear from the road for four hours to allow the armour to get through. The Battalion was to supply the guides to the river crossing. When "A" moved forward it met opposition from Spandaus and shell fire, which was quickly overcome, so that shortly before dawn on 24th September the company reached their objective. The armour began to arrive and was very soon across the river, which was in effect no more than a stretch of shingle a quarter of a mile wide.

When the armour was across the river, the Battalion moved into a position in close country on the plain, between Sant Archangelo on the left and Casale on the right. On 26th September, when the next river, the Uso, had been crossed, the Battalion moved to a concentration area, where it remained for a sufficient length of time for some training to be done. It was during this time that on 11th October the very lively unit magazine *Tiger Rag* first went to press. This respite lasted until 24th October and, as well as a very thorough training programme, there was a welcome allowance of entertainment and sport.

The 4th Division commenced the relief of the 46th Division south-east of Forli on 19th October, and the Battalion moved forward to Longiano on the 24th, though immediate operations seemed unlikely as heavy rain continued.* The Battalion was moved to a position north-west of Cesena and it was here that the unit suffered two serious tragedies in three days. The first was on 6th November when Colonel Mitchell, with his Second-in-Command and Company Commanders, was looking over the battlefield from a vantage point, and one of the party stepped on an "S" mine. Major G. E. Morgan was killed, Major Bichard was mortally wounded, and Major Deedes, the Second-in-Command, and Major Wakeford, V.C., were wounded. Colonel Mitchell happened to be a little forward of the rest at the time and very fortunately he escaped unscathed. The second tragedy occurred two days later when an enemy long-range shell burst on an ammunition carrier standing outside Battalion Headquarters. Captain Horne, the Adjutant, Captain Meakins, O.C. "H" Company, Lieutenant Valgreen, the Signal Officer, and two other ranks were killed, and the Chaplain, Captain the Reverend R. Edwards, Lieutenant Russell, Lieutenant Ross and twenty-four other ranks were wounded.

These tragic casualties to key personnel in the Battalion were not permitted, of course, to affect the Battalion's commitments. Fierce fighting was going on at Forli, where the 128th Hampshire Brigade was in the thick of it, and the Battalion was committed to stand by as immediate relief. At eleven o'clock that night it moved forward by march route and formed up ready for action. At midnight Somerset L.I. patrols reported that they had found houses on the outskirts of Forli unoccupied and they believed the enemy was withdrawing. Accordingly, in the early hours of 9th November the Battalion moved forward towards Forli to fight beside their comrades of the Hampshire Brigade. Dawn came with a heavy fog and at seven o'clock the Pioneer Platoon entered the town, clearing the mines just ahead of "A" Company, which entered the town followed by "B," and the two companies patrolled the streets and dealt with snipers. The Battalion remained in Forli for two or three days, disturbed only by moderate shelling.

On 14th November the Battalion advanced again and captured Villafranca with little opposition, though once in position the companies were subjected to heavy mortar fire. Patrols went forward to investigate the crossing of the River Montone, which was found to be dangerously swollen by the recent rain. Two companies were thereupon withdrawn to practise boat drill, but a change of plan occurred on 18th November and the Battalion was relieved by the 4th Reconnaissance Regiment.

After a further three days at Forli the advance was resumed, the Battalion being committed to the task of forming a bridgehead. At ten o'clock on the morning of 22nd November, therefore, they moved forward to a concentration area from which, with the Somerset L.I., they were to pass through the forward battalions across the River Cosina and capture objectives beyond. At 7.30 that evening, while forming up for the attack, "A" and "D" Companies lost men through being heavily mortared. The attack went in with great spirit,

* See map on page 194.

however, and both companies were firm on their objectives an hour and a half later.

This attack was a commendable feat as it was made in darkness over saturated ground. When the positions were consolidated, patrols were sent out and made contact with the enemy. Next morning "B" and "C" Companies were given their orders to continue the advance by cutting Route 9 and attacking houses and a bridge. While Major Stevens, commanding "C" Company, was discussing his plan at a Company "O" Group he was seriously wounded by an enemy shell, and Lieutenant Pennington assumed command of the company.

This attack had to be made over open country consisting of ploughland and meadows, all under observation from the enemy. Consequently very heavy enemy shell fire was brought to bear on the start line and many men fell, but both companies were quite undaunted and pressed forward, through heavy machine-gun fire, and the enemy strong-points were soon dealt with. One platoon, commanded by Lieutenant Evans, captured a German headquarters in a house where a German officer was still sending out messages on his radio when the leading section entered the building. A burst of sub-machine-gun fire through the set interrupted his transmission and he surrendered meekly. All objectives were quickly captured and securely held; the whole operation was a typical example of the fine fighting spirit of the Battalion.

This gallant and efficient action was to be the last fought by the 2/4th in Italy, and brought a brilliant campaign to a close. In every action in the campaign in Italy the 2/4th Hampshire Battalion had captured and held its objective. So heavy had its losses been that of the officers with the Battalion in February, only one was still on the strength in December, Lieutenant-Colonel Mitchell, D.S.O., M.C.

The fact was that the time had come for the 4th Division to leave Italy for Palestine for a long spell out of action. Accordingly the Division moved south in early December and pulled up at Taranto to await shipping. This plan was suddenly changed, however, by the outbreak of civil war in Greece, and accordingly on 11th December the 2/4th Hampshire Battalion was flown to Greece in bombers to take part in the operations against the E.L.A.S. forces. A month later the three Hampshire battalions of 128th Brigade were also sent to Greece, and the story of the Hampshire battalions in Greece and Crete will be told in a later chapter.

CHAPTER XV

THE HAMPSHIRE BRIGADE IN ITALY—II

JUNE TO DECEMBER, 1944

THE 128th Infantry Brigade was taken out of the line in Italy with the rest of the 46th Division in March, 1944, after six months' continuous fighting, and sailed from Naples to Port Said. The Brigade was first quartered at Qassasin, and there was leave in Cairo. After the grim and desperate months in Italy, the flesh-pots of Egypt provided a costly but attractive opportunity for jollification. Everyone relaxed, some men to such a degree that a formidable number of charges came in from the Military Police in Cairo for minor infringements of rules and regulations. It was, of course, not easy for seasoned warriors very much on holiday to observe all the meticulous regulations of Cairo. Fortunately their own officers understood this, and one Commanding Officer returned a pile of charges to Higher Authority with, in the column marked "Punishment awarded," the laconic report "beheaded."

The holiday was soon over, however, and after two weeks the three battalions moved up to Nathanya in Palestine for intensive battle training. The battalions were considerably reinforced and brought up to full strength, mainly by officers and men from disbanded A.A. units in the Middle East. Training was vigorous and the gunners soon became excellent infantrymen, and the three battalions had every reason to be satisfied with their new men. The war was not left behind altogether, as it was necessary to be on the alert and ready for action as serious Arab-Jewish trouble was brewing up.

In the middle of May the Brigade moved up to Djaida, north of Baalbec in the Lebanon valley, for realistic battle training. The Brigade's camps were a long way from any large town, but thirty-six-hour passes were available for visits to Beirut, reached by a journey over the mountains in unit transport. As news of the invasion of Normandy came through the men wondered hopefully whether the war would be over before they were called into battle again.

There was, however, still to be a great deal of battle for the Brigade, and the first step towards it was the return to Qassasin on 19th June. Final adjustments were made to the battalion strengths. In the 2nd Battalion Lieutenant-Colonel Rotherham had Major P. C. Taylor for his Second-in-Command, and Captain Goode as Adjutant. The rifle companies were commanded by Majors Sanguinetti, Brehaut, Hutchinson and Davey, while Captain Lehmann commanded H.Q. Company and Captain Drewell the Support Company.

The 1/4th was still commanded by Lieutenant-Colonel Chandler, with Major A. G. Ryshworth-Hill Second-in-Command *vice* Major Portsmouth, who had gone to a Staff appointment on promotion. Captain Leader was Adjutant and Majors Dolman, Powell, Salmond and Bird commanded the rifle companies, Captain G. M. B. H. Moore Support Company and Captain Elwin Headquarters. In July Captain Elwin became Adjutant, a position he held with marked ability and cheerfulness until some months after the war was over.

The 5th Battalion was still commanded by Lieutenant-Colonel J. H. H. Robinson, with Major Boyce as Second-in-Command and Majors Keane, Gater, Williams and P. R. Sawyer commanding the rifle companies, and Captains Ayles and Mordaunt Headquarters and Support Companies. The 46th Division's three months' respite from war came to an end on 27th June, and it sailed from Alexandria to return to Italy, arriving in good time to take part in the assault on the Gothic Line two months later.

The 128th Brigade disembarked at Taranto and moved by train to Pignataro, north of Capua, where battalions were re-equipped with vehicles and weapons which had been left behind by the 5th Division. The stay at Capua was brief and the Division moved northwards up Italy by easy stages. The 128th Brigade passed through familiar country ; they saw the well-known hills where they had fought in the winter, and drove through the rubble and desolation that had been Cassino. The Brigade passed on through Rome in fine style and felt, not without justification surely, that it was something of a triumphal march ; had they not fought as hard as any to smash the gateway to Rome six months before? In the last week in July the Brigade was able to see the King when he visited the Eighth Army ; the same visit in which His Majesty decorated Major Wakeford with the V.C. The Brigade was among those who lined the route from Perugio aerodrome and gave the King a most enthusiastic welcome as the Royal car drove slowly past.

As the Brigade moved up Italy there was opportunity for both training and relaxation. On 1st August they were in a pleasant and peaceful rural district and it was possible to celebrate Minden Day in a fitting manner. The 1/4th Battalion, for example, organized an English Country Fair, "Winchester Fair," held in the harvest fields with all the appropriate sideshows. In the evening there was a concert, marred, however, in the pleasantest manner by the fact that performers and audience, loyally recognizing the significance of Minden Day, had indulged rather too deeply in the local wine. It was about this time that the 1/4th lost a great character in Lance-Corporal Mitchell, M.M. He was fifty years old—he had won his M.M. in 1917—and he had become a kind of battalion institution. To his own and everyone else's disgust, he had to be relegated to a Base Depot under an order forbidding men over forty to remain with battalions. It was at this time, too, that the 5th Battalion was able to welcome back Captain Lytle, who had been taken prisoner at Sidi Nsir and had escaped.

The Assault on the Gothic Line

(*See map on page* 178)

The Division reached the rolling country round Bevagna, south of Assisi, and it was soon known that important battles lay ahead, for the next move in the campaign was the assault on the Gothic Line. The Germans were determined to make a stand on the formidable natural defences based on the Etruscan Apennines to deny our entrance to the valley of the Po. The huge natural barrier through central Italy to the flat lands of the north-east was well suited to the enemy's purpose, and great defensive work had been carried out. The breaking of the Gothic Line was a fresh chapter in the campaign, on a par with the landing at Salerno and the battles for Rome. Ever since the fall of Rome the Germans had worked hard with forced Italian labour to make their Gothic Line impregnable. To break it was the Eighth Army's next task, and in this the 128th Brigade was to play an important part.

On 10th August the 46th Division became part of V Corps in the Eighth Army, and to V Corps, commanded by Lieutenant-General Keightley, was given the major role in the offensive. The infantry in the Corps consisted of the 4th Division, in which the 2/4th Hampshire were serving, the 46th and 56th Divisions, and the 4th Indian Division. The Allied Commander had decided to switch his attack from the area of Florence to the Adriatic coast, and with great care and considerable security precautions the Eighth Army had been moved across to appropriate positions without the enemy knowing what was afoot. The plan was for V Corps to assault the Gothic Line in its eastern sector with the 46th Division on the right and the 4th Indian Division on the left.

The plan depended very greatly on the secrecy of the preliminary moves, and the 46th Division moved to the concentration area fifteen miles south of the River Metauro at night without lights, and all communication with civilians was forbidden. The first task of the Division was to cross the River Metauro and then to fight its way to the Foglia, a dozen miles beyond. It was here that the defences of the Gothic Line began, following the line of the Foglia and running back as far as the River Conca. The main objective given to 46th Division was the mass of Monte Gridolfo. It promised many difficulties, for beyond the Foglia the hills rose very sharply to a thousand feet or more and the river banks were high and steep ; just as secrecy was vital before the attack began, so was speed essential when it was on, to cross the hilly ground between the Metauro and the Foglia, and to assault the bastions on the Gothic Line itself before the enemy could bring up more troops.

The operation order for the battle issued by General Hawkesworth braced everyone ; it was simply : *46th Division will BUST the Gothic Line.* The 128th Brigade was ordered to lead the divisional assault with the 46th Reconnaissance Regiment on the left and the 139th Brigade close up behind. The Recce Regiment was commanded by Lieutenant-Colonel John Cotton, of the Hampshire Regiment. Momentum in the attack was to be maintained at all costs by "violent and sustained armour and infantry by day, and fresh infantry by night." It was to start an hour before midnight on 25th August, and the 128th Brigade's first objective was Monte Bartolo ; that taken they were to probe forward with all speed to the Gothic Line itself. The Brigade had under command the North Irish Horse, whose tanks had supported the

Brigade in the battle for Bèja in North Africa. There was ample air support, for the army had twenty-seven squadrons of the Desert Air Force on call. Everyone was fully aware of the importance of the great operations ahead, and spirits were high when the Hampshire Brigade moved up to the River Metauro on the night of 25th August, 1944.

The first phase of this very important operation went quite according to plan; the enemy had not had time to man his defences properly, and his rear-guards were quickly dealt with by the fresh and eager battalions of the 128th Brigade. The 2nd Battalion crossed the Metauro first, followed by the 1/4th, with the 5th in reserve. The advance parties of the 2nd Battalion had to run the gauntlet of a self-propelled gun trained on the corner of a road near San Ippolito, and there were scattered pockets of resistance here and there. But the three battalions of the Hampshire Brigade and the 46th Recce Regiment moved steadily forward across country and up narrow sunken tracks.

It was gruelling progress for the infantry; the going was rough and there were many hills, but they pressed forward, and by 8.30 on the evening of 26th August the 2nd Battalion was chasing the enemy from Isole del Piano and still going well. At 7.15 on the morning of the 27th the 1/4th had captured Monte San Bartolo and the 5th Battalion were fighting hard for Monte Grosso, assisted by the North Irish Horse. Before midnight on the 27th the 2nd Battalion had cleared Mount Abullo. Apart from their success in capturing their objectives, the three battalions had performed no mean physical feat. For example, Mount Bartolo represented a climb of some 1,500 feet from the river-bed of the Metauro. To have covered the twelve miles in a direct line on the map they had marched and fought twenty-five miles.

There was much more to be done yet, however, for it was essential that the impetus be maintained. The advance went on, and by six o'clock on 28th August the 5th Battalion were relieved on Monte Grosso so that they could push on again, and that night, in quick succession, captured two more hilltops, and by six o'clock the next morning had taken Monte Busetto. This advance of the 5th Battalion, following as it did the arduous work of the preceding two days, was a truly magnificent achievement. At first light on 29th August the 2nd Battalion passed through the 5th and by midday had captured Colbordolo.

The 1/4th had come up against very serious opposition at Montegaudio and only the most desperate fighting brought about its capture. During this action Major J. P. Salmond, of the Royal Warwickshire Regiment, was killed most gallantly leading "A" Company. Major Salmond had joined the Battalion at Bou Arada in April, 1943, and led his company through all the important battles since then. His very distinguished service to the 1/4th Battalion and the gallantry which was so characteristic of him was recognized by the award of the Military Cross. At this time Colonel Chandler was sent back to hospital and the command of the 1/4th Battalion was given to Lieutenant-Colonel A. Boyce, of the 5th Battalion. Major Keane became Second-in-Command of 5th Battalion, and Captain Mordaunt took over his company.

Monte Gridolfo

The Brigade were now at the Gothic Line proper, with the River Foglia before them and the grim massif of Monte Gridolfo a couple of miles beyond. Monte Gridolfo was indeed a formidable objective ; all houses had been pulled down, trees felled and avenues prepared between extensive minefields for machine-gun fire. Gullies which could have given cover had been filled in with logs, and the assault of the bare slopes of the hill looked suicidal. It required courage of no mean order to assault those formidable slopes in the broad light of an August day.

Yet they were assaulted. The 2nd Battalion advanced on them with great determination, crossing the Foglia at one o'clock in the afternoon of 30th August with little opposition. The road below Belvedere Fogliensi was crossed and then the two leading companies were held up by very intense mortar and machine-gun fire and forced to take what cover they could until darkness came down. Then they moved forward again and attacked and cleared the fortified houses on the first ridge, in spite of very bitter opposition. Major Brehaut and Major Hutchinson led their companies with great spirit and dealt with one machine-gun post after another. By dawn on 31st August the first height was captured and held by the 2nd Battalion.

Then the 1/4th Battalion passed through and carried on the furious assault. Nothing could stop them, and with great heroism they dealt with strong-point after strong-point, driving deeper into the Monte Gridolfo feature. The Battalion was at the top of its form, but "D" Company led by Major Baillie was outstanding, and Lieutenant G. R. Norton, M.M., commanding a platoon of that company, fought with such gallantry that he won the Victoria Cross. Lieutenant Norton was one of the officers seconded to the Brigade from the Union Defence Force. He had joined the army at the beginning of the war in company with a colleague of his from a bank in East London, South Africa. This colleague was Major Baillie, his Company Commander at the battle of Monte Gridolfo. They had fought together in Tobruk, escaped together when it fell, and had walked 500 miles to Alamein. Lieutenant Baillie, as he was then, had won the M.C. and Sergeant Norton the M.M. When Lieutenant Norton joined the 1/4th Battalion in July, 1944, he found that his old colleague was now his Company Commander.

The action in which Lieutenant Norton won the Victoria Cross was on 31st August. Major Baillie's company attacked strongly held German positions protecting the village of Monte Gridolfo. Lieutenant Norton led his platoon in an attack on one of the strong-points which was constructed with well-sited concrete emplacements, and it was soon pinned down by heavy machine-gun fire from a valley on the right flank of the advance.

On his own initiative Lieutenant Norton at once went forward alone and engaged a series of enemy positions in this valley. He attacked the first machine-gun position with a grenade, killing the crew of three ; then, still alone, he worked his way forward to another enemy position containing two machine guns and fifteen riflemen. After a fight lasting ten minutes he wiped

LIEUTENANT G. R. NORTON, V.C., M.M.

Face page 188

out both machine guns with his tommy-gun, and killed or took prisoner the rest.

Throughout these engagements Lieutenant Norton was under direct fire from an enemy self-propelled gun, and, still under fire from this gun, he led a party of men who had come forward against a house and cleared the cellar and upper rooms, taking several more prisoners and putting the rest to flight. Although by this time he was wounded and weak from loss of blood, he went on calmly leading his platoon up the valley and captured the remaining enemy positions.

The official citation said : "Lieutenant Norton displayed matchless courage, outstanding initiative and inspiring leadership. By his supreme gallantry, fearless example and determined aggression, he assured the successful breach of the Gothic Line at this point."

There is a charming postscript to this tale of great gallantry. When Lieutenant Norton was taken back to the base hospital he discovered that the nurse who was to look after him was his twin sister. The next day was their birthday.

With the capture of Monte Gridolfo the Gothic Line was breached, and within thirty hours of the beginning of the assault the three battalions of the Hampshire Brigade were within the enemy defences. The 5th Battalion, which had been in support, took up the lead early on 1st September and made good progress until they came up against strong resistance at a road junction. They called for tank support at first light, the resistance was cleared, and the Battalion took up forward positions above Meleto, just north of Monte Gridolfo, from which they fought off several enemy counter-attacks, and captured Meleto by the evening of 2nd September.

This successful breaching of the much-vaunted German Gothic Line gave the men of the Hampshire Brigade ample reason to be pleased with themselves. They had been splendidly helped by the squadrons of the North Irish Horse ; their Churchill tanks had always been there, supporting the battalions over appalling tank country. Squadron leaders on foot led their tanks up seemingly impossible slopes ; nothing daunted them. The G.O.C. Eighth Army, General Sir Oliver Leese, sent a signal to the Commander, 128th Brigade : "My best congratulations to you and your Brigade on your hard-fought four days' advance, including the capture of Monte Bartolo and culminating in the forcing of the Gothic Line, and the capture of Monte Gridolfo. This was a fine achievement."

It was not only a fine achievement by the rifle companies ; the whole Brigade threw themselves passionately into those violent and exhausting days. The advance was so fast at first that supporting supply echelons had great difficulty in keeping up. They raced through the thick clouds of dust, often under shell fire, and got the rations and ammunition up in spite of very great difficulties. Drivers, cooks, quartermasters' staffs, all suffered casualties, and all kept hard on the go with only a couple of hours' sleep snatched here and there. It was a fully concerted effort by everyone. The orders were to "Bust the Gothic Line." It was duly busted.

San Clemente

The advance was continued by the 5th Battalion, who went on to the Ventena, reaching Ponte Rosso behind the 138th Brigade by midday on 3rd September. Here they concentrated, and the other two battalions were brought up on transport. The troops were well-nigh exhausted from their ten days' continuous fighting over rough and mountainous country, but General Hawkesworth called for a final effort from the Brigade. It was ordered to cross the River Conca, and then to seize the bridge over the next river, the Marano, at Ospedaleto more than five miles ahead. The purpose of this was to speed the passage of the 1st Armoured Division. This order, with all it portended of relief and the final exploitation of the successes which had been attained with so much effort, gave the weary battalions the necessary spark of exhilaration ; exhausted though they were, they found new energy for this last assault.

The 6th York and Lancasters forced a crossing of the River Conca after a stiff battle on 3rd September, and the 2nd Hampshire crossed the river under very heavy fire and established themselves on the slopes below San Clemente. By this time the enemy defensive positions were much more strongly manned and he had brought up considerable artillery strength. Nevertheless the 2nd Battalion fought their way resolutely up the ridge and on to Monte Annibolina.

The 1/4th Battalion followed up, passed through the 2nd and attacked Monte Gallera with great spirit and took it. At midnight the 5th Battalion went into action, two companies attacking Clemente itself and the other two by-passing the village and making for Castelleale, a couple of miles ahead. There was furious fighting in Clemente, and as no progress was being made the two companies attacking it were switched to the right and joined those making for Castelleale. Here, too, the enemy resisted with great spirit and considerable fire power, and the forward company had a bad time, being shelled by several kinds of artillery as well as being under heavy small-arms fire from Coriano ridge. The companies of the 5th Battalion were held in their positions spread out along the road until they were pulled back to San Clemente. The Battalion suffered heavy casualties, both in the attack towards Castelleale and in the withdrawal.

On 5th September the 128th Brigade was relieved in the positions it held at San Clemente and moved back to Pian di Ventena for a few days' rest. The battle to break into the Gothic Line was over ; it had called for great feats of endurance and verve. The Hampshire Brigade had advanced 26 miles on the map, and something between 45 and 50 marching miles. Casualties had been heavy and the battalions were getting short of officers and men. Among the changes made at this time was the appointment of Major P. R. Sawyer as Second-in-Command of the 5th Battalion.

All three battalions had suffered heavily, but the enemy had been savagely mauled and the extent of the opposition can be gauged by the fact that the 322 prisoners taken by the Brigade came from five different German divisions.

The 46th Division's achievement in piercing the Gothic Line was fully recognized and received considerable publicity; it was quite justifiably compared with the smashing of the Hindenburg Line by the 46th Division in 1917. For five days the 128th Brigade could lick its wounds, take stock of the situation, sort itself out and get some rest. On 9th September all ranks of the Brigade wore oak leaves in their caps to mark the first anniversary of Salerno. At this time the 1/4th Battalion lost an old friend in R.S.M. A. Brown, a Regular soldier who had been with the 1/4th since it was formed from the Territorial 4th Battalion in September, 1939. The new R.S.M. was a Territorial, R.S.M. G. Bugden, who was to be in the re-formed 4th after the war.

Montescudo and Trarivi

While the 128th Brigade were resting, fighting continued fiercely along the hills from Gemmano to Coriano. The weather broke and two days' rain changed rivers from trickling streams to torrents. There was a great deal of shelling and bombing of the German positions while the Eighth Army continued to fight its way towards Rimini and the valley of the Po.

The 128th Brigade moved forward on 11th September to an area north of Tavoleto, and reconnaissance parties went forward to Farneto, but the intended operation was called off. On 14th September the Leicesters captured Monte Colombo after a violent attack against fierce opposition, and at midnight the 5th Hampshire passed through the Leicesters in Monte Colombo bound for Montescudo and a bleak feature known as Hill 475. This was the beginning of a new fighting advance by the Brigade, in a north-westerly direction from Monte Colombo, parallel with the coast. The 5th Battalion advanced up the road amid the debris of the day's battle. The dead still lay by the side of the road ; a ruined house and an abandoned tank, the stench of rotting cattle, all told their grim story in the dim half-light. The Battalion occupied the cemetery outside the village of Montescudo, and one company moved to the right to come in against Montescudo from the north. As the company crept forward in the darkness they heard enemy talking, and they surprised a platoon standing on the Trarivi cross-roads to the north of Montescudo. The company attacked and killed many of the enemy ; the rest ran wildly and a heavy toll was taken of them until the alarm was given.

They were units of the 100th Mountain Regiment, picked Austrian troops and first-class fighting men, and they soon settled down grimly to defend the village from positions dug in the roadside and from strong-points in houses. For a while no progress could be made against the defensive fire, but eventually Major Heald led "D" Company against the defences with such determination and dash that he took them into the houses on the outskirts of the village. Major Heald, who was wounded, received the D.S.O. for this action, and Sergeant Cooke, M.M., of the Ornito battle, won the D.C.M. Private Roberts, who had particularly distinguished himself with the Bren gun in the assault, was awarded the M.M.

At the same time "C" Company, advancing on the north of Montescudo, suffered an initial shock when their Company Commander, Major Williams, was killed leading them forward ; but Lieutenant Roux and C.S.M. Maclean, who won the M.C. and M.M., rallied the company and led it into the village on their side. The fighting in Montescudo was some of the bitterest the Brigade had ever met. Every house had to be cleared one after the other, and the enemy fought with heroic fanaticism. Throughout the fighting our positions were shelled and mortared intensely. Colonel Robinson and Major Heald with the leading company set about the enemy in no uncertain manner. Our tanks had come up soon after dawn, and when they could join in the house fighting they put anti-personnel shells into the houses and followed it with shrapnel. Even so, bazookas appeared and our tanks were shot at from behind corners and tops of houses. A carrier in which C.S.M. Race of "S" Company was bringing up ammunition to the forward company was blown to pieces. The enemy were most obstinate and small isolated groups continued to fight to the end. Even when the front of the village was occupied, the enemy's defensive fire was still intense on all the approaches, and they had observation on the road up from the near-by Hill 475. Gradually the enemy was dislodged from his remaining positions and by 10.30 in the morning all Montescudo was in our hands.

With the village taken, Colonel Robinson tried to get forward, but he was concussed by a near miss from a heavy shell and Major Sawyer took over command. The next task was to capture Hill 475 that evening, a formidable task as the bare commanding feature was strongly protected by strong defensive positions.

While the 5th Battalion were fighting so desperately for Montescudo, the 2nd Hampshire moved north towards Trarivi. They made good progress at first, but when they were some 500 yards from the village they were held up. Here the 1/4th Battalion relieved them, and they concentrated south of Montescudo on the southern slopes of Hill 475 to join the 5th Battalion in the assault of that feature. Patrols from both battalions went forward and inflicted casualties on the enemy before being driven back by heavy mortar fire and shelling. Then the 5th Battalion formed up and moved in to attack, but their leading companies came under such heavy mortar fire as they crossed the start line that they could make no progress. Major Keane went on alone up the slope of the hill through the inferno of the shelling, calling his men on, but he was killed and the attack was halted. One company of the 2nd Battalion which had penetrated far round on the flank was pulled back, and the 1/4th Battalion, who were advancing on their side and had managed to gain a foothold, also had to be brought back, much to their disgust, to deal with an unexpected development at Trarivi.

In the Gothic Line the enemy had very strong artillery and mortar defensive fire arranged well beforehand. The infantry did not have to fight infantry only ; they had to get through curtains of shell and high explosive. When they had passed through the fire and reached their objective they had to penetrate close-range fire and get to grips with a resolute enemy in excellent defensive positions. Hill 475 was no exception. Throughout 16th September the 2nd and 5th Battalions stuck to their positions in Montescudo and at the base of the hill under incessant shelling, with the enemy still above them on Hill 475. The worst tragedy of the action was when the regimental aid post was hit ; the Medical Officer, Captain Bergin, the stretcher-bearers, the pioneers helping them and all the casualties were killed.

During the night the enemy withdrew from the hill, and early on 17th September the 2nd Battalion occupied it. Thus both Montescudo and Hill 475 were taken, but only after most bitter and costly fighting. All the while the approach roads to the position were under constant shelling and the convoys bringing supplies and ammunition suffered many casualties. To add to the difficulties, the weather, for all it was September in Italy, was dreadful. There was rain and there was mud ; rivers changed overnight from gentle brooks to serious obstacles.

The 1/4th Battalion had been withdrawn from their positions in front of Trarivi to assist in the capture of Hill 475. But when no progress was made they were sent back, and returned to the attack in the morning of 16th September. They had with them a squadron of the 46th Recce Regiment, a squadron of tanks and one company of the Manchesters, a machine-gun battalion. Even so progress was slow on account of the violent defensive fire from the village, and the attack was held up at the cross-roads outside the village.

The village was thereupon subjected to a heavy artillery attack ; hundreds of rounds of H.E. were pumped into the position by tanks and artillery, and the area was sprayed with machine-gun and mortar fire. Then, at a given signal of three green Very lights, Major Baillie led his company of the 1/4th to assault the position from the valley. The defenders were certainly made of stern stuff ; even after six shells had been put through the church tower, sniping still came from it. The attack was developed with great zest. Each house had to be dealt with separately. It was a hard battle, extremely well handled by the 1/4th Battalion. By nine o'clock in the evening of 16th September Trarivi was taken ; patrols went forward, but no contact was made with the enemy. By dawn on the next day the 1/4th were firmly established well beyond Trarivi at Vallecchio.

With Montescudo, Hill 475 and Trarivi taken, resistance in the immediate area was broken and the pursuit was on. This was taken up by units of 138th and 139th Brigades, and the enemy were chased as far as the neutral state of San Marino, from which they had to be driven out. In this operation the Allies had the enthusiastic assistance of the diminutive San Marino Army. Meanwhile, 128th Brigade, which had again fought itself to a standstill, was moved on 18th September back to Taverna to rest and reorganize. Reinforcements were sent from the 1st Battalion The Buffs, but even so all three battalions were still short. The battles for the Gothic Line had been costly in men and equipment ; there was, however, still more stern fighting ahead, mostly in the rain and mud of the Italian autumn.

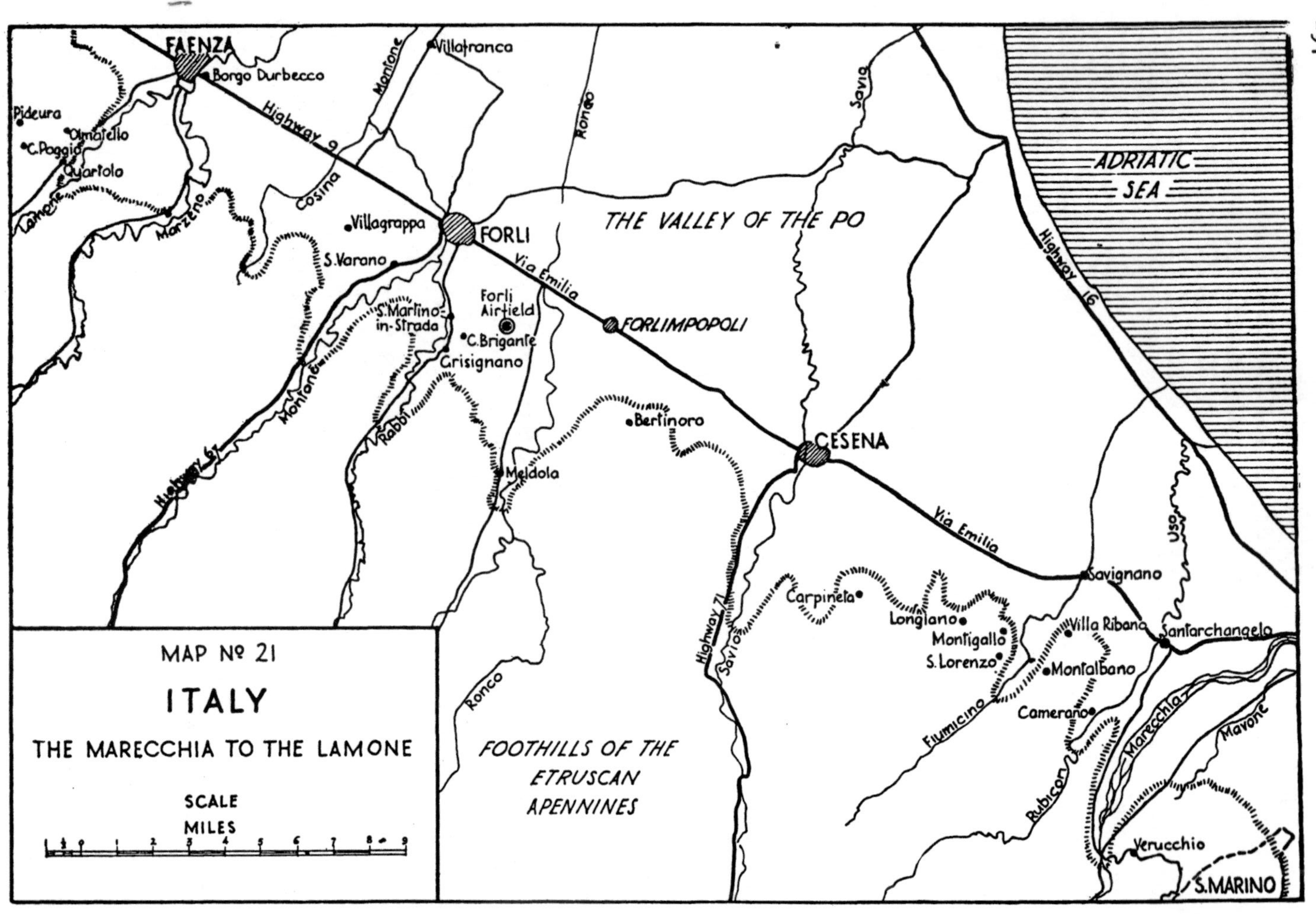
MAP No 21
ITALY
THE MARECCHIA TO THE LAMONE
SCALE
MILES
1 0 1 2 3 4 5 6 7 8 9
ADRIATIC SEA
THE VALLEY OF THE PO
FOOTHILLS OF THE ETRUSCAN APENNINES
FAENZA
Borgo Durbecco
Villafranca
Pideura
Olmatello
C.Poggio
Quartolo
Lamone
Marzeno
Highway 9
Cosina
Montone
Ronco
Savio
Villagrappa
FORLI
S.Varano
Via Emilia
Forli Airfield
S.Martino-in-Strada
C.Brigante
Grisignano
FORLIMPOPOLI
Highway 16
Montone
Rabbi
Highway 67
Bertinoro
Meldola
CESENA
Uso
Via Emilia
Savignano
Highway 71
Savio
Carpineta
Longiano
Montigallo
S.Lorenzo
Villa Ribano
Santarchangelo
Montalbano
Camerano
Fiumicino
Rubicon
Marecchia
Mavone
Ronco
Verucchio
S.MARINO

The Crossing of the Fiumicino

While the 128th Brigade spent ten days out of the line, the advance went on and two more of the apparently endless series of rivers across the Allies' path were crossed, the Marecchia and the Rubicon. Then on the night of 28th September 128th Brigade went back into the line, to take the lead once more for the crossing of the River Fiumicino.

It was raining heavily as the Brigade left Taverna, and transport presented a very serious problem along the muddy tracks. The 5th Battalion, misdirected for the crossing of the Marecchia, were completely bogged down on the approaches to the ford, so that they had to change vehicles and move round over the bridge to Verucchio. During the day rivers rose several feet and the Rubicon, which two days before had been no deeper than men's boots, had to be waded with the water above the men's waists. The scene of the troops splashing through the river reminded some of the celebrated crossing of the Rubicon by Julius Cæsar two thousand years before. Overcoming the difficulties and discomfort brought about by the unkind weather, the Brigade took up its new positions and went into action on 30th September.

Between our positions and the Fiumicino was the Montalbano Ridge. The 2nd and 5th Battalions took this without much difficulty, but their efforts to exploit the slopes down to the river were sternly resisted. The enemy were established in strength in good positions on the farther bank, and the two battalions were held up in their positions overlooking the river, the 2nd forward of Villa Ribano and the 5th in Montalbano. They had to stay there under most uncomfortable circumstances for six days. The cause of this delay was the worsening of the weather so that the Fiumicino itself and the rivers to the rear over which supplies and reinforcements had to be brought were in full flood.

Vehicles were bogged down, guns were up to their axles in mud and tanks could not be moved. There was also considerable shelling, including phosphorous shells, and constant patrol clashes caused a steady drain in casualties. Another unpleasant feature of this most disagreeable phase in the battle was the first meeting with the new German non-metallic mines, for which mine detectors were useless. The supply of rations and ammunition was a nightmare problem ; even mules were immobilized and everything had to be manhandled to the forward positions. Drivers, clerks, cooks, batmen and all available men were mobilized and magnificently they toiled, often knee-deep in mud, loaded down with heavy burdens, and often struggling back to base bearing the wounded. So, constantly harassed by the near-by enemy, within range of many types of artillery ; cold and wet ; living a kind of a troglodyte existence in a world of mud, the troops waited grimly for the weather to improve.

Every day the crossing of the Fiumicino was postponed because of the transport problems in the rear. Two officers on recce were captured and the crossing plan had to be changed, an event which turned out to be of considerable value to us. For several days diversionary bombardments and false crossing preparations had been made on other points on the river. Then at last, on 7th

October, the weather improved enough for the attack to be made, much to the relief of the marooned and much-shelled troops of the two Hampshire Battalions holding the ridge.

In the evening of 7th October the 2nd Battalion led off the attack, with the task of crossing the Fiumicino and capturing the Montigallo spur. The Battalion moved down to the river under cover of a very heavy bombardment on the enemy positions by guns, mortars and machine guns. Two companies attempted the crossing, through heavy fire laid down on the slopes to the river by the enemy. One company was held up but the other got over, and another passed through it with the Battle Patrol, stormed the Montigallo spur and took it with an impressive bag of prisoners. Soon the whole Battalion was over and all the objectives were taken. The enemy counter-attacked several times, but every time he was driven off.

The 5th Battalion forded the river on the left, below Montalbano. The leading company was held up by an enemy strong-point, but another company attacked it on the flank and cleared the obstruction, and the Battalion took the village of San Lorenzo, beating off a dangerous counter-attack within the hour. The 1/4th crossed the Fiumicino at midnight, passed through the 2nd Battalion and made good progress along the spur towards Longiano. Continual rain was falling, and the river rose rapidly—some six feet in two hours—so that neither of the two fords which had been used was passable. At dawn work was begun on a bridge, but for the time being no supplies or follow-up troops could cross. The 56th Division on the right of the Brigade had not been able to get across, and the right flank was therefore exposed. Fortunately an enemy wireless message was intercepted which disclosed an impending counter-attack. Consequently the 1/4th were ordered to pull back a little and stand by, much to their disgust as they were making good progress. The attack came in, but very heavy gun-fire was concentrated on it and only a few men got through, to be driven off at great cost to themselves.

Thus the Fiumicino was crossed, with the 2nd and 1/4th Battalions on the Montigallo spur, and the 5th in San Lorenzo. The bridgehead was established, but the weather prevented it being exploited. All the Brigade could do was to dig their toes in and stick to their positions until the weather improved sufficiently for the rest of the Division to get over. There followed a very difficult two days. The Battalions were heavily shelled. Colonel Boyce, visiting his companies, was severely wounded by a shell which killed the runner beside him, and Major Ryshworth-Hill took over command of the 1/4th. The Command Post of the 2nd Battalion was hit, and the resulting casualties left Colonel Rotherham with a Headquarters consisting of himself, the Battery Commander, and a lance-corporal acting as adjutant. Men toiled valiantly heaving hundred-pound boxes of ammunition up the slippery and muddy slopes from the river, and they were passed forward from platoon to platoon. All support was behind them over the swollen Fiumicino ; the wounded had to remain in the regimental aid post.

The enemy counter-attacked several times, but always they were driven off. One platoon established in a house was surrounded by Germans, who advanced firing and throwing grenades, shouting "O.K., come on out." A sergeant-major, an ex-gamekeeper, led the reply by killing four Germans with four shots. The fight was furious, but before long the enemy had to give in and they went back leaving many dead around the position. It was the same everywhere. The enemy counter-attacked violently, and shelled our positions with all he had. But we were well able to reply in kind, for the Gunner officers attached to each headquarters could call on some nine regiments, with the result that the enemy were blasted at will. It was exceedingly noisy, very wet and altogether uncomfortable.

The battalions held the bridgehead for thirty-six hours, cut off in their rear by the swollen Fiumicino. Then on 9th October the weather improved and the river fell as swiftly as it had risen. The Bailey bridge was finished and the follow-up brigades crossed, passed through the 128th Brigade and the advance was taken up again. One more river had been crossed.

An excerpt from the diary of R.Q.M.S. Smith of the 1/4th shows what it was like on the ridge across the Fiumicino: "Battalion in Brigade attack. Most severe stonking yet. Lieutenant-Colonel Boyce wounded. River in flood. Great difficulty with mules. Had to manhandle all rations and ammunition over rickety bridge. Then stiff climb to Bn. H.Q. in liquid mud. B.H.Q. in Montigallo church. Almost intact when they went in. Completely ruined and flattened when they left. All safe in vault under church. C.S.M. Algie Fry very active sniping Germans."

The crossing of the Fiumicino was a magnificent achievement. The attack was made over slippery mud in the teeth of most violent opposition from guns, mortars and machine guns. That the attack succeeded was very largely due to Colonel Rotherham's brilliant leadership of the 2nd Battalion; their superb fighting spirit was on a level with the Battalion's achievement at Tebourba. For his distinguished leadership of his Battalion, Colonel Rotherham received the D.S.O.

When the 138th and 139th Brigades passed through to continue the advance, 128th Brigade was given a short rest in the Verucchio area while the other brigades fought forward and took Carpineta and Cesena. On 21st October the whole Division came out of the line for ten days. General Hawkesworth received this message from the Commander of V Corps: "I would like to take this opportunity of congratulating you most sincerely on your brilliant successes in the fighting of the last few months. Throughout this phase of the battle of Italy, which has resulted in forcing the enemy through the much publicized Gothic Line, 46 Division has been engaged in all the toughest and most bitter actions. Throughout all your operations your commanders have shown skill in leadership and your troops the greatest gallantry."

The Commander of the Canadian Corps, which had fought beside the 46th Division, said to General Hawkesworth, "I think if ever a Division has earned the title of 'The Iron Division,' 46 Division has."

Having played no small part in the Division's battles for the Gothic Line, the Hampshire Brigade could well be pleased with itself as it took its well-earned rest at Verucchio. It had lost many officers and men ; companies were nearly down to half strength, and the newcomers who had joined the battalions in the Middle East were already fully experienced in battle. But all three battalions were in fine spirit, they were remarkably well led, most of the officers and N.C.Os. were veterans of the whole Italian campaign. From Verucchio it was possible to visit the 2/4th Battalion, in the 4th Division on their right, and to renew old friendships and exchange experiences.

It was while the Brigade was at Verucchio that Lieutenant Norton returned from hospital, to receive the news of the award of the V.C., and a Special Order of the Day was issued for the 1/4th Battalion on 26th October announcing this award and the D.S.O. to Lieutenant-Colonel Boyce, one D.C.M. and three M.Ms., and a battalion holiday.

San Martino, The Lamone and Faenza

The Hampshire Brigade moved into the line again on 1st November, going forward to a concentration area in the hilltop village of Bertinoro. There was a magnificent view right over the plain, and Forli with its airfield could be clearly seen in the sunshine of a fine autumn afternoon. But the next day the Brigade moved forward towards Forli through heavy rain, with mud everywhere. The River Ronco was crossed ; there was no bridge, but jeeps could cross by an aqueduct which was still standing, though most of them got stuck on the slippery mud tracks on the other side.

The immediate objective of the 46th Division was to assist in the capture of Forli, the next large town after Cesena on Highway 9, the Via Emilia. On the right of the 46th Division was the 4th Division, with the 2/4th Battalion on its left. Thus, when the 128th Brigade went into action in the battle for Forli, there were four Hampshire battalions in line.

In the past twenty-four hours a considerable advance had been made and Grisignano on the River Rabbi had been reached, some three miles south of Forli. It was to this village that the 5th Battalion made its way after it had crossed the Ronco. There was no route forward and the Brigade had to march along tracks ankle-deep in mud, through a countryside pitted with craters where even the smallest bridge was demolished. Again the bringing forward of rations and supplies was a difficult problem. There was heavy shelling as well as constant rain. It was another of the many miserable days of campaigning in Italy.

As the 5th Battalion moved into Grisignano to take over from 1st King's Own, they were greeted with a violent and general demonstration of machine-gun fire. The 2nd Battalion came into position on the right and the 1/4th on the left of the 5th, so that the three battalions were in a semi-circle facing towards Forli, with the suburban village of San Martino-in-Strada a mile in front of them.

The brigade plan was to attack northwards through San Martino-in-Strada to help the 4th Division in their task of clearing the aerodrome and taking

Forli. Before this could be done a route forward had to be cleared and made so that tanks could be brought up to take part in the street fighting in San Martino-in-Strada, and in the deplorably wet weather this took several days.

The enemy was putting up a stubborn resistance against the 4th Division on the Forli aerodrome and south of Highway 9. He had strong positions at Casa Brigante and along the dykes south of the airfield, to prevent his flanks being turned by an attack from the south. He also had abundant artillery in operation and a force of tanks at call. The Hampshire Brigade had patrols out nightly and the days of waiting were tense, active, and very noisy.

All was ready on 7th November and the attack started at eleven o'clock that night. The 5th Battalion went for the village itself while the 2nd advanced on their right. The 2nd Battalion made effective use of their knowledge that the enemy occupied houses at night and abandoned them in daylight ; they got into the houses first and so got a good start. The 5th Battalion were held up for some time by enemy posts on their left flank across the river and progress was slow and costly, so that it was nearly dawn before the blocks of flats and the cinema in San Martino had been cleared. From that point onward, however, the advance was swift. It became a copy-book battle, with the infantry co-operating perfectly with the tanks of the 9th Lancers. As the Lancers shot their way down the road the 5th Battalion searched and cleared the houses on either side. By nightfall an advance of two miles had been made and 150 prisoners taken.

The battle for San Martino-in-Strada was a remarkable one. Not only did it go beautifully according to plan, with tanks and infantry working together as a pair of hands, but two new weapons were used by us. Our troops had their first experience of rocket-firing aircraft, and watched Tempests attacking German tanks on the far side of the River Rabbi. The results were startlingly successful. New anti-tank guns were used for the first time, too. Littlejohn anti-tank guns were issued just before the battle, laboriously manhandled up to Grisignano, and there the Gunners learned how to use them with the enemy only 200 yards away ; in this case, too, the result was most effective.

Immediately after the battle General Hawkesworth gave up the command of the Division, which he had commanded since Salerno, to take over X Corps. General Hawkesworth, "the little man with the big stick," was known to every man in his Division. His dapper figure was a familiar sight to front-line troops wherever they were. When the Division was resting and refitting in the Middle East, General Hawkesworth was recalled to take over the 1st Division at Anzio. But he returned to the 46th Division in time for the Gothic Line battles. He was succeeded by Major-General C. E. Weir, who had commanded the New Zealand Division in the absence of General Freyberg.

The battle had gone well all along the line ; the 4th Division had taken the aerodrome and the first part of the plan had been achieved. The Hampshire Brigade had now to swing left and cross the Rabbi and, if possible, to cross the Montone and take San Varano. Accordingly on the night of 9th November the 1/4th crossed the Rabbi near San Martino. A swift advance, practically unopposed, brought them up to the River Montone in the afternoon, when dark lowering thunder clouds began to pile up. Patrols from the 1/4th went over the river, but they encountered Tiger tanks on the other side. When the storm broke the Montone, as was the maddening habit of these endless rivers, promptly rose behind them and became a raging torrent in a few hours.

Crossing the Montone and Lamone

The weather had cleared on the morning of 9th November, and the Sappers toiled to build a 220-foot bridge over the Rabbi south of Grisignano, while our guns and fighter bombers dealt with enemy tanks at San Varano. Fighting patrols crossed the Montone after dark, though it was still waist-deep.

The Montone was crossed in the early hours of 12th November, the 1/4th getting over opposite San Varano, while two other crossings were made farther south. The 1/4th obtained a precarious foothold on the far bank, where they held on under heavy shelling, trying in vain to enlarge their bridgehead. But the pressure against them was relieved as the two other crossings were exploited and they then attacked and captured San Varano. Here the 2nd Battalion passed through and advanced against strong opposition to within a mile of Villagrappa.

It was flat country, with lines of vines separating the fields, with houses scattered everywhere ; splendid country for the enemy machine-gunners. Our tanks became bogged and every house had to be cleared ; enemy tanks and self-propelled guns were always being encountered. The 1/4th captured Villagrappa, and when they were relieved they went back and joined the 5th in Meldola. The 2nd moved to Forli, now in the hands of the 4th Division.

The other brigades of the Division took the lead, and for nine days they fought forward slowly against tough opposition over the flat, muddy country. By 23rd November the Cosina Canal was bridged, and the 128th Brigade came into the picture. They were to pass through the forward positions of the Division at dawn on 24th November and take the lead towards Faenza.

It promised to be a difficult assignment, and a most elaborate fire-plan was arranged to support the three-battalion advance. But for a change all went well—at first. Indeed the advance became a triumphal progress through farms, where everyone turned out to welcome them with cheers, wine and fruit as they hastened past. By eleven o'clock in the morning a company of the 5th Battalion had got in Borgo Durbecco, looking across the River Lamone at the walls of Faenza itself. All the bridges over the river had been demolished, and a crossing was impossible.

The 1st K.R.R.C. were under command 128th Brigade for this operation, and shortly before noon came the welcome news that they had been able to force a crossing of the River Marzeno, which joined the Lamone south of Faenza, on the left of the Brigade. Brigadier Kendrew therefore switched the other battalions of the Brigade to the south to cross at this point, on to the tongue of land between the Marzeno and the Lamone, while the 139th Brigade took over their positions in front of the city.

The 5th Battalion, and then the 2nd, got companies over the Marzeno in the late afternoon, but the bridgehead was small and soon uncomfortably crowded, and the enemy shelled the bridgehead heavily. Machine-gun posts in houses, and a few tanks covering the few roads out of the bridgehead, made any advance extremely difficult ; when our own tanks were over the Marzeno they got bogged down as soon as they left the roads. Then it rained and the Marzeno ran true to type and rose rapidly behind the companies in the bridgehead, and the crossing-place was washed away. But a weir was found just wide enough for carriers to cross, and the drivers showed considerable skill and courage easing their vehicles across, the tracks lapping the fall of the water. They brought over ammunition, anti-tank guns and supplies.

Slowly the outward pressure gained impetus and the Lamone was reached on the 26th, and patrols were sent out to the river that afternoon. They were not interfered with, but when fighting patrols crossed the Lamone they at once encountered strong enemy posts and were violently engaged by machine guns and mortars. The Lamone was yet another case of "one more river," and it promised to be a tough crossing.

It was necessary to cross the Lamone in strength, and much had to be done first. The Sappers had erected numerous temporary crossings over the turbulent Marzeno, but all failed, and when a site was found they set to work to build a 110-foot Bailey bridge. The only road between the two rivers was unmetalled and narrow, and had to be improved for the moving up of tanks, guns and bridging lorries.

The three battalions of the 128th Brigade had to wait a week in their positions before the Lamone, while hectic work went on in the rear. Intermittently it rained, intermittently the enemy sent over angry outbursts of shelling. Every night patrols were out looking down at the river, which was, of course, swollen and torrential, while the Sappers were out selecting bridging sites and crossing-places. One bright spot in a rather dreary week was when the enemy fired propaganda leaflets into our positions, thus providing the troops with highly entertaining literature.

The plan for the crossing of the Lamone was to make a bridgehead from Olmatello on the right to Casa Poggio on the left, and then to extend it to Pideura. The 2nd Battalion was to cross and capture Olmatello, the 1/4th to cross, capture two intermediate hills, and then to advance through Casa Poggio towards Pideura, and the 5th were to pass through the 2nd Battalion and make their way along a narrow ridge to capture Pideura. The 1st K.R.R.C., still under command, were to take care of the left flank of the brigade advance. The attack was timed to start at seven in the evening of 3rd December, with an elaborate artillery programme in support. The 169th Brigade of 56th Division and the guns of the New Zealand Division were to carry out a large-scale diversionary attack on Faenza itself.

Just after dark on 3rd December the opening barrage broke the uneasy silence with its thunder. The 2nd and the 1/4th Hampshire Battalions moved down to the river, and patrols of the 2nd Battalion were soon across and in action, clearing houses on the lateral road. Meanwhile a ladder bridge was constructed, not without difficulty. The 2nd Battalion crossed, and as the moon rose two companies began the stiff climb up the steep, slippery fields to the village of Olmatello, standing on a 500-foot ridge. An enemy post was overrun, but machine guns on the crest of the ridge held up the leading platoons and they were forced down in the hollows below. It began to look like a deadlock, but just before dawn Colonel Rotherham took the situation in hand and led the two companies in a headlong charge up to the ridge and into Olmatello ; a magnificent full-hearted charge which swept the enemy off their feet.

The 1/4th Battalion, on the left of the 2nd, got across the river, but were faced with a difficult situation once they had made good the line of the main road parallel with the river. Opposition was very severe, and only by pushing out well to their left, and keeping going whatever happened, could they make their way into the hills and settle themselves above Quartolo.

The 5th Battalion passed through the 2nd at Olmatello and advanced towards Pideura. But it was already light, and they fought their way on until they were held there by the enemy who were holding a ridge and it was impossible to deploy the Battalion on their narrow front. Accordingly they made good their ground and prepared to hold it.

The initial bridgehead over the Lamone was complete, and the Sappers, with everything prepared most thoroughly before the assault, went into action with their customary enthusiasm to bridge the river. Meanwhile the three battalions tried during the day to enlarge their sectors of the bridgehead, but with little success. Forty men manhandled a Littlejohn anti-tank gun up to Olmatello, and a stream of porters kept going continuously up and down the hillside ; even water had to be taken up, for the wells had been fouled by the Germans. In some, corpses of Italian partisans were found. The rain was continuous and the enemy shelled routes forward and the crossing-places, and the men mustered from "B" Echelon of the battalions had a most trying time, floundering through the mud and suffering constant casualties. But the stream of supplies was maintained.

After a night of desperate toiling up muddy hill-faces, the 1/4th Battalion occupied Casa Poggio at dawn on 5th December and the 5th Battalion tried to advance from their positions. But they found that the ridge above Olmatello was more strongly held than they had expected, and no progress could be made in the face of very heavy machine-gun fire. That night, however, they stormed the ridge, though they suffered very heavily as they debouched along the narrow ridge.

While the men of the Hampshire Brigade were battling valiantly under atrocious conditions, their comrades in the Quartermasters', transport and clerical staffs were taxed to the utmost in an exhausting struggle to keep open the lifeline of supplies. The system for getting supplies forward was divided into three phases. Three-tonners and 15-cwt. trucks ferried stores forward in company and platoon lots to "A" echelons, where they were transferred to jeeps. These set off in convoy on times stipulated by Brigade Headquarters.

The route forward took the jeeps over muddy roads, along narrow tracks and across Bailey bridges approached through lines of white tape. At forward dispersal points, which could only be approached under cover of darkness, the stores were unloaded and then manhandled forward. The whole operation was within enemy artillery range and the jeeps often came under machine-gun fire. One-way roads and shell-plastered junctions and heavy rain added to the perils of the long nightly supply route.

On 6th December, when the countryside was blanketed in mist, the 1/4th advanced again, with tanks in support, and after a stiff climb and a brisk battle captured Casa Nova. They were well-nigh exhausted by the effort, but nevertheless the remnants of one company went on and most gallantly forced their way into Pideura. But a sharp counter-attack at nightfall drove them back. The 1st K.R.R.C. came up and attacked Pideura with artillery support and tanks, fought for the village all day, and after a most costly and bitter battle took the place.

On the night of 7th December, 25th Indian Brigade relieved 128th Brigade. The Hampshire Brigade had fought its last battle in Italy, and the long campaign against the Germans from Tebourba to the outskirts of Faenza was at an end. The final battle had been as tough as any, in rain and mud, leading an attack, making their ground, and holding it against violent opposition. They were withdrawn from the line and moved back to Forli to take part in a deception plan. Three days later they were well out of the battle, away on the Adriatic coast south of Ancona, living in billets and preparing for Christmas. For this celebration the Quartermasters had been zealously collecting poultry and all the necessary details.

So the Eighth Army was left to continue driving the Germans up Italy without the assistance of any Hampshire battalion. The battles they had fought were landmarks in the campaign, from Tebourba, Sidi Nsir and Hunts Gap; Sicily, Salerno, the Volturno, the Garigliano, Monte Camino, Monte Ornito and Cerasola, and finally the Gothic Line. To that list of names, which sound very like Battle Honours, must be added the crossings of the Foglia, the Conca, the Fiumicino and the Lamone.

From 24th August, 1944, until it was relieved on 7th December, the total casualties of 46th Division were 4,396, of which 3,797 were in the infantry. Of these 1,276 were of the Hampshire Brigade:

	KILLED		WOUNDED (including died of wounds)		MISSING	
	Officers	Other Ranks	Officers	Other Ranks	Officers	Other Ranks
128th Brigade Headquarters ...	1	1				
2nd Battalion	9	68	25	350	1	17
1/4th Battalion	5	51	20	354		39
5th Battalion	5	52	25	245		8

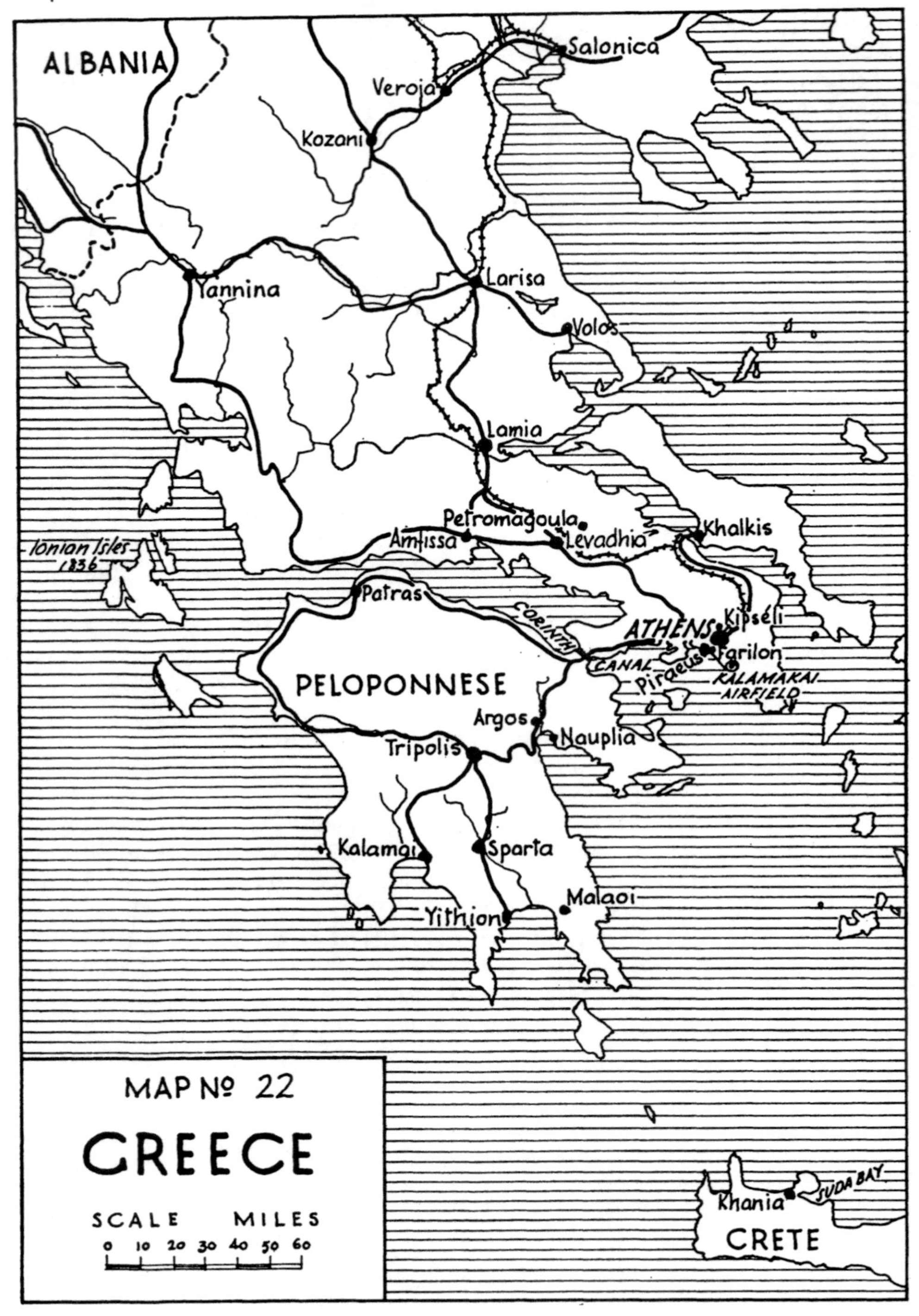
ALBANIA
Salonica
Veroja
Kozani
Yannina
Larisa
Volos
Lamia
Petromagoula
Amfissa
Levadhia
Khalkis
Ionian Isles 1836
Patras
CORINTH CANAL
ATHENS
Kipseli
Argilon
Piraeus
KALAMAKAI AIRFIELD
PELOPONNESE
Argos
Nauplia
Tripolis
Kalamai
Sparta
Malaoi
Yithion
Khania
SUDA BAY
CRETE
MAP No 22
GREECE
SCALE MILES
0 10 20 30 40 50 60

CHAPTER XVI

THE HAMPSHIRE BATTALIONS IN GREECE AND CRETE

The 2/4th Battalion

On 12th December, 1944, the 2/4th Battalion, in company with the 2nd King's, were flown to Greece in Wellington and Liberator bombers, while the rest of the 4th Division, diverted from the intended move to Palestine, followed by sea. The overthrow of the Germans in Greece had brought about a critical situation. The E.L.A.S. army, which had been trained by British officers and armed with British weapons, was now attempting to bring about an armed *coup d'état*. General Scobie was trying to negotiate a peaceful settlement with the E.L.A.S. leaders, but serious political tension and local clashes between E.L.A.S. and the Greek gendarmerie made the reinforcement of the British and Greek Government troops in Athens urgent.

There had been no stable government in Greece for four years; German or Italian garrisons had occupied the towns, while partisan bands roamed in the hills. When the Germans were driven out the partisans, ardent young men organized under E.L.A.S., threatened a new reign of terror. It was essential that law and order should be established. The E.L.A.S. forces had to be dislodged from Athens and induced to lay down their arms, and the Greek people impressed by the strength and discipline of British arms. It was in this task that the 2/4th Battalion, and later the three battalions of the 128th Brigade, were to play their part.

The 2/4th Battalion, like most of the 4th Division, was split up when it flew to Greece. There was an advance party in Palestine, a quartermaster's party up in the north of Italy, and a rear party in southern Italy. The men travelled in the bomb-bays of the aircraft and landed at Kalamaki aerodrome near Athens at noon on 12th December. The King's at once moved into Athens itself while the Hampshire battalion undertook the all-round defence of the aerodrome. It was believed that E.L.A.S. were preparing to attack the airfield from the north, but no attack was made.

More battalions of the Division arrived in a few days, and a full-scale operation was launched to clear Athens of the E.L.A.S. forces. The 2/4th Hampshire was given the task of clearing the main road leading from Farilon into Athens and through to the isolated Headquarters of III Corps. Other battalions were to clear blocks of buildings on the left and right of the Battalion simultaneously. The main enemy strong-point was a brewery which dominated the road, and this was the Battalion's main objective.

The attack was planned for the early morning of 18th December. As the companies marched up to the forward assembly area no opposition was encountered, and they were dispersed in the buildings surrounding the brewery to await the attack. At a quarter to seven tanks under command moved forward and blasted the end wall of the brewery, and the Battalion pioneer platoon made for the main entrance to force the doors with pole charges. E.L.A.S. snipers, well concealed in houses round the assembly area, opened fire with automatics and rifles, but the houses were soon entered and the snipers dealt with.

At seven o'clock "C" Company assaulted the brewery and very quickly killed, captured, or drove out all the E.L.A.S. men ; a thorough search of the building yielded some thirty prisoners and a store of arms and ammunition, as well as some valuable documents giving lists of names of E.L.A.S. men and orders. Meanwhile "A" Company stormed a block of buildings under brisk fire by snipers and quickly cleared them. "B" Company followed up and in gaining their objective lost Private Baxter, M.M., who was killed. Throughout the morning buildings around the brewery were systematically cleared of the enemy and all the positions in the battalion area were consolidated.

The opposition was, of course, infinitely easier than the German armies the Battalion had been fighting in Italy. The regular guerilla troops, however, were slippery customers. They had no distinctive uniform, they wore British battledress or the blue and white brassard of the Greek National Guard. E.L.A.S. was well supplied with miscellaneous weapons, some of them German, and they were desperate young men. They could always assume the role of civilians at a moment's notice, and they paid no attention to the Usages of War ; they used ambulances to bring up reinforcements and ammunition. Children and women were used to pass messages and to carry ammunition ; and snipers would open fire from behind the full skirts of a woman standing in a doorway. The first few weeks in Greece were a nerve-racking experience. On the one hand there was the ever-present and ruthlessly murderous enemy, on the other the pathetic and starving civilian population. As soon as an area was cleared of E.L.A.S. the British army organized soup kitchens and food distribution centres.

The Battalion spent Christmas Day in its positions around the brewery, but the actual celebrations were postponed. Fortunately sufficient beer had been "liberated" when the place was captured to induce some feeling of festivity, to compensate for the enemy mortaring and spasmodic sniping. There was a great deal of work to be done searching houses, rounding up suspects and extending the Battalion perimeter.

The Battalion's area round the brewery was taken over by the Greek National Guard on 29th December, and the Battalion moved to the north-east to clear more districts of Athens. On the outskirts of the town near a barracks the Battalion came across a strong E.L.A.S. area, which it attacked late at night on 2nd January. This was a more difficult proposition than the brewery had been, as the enemy were well situated in houses and in strong sangars at street corners. Their positions had to be taken one by one, moving on them with great care, and it was not until early on 3rd January that the area was reported clear. By that time the enemy who had not been caught or killed had fled northwards out of the city. This was the end of the more difficult operations in Greece, in which the Battalion lost three other ranks killed and Lieutenants Barker and Evans and twenty-two other ranks wounded.

On 6th January it was officially announced that the whole of Athens was clear of the enemy, and the Battalion was able to settle down in Kipséli to enjoy a well-earned rest for three weeks. On 29th January the Battalion moved to Petromagoula to police the village until the local police could be properly organized, and it was here on 3rd February that the Battalion celebrated Christmas. Each company occupied an outbuilding in a cotton factory and everyone entered into the spirit of the occasion most enthusiastically. In the evening a deputation arrived from the village and speeches were made thanking the British, and particularly the 2/4th Hampshire, for their friendly attitude towards Greece. It was all very cordial, and before the deputation left it presented Colonel Mitchell with a live lamb, charmingly decorated with blue ribbon.

At the beginning of March the Battalion went back to its old billets at Kipslié, and from there to Khalkis, where training, which had been carried out ever since the E.L.A.S. forces were overcome, was continued in a more advanced form. On 6th May the Battalion was informed by Colonel Mitchell that it was to move to Crete directly the German garrison there surrendered, and for this reason the Battalion was not able to take part in the triumphal march to Athens on VE Day.

A small advance party, including the Commanding Officer, left Greece in a destroyer for Crete on 13th May, and the remainder of the Battalion followed a few days later. They found some 10,000 German prisoners of war contained in a small area. The Battalion's duty was to take over the prisoners, to guard all German stores, and to assist at their embarkation at Suda Bay. This duty was somewhat delicate as the Cretans were, quite naturally, most eager to take their revenge on the Germans, who had for so long been their oppressors. The Cretans strongly resented the restraint of the British troops towards their hated and conquered foes. The situation was resolved by the tolerance and cheerful fairness of the British soldiers.

128TH BRIGADE

The battalions of the 128th Brigade celebrated Christmas, 1944, in memorable style. The 2nd Battalion was at San Benedetto, the 1/4th in the mountains at Ripatransone and the 5th at Grottemare. A supply of turkeys and pigs, carefully collected over the past weeks by rear echelons, was augmented by a generous allocation of vermouth. This was supplied free from a captured factory near Forli, and lorries loaded high with receptacles of all sorts, and even unit water-carts, queued outside until someone of high authority put a stop to it. But it was indeed a merry Christmas.

Rumours had been rife that the 46th Division was to go to Greece, but no orders came, and in the New Year training began in earnest, until on 6th January the word to pack up and move south came through ; it was to be Greece. The long and uncomfortable journey south to Taranto was made through snow and rain, and the 2nd Battalion and the 5th embarked on the *Hai-Lee* and the *Maregot* on 13th January, and two days later disembarked into landing-craft to go ashore in Piraeus harbour. The craft of the advance party of the 5th Battalion struck a mine in the harbour mouth and there were serious casualties. On 22nd January the 1/4th crossed to Piraeus on the Canadian miniature liner *Princess Catherine*.

For the operations in Greece the Brigade became "Tigerforce," and after a few days outside Athens moved across the Corinth Canal by Bailey bridge, the 2nd Battalion to Argos and the other two to Nauplia. By this time the E.L.A.S. resistance had been broken and there remained only scattered bands in remote and usually inaccessible places. The British Army had the task of rounding up these bands and disarming them, as well as restoring the people's confidence in law and order and helping to re-establish local government and the public services. Civil tension, total disorganization of local government, poverty and fear, was the background against which the Army had to work. It was important that the ordinary Greeks should be impressed with the power of British arms, and ceremonial parades and the natural efficient and friendly bearing of the army brought new and salutary hope to the bewildered Greek population.

The soldiers were welcomed with enthusiasm everywhere ; when the 2nd Battalion entered Argos, the streets were lined with cheering crowds, and flowers and garlands soon made the column look like a carnival procession. The 5th Battalion found the streets of Nauplia lined with coloured lights and the usual wildly demonstrative crowds. Battalions immediately took over the administration of the towns, started public services, cleared minefields, opened food distribution centres and did everything they could to restore morale and a normal way of life. The hospitality of the Greek people was formidable. They gave generously from their meagre supplies to entertain the British soldiers. Their national drinks, retsina and ouzo, were offered with embarrassing generosity, and it became necessary in the interests of international relations for the men to acquire both a taste and a head for these powerful drinks as soon as possible.

Behind the moving friendliness and gratitude of the Greek people there was constant tenseness ; the rival factions, Communist and Royalist, were always ready to fly at each other's throats. The tension was somewhat eased, however, on 17th February when political agreement was reached and the E.L.A.S. army was disbanded. Almost at once the Brigade moved more deeply into the Southern Peloponnese ; the 2nd to Kalamai, the 1/4th to Tripolis, and the 5th to Sparta.

Again there were scenes of wild excitement. When the 1/4th marched into Tripolis, cheering crowds lined old streets and the soldiers were garlanded with flowers and bay leaves. The E.L.A.S. commander handed over the city to the Commanding Officer, and the civilians paraded jubilantly for the benefit of the Hampshire Battalion. The two factions marched amicably backwards and forwards before Battalion Headquarters, eager to show that they did not resent our intrusion; the Communists carried a placard showing the Union Jack and the Stars and Stripes, and raised a cheer for the Regimental Quarter Guard. The Royalists paraded in Greek national costume, carrying a framed portrait of their King George, and sang "Tipperary" in English. On 25th March, the Greek National Independence Day, the 1/4th put on a big parade in the square, and the whole town turned out with banners and flags; many wore national costume, and afterwards there was dancing. The Battalion set to work in its dual role of hunting down obstinate E.L.A.S. bands hiding in the mountains around Tripolis and restoring local administration. Battalion Headquarters was regarded by the Greeks as a sort of fairy godmother, whither they flocked with all their problems.

It was the same everywhere; the 2nd and 5th Battalions came up against the same enthusiasm and hospitality, the same poverty and disorganization. When the 5th Battalion entered Sparta, the E.L.A.S. Mayor begged Colonel Robinson to make a speech from the balcony of the Town Hall to a large crowd in the square, but a bomb thrown in the middle of the crowd spoiled the occasion. When the rest of the Battalion arrived, however, things settled down, the E.L.A.S. mayor disappeared and the crowd took up the cry "Zeeto Churcheel."

The Brigade served in Greece until the beginning of April. As well as the restoration of administration, there was plenty of training and expeditions by companies and platoons to round up isolated E.L.A.S. groups. Companies or platoons foot-slogged their way over snow-covered mountain passes to villages where British soldiers had never been seen before. It was always the same; the people were always overjoyed to see them, and after cheers and tears they loaded the men with gifts of fruit, wine, nuts and eggs.

From the Headquarters point of view the scattered detachments meant many supply routes extended over scores of miles in different directions. Long and difficult journeys had to be made by jeep every day. One company, which marched many miles through the mountains, were marooned for a fortnight with ten-foot snowdrifts separating them from their base camp. Rations were carried through to them by men of other companies loaded with rucksacks, making a trek of thirteen miles each way over mountain tracks.

It was while the 5th Battalion were at Sparta that they said good-bye to Lieutenant-Colonel J. H. H. Robinson. Colonel Robinson had commanded the 5th Battalion since October, 1943, with notable and spirited efficiency. He left the Battalion to take command of the Infantry and Reinforcement Training Depot in Italy, and he was succeeded by Lieutenant-Colonel A. Boyce, who had just returned to duty after recovering from wounds sustained in Italy.

On 5th April the 46th Division handed over its commitments in Greece to the 23rd Armoured Brigade and began to return to Italy. The 1/4th and the 5th Battalions went back to Navplion and the 2nd to Argos, on to a Transit Camp at Athens, and then back to Taranto. In record time the battalions prepared themselves to go back into the fighting line, and they had soon started their three-hundred-mile journey northwards to Forlimpopoli.

The journey began on May Day, with everyone grimly aware of the kind of life awaiting them ; but it ended with spirits gloriously high at the splendid news of those days. At every halt there was a crowd round the wireless sets, and cheers went up at the heartening announcements telling of the disorderly retreat of the Germans before the final onslaught of the Fifth and Eighth Armies. There was also great news of victory in Germany, and of Hitler's death.

But the day after the Brigade arrived at Forlimpopoli came the greatest news of all, the announcement by Field-Marshal Alexander of the surrender of the German armies in Italy and southern Austria. Then came VE Day, and that night the sky was magnificently illuminated by the whole of 46th Division's tracer ammunition. It was indeed fitting that it should be in Italy, amid the scene of some of their toughest battles, that the Hampshire Brigade celebrated the victory for which they had fought so resolutely.

CHAPTER XVII

THE 1ST BATTALION ON D DAY

6TH JUNE, 1944

(*See maps on pages 70 and 212*)

ON 4th November, 1943, the 1st Battalion arrived back in England, for the first time for twenty-three years, with 231st Infantry Brigade in the 50th (Northumbrian) Division. The Battalion went to Long Melford, near Sudbury, and immediately the troops went on leave for periods varying from fourteen to twenty-eight days according to the length of service served overseas. It was well known, of course, that this return to England was by no means designed to keep the Division out of the war ; the Battalion knew that the Division was to be part of the "follow-up" in the landing to be made in North-West Europe. But when General Sir Bernard Montgomery was appointed Commander-in-Chief, 21st Army Group, the plan was changed, and the 50th Division became an assault division in Operation "Overlord." The further news that the 231st Brigade was to be an assault brigade was given personally to the Brigade early in 1944 by General Montgomery when he visited it at Sudbury. To be specially selected to lead the most vital operation in the war was a considerable honour for the 231st Brigade, though the news was received with mixed feelings as it had already made two assault landings in the Mediterranean.

In February, 1944, the King visited the Battalion at Long Melford and spent an hour watching assault demonstrations. His Majesty was particularly interested to meet Captain G. A. Greenway, who had forsaken his Quartermaster's commission for a combatant one, and who was then commanding a company. His Majesty knew quite as much about the A.C.I. which permitted this change as anyone else. In May General Eisenhower inspected the Battalion on a brigade parade and said how much he was impressed by the bearing of the men.

The Battalion went from Long Melford to Southwold in Suffolk in February, 1944, until the end of March, when it moved into Hampshire to Cadlands Camp, Fawley, near Southampton. From Fawley it went to the Combined Training Centre, Inverary, for three weeks' practice at seaborne operations, where the details of the problem of landing on the Channel coast of France were explained. The final move was from Cadlands camp to another near by, between Lyndhurst and Beaulieu.

Very comprehensive exercises were carried out on the south coast, in full co-operation with armoured vehicles and with the Navy and the R.A.F. The new and secret monsters of armoured warfare were used, the flail tanks, Scorpions, Snakes and Crocodiles, and the Assault Vehicles, R.E., known collectively as "Funnies."

While at Southwold the Battalion was selected to give a demonstration with these "Funnies" in front of General Montgomery. He wanted to see for

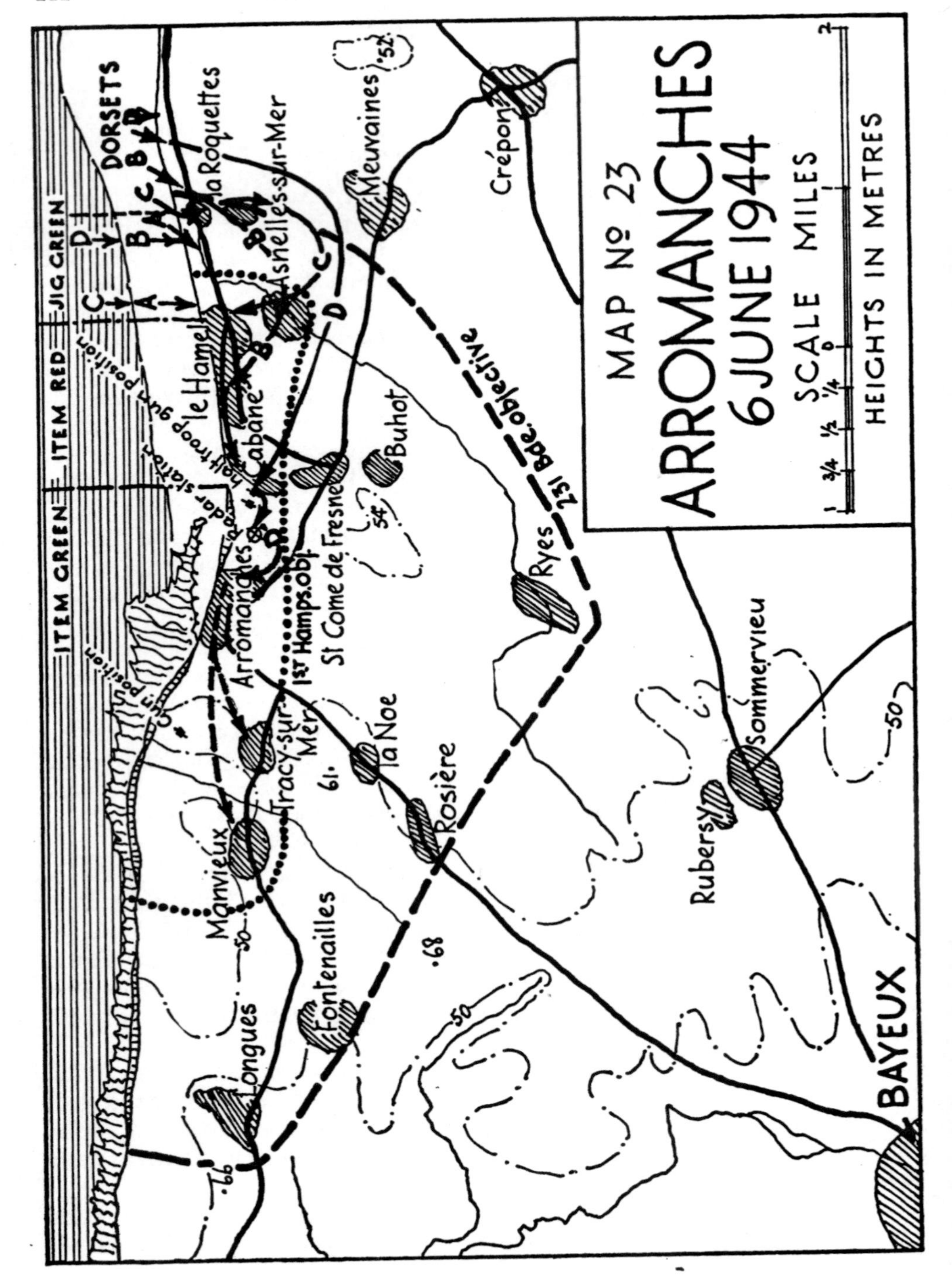
MAP No 23
ARROMANCHES
6 JUNE 1944
SCALE MILES
HEIGHTS IN METRES
ITEM GREEN
ITEM RED
JIG GREEN
DORSETS
le Hamel
La Roquettes
Asnelles-sur-Mer
Meuvaines
Crépon
Cabane
Buhot
St Come de Fresne
1st Hamps.obj
Arromanches
radar station
half troop gun position
gun position
231 Bde. objective
Ryes
Tracy-sur-Mer
La Noe
Rosière
Manvieux
Fontenailles
Longues
Sommervieu
Rubersy
BAYEUX

himself the technique being used by an infantry battalion when it left the landing-craft and attacked over the beach. All went well, the assault technique was given the final stamp of approval, and all that remained was to practise the drill as much as possible.

From Cadlands Camp two brigade rehearsals took place in Studland Bay, in co-operation with the Navy and the R.A.F. The same ships were used as for the real invasion. Two of these exercises, "Smash II" and "Smash IV," were most comprehensive, including the moving from the marshalling area at Southampton, a sea voyage round the Isle of Wight to equal the length of the crossing, and the landing on a replica of the West Wall, with full naval and air support and live ammunition. The final rehearsal was Exercise "Fabius," which entailed a landing on Hayling Island.

On 24th May, just before the camp was sealed, the Battalion marched past the Colonel of the Regiment, after a field firing exercise at Dibden Purlieu. The Regimental Band had come down for the occasion and led the march past. It was pouring with rain, but when General Haking saw that the men were coming past without greatcoats or groundsheets the grand old soldier took off his own raincoat, and ordered Major Jeffery, who was with him, to take off his coat as well. This was General Haking's last appearance, and this salute from the 1st Battalion of his Regiment, about to go into battle, was the last he was to receive on a ceremonial occasion.

When the camp was sealed a very complete briefing began, but with bogus place-names, as only Company Commanders and above knew the exact location of the landing. There was an accurate scale model and a large-scale map of the battalion assault area, and a great number of excellent aerial photographs.

While the camp was sealed a most disturbing situation arose, for a number of officers and men had to be sent to hospital with malaria. At one time men were going down with malaria at the rate of about a section a day, and it was mainly the men who had been in the Battalion a long time and who had already taken part in two assault landings ; experienced men on whom the Battalion was counting for the third landing. This serious situation was caused by the dampness of the New Forest, which seemed to revive the malarial "bugs." It was, however, a situation which had to be faced, and the Battalion was at full strength and at the highest point of morale when the day came to embark, and on 31st May, 1944, the 1st Battalion left its sealed camp for Operation "Overlord."

When the Battalion drove through the streets of Southampton, the civilians took no notice of them at all. They had already been "taken in" on five other occasions recently when the men had gone to the docks in exactly the same way for various rehearsals, returning to camp again by another route after the practice landing. So there were no cheers for the soldiers. Yet how apt and proper it was for the 1st Battalion of the County Regiment to leave the port of Southampton with the purpose of assaulting the enemy's defences at Arromanches. The men embarked on two L.S.Is., the *Empire Arquebus* and the *Empire Sword*, on 31st May, and waited on board until the convoy sailed five days later. Lectures and indoor games were organized on board the ships, and the scale model and the photographs were still available for study. The only criticism of the amazingly efficient arrangements for this mighty operation seems to be that no beer was available in the ships' canteens.

D Day had been fixed for 5th June and the whole intricate organization had been geared up to that date. Bad weather, however, presented General Eisenhower with the tremendous responsibility of deciding whether the gigantic operation should be postponed. He made that decision, and the troops were told that the day of the landing was changed to 6th June. Accordingly at 6.30 in the evening of 5th June, 1944, the assault convoy sailed. The sea was choppy and there was some sea-sickness ; it was indeed the roughest weather for June for twenty years. The convoy, Force "G" of the Royal Navy, sailed down the Solent and out to sea past the Needles.

Thus the 1st Battalion The Hampshire Regiment sailed with the 231st Brigade on one of the most dramatic military expeditions in our history. With their comrades of the Malta Brigade, the 1st Dorsets and the 2nd Devons, the Battalion was entrusted with the vital task of piercing the elaborate defences on the Normandy coast between Le Hamel and Arromanches, to enable the British Second Army to get a foothold in Normandy. When the Battalion sailed for Operation "Overlord" it was commanded by Lieutenant-Colonel H. D. Nelson Smith, M.C., with Major A. C. W. Martin, D.S.O., his Second-in-Command, and Captain F. H. Waters his Adjutant. The Company Commanders were Majors R. G. T. Baines, A. R. C. Mott, D. J. Warren, M.C., and J. L. G. Littlejohns, commanding the rifle companies, and Major J. M. C. Wicks and Captain T. G. Wilmer, commanding Support and Headquarters Companies.

The over-all object of Operation "Overlord" was "*to secure a lodgement on the Continent of Europe from which further operations could be developed.*" The intention was to assault simultaneously beaches on the Normandy coast immediately north of the Carantan estuary and between that estuary and the River Orne, with the object of securing an area including airfield sites and the port of Cherbourg. The left flank of the area was to include the road centre of Caen. For the assault General Montgomery, commanding 21st Army Group, had under his command the First United States Army, supported by Western Naval Task Force, and the Second British Army, supported by Eastern Naval Task Force. The First United States Army was to assault with three divisions between Varreville and the Carantan estuary and between Vierville-sur-Mer and Colleville-sur-Mer. The Second British Army was to assault with three divisions, the 50th, 3rd Canadian and 3rd British, between Port-en-Bessin and the River Orne, and to develop a beach-head and to protect the flank of the Americans while they captured Cherbourg and the Brittany ports.

The 50th Northumbrian Division was to go in on the right of the three assault divisions of 2 Army, with the 69th and 231st as the two assault brigades. The 231st Brigade was to land two assaulting battalions on "Jig Green" beach, the 1st Dorsets on the left and the 1st Hampshire on the right, followed at

H hour + 40 by the 2nd Devons. Thus the Hampshire Battalion was assaulting on the right of the line, the traditional post of honour.

The Battalion plan was to land "A" and "B" Companies at H + 5, preceded by one squadron of amphibious tanks at H − 3, and three breaching teams of flail tanks at H hour. At H + 20 "C" and "D" Companies were to land. The Battalion tasks were for "A" Company on the right to capture Le Hamel East, "B" Company on the left to capture Asnelles-sur-Mer, and "C" Company to capture Le Hamel West. In the second phase "D" Company was to capture a gun position near Cabane. The third phase, following the capture of the gun position by "D" Company, was for "B" and "C" Companies, supported by one squadron of the Sherwood Rangers, to capture a radar station some 500 yards along the coast to the west. The next phase, to follow the capture of the radar station, was for "D" Company to advance farther west to capture enemy positions on the cliffs west of Arromanches and to patrol to the village of Tracy-sur-Mer and to Manvieux. The fifth and final phase was for one company to move into Arromanches to clear the enemy positions. Thus it was that the Battalion, by landing and swinging right along the coast, was thereby made responsible for the clearance of no less than three miles of the much-vaunted "Western Wall" of Europe; a formidable assignment.

The support was most impressive. There were to be two regiments of self-propelled artillery, the Sherwood Rangers with their "D.D." tanks, a squadron of Centaurs mounting 95-mm. guns and manned by the Royal Marines, a squadron of Armoured Vehicles R.E.—A.V.R.E.—a squadron of flail tanks of the Westminster Dragoons and the 47th Marine Commando. Among the larger warships in support of the Brigade were the cruiser *Emerald*, the destroyers *Cottesmore*, *Grenville*, *Undine*, *Jervis*, *Urania* and *Ulysses*, as well as a Polish destroyer. Four fighter-bomber squadrons of the R.A.F. were to be on call, and there was to be a tremendous pre-arranged bombing programme.

Thus was the assault planned, a most elaborate operation in which everything possible had been done by way of preparation, training and organization. As always, however, all depended finally on the courage and determination of the first infantry ashore, whose duty it was to grapple personally with the enemy defences. If they failed to gain the initial foothold all could be brought to nought.

A special message was sent to all ranks of the 50th (Northumbrian) Division on D Day by the Divisional Commander, Major-General D. A. H. Graham:

> The time is at hand to strike—to break through the Western Wall and into the Continent of Europe.
>
> To you, officers and men of the 50th (Northumbrian) Division, has been given the great honour of being in the vanguard of this mighty blow for freedom.
>
> It is my unshakeable belief that we, together with Force "G" of the Royal Navy, the special regiments of the Royal Armoured Corps, the Royal Artillery and the Royal Engineers attached to us and with the

help of the R.A.F. and American Air Force, will deliver such an overpowering punch that the enemy will be unable to recover. Thus we shall be well set to carry through to a glorious and successful end all that is now entrusted to us.

Much has been asked of you in the past and great have been your achievements, but this will be the greatest adventure of all. It will add yet another fine chapter to your already long and distinguished record—the grandest chapter of all.

Very best of luck to every one of you.

So the great enterprise was afoot, with the 1st Hampshire on the right of the line of the initial assault. Everyone knew how historic the occasion was, and spirits were high. When it came to the assault, however, things did not turn out quite as had been expected. First there was the rough sea, which caused serious dislocation in important parts of the programme. The secret "D.D." swimming-tanks were to have been launched some four miles out to swim ashore, but the first few were sunk in the rough seas and the remainder remained on their craft and were landed on the beach in the ordinary way. They were to provide valuable support, but they were not there, as had been planned, before the infantry landed. The expected support of the Centaurs was also missing at the landings. These Centaurs were mounted in pairs in landing craft and they were intended to cover the run-in of the infantry to the beach. Of the sixteen craft which should have reached the beach only two arrived on the 50th Division front ; the rest were delayed or turned back because of the rough sea. The supporting fire did not in effect silence the enemy defences in the battalion area as much as had been expected, particularly in the hospital at Le Hamel East, and another complication for the assaulting infantry was that the breaching team of flail and A.V.R.E. tanks were either knocked out or bogged down on the beach, so that they were not there to make the gaps in the mines and wire at the top of the beach. Finally, the bombers which were to have attacked Le Hamel to "soften up" the many strong-points in the area had missed their mark in the uncertain light and had dropped their bombs too far inland.

The assault convoy anchored at 5.30 on 6th June some seven miles off shore. It was very choppy with a four-foot sea running. The men were on their troop decks by a quarter to six and embarked at six o'clock. H hour was 7.25. The L.C.As. were lowered, and although the run-in was uneventful from the military point of view, most men were very sea-sick and all were drenched. The beaches were invisible until the craft were some four miles off shore. A very heavy naval bombardment was in full swing and the troops, in spite of their acute sea-sickness, and resultant depression, were much heartened by the roar of the broadsides from the 6-inch guns of H.M.S. *Ajax* as they passed close to her. They took more comfort, too, when the supporting S.P. regiment began its run-in shoot. During the last half-mile enemy mortar and artillery fire, as well as small-arms fire, came down on the sea, but fortunately without much effect. Some of the landing-craft were lost through striking the underwater obstacles which had been dug deep into the beach. These were stout wooden posts and pieces of steel rail about four feet high, with mines or explosive charges fixed to the top. The beach was thickly sown with these, and although Royal Engineer "frogmen" had gone in with the breaching party and had gallantly set about disarming them, enough remained to cause some casualties to craft.

The landing-craft beached some thirty yards from the edge of the sea and the men leapt into the water ; some were up to their armpits in the sea, others up to their thighs, and at once they came under concentrated small-arms fire, so that many were killed. There were casualties, too, as the craft, lightened as the men jumped out, became water-borne again and were swept inshore by the sea, overrunning some of the wading soldiers. It was apparent that the assault of the beach was going to be more difficult than had been expected. There were to have been two or even three gaps through the mines and wire, but there were none in the battalion sector, and it was uncomfortably apparent to the men that the beach defences were by no means softened up.

The situation was such that less seasoned or less determined troops might well have been helplessly pinned down and the whole great venture brought to a standstill. But in spite of the demoralizing effects of sea-sickness, in spite of the violent machine-gun and mortar fire, and in spite of the constantly rising number of casualties, the assault companies, of the Hampshire on the right and of the Dorset on the left, resolutely made their way on to the beach and up it towards the dunes. The Battalion was unsupported by any armour ; a number of tanks of various descriptions were ashore, but they were either helplessly bogged down or lay crippled and blazing.

"A" Company was first ashore, landing in the thick of very heavy fire slightly east of their intended position, so that they could not get forward to deal with the enemy at Le Hamel East, nor could they get up the beach to make their own gaps through the mines and wire, which were very thoroughly covered by enemy fire. The left-hand platoon got inland and dealt effectively with two pill-boxes at the edge of Les Roquettes, while the other two tried to work their way towards Le Hamel, but they ran into such violent machine-gun and mortar fire from the village that they were pinned down.

"C" Company, following "A" in the assault, were caught on the beach in the same way and tried in vain to get up the beach to get into Le Hamel. "B" Company made good progress up the beach and dealt with the Dorsets' objective at Les Roquettes, and then fought their way into Asnelles. "D" Company also forced their way inland towards the forming-up position to attack the gun positions near Cabane.

It was apparent that no progress could be made until the enemy in Le Hamel were silenced. To help in this, one flail tank which was still operative was asked to fire at the hospital, from where most of the enemy fire was coming. When he opened fire, movement across the beach towards the village was possible, although not without further casualties. However, the tank commander decided to move to a better position, and his tank was immediately hit by an 88-mm. shell from Le Hamel and was soon blazing.

At this stage Lieutenant-Colonel Nelson Smith was wounded for the second time, and so seriously that he had to be evacuated. As the Second-in-Command was still at sea, Major Warren, commanding "C" Company, took over for the time being. Unfortunately, when Major Martin landed two hours later he was immediately killed by a sniper.

Major Warren handed over the command of his company to his second-in-command and went to Battalion Headquarters in Les Roquettes to collect all the information about the Battalion he could. He saw that it was not possible to take Le Hamel by frontal attack, so he ordered the withdrawal of "C" Company with the remainder of "A," brought them to Les Roquettes through the gap in the mines and wire on the Dorsets' sector, and reorganized them as one composite company. He sent this, now called "C" Company, farther inland to join "B," so that the two of them could advance on Le Hamel from the rear. "C" Company made contact with "B" and moved into Asnelles-sur-Mer, where Battalion Headquarters moved at the same time. "B" Company moved on and took up a position at the cross-roads south of Le Hamel and remained firm there to give supporting fire to "C" Company, which was to advance across country and establish itself on the lateral road south of Le Hamel. "B" Company would then assault the position, supported by fire from "C" Company.

"C" Company's advance began at a quarter to one in the afternoon, and it took them an hour to break down enemy opposition and reach their position on the lateral road. "B" Company then advanced grimly on Le Hamel, but they were held up about fifty yards from the hospital by a torrent of fire. By good fortune an A.V.R.E. came down the road from Asnelles at this critical moment. This drove close to the hospital and fired a petard bomb which exploded with its typical violence. The enemy machine-gun fire was only checked for a second or so, however, and it was not until five rounds had been fired by the A.V.R.E.'s petard that "B" Company was able to close with the hospital and silence this very obstinate and costly enemy position. While "C" Company were mopping up the hospital position, "B" attacked Le Hamel West. Here again the enemy fought it out until the end, but, as at the hospital, the tremendous bombs of the A.V.R.E.'s petard on fortified houses enabled the company to close with the enemy, and by four in the afternoon both parts of Le Hamel were reported clear and in our hands.

While the attack on the hospital was in progress, "D" Company reported that the enemy gun position beyond Cabane had been taken, and Major Warren sent the company to attack their next objective, the radar station, which was quickly captured with some forty prisoners. Sniping was reported, coming mainly from the cliffs west of Arromanches, so fire was called down on the enemy positions from the S.P. guns of 147 Field Regiment, and from one of the destroyers. This naval support was arranged direct with the ship by the Forward Bombardment Officer, attached to each of the assault battalions. This fire, from the S.P. guns and the destroyer, was thoroughly effective. At four o'clock the Battalion's priority trucks arrived at Le Hamel, together with further A.V.R.Es. which were most welcome as companies were getting very short of ammunition.

The crisis of the great day was now well past. The assault brigade were ashore, all their principal objectives were taken, and the bridgehead was established. The machine-gun posts which had inflicted such cruel casualties on the assault battalions were silenced, and troops, vehicles and stores were flowing on to the beaches. There still remained, however, the final phase for the Hampshire Battalion ; the clearing of Arromanches itself. Major Warren held an "O" Group at the captured radar station and ordered "D" Company to move down and around the southern end of Arromanches to attack it from the rear. He arranged a fifteen-minute bombardment from the destroyer, followed by a ten-minute concentration by the S.P. guns of 147 Regiment, R.A. "B" and "C" Companies were to support the attack with small-arms fire from the forward slopes of the radar station. The attack on Arromanches was completely successful ; the resistance was slight, twenty prisoners were taken for no casualties, and the town was clear of the enemy by nine o'clock that evening.

Thus ended the memorable day, the great D Day when Hitler's West Wall was broken and entered. It had been done in spite of many forbidding difficulties in the earliest and most vital hours. Because so much of the planned pattern had gone wrong through various circumstances, what was to have been an intricate and scientific combination of assaulting arms became a simple infantry problem. In the first hours there was little or no support, and the infantry had to get on with the task of overcoming a determined enemy as best they could with their own weapons.

That the great assault succeeded is a fine testimony to the fighting qualities of the men who made the assault ; to their leadership and their aggressive spirit. The infantry grappled with the foe on their own, suffering terrible casualties but never hesitating, and not one Hampshire man was taken prisoner. Every man knew the full importance of the task the Battalion had been given ; they understood the honour of being in the very spearhead, and they knew that no price was too high to pay for success. That way success was won.

The casualties to the 1st Battalion on 6th June, 1944, were one hundred and eighty-two all ranks. Of these five officers were killed and eleven wounded—Majors Martin and Baines, and Lieutenants Williamson, Bawden and Westley killed ; and Lieutenant-Colonel Nelson Smith, Captains Arnett, Edkins and Hughes, and Lieutenants Elliot, Boys, Davison-Lungley, Lauder, Layton, Miller and Norman wounded. Lieutenant Elliot died of his wounds the next day. The casualties among the other ranks included six sergeants, twelve corporals and one hundred and forty-eight privates. Among the awards for gallantry were the D.S.O. to Major Warren, the M.C. to Major Littlejohns, and the M.M. to Sergeant G. J. B. Slade and Lance-Corporal W. R. Butt.

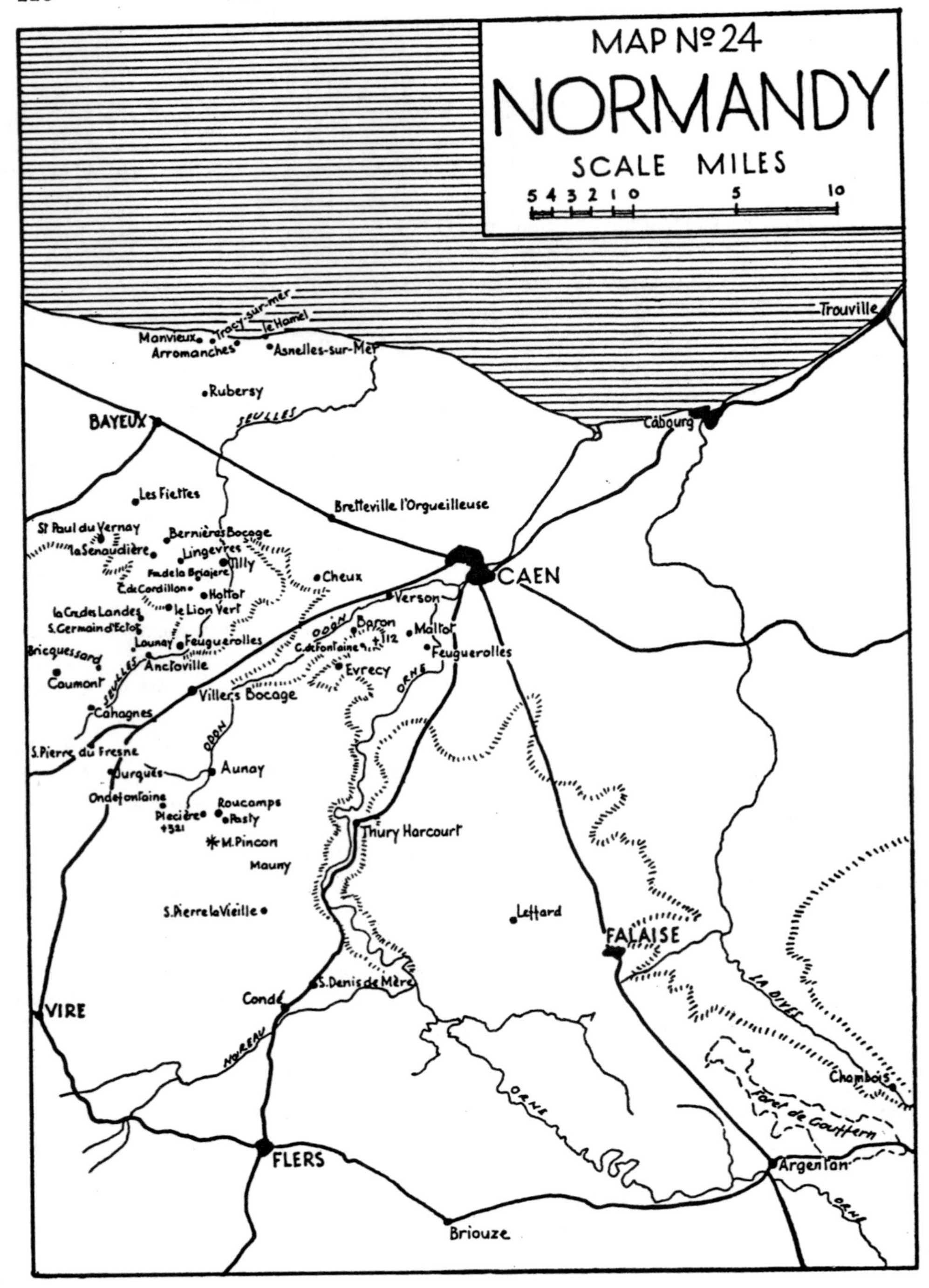
MAP No 24
NORMANDY
SCALE MILES
5 4 3 2 1 0 5 10
Trouville
Manvieux
Tracy-sur-mer
le Hamel
Arromanches
Asnelles-sur-Mer
Rubersy
SEULLES
BAYEUX
Cabourg
Les Fiettes
Bretteville l'Orgueilleuse
St Paul du Vernay
Bernières Bocage
la Senaudière
Lingevres
Tilly
Fe de la Briajere
Cheux
C de Cordillon
Hottot
CAEN
la Cr des Landes
le Lion Vert
Verson
S. Germain d'Ectot
ODON
Baron
Maltot
Launay
Feuguerolles
C de Fontaine
+112
Bricquessard
Feuguerolles
SEULLES
Anctoville
Evrecy
Caumont
ORNE
Villers Bocage
Cahagnes
ODON
S. Pierre du Fresne
Jurques
Aunay
Ondefontaine
Roucamps
Pleciere
Pasty
+321
M. Pincon
Mauny
Thury Harcourt
S. Pierre la Vieille
Leffard
FALAISE
S. Denis de Mère
Condé
LA DIVES
VIRE
NOIREAU
Chambois
ORNE
Foret de Gouffern
FLERS
Argentan
ORNE
Briouze

CHAPTER XVIII

THE 1st BATTALION IN NORMANDY

JUNE TO AUGUST, 1944

THE morning of 7th June, 1944, found the Allied armies established firmly in Normandy. The enemy had failed to repel the assault troops, and his object now was to try to contain our bridgehead and to counter-attack with such concentration of armour that the assault forces would be speedily eliminated. Our task was the precise reverse : to expand the bridgehead as quickly as possible and to build up reinforcements and supplies faster than the enemy could bring his forces to bear.

The Germans quickly got their armoured reserves on the move, and two divisions were already in the battle on 7th June. There was also the Panzer Lehr prepared for battle ; a "demonstration" division which was to be the 50th Division's implacable and skilful enemy during the protracted and bitter fighting that lay ahead. The 50th Division's part in the early stage of the Allied plan was to contain as many of the enemy as possible by aggressive action. A very important part of the army plan was the capture of Villers Bocage, a small town nearly twenty miles south of the beaches.

Villers Bocage and the country around it were to be the scene of grim fighting by the 231st Brigade in the days to come. The little Norman town stood on fairly high ground surrounded by hills at the junction of five important roads. About five miles north of Villers Bocage is the village of Hottot, and in the fighting for Hottot the 1st Hampshire were to be particularly concerned.

A strong divisional attack with the complete 7th Armoured Division was launched against Villers Bocage in the first few days ashore, but the place could not be taken and there followed a prolonged period of very bitter fighting in which every yard gained had to be fought for and then grimly held. In fact, Villers Bocage did not fall until 4th August, two months later.

On 7th June Lieutenant-Colonel C. R. Howie took over command of the 1st Battalion, which remained static except for patrols in the early morning to Tracy-sur-Mer and Manvieux. When the perimeter Le Hamel–Asnelles-sur-Mer–Arromanches–Tracy-sur-Mer–Manvieux was finally cleared, the Battalion moved to Rubersy, where the companies were formed in a close "box" and patrols probed outwards.

On 9th June the Battalion moved forward to a position south-west of Bayeux. Mopping-up operations continued, the Battalion moving all the while, to St. Paul du Vernay and to Bernières Bocage. Here, on 10th June, the Battalion launched an attack on an enemy pocket of resistance, the first of many costly battles to come. The tanks in support were soon held up by a well-camouflaged 80-mm. gun at a sharp bend in the road, and the advance was made exceedingly difficult by enemy Spandau teams behind the high hedges, in the orchards and in the woods. The road, the tracks and the fields were all covered by enemy mortars. It was typical of the fighting in the Normandy bocage, in close country with an abundance of cover, lush with summer. In spite of these natural advantages of the enemy, the rifle companies gained ground and dug in in a defensive arc south-west of Bernieres Bocage. These positions were subjected to many fierce counter-attacks, which were all successfully repelled with considerable casualties to the enemy. A whole series of grim battles followed in the close bocage country, all part of an offensive to capture the village of Hottot, a necessary preliminary to the assault on Villers Bocage.

On 12th June the fighting continued with renewed vigour. The Battalion tried to destroy the enemy resistance beyond Bernières with the support of flail tanks and A.V.R.Es. But these moved too far forward and got knocked out. The battalion start line forward of the village was dominated by ridges from the enemy side, and a strong counter-attack was launched when the Battalion was lined up on the road. Fighting was very fierce, but the counter-attack was driven off, with heavy loss to the enemy, and the Battalion regained its position south-west of Bernieres. The Battalion suffered many casualties, including three officers killed—Major Wicks, commanding "C" Company, Major Boyd, commanding "A" Company, and Lieutenant Paul.

On 13th June the Battalion was withdrawn slightly to the northern end of Bernières Bocage to clear the way for a heavy air bombardment of La Senaudière. Once more the Battalion was ordered to put in an attack, with an artillery barrage covering a hundred yards every three minutes, and the Battalion advanced with the support of a troop of "Crocodiles" and a troop of tanks. The enemy had occupied the positions vacated by the Battalion, and strong opposition was encountered north-east of La Senaudière. Once again the armour failed in the effectiveness of its support by venturing too far ahead, and, penetrating into the village, the tanks were knocked out, though not before they had inflicted severe damage on the enemy.

Captain Hammond and a section of the Carrier Platoon were sent on foot to find an enemy mortar detachment, on the high ground west of La Senaudière, which had been causing a lot of trouble. In this action Captain Hammond and four of his patrol were killed. For his share in this battle Sergeant R. F. Curley was awarded the D.C.M. Very fierce fighting followed for the Battalion, who advanced against furious opposition to the cross-roads outside the village; a counter-attack was repulsed and the Battalion consolidated their position. Several German Panther tanks were knocked out at the cross-roads. On the following night the Germans made an attempt to recover one which stood opposite "B" Company's position, but they were severely mauled and did not try again. Again the Battalion lost many men, among them Lieutenant E. R. Brown, killed, and two other officers wounded—Major Thomas, who had won the D.S.O. in particularly gallant circumstances with the 2nd Battalion at Tebourba, and Lieutenant Hughes.

Then followed the first breathing-space for the Battalion since the landing, while the Brigade went into divisional reserve for three days. It was still necessary to have units standing to, and shelling continued. But some attention could be paid to domestic affairs, and there were visits to Bayeux for baths, sight-seeing and a glimpse of civilization. Then on 18th June the respite ended and the Battalion moved forward from La Senaudière to take part in a brigade attack on Hottot. The defences of Hottot had been very thoroughly prepared, and all the approaches were heavily mined and booby traps were set in every likely spot. Snipers were particularly active, and operated from both front and rear. They were tied in the trees, where they stayed all day, taking a steady toll of the unwary, making every movement difficult.

Hottot

The attack started early in the afternoon of 19th June in pouring rain. At once the start line was heavily mortared. The companies advanced, however, under a heavy barrage and went forward stubbornly over the difficult country. The method was to get to a ditch or hedge, take breath, and then dash forward again through a hail of mortar bombs and bullets. The enemy were holding Hottot in strength and it was only by dint of quite reckless determination that the village itself was reached. That achieved, the enemy counter-attacked most violently with Panther tanks, and those who had made the village were forced back. Later the 2nd Devons fought their way into the village and after repelling several counter-attacks maintained a precarious hold on it ; so precarious, indeed, that during the night the Brigade withdrew slightly to the north and the enemy occupied Hottot once more. This excerpt from the diary of Lieutenant M. Blackmore of "A" Company tells some of the story :

"The attack on Hottot started in pouring rain, which began before noon. The start line was neatly marked with white tape, and the enemy gave it (and us) a terrific plastering with his mortars. We pushed forward under a heavy barrage with our Brens fighting a staccato duel against the faster b-r-r-r-p of Jerry's Spandaus. In the din it was difficult at first to know which was his artillery and which was ours, but one soon realized where the 'receiving end' was when we reached a sunken lane, evidently well pin-pointed by the enemy. Several men in 'D' Company (the leading formation) were also held up in this lane. But the place was decidedly too hot for comfort ; so we climbed up the bank and dashed across the next field through a hail of mortar bombs and bullets, luckily without any casualties. We shoved over a lot more artillery than the enemy ; he seemed to rely more on his mortars.

"We got to close quarters with him at a farm. One of his Panther tanks came rumbling forward right up to our position, firing everything it had. With great presence of mind, one of our anti-tank gunners caught the Panther amidships, but not before it had managed to get one of our Shermans belonging to the Sherwood Rangers, who were in support. Both caught fire, but the Sherman crew managed to get out all right. The 'brewed up' tanks, now well ablaze, began to attract heavy mortar fire, and although 'A' Company were still supposed to be in reserve, we moved forward towards the farm where Major J. Littlejohns (commanding 'D' Company) had set up his headquarters.

"No sign of the rain stopping after ten hours. Everyone is tired and wet, but we have moved forward nearly a mile from La Senaudière, with Hottot another thousand yards ahead."

This first attack on Hottot—it was not captured until a month later—was another costly day to the Battalion. Among the many casualties were Lieutenant Needham who was killed; and four officers wounded, Major Warren, the Second-in-Command, Major Mott, commanding "B" Company, and Lieutenants Hand and Dougherty.

The Battalion held their positions north of Hottot, with the 69th Brigade on the right of the 231st Brigade and the 151st Brigade on their left, in the general direction of Tilly. This was the situation for nearly three weeks, in which there was no general advance, though we were in constant contact with the resolute enemy of the Panzer Lehr Division. Sniping, mortaring and shelling were almost incessant. It was a grim state of affairs which called for constant vigilance and steady nerves. If no progress towards Villers Bocage through Hottot could be made, the enemy was constantly pressed and contained resolutely in his positions.

Both sides suffered casualties all the while, and in this period the Battalion lost very many good men, and five officers wounded—Major Dewar, commanding "A" Company, Captain Bradley, and Lieutenants Hunter-Smith, Florence and Bennett. Throughout the long battle for Hottot many officers and N.C.Os. won the admiration of their fellows by their constant devotion to duty and unflinching good spirits. Among them was the Medical Officer, Captain Ivor Joseph, M.C., who worked day and night with the casualties quite regardless of his own safety; a splendid example of the traditions of the R.A.M.C. It was during the seemingly endless days at Hottot that General Graham visited Battalion Headquarters, and an 88-mm. shell whistled past his head, so closely that even he raised his eyebrows and observed that it was a most unhealthy spot. The men called it "Hot Spot." The Brigade Commander, Brigadier Sir Alexander Stanier, was a constant source of strength to all of the 231st Brigade throughout the fighting in Normandy and afterwards.

The three weeks of incessant fighting north of Hottot reached the climax on 11th July when, as part of an all-out divisional attack to reach Villers Bocage, the 231st Brigade was ordered to capture Hottot. The attack began at seven o'clock in the morning of 11th July with the three battalions and the Sherwood Rangers in their Sherman tanks. The Brigade was to attack with the 1st Hampshire on the right and the 2nd Devons on the left, preceded by a massive R.A. barrage moving at fifty yards every two minutes, and governed in its lengths of pause on various objectives by the battalion commanders. Flail tanks, A.V.R.Es., mortars and medium machine guns were also in support.

As soon as "A" and "D" Companies crossed the start line they came under heavy fire. "A" on the right flank had an early success by overcoming enemy resistance and taking fifteen prisoners in the first quarter of an hour. They moved forward again and tackled enemy in entrenched positions in an orchard, taking more prisoners, and within an hour the company was in possession of its first objective. "D" Company, however, on the left was less fortunate, and advanced only fifty yards before being pinned down by merciless mortar fire. They also suffered badly from clever sniping. The Company Commander, Major Littlejohns, was seriously wounded and the C.S.M. was killed ; in fact, the company was reduced from ninety-three to about thirty within two hours of the start of the attack. In spite of their heavy losses, and with the enemy firing at almost point-blank range, Lieutenant Ricketts led the remnants of "D" Company forward and they fought so doggedly that they eventually captured their objective.

The second phase of the attack began at ten o'clock in the morning, when "C" Company passed through "A" Company on the right and "B" went through "D" on the left. "C" Company made splendid progress, capturing Spandau posts and killing the enemy manning them, forcing the enemy back and gaining their objectives. "B" Company advanced steadily through a veritable hail of mortar bombs and flying shrapnel, suffering in their turn heavy casualties, including their Company Commander, Major the Lord Carew, who was wounded. Reaching their objective, they stormed and took it. Three enemy tanks complicated matters by appearing on the left, but the Sherman tanks of the Sherwood Rangers knocked out one and drove the other two off.

By one o'clock the battle, one of unceasing noise with no respite, went into its third phase. The enemy mortar fire increased in intensity on the battalion front and our mortars and guns replied with equal ferocity. A counter-attack on the right flank was sternly repulsed by "C" Company. "D" Company, owing to its sadly reduced strength, was joined to "B" on the left. The next task was the final assault by the whole Battalion on the enemy positions north of the village and so into Hottot itself. Two incidents occurred at this stage which caused considerable discomfort to the troops, who had already been fighting through the heat of the very hot day in the sternest manner. While waiting for the order to move forward, shells from our own guns began to fall among the troops, and then a small force of R.A.F. Typhoons mistook the Hottot road for the Tilly road and began to dive-bomb our positions. These events naturally caused some confusion and delay, and gave the enemy time to withdraw into Hottot.

At this time the situation was very confused. Battalion Headquarters was not in touch with any of the companies by wireless. Accordingly Lieutenant-Colonel Howie went forward to see the situation for himself, and was killed as he was directing the two forward companies to the final assault. In the month in which Colonel Howie had commanded the Battalion his fearlessness, at a time when nerves were stretched to the uttermost, had been a splendid example to his men. Major Drewitt took over command of the Battalion, and, with the enemy strongly entrenched within the village, the Battalion was reorganized to hold the positions already taken. A patrol of "C" Company was sent into the village after dark and found it strongly held.

In the day's fighting for Hottot on 11th July the Battalion suffered heavy casualties. Among the officers, Lieutenants Hastings and Godfrey were killed, as well as Lieutenant-Colonel Howie, and Majors Littlejohns, commanding "D" Company, and the Lord Carew, "B" Company, and Lieutenants Ricketts, D. B. Evans, Connor and King were all wounded.

Lieutenant Blackmore's personal narrative again gives a vivid picture of the fighting for Hottot on 11th July:

"We began the attack on Hottot at 0700 hrs., starting off with a hand-to-hand party in the orchard. I got the leading section of 7 Platoon near the southern end under covering fire without much trouble, and then Jerry gave us everything he had at point-blank range.

"At this stage Horace Wright, who was in the adjoining field, crawled up to give me further orders through the hedge, and while he was talking I had the uncomfortable sensation that my backside was being made a target for Spandau fire. From his position in the ditch on his side of the hedge he couldn't see the ground being churned up behind me, whereas I was uncomfortably well aware of the fact! Luckily the gunner was a bad shot.

"For a while things were somewhat hectic, but Private R. Robins did a good job single-handed with a Bren gun, charging into a heavily defended post and silencing it, after which we had things our own way. The enemy now began to surrender, and fourteen of them came out—two or three of whom were boys of about eighteen years or so, but fierce fighters for all that. I counted seven enemy dead in the orchard, and there were also several badly wounded Huns who seemed glad enough to be put 'in the bag' after their ordeal.

"After a brief pause to regroup, 'A' Company then advanced and reached its first objective (known as 'Orange') without meeting anything worse than moderately heavy mortar fire. But after we had consolidated the position, hell was let loose on us by mortars and 88-mm. shells for two or three hours, causing further casualties among the company.

"In the afternoon we moved forward again and reached the outskirts of Hottot at about 1530 hrs., after getting through some really heavy mortar fire. Here we dug in. There were woods to our left and right, and the houses of Hottot itself could be seen about 500 yards to our immediate front. Tanks from the Sherwood Rangers—complete with flails and flame-throwing Crocodiles—were now in close support. Then at about 1600 hrs. I heard the drone of approaching aircraft—our Typhoons were coming over.

"The engines of the nearest aircraft roared as the plane began to dive, but with a feeling that quickly changed from one of relief to horror, I realized that our R.A.F. friends were attacking our positions! Not altogether surprising because the whole picture was very confused, our tanks being in close combat with the enemy's. The first rocket came down with a mighty roar and I felt a somewhat queasy sensation in the pit of my stomach as the rocket exploded in a wood about seventy yards away. The Typhoon in question banked for a second attack, and one of our tanks managed to fire a yellow identification signal just in time to warn the pilot. He rose steeply and flew on without firing. Then a Panther tank opened up on our right flank and moved towards us, but another of our Typhoons spotted it and attacked immediately. There was an ear-splitting explosion and the Panther rocked sideways, then halted abruptly, while red and orange flames rapidly engulfed it and set fire to its ammunition. Another tank was also hit, judging by the flames that rose from a near-by copse, but it was now becoming impossible to see anything clearly through the thickening smoke.

"Despite a prolonged and accurate bombardment, we hung on to our forward positions, with our right flank dangerously exposed. During much of the time there was a lot of confused firing in our rear and it seemed as if the enemy were launching some kind of counter-attack from the woods south of the Château de Cordillon. We heard later that they had done so twice, but with limited success, against the 1st Dorsets, who were able to prevent them from making any serious penetration.

"After nightfall 'A' Company was given orders to withdraw, which we managed to do in orderly fashion and without further incident, passing silently within less than 200 yards of the enemy, who made a great deal of noise digging in. However, they didn't hear us and we got back to a position some 250 yards north-east of the Ferme de la Briajére. Although most of us could cheerfully have fallen asleep standing up—we were pretty tired—it was irritating to yield the ground that we had won at the cost of severe casualties."

Next day, 12th July, the Battalion was relieved in its forward position by the 1st Dorsets, and moved back. While still near enough to the enemy to suffer occasional mortaring and to require constant alertness, opportunity was taken for training and reorganization.

On 18th July came the news that the enemy had at last withdrawn from Hottot to positions farther south, and the Battalion advanced through the shambles that had been the village of Hottot and took up a position south of the village on high ground overlooking the Seulles valley; there was no opposition, but the enemy shelled and mortared our positions with monotonous regularity. Fighting patrols probed forward, clearing the area around Hottot, the area which the enemy had for so long held in such a determined manner and at such great cost to himself. On 19th July Lieutenant-Colonel A. J. D. Turner, M.C., took over command of the Battalion, and on the 23rd the 231st Brigade was relieved in the line and the Battalion moved back to a rest area near Les Fiettes, where they spent four days.

Villers Bocage

The general situation was that the Allied armies in Normandy now stood poised ready to make the break-through which was eventually to send them swiftly north-east through France, Belgium and Holland to the frontier of Germany. The Allies were tremendously strong, thoroughly equipped and had enormous air power. The enemy, forbidden to withdraw by their Führer, were ruthlessly bombed and shelled, and when their main retreat lines were cut they were massacred. But first the Allies had to pierce the enemy positions, and in this great battle the 50th Division had an important part to play, and the 231st Brigade had a post of honour in the van.

The Division's first task was to advance on Villers Bocage and occupy the high ground to the west and north-west of that strategically important centre. For one of the first phases in this operation the 231st Brigade were moved forward on 27th July to the sector La Croix des Landes–Le Lion Vert. When the attack was launched on 30th July the Battalion was on the right, with the Dorsets on the left. The attack began at six o'clock in the morning, and the Battalion's first objective was a high feature north of St. Germain d'Ectot. The advance, through very closed country, began well, and "A" and "B" Companies, who were leading, got near to their objective without meeting any opposition. Then the enemy opened up at close range with Spandaus. These posts were successfully silenced, but both companies then found themselves under direct observation from the next range of hills and they were bombarded heavily with artillery and mortars. They held their ground, however, and dug themselves in in the new positions. The advance through these positions to the next objective was begun by "C" and "D" Companies at a quarter to seven in the evening, supported by tanks of the 13th/18th Hussars, who fought with great dash and daring. The opposition was again violent, but the position was taken and consolidated. Again the Battalion lost men, and three officers were wounded, Lieutenants Wynne-Owen, Heald and Higginson.

Minden Day, 1944, was celebrated by the 1st Battalion by going into battle at seven o'clock in the morning wearing in their steel helmets red roses taken from the wall of a ruined building. The object this time was a high feature at Launay which the enemy had held strongly. There was a heavy morning mist and "A" and "D" Companies reached their objective with but little opposition, and fighting patrols sent down the Anctoville–Feuguerolles-sur-Seulles road came across no enemy. In fact the enemy had withdrawn farther south, though he still continued very consistent shelling and mortaring on our lines. The great concerted attack by the Allies was stretching the enemy line to its limit. On 4th August Villers Bocage was abandoned by the enemy, and at long last this important and most obstinate objective was ours, and on the same day the 50th Division was taken right out of the line for the first time since the landing two months before.

For four days the Battalion was able to reorganize, rest and train. It was visited on 6th August by General Horrocks, who had just taken over command of XXX Corps. The General spoke to all officers and N.C.Os. about the current situation, and had some most complimentary things to say about the 231st Brigade and about the 1st Hampshire in particular. The brief respite ended on 8th August when the Battalion moved in transport to a concentration area at Aunay-sur-Odon. The battle to come was to be the climax of the Normandy campaign, part of the historic break-out which was to alter completely the tempo of the campaign.

St. Pierre la Vieille

The task of the 50th Division was to advance southwards towards Condé-sur-Noireau, a small town at the confluence of two rivers and at a road bottle-neck. It was one of the vital points along the enemy's northern line of withdrawal from the rapidly forming pocket between Vire, Condé and Falaise. To seize Condé would be to close the trap still further.

To 231st Brigade was given the all-important task of forcing the way towards Condé, and a Brigade attack was launched at 8.30 on the morning of 11th August with the 1st Hampshire on the right and the 2nd Devons on the left, each with a squadron of Sherman tanks in support. The Battalion's first objective was the village of St. Pierre la Vieille and the high ground to the west. The 2nd Battalion East Yorks had attacked this locality the day before, but had had to fall back on the high ground to the north. Between this high ground and the village lay a deep ravine with a muddy stream, which provided a natural tank obstacle.

When "B" Company, commanded by Major A. W. Anstey, moved forward to open the attack, there was considerable fog, and the company crossed a gully and made good progress to the edge of an orchard, where they came under machine-gun fire. This enemy strong-post was immediately dealt with, and the company continued its advance until it was temporarily held up by a great deal of fire from Spandau positions in the orchards surrounding the village.

"C" Company (Major Broughton) had advanced successfully over the ridge and dropped down to the main road, where two platoons lined the hedge at right angles to the main road while the third worked its way up a sunken lane, between orchards. Enemy were encountered in the lane and shot, but the platoon could make no progress beyond the end of the lane as it was covered by heavy machine-gun fire.

At half past nine in the morning "D" Company, commanded by Major Harley, was ordered to advance, swinging to the right of "B" Company, to take the high ground west of the village. The company was heavily shelled and mortared as it crossed the valley, and two of its platoons suffered very heavy casualties. Nevertheless "D" Company kept going and made a very determined assault on the orchards on this high ground. There was fierce fighting for a long while, but the enemy fire was so intense that the company, now only twenty strong, was driven back and took up positions on the reverse slope of the ridge. Stretcher-bearers worked heroically in the exposed forward ground to get in the casualties, though the whole area was under extremely heavy shell fire.

With "B," "C" and "D" Companies pinned down short of their objectives and all grievously depleted by casualties, Colonel Turner ordered "A" Company to by-pass "D" and attack the high ground. As soon as the company got into the open it came under heavy fire, but pressing on it reached some dead ground in the valley, where the Company Commander, Captain E. G. Wright, led two platoons on a line towards the village church while the third platoon gave him covering fire. This platoon was to join the others in the village. The two platoons advanced, went through a number of unoccupied enemy positions on the side of the hill, and then assaulted a strong enemy position on the top. The attack was driven home with fine spirit and a number of Germans were killed and others taken prisoner. They then came under very heavy fire from an orchard, where the enemy battalion headquarters was situated, so they dug themselves in on the reverse slope.

Meanwhile the other three companies had worked forward and had infiltrated into the orchards before them. All went well until artillery fire from our own guns, supporting "A" Company's attack, made them withdraw to their former positions. It was by now seven o'clock in the evening, and the troops had been fighting continuously for eleven hours in the most intense way. They were, however, still undaunted, and it was decided to make yet one more combined effort by "B," "C" and "D" Companies. Grimly the three companies moved forward once more against the orchards and ruins of the village of St. Pierre, but at once "B" and "D" came under very heavy enemy shell fire and a lot more men fell, and this gallant attack by battle-weary men was broken up while they dealt with the wounded. Finally "C" Company, which had lost its Company Commander, Major Broughton, who was wounded, moved into the orchard again and worked its way right through the village to the houses on the far side, and here it consolidated. The three platoon commanders of "C" Company had no communication with "B" or "D," or with Battalion Headquarters, and as ammunition was running low they decided to withdraw. They got back with only a few casualties and took up a position with "B" and "D" Companies. The three companies could muster only seventy-two men between them, for they were desperately reduced. "C" Company was thirty-five strong, "B" twenty-five, and "D" had only twelve men.

Early next morning "B," "C" and "D" Companies were withdrawn with the object of attacking the village again from a different angle, for the enemy still held it grimly. It was found, however, that the men were so exhausted that the attack was impossible, so later in the day "A" Company was withdrawn as well, and the Battalion moved on behind the Devons and Dorsets. At six o'clock in the evening of 12th August, St. Pierre was shelled by the Army Group and Corps Artillery and a hundred Germans came out and surrendered. Thus ended the final battle for the Battalion in Normandy. In his book "The Path of the 50th" Major Ewart Clay writes of the battle for St. Pierre :

". . . The story of that day is of wonderful persistence by our infantry in the face of determined opposition, and as an example of the pluck and stamina displayed one can do no better than quote the fact that at 1900 hours after a day of continuous fighting and casualties, the Hampshire Regiment tried to mount a three-company attack."

In the fighting for the village of St. Pierre on 11th August the 1st Battalion, already savagely reduced, suffered its last heavy toll of killed and wounded, nearly a hundred men, including three officers wounded—Major Broughton and Lieutenants Blackmore and Keene.

So ended the long tussle in the Normandy Bocage ; the two months of close battle were over ; no longer was it a matter of fighting from hedge to hedge, of continuous sniping from summer orchards, of desperate assaults of ruined villages along sunken lanes ; now it was to be a great and triumphant pursuit across a jubilant France into Belgium. At first 231st Brigade advanced slowly, probing forward with fighting patrols south of St. Pierre, but no Germans were found except dead ones. On 23rd August the Battalion was moved forward in transport to Laigle, and had a couple of days' rest.

The Break-out

Then the great advance began. The general plan was a wide sweep to the Seine, the British and Canadians north-east and east to the river from the coast to Vernon, and the Americans eastwards to Paris, Château Thiery, Troyes and Orleans. The 50th Division's part was to support the 11th Armoured Division, and once more the 231st Brigade was to the fore. The Brigade had no actual fighting, but the Battalion was called upon to do a good deal of picketing, searching of woods, and had to be in constant readiness to support the armour if it should encounter any opposition.

So began long days of motoring through the summer countryside, with ecstatic welcomes from the French. The Battalion crossed the Seine at Vernon on 31st August, and swept on to Amiens, which was entered the next day. There was an additional spur to the British troops at this stage, as they were approaching the country of the German flying-bomb sites. At Amiens there was a very enthusiastic welcome for the leading British troops.

The Brigade now came under command of the Guards Armoured Division and advanced from Amiens to Arras, and from there on 3rd September in the historic advance to Brussels, covering ninety-seven miles in fourteen hours, and at five o'clock in the evening of 3rd September the Guards Armoured Division and the 1st Hampshire entered Brussels. There the Battalion, who had been the first British infantry ashore in France on 6th June, were also the first across the Belgian frontier and the first to enter Brussels itself. The welcome surpassed anything yet seen ; there were cheers, flags, wine, fruit and kisses. People wept openly for joy. "A" Company were detailed to take part in a Victory Parade through the city, a parade which was received with tremendous and unforgettable enthusiasm. It was all very difficult from the administrative point of view. A sentry would be posted, but at once a crowd of civilians would bear the man away, regardless of his protests, to regale him and pay tribute to the liberators. These were the very sweets of victory.

CHAPTER XIX

THE 7TH BATTALION IN NORMANDY

JUNE TO SEPTEMBER, 1944

(*See map on page* 220)

ON 22nd June, 1944, the 7th Battalion The Hampshire Regiment landed on the Normandy beaches. At that time the 1st Battalion was locked in battle north of Hottot, and away in Italy the 2/4th was engaged in the assault of Vaiano, while the three Hampshire battalions of the 128th Brigade were returning to Italy from the Middle East to resume their battles with the Germans. Thus, with the landing of the 7th Battalion in the theatre of war, there were six battalions of the Hampshire Regiment in action, and ten days later yet another joined them when the 147th Regiment, R.A.C., landed in Normandy. This was the old 10th Battalion, converted to tanks and destined to fight a distinguished campaign in the 34th Armoured Brigade.

When it landed near Le Hamel, on the beach where the 1st Battalion had fought so magnificently sixteen days before, the 7th Battalion achieved the ambition it had waited for so long. The Battalion had prepared itself diligently against this day, through the long months at home, and, toned up through the whole course of battle training, it landed in full fighting trim and very eager to prove itself.

The Battalion was commanded by Lieutenant-Colonel D. W. G. Ray, with Major J. R. C. Mallock Second-in-Command, and Captain J. F. Johnson Adjutant. The Company Commanders were Major C. G. T. Viner, Major J. J. Tompkins, Major R. J. McPhillips, Major H. Eastwood, Captain J. L. Braithwaite, and Captain T. G. Stevenson. The Medical Officer was Lieutenant R. L. Waddell, and the Chaplain was Father Fisher, an unfailing source of inspiration to the Battalion in the difficult days which lay ahead. The Battalion was brigaded with the 4th and 5th Battalions The Dorsetshire Regiment in 130th Brigade, commanded by Brigadier N. D. Leslie, in the 43rd (Wessex) Division, commanded by Major-General G. Ivor Thomas.

Disembarkation had been delayed by unusually heavy storms in the Channel, but by 24th June the Division was concentrated in the Bayeux area with the Battalion north of the town. For the first two weeks the men were able to become acclimatized by taking over various sectors of the line. Their first move was to a defensive position on the Bayeux–Caen road, near Bretteville L'Orgueilleuse. They went forward after a few days to act as a counter-attack battalion on Cheux, where Private Hayes was killed, the first of the 7th Battalion to die in action in North-West Europe. From Cheux the Battalion moved forward again on 5th July into the line at Baron, south-west of Caen. On the move forward the Battalion was heavily mortared and lost some men, including Captain Collier, of "A" Company, who was wounded. In this preliminary campaigning the Battalion quickly became acquainted with the bocage country and the nature of the close fighting in which they were so soon to take part. They had their christening of fire at once, from the shelling and mortaring which seemed almost to be a natural phenomenon.

MALTOT, CAHAGNES AND JURQUES

Their initiation into the full realities of battle against very good troops in country which was maddeningly suitable to defence was, however, far from complete ; for the 130th Brigade had of necessity been kept in reserve. The result was that the Battalion's first battle on 10th July was to be tragically costly. The Battalion was given the task of capturing and holding the village of Maltot, which was the third and last objective in a brigade operation. This in itself was part of a divisional operation, which had the objective of securing high ground between the Rivers Odon and Orne, and of exploiting as far as the Orne at Feuguerolles. The task of the 130th Brigade was to capture part of the ridge, including the Château de Fontaine to the west of Hill 112. The 5th Dorset on the right and the 4th Dorset on the left achieved this, and the 7th Hampshire were set the task of exploiting this success by capturing Maltot and the woods beyond. This entailed a long advance down the forward or enemy slope of the ridge through tall ripe corn with but little cover.

The Battalion moved in to the attack at 8.15 on the morning of 10th July, preceded by a heavy artillery barrage. It was supported by tanks of 44th R.T.R., but owing to the nature of the ground and the amount of enemy armour, the tanks suffered very heavy casualties. As the Battalion advanced towards Maltot it met violent opposition and at once sustained severe losses. Nevertheless part of the Battalion succeeded in getting into the village and attempted to secure defensive positions. It seemed at first to be a successful operation, but that was far from the case. What had actually happened was that they had superimposed themselves on top of a very strong enemy defended locality. Many Tiger tanks lay concealed dug in on the outskirts of the village. Consequently the enemy were able to counter-attack with great power, and although the companies in the village stood their ground and fought back desperately, the situation was well-nigh hopeless.

In the early afternoon Brigadier Leslie ordered the 4th Dorsets to advance on the village to reinforce the Hampshire battalion. It was impossible, however, to make any impression on the very strong enemy defences manned by first-class troops of S.S. divisions, and eventually the battalions were withdrawn, the 7th Battalion concentrating in an area to the west of the village of Verson, where it was reorganized into three rifle companies.

The Battalion's casualties in this, its first major action, totalled eighteen officers and two hundred and eight other ranks killed, wounded and missing. Four officers were killed : Captain Terry and Lieutenants T. P. Evans, Sandy and Waddell. Colonel Ray was twice wounded, but remained on duty until wounded again, this time so seriously that he had to be evacuated, and he died on his way home to England. Lieutenant Waddell, the Medical Officer, was killed while attending the wounds of the Adjutant. The officers wounded were Major Eastwood, Captains J. F. Johnson, J. Reid, Stevenson and Game, and Lieutenants Rowe, Friend and Hall. Captains Game and Reid and Lieutenant Rowe rejoined the Battalion later in the campaign. Among the five officers missing after the battle was Major Tompkins, commanding "B" Company. The supporting battery of 112 Field Regiment also suffered very heavily. Two of the F.O.Os. were killed and the Battery Commander, Major J. H. Penrose, was wounded.

When Colonel Ray was evacuated, Major Mallock took over command of the Battalion, with Major McPhillips as Second-in-Command, but both these officers were tragically killed on 13th July. They had just completed their reconnaissance and were arranging the take-over with the Commanding Officer of the 7th Somerset Light Infantry in the latter's Headquarters in the Château de Fontaine when all three were killed by the same shell. Lieutenant-Colonel D. E. B. Talbot then joined from the 5th Dorsets and took over command. Casualties continued while the Battalion was at Verson, through constant mortar and artillery fire.

It was disastrous indeed for the Battalion to suffer such cruel casualties in its first major action, but morale remained good. Two of the Battalion particularly distinguished themselves at Maltot, Captain Braithwaite and Corporal Henry of H.Q. Company. Throughout the day Captain Braithwaite was continually in evidence either in his jeep or carrier, showing a complete contempt for enemy fire. When the Medical Officer was killed, Captain Braithwaite organized the collection and evacuation of the wounded and directed detached groups and supporting arms to positions. He was himself hit several times by shrapnel, but took no notice of his wounds. For his gallantry at Maltot, Captain Braithwaite was awarded the M.C. Corporal Henry was similarly an example of coolness throughout the battle. He crossed open ground under short-range fire to assist a party of wounded men, and later in the action himself engaged the crew of an enemy tank. For his verve and dash Corporal Henry was awarded the M.M.

In spite of the heavy losses in its first battle, the 7th Battalion was back in the line two days later, near Château de Fontaine, as a forward battalion on the divisional front. The troops had recovered amazingly quickly from their ordeal at Maltot, and although kept busy with regular patrolling and under frequent shelling and mortaring, the Battalion was able to build itself up again and absorb its reinforcements. Amongst these was Major D. B. Rooke, who became Second-in-Command and remained with the Battalion for the rest of the campaign, during which he greatly distinguished himself.

The Battalion was in the line for eleven days, until the local situation changed when the village of Maltot was finally cleared by 129th Brigade. In this operation "B" Company of the 7th Battalion, temporarily commanded by Captain C. J. G. Mumford, was given a subsidiary role clearing the wheat-fields near the village. This was very successfully done, at the cost of one officer and eight other ranks wounded, and twenty-five prisoners were taken.

From 25th to 28th July the Battalion had a short rest near Bayeux, and then it moved back into the line to take part in the general operation for the break-out. Its task was to attack the village of Cahagnes from the north, as part of a brigade operation to pierce the enemy's defences between Bricquessard and

Caumont. That done, 214th Brigade was to pass through and advance to St. Pierre du Fresne, and finally 129th Brigade was to continue the advance. The attack commenced at eight o'clock in the morning of 30th July, with the 4th Somerset Light Infantry, under command of 130th Brigade for this operation, advancing on the left and the 5th Dorset on the right, the 7th Hampshire being in reserve. Unfortunately, both battalions soon found themselves in considerable difficulties, and the Dorsets became entangled in a dense minefield some three hundred yards from the start line, and were pinned down by heavy fire. It became obvious that the clearing of the obstacles in the very close bocage country would have to be done at night. Accordingly Brigadier Leslie ordered the 7th Hampshire to advance later in the evening round the right flank of the Dorsets, towards a spur immediately north of Cahagnes.

The battle for Cahagnes was fought out in the typical and difficult close wooded country of the bocage, on the slopes leading up to the ridge on which the village stood. The Battalion advanced astride the road leading to the village, but it was soon seriously held up, "A" Company on the left by minefields, and "D" on the right by very strong enemy opposition in the orchards. But the attack was sustained and by midnight of 30th July all four rifle companies were deployed in positions about three-quarters of the way up the slope. The Germans put in several counter-attacks, but they were all repulsed. They made their final attempt just before dawn ; again it was unsuccessful.

After this final counter-attack the enemy's pressure ceased and the Battalion was able to advance on to the ridge without much opposition and went forward into Cahagnes, which was badly damaged and still burning from a heavy raid by the R.A.F. Positions were taken up round the southern end of the village on 31st July, when it was involved only in minor patrol activity.

The Battalion remained in its positions around Cahagnes on 1st August, and wore roses in their steel helmets. Their next task was to form part of a divisional thrust straight through to Jurques and Ondefontaine, and during the night 1st/2nd August the Battalion concentrated ready to move forward the next day in its own trucks, on the tanks of "B" Squadron of the Sherwood Rangers and the vehicles of 236 Anti-tank Battery, R.A. The concentration area was bombed during the night and there were several casualties. Some of the bombs fell uncomfortably close to the cottage where Colonel Talbot was giving out his orders to a large "O" group, much to everyone's consternation.

The move forward to Jurques the next morning was accomplished without difficulty, and the Battalion formed a firm base to hold the Jurques ridge and the main cross-roads. A ridge which ran parallel to theirs about a mile to the south was strongly held by enemy infantry, supported by self-propelled guns and tanks. It was consequently most unpleasant as the day was spent under heavy shell fire from these 88-mm. guns. All efforts to advance met obstinate resistance, and even the Typhoons of the R.A.F. directed against them failed to dislodge the enemy.

A night advance was ordered, and "C" and "D" Companies, under Majors Nayler and Braithwaite, moved forward with the object of seizing the feature the enemy held and clearing the main road. At first the companies advanced well, but when they were well forward they met very heavy machine-gun fire from well-sited positions and dug-in tanks, and were brought to a standstill short of the objective. At dawn Major Viner, commanding "A" Company, made two attempts to work round the right flank, but both times his company was furiously repulsed by heavy fire. No tanks were available to support this attack, and a very heavy mist made control difficult, prevented observation, and interfered with close artillery support.

The situation was the same all along the line of the divisional attack, but constant pressure was maintained, and on the night of 3rd/4th August the enemy withdrew. "B" Company, commanded by Major Chesham, a Canadian, was able to secure the high ground at Point 321 on the right at dawn on 4th August, while the 214th Brigade continued the advance towards Mount Pincon. Mount Pincon dominated a large area and it was well fortified. It was essential that this feature be taken, and the battle in which it was stormed and captured by 129th Brigade may well be considered among the finest infantry actions in the war.

Mount Pincon and St. Denis de Mère

In the divisional plan 129th Brigade was to assault Mount Pincon by a right flanking attack while 130th Brigade made a frontal attack from the north-west, to give the enemy the impression that the main attack was to come from that direction. This deceptive frontal attack was made by the 7th Hampshire. As Colonel Talbot had returned to "B" Echelon for a few days' rest, Major Rooke commanded the Battalion in his place.

The objectives of the Battalion attack were Plecière, Roucamps, and Pasty. The attack started at eleven o'clock in the morning of 6th August, with "C" Company, commanded by Major Nayler, on the right, and "D" Company (Major Braithwaite) on the left. The first objective was taken without much difficulty. Thereupon phase two started, and the enemy, now fully alert, opened up with heavy mortar fire. "B" Company, commanded by Major Chesham, passed through "D" successfully to reach its objective, Plecière. On the left, however, "A" Company, under Captain Wright, was soon in difficulties from heavy machine-gun fire as it advanced towards Roucamps. Captain Wright was wounded and the company suffered severe casualties and was withdrawn behind "D" Company.

An effort was now made to by-pass this opposition by crossing a stream to the south of Plecière, while the supporting Field Regiment engaged Roucamps with three separate concentrations of fire. "C" Company was brought up to the left of "B" and then, at two o'clock in the afternoon, both companies advanced to cross the stream, but were at once held up; "B" by heavy machine-gun fire from the opposite bank and "C" from the far bank and from Roucamps itself. In spite of the violent machine-gun fire, Lieutenant Taylor, a Canadian officer of "B" Company, managed to cross the stream with one section and most gallantly led them forward right up to an enemy machine-gun post. The enemy tried to withdraw, but Lieutenant Taylor killed two of them and captured the other two. As the rest of his company was still held up by enemy fire, he then skilfully withdrew, taking his two prisoners with him. For his gallant action Lieutenant Taylor received the M.C.

Private Haseley, one of Lieutenant Taylor's section, also displayed great gallantry, and won the M.M. It was almost entirely due to the determined manner in which he used his Bren gun that Lieutenant Taylor was able to lead the section up to the machine-gun post, and he covered the withdrawal across the stream by firing with the utmost coolness.

Meanwhile "C" Company had suffered very heavy casualties, including all their officers, and it was apparent that no further progress could be made. Both companies were accordingly withdrawn to enable a timed artillery bombardment to be put into operation to prepare for a further attack that evening. Orders were then received from Brigade cancelling the evening attack, and the Battalion took up a defensive position round Plecière. The Battalion's operation had been most successful, for they had engaged the attention of at least three companies of the enemy and had advanced to the very foot of Mount Pincon, thus carrying out their task to the full; for while they had fought in such a determined manner, the 129th Brigade had been able to attack the mountain from the right with startling and well-deserved success.

The next day, 7th August, it was found that enemy resistance had ceased over the whole Mount Pincon area, and the Battalion was given the task of clearing the area round Roucamps and Pasty, and then it took over the defence of the reverse slopes of Mount Pincon, which was to be held at all costs. The Brigade advanced on 8th and 9th August, and on the 10th it concentrated around Mauny. The Battalion had lost many men in the fighting of the past fortnight, including nine officers. Of these, three had been killed, Lieutenants H. A. Talbot, A. J. Lester and L. J. Campion.

From Mauny the Battalion moved forward on 14th August for an assault on St. Denis de Mère, supported by "B" Squadron, Sherwood Rangers Yeomanry. The attack was made under a heavy artillery barrage from six field regiments and three medium regiments. The start line was crossed at two o'clock, and by seven o'clock that evening the Battalion had completely secured the village, despite considerable trouble caused by four enemy self-propelled guns. These guns knocked out four of our tanks, but their positions were overrun and one of the guns was captured intact. The Battalion lost one officer and twenty-eight men, and captured seventy-four prisoners.

The Break-out

On 15th August the 214th Brigade passed through, and for the next three days the Battalion was occupied in clearing up the area, patrolling forward to the town of Condé-sur-Noireau, and dealing with civilian refugees. For three or four days the Battalion had no operational role, and was able to attend to internal administration and general cleaning up before it moved forward again on 22nd August.

This move was, as it were, the reward for the grim fighting since the Battalion had landed ; it was part of the historic break-out through the ruins and the wreck of the defeated German army. The 130th Brigade Group moved to the Falaise Gap area to protect the left flank of XXX Corps, by taking up a position around Chambois. The 7th Hampshire travelled in T.C.Vs. through Argentan and the Forêt de Gouffern through scenes of indescribable confusion, with German guns and vehicles lying wrecked everywhere. Chambois and all the roads leading to it were littered with abandoned equipment and there were many dead Germans awaiting burial.

On the afternoon of 25th August the Battalion moved fifty miles north-east to a brigade area at Conches, now travelling through a countryside hardly marked by war, and were received ecstatically by jubilant French civilians at every village. The next move was to a concentration area near Pacy-sur-Eure. The 129th Brigade was already brilliantly forcing the crossing of the River Seine at Vernon. This was indeed the first check in the army's triumphant surge north-east from Normandy, and the Germans were trying desperately to delay the advance. The 129th Brigade established its bridgehead, and the Sappers quickly built a class 9 bridge, and then a class 40, and early in the morning of 27th August the Battalion advanced towards Vernon to cross the Seine after the 4th Dorsets. The Dorset Battalion crossed under mortar fire, but one of the bridges was hit and damaged, which caused some delay. However, at four o'clock in the afternoon the Battalion crossed the Seine and took up a defensive position some thousand yards on the other side of the river. During the night, pitch black and pouring with rain, Colonel Talbot was summoned back to Brigade Headquarters, which was still on the other side of the river. Here he received orders that the 130th Brigade was to extend the bridgehead, the Battalion being directed to capture the village of Tilly. By the time Colonel Talbot had recrossed the river and returned to his Headquarters there was very little time left to plan the battalion operation and issue the necessary orders.

The operation for the capture of Tilly began with the clearing of a large wood to secure the start line. Three wide rides ran through the wood, and the Carrier Platoon, under Captain K. M. White, supported by "A" Company commanded by Major Viner, quickly cleared them and secured the start line. There was some opposition from pockets of enemy infantry in the wood, but one carrier section disposed of an enemy party of eleven, killing two and wounding nine, while another section knocked out an anti-tank gun with one of the same type which had been captured at St. Denis de Mère. The attack on Tilly began at a quarter to one in the afternoon, with "B" Company under Major Chesham on the left, and "D," Major Braithwaite, on the right. Some opposition on the left was quickly silenced by our tanks, and by two o'clock the village was in our hands, with ninety-five prisoners.

With the Seine crossed there followed the rapid advance of Second Army right into Belgium, and for this purpose much of the transport of the 43rd Division was detached, so that the Division itself remained in the area of the bridgehead. The Battalion therefore spent eleven days at Tilly. This provided an excellent opportunity for reorganization, for taking in reinforcements, training, entertainment and rest.

On 8th September Colonel Talbot was summoned to Divisional Headquarters, where Major-General Thomas informed him that his Battalion had been specially selected to go at once to Brussels for temporary garrison duty. Transport was provided and the Battalion left that afternoon and bivouacked for the night eighty-five miles away, near Amiens. The Battalion drove into Brussels on the evening of 9th September. As with the 1st Battalion six days before, the Battalion's progress through the city was in the nature of a triumphal procession. The population were still *en fête*, and the Battalion found itself in the slightly embarrassing role of victors and heroes.

The Battalion was billeted in the Hospital St. Jean, which had been used as a German barracks, to act as mobile reserve in the event of any enemy infiltration into the city. Apart from the general junketing, there was much work to be done. One company was employed escorting prisoners to the rear, while another provided guards on food, wine, petrol and coal dumps, map depots, and a military hospital. The Battalion was greatly assisted in its many tasks by the Belgian Liaison Officer, Captain the Count D'Asche. Two other duties carried out in Brussels were an operation to clear the Bois de la Cambre and the Forêt de Soynes of suspected enemy, and the starting of the Palace Hotel as an officers' transit hotel. The first task was fruitless as no enemy were found, but the Palace Hotel became a most successful venture, and was well known to officers on leave for the rest of the war.

The Battalion had landed in Normandy on 22nd June and it made its triumphant entry into Brussels on 9th September. In that short time it had proved itself in battle, but at a grievous cost. Two Commanding Officers had been killed, and of the thirty-six officers who had landed at Le Hamel, only twelve were still with the Battalion on 19th August. Of these only Major Viner, still commanding "A" Company, held the same position. On 19th August Lieutenant-Colonel Talbot's key men were Major Rooke, Second-in-Command; Majors Viner, Chesham, Nayler and Braithwaite, and Captains Boschetti-Birch and Mumford, commanding the companies; with Captain A. T. Davies, Adjutant, and Captains K. M. White, Elwell and Quy commanding the Carrier, Mortar and Anti-tank Platoons. The Battalion had lost, killed and wounded, since 22nd June, 1944, thirty-five officers and approximately four hundred and fifty N.C.Os. and men, of which casualties eighteen and two hundred and eight had occurred at Maltot.

The 7th Battalion had fought hard, and had won its spurs. There was stern work ahead, however, fighting in XXX Corps with the 1st Battalion in Holland and Germany. But for a brief respite in Brussels it could rest from battle, and feel proud of the good name it had won in the 43rd Division.

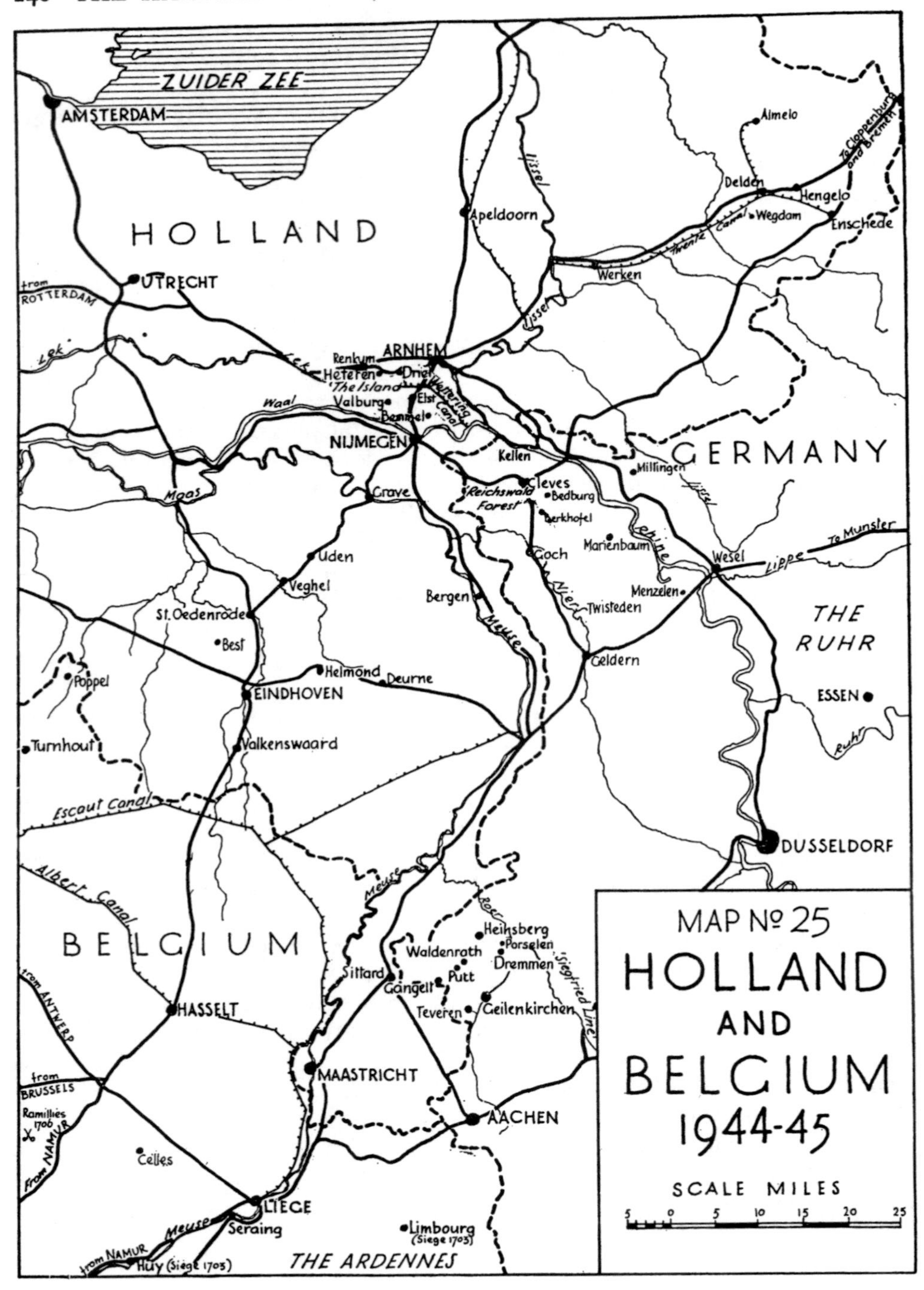
ZUIDER ZEE
AMSTERDAM
HOLLAND
UTRECHT
from ROTTERDAM
Lek
Apeldoorn
Ijssel
Almelo
To Cloppenburg and Bremen
Delden
Hengelo
Wegdam
Enschede
Twente Canal
Werken
ARNHEM
Renkum
Heteren
Driel
'The Island'
Wettering Canal
Elst
Valburg
Bemmel
Waal
NIJMEGEN
Kellen
Cleves
Bedburg
Millingen
GERMANY
Reichswald Forest
Moas
Grave
Uden
Veghel
Marienbaum
Goch
Rhine
Wesel
Lippe
To Munster
Menzelen
Niers
Twisteden
Bergen
Meuse
St. Oedenrode
Best
THE RUHR
Geldern
Helmond
Deurne
Poppel
EINDHOVEN
ESSEN
Ruhr
Turnhout
Valkenswaard
Escaut Canal
DUSSELDORF
Albert Canal
Roer
Heinsberg
Porselen
Waldenrath
Dremmen
BELGIUM
Sittard
Putt
Gangelt
Siegfried Line
Teveren
Geilenkirchen
HASSELT
from ANTWERP
MAASTRICHT
from BRUSSELS
Ramillies 1706
from NAMUR
AACHEN
Celles
LIEGE
Seraing
Limbourg (Siege 1703)
from NAMUR
Huy (Siege 1703)
THE ARDENNES
MAP № 25
HOLLAND AND BELGIUM 1944-45
SCALE MILES
5 0 5 10 15 20 25

CHAPTER XX

THE HAMPSHIRE BATTALIONS IN HOLLAND AND GERMANY

SEPTEMBER, 1944, TO MAY, 1945

I—THE 1ST BATTALION

ON 5th September, two days after it had entered Brussels, the 1st Battalion was ordered to advance at once to Antwerp, immediately behind the Guards Armoured Division. The armour swept into this great port with such impetuosity that the enemy were taken completely by surprise, and did not have time even to wreck the dock area. He offered a stubborn resistance at some points, but the valuable docks, with all the installations, were captured intact.

There was none of the Brussels jubilation in Antwerp; the people seemed dazed. The 1st Battalion moved into positions on the north bank of the Albert Canal, suffering some casualties from shelling. After twenty-four hours the Battalion moved on again, still behind the Guards Armoured Division, and advanced to the Escaut Canal. Here the Irish Guards brilliantly forced a crossing, which the Battalion took over on 14th September, while the Guards withdrew a little to prepare for the advance on Arnhem. The Battalion toiled at building up the defences of the bridgehead and carried out ceaseless reconnaissance patrols. The enemy were very active in their patrolling too, and there were many clashes of patrols. It was an exciting, jubilant campaign, this sudden thrust into Holland, and in it the 231st Brigade were right to the fore. While the Battalion held the bridgehead over the Escaut, the Devons and Dorsets went forward with the Irish Guards Group as they thrust on as far as Valkenswaard.

This brilliant thrust into Holland was the preliminary to the great operation "Market Garden," a bold plan to secure the crossings over all the Dutch waterways, including the Rhine, and so to put the British Second Army into a position from which it could strike into Germany north of the Ruhr. This stroke, if successful, would carve a corridor northwards across Holland and would isolate the Germans in western Holland. "Market" was the code name for the airborne part of the operation, "Garden" for the simultaneous thrust by the Second British Army. The plan was to lay a carpet of airborne troops in the path of the advancing Second Army, to seize the vital bridges over rivers and canals with which the country is laced. At the same time the Second Army were to thrust north from their Meuse–Escaut bridgehead along a very narrow front, a corridor with only one road most of the way, through Eindhoven, Oudenrode, Veghel, Ouden, Grave, Nijmegen, Arnhem and Apeldoorn.

The Second Army part of the operation devolved mainly on XXX Corps, which was to lead the advance with the Guards Armoured Division in the spearhead. XXX Corps, of course, contained both the 1st and the 7th Hampshire Battalions in the 50th and 43rd Infantry Divisions, although for this operation the 1st Battalion, with 231st Brigade, were under command the Guards Armoured Division. Also in XXX Corps was 147 Regiment, R.A.C., converted from the 10th Hampshire.

Operation "Market Garden" began on 17th September and a vast air fleet became airborne over England. It was a most exhilarating and exciting day for the troops who saw the gigantic air armada. There were 1,544 planes and 478 gliders, of which 1,481 planes and 425 gliders reached their destination, landing about half of three divisions, some 20,000 men. Soon after noon XXX Corps was given the order to advance, and the tanks of the Guards, lined up nose to tail, moved forward. It was very dramatic. Although at first they only ran into a little Spandau fire, the resistance suddenly became strong, and it was only after bitter fighting that the leading tanks of the Irish Guards managed to enter Holland soon after three o'clock. A heavy artillery barrage was laid along a road and rocket-firing Typhoons flew low over the column of tanks and the advance became easier, so that just before last light the Irish Guards Group reached Valkenswaard.

Next day the Guards headed for Eindhoven, and the 1st Battalion, relieved by the Dorsets, moved from the Escaut bridgehead into "The Corridor." Here life was uncomfortably precarious, with enemy counter-attacks on both flanks. The country was difficult, with the roads built up above the marshy countryside; the weather had turned bad, and the Germans quickly got over the surprise of the attack and counter-attacked strenuously against the corridor. The Battalion lost some good men, including Captain Hand, wounded for the second time. They were desperate, dangerous days, but "The Corridor" remained intact and was gradually widened.

The progress of the gigantic operation had been remarkable, but there was one essential gap, between the Nijmegen and Arnhem bridges, from which the enemy could not be dislodged. The Germans had made an uncanny recovery; their troops were good, and the bad weather after the first two days prevented the reinforcement and proper supplying of the airborne troops. Moreover the Second Army were unable to reach Arnhem bridge in time to achieve the complete break-through.

The result was that the 1st Airborne Division could not be reached by the Second Army; it was surrounded and very hard pressed. It continued, however, in spite of the greatest difficulties, in making a most heroic stand at Arnhem. The 231st Brigade held their positions in the corridor until the 43rd Division passed through, and then the Brigade moved towards Nijmegen, where the great bridge over the Waal had been captured intact after a most gallant operation, in which the 504 U.S. Parachute Infantry Regiment distinguished themselves.

At the beginning of October 231st Brigade moved forward through Nijmegen, crossing the famous bridge, and took over a sector between Elst and Bemmel on the "Island," the area between the Waal and the Lek, to hold part of the all-important bridgehead. This area had been heavily counter-attacked for two days, and the brigade task was to drive the enemy from positions they had gained, which threatened the vital Nijmegen bridges. The enemy had all the advantages of ground and excellent observation posts north of the Lek; he also had plenty of artillery, and he was rushing up all available reserves.

An attack was launched to widen the bridgehead on 4th October. The 231st Brigade were given the task of attacking the enemy's positions north of Bemmel, and the 1st Hampshire was the spearhead of the attack, with "A" Company leading, with the Dorsets on the left and the Devons attacking on the right slightly later. The battle of Bemmel was a bitter and a bloody day's fighting, with the German S.S. troops resisting fiercely in every dyke and orchard, and their artillery and mortars bringing down heavy defensive fire. Casualties to the 1st Battalion were unfortunately heavy, for the supporting tanks of the Coldstream had been hampered by the difficult country and many had been knocked out by the enemy bazookas. Colonel Turner commanded the battle from a tank, but soon so many wireless sets had been hit that the Second-in-Command, Major Drewitt, took over command temporarily from Battalion Headquarters. The enemy's fire was so heavy that every vehicle at the Battalion Command Post was riddled with shrapnel, and a carrier loaded with ammunition caught fire and blocked the route back for a considerable time.

The heavy enemy fire, however, and the stubborn resistance of the Germans were of no avail, and towards the end of the afternoon all the Battalion objectives were taken and the enemy were driven back to the line of the Wettering Canal. They had been so severely mauled that they were not able to counter-attack, and the Battalion held its new positions, which were heavily shelled and mortared.

In the Bemmel battle, Major E. G. Wright was wounded by a shell that landed virtually in his slit trench so that it was indeed a miracle that he was not killed. In spite of his serious wounds, great difficulty was experienced in getting him to go back to "B" Echelon for a few days. He was awarded a bar to his M.C. for his share in the attack. Sergeant Slade, M.M., an N.C.O. who had fought with magnificent spirit throughout the campaign, was killed when his section overran its objective, and Sergeant Medway, commanding the left-hand platoon, won the M.M. He hated Germans and he had been killing them on every possible occasion since he first encountered them in Sicily; he was a most aggressive fighter who had seen as much action as anyone in the Battalion. Among the many casualties were Lieutenant J. A. Reed, who was killed, and Lieutenants W. R. Dugmore, W. A. Hughes, F. T. MacGowan, T. C. Austin, and G. F. B. Layton, all wounded.

Although the Battalion was to put in hard, dangerous and most uncomfortable service on the "Island" until the end of November, the battle of Bemmel was the last the 231st Brigade was to fight. It continued with the pattern of a week on duty on the "Island" and a few days at rest. The Battalion occupied several defensive positions, and as the weeks passed the weather grew worse. The enemy were always close on the other side of the canal and were very active every night at stand-to. Transport in the bridgehead was cut down to a minimum on account of the easy target it presented to enemy Spandau fire. The ground was waterlogged, there was much rain, and it was very cold. Patrolling was maintained down to the canal and occasionally across to the other side.

Soon the ground became so thoroughly waterlogged that no wheeled or tracked vehicle could get to forward company positions, and a horse and cart was sometimes brought into service. Men walking up to the forward companies were apt to be stuck in mud up to their knees. Although there was no fighting, shelling, mortaring and sniping were ever recurrent, and there was a great deal of difficult patrolling in the flat and always wet country.

The disagreeable service on the "Island" eventually came to an end with the surprising news that the Battalion was to go home. Accordingly on 29th November it moved back in brigade convoy to Ypres, to be accommodated in billets in the north of the town. Here more details were learned : the Battalion was to take a training cadre home to England, to train men from other arms of the services to become riflemen. Consequently a number of men of the Battalion were posted to other infantry units ; some were posted to garrison battalions and the remainder went home as the training cadre.

The senior officers of the 1st Battalion at the end of its long and varied service in the war were Lieutenant-Colonel A. J. D. Turner, D.S.O., M.C., with Major O. B. Drewitt, Second-in-Command. Majors A. W. Anstey, F. L. Harley, F. H. Waters, M.C., E. G. Wright, M.C., and Captains T. G. Wilmer and D. E. H. James all commanded companies. Captain A. B. Stone, M.B.E., was Quartermaster and Captain J. H. Dracott, Adjutant.

This was the end of the war for the 1st Hampshire Battalion ; a war which had begun for them with the siege of Malta and had included landings in Sicily and Italy and in Normandy, as the very spearhead of the most momentous operation of all. It had taken them through the grim and costly fighting of the bocage country, up through France and Belgium in the splendid triumphal advance, and had ended with grim and unspectacular fighting at the very focus of the final struggle with the Germans in Europe. The awards for gallantry not already mentioned included the M.C. to Major J. L. G. Littlejohns and the M.M. to Sergeant B. J. Edmonds, Corporals W. R. Butt and V. L. Waller, and Private R. J. Playford.

The Battalion went home to Dunscombe Park Camp, Helmsley, near York, where they were able to celebrate VE Day. Soon after this, however, 231st Brigade was called on for active service again and moved to Louth to train and re-equip as part of a special Light Division for service in Burma. But this was not to be, because before their training was completed came VJ Day and the end of the war in which the 1st Hampshire Battalion and 231st Brigade had won so splendid a name.

II—The 7th Battalion

The 7th Battalion was in Brussels for six days, and then it rejoined the 130th Brigade at Deurne in Belgium on 15th September for the operation

"Market Garden." After a series of conferences at Army, Corps and Divisional levels, the Brigade moved through Eindhoven to Grave on 20th September. The first task for the 7th Battalion was to clear part of Nijmegen, but no enemy were encountered. The Battalion then took over the responsibility of protecting the southern ends of the two great bridges over the Waal, with one troop of tanks, one section of anti-tank guns and one of 3-inch mortars in support of each pair of companies.

At this time strenuous efforts were being made to link up with the Airborne Division at Arnhem, and 214th Brigade was already in action south of Elst while 129th Brigade was over the Waal ready to pass through it to secure a bridgehead over the Lek at Arnhem. The 130th Brigade was then to pass through 129th Brigade into Arnhem itself and clear the town of the enemy. But when the break-through into Arnhem failed, 130th Brigade received new orders and was sent forward on 23rd September to Driel to the west of the other two brigades, who were still battling furiously in the Valburg–Elst area.

The objective of 130th Brigade was to occupy the south bank of the Lek from Driel to Heteren and to try to contact the airborne troops cut off on the north bank. The 7th Hampshire, on the left of the 5th Dorsets, were to link up with the 43rd Reconnaissance Regiment, who were protecting the Division's left flank.

THE "ISLAND"

The Battalion reached its allotted area without incident and found that the high bank which ran along the south side of the river varied in distance to the water's edge from about two hundred yards to half a mile or more. The situation was further complicated by the fact that the opposite bank rose steeply and dominated the south bank, which was without a vestige of cover. The Battalion had three companies up: "B" Company (Major Chesham) on the right, in patrol touch with the 5th Dorsets, "A" Company (Major Viner) in the centre, and "D" (Major Braithwaite) on the left. "C" Company (Major Nayler) was in reserve, and there was a squadron of 13th/18th Hussars, and one platoon of medium machine guns from 8th Middlesex. When the Battalion took up their positions, a number of enemy anti-aircraft guns in the open were gleefully engaged by the Battalion's mortars and supporting artillery with very good results. The Battalion was in this position for eleven days, until the 4th October, during which the snipers on the dyke road did some excellent work. In the eleven days continuous action the Battalion was involved in three different affairs.

The first was on the night of 24th September when "B" and "C" Companies, commanded by the Second-in-Command, Major Rooke, helped in the very gallant crossing of the River Lek made by the 4th Dorsets. "C" Company assisted in loading the assault boats with stores, while "B" Company helped to ferry the boats across. Unfortunately, boat casualties and the strong current made the task exceedingly difficult and only about five loads of medical equipment, food and ammunition were ultimately landed on the other bank.

The second affair was on the night of 27th September when a small force of enemy managed to cross the river in front of the 43rd Reconnaissance Regiment, opposite to Renkum and began to infiltrate towards Heteren. "C" Company, supported by a troop of tanks, went to deal with this situation and a violent battle flared up. The enemy were numerically stronger than "C" Company, but the company contained them all day until they were mopped up by a battalion of 214th Brigade attacking from the south.

The third affair was on 1st October when a party of the enemy got across the river and occupied a factory in front of "B" Company, holding the bridgehead they had won with the greatest determination. For the next four days repeated attempts were made by various companies in turn to dislodge him, but in vain. The enemy fought off every attack with fanatical bravery, and although, in all, six assaults were made on his position none were completely successful.

The conditions presented several problems. Between the battalion positions and the factory area was some five hundred yards of marshy exposed ground. Several of the Battalion's attacks were made more difficult by a heavy river mist which reduced visibility to a yard. Moreover the enemy had well-sited machine guns among the confused tangle of factory buildings.

During the many attacks on the factory buildings there were many examples of personal gallantry. The second-in-command of "D" Company, Captain H. J. Anaka, a Canadian officer serving with the Battalion, attacked a machine-gun post single-handed with a Bren gun and slew several of the enemy before he himself fell mortally wounded. Private Barlow went in firing his Bren gun from the hip and killed at least four before he was himself killed by a grenade. On another occasion Sergeant A. R. Powell led his platoon in several gallant but unsuccessful efforts to work his way closer to the enemy, until he was ordered to withdraw. He controlled the withdrawal with the greatest skill, though he himself was wounded, and he carried one of his own wounded men to safety across a distance of over two hundred yards, over ground swept by fire. Sergeant Powell received the M.M.

Sergeant H. Bailey, commanding a platoon in an attack on the factory buildings, succeeded in getting his men so close to the enemy and in such a commanding position that he was able to use his Bren guns with devastating effect. Unfortunately, it was not possible to get the remainder of his company up to him and Sergeant Bailey was ordered to withdraw his platoon. This he did brilliantly, although they had now been brought under very heavy fire. Sergeant Bailey's coolness and personal courage in the action of 27th September, and again in the attack on the factory, were recognized by the award of the M.M.

Another M.M. was won by Sergeant S. Mussell in one of the last attacks on the bridgehead in the early hours of 4th October. Sergeant Mussell personally controlled his sections in the confused enemy positions, moving from one to the other and exposing himself to heavy and close enemy machine-gun and grenade fire. When a grenade burst near him he calmly removed the pieces of phosphorus from his legs and carried on, taking his platoon right on to its objective, destroying several enemy machine-gun positions and killing at least twenty of the enemy.

Throughout this bitter and close fighting at the bridgehead which the enemy defended so very stubbornly, every one of Colonel Talbot's men fought magnificently, and none more so than Major C. G. T. Viner, who was awarded the M.C. He manned an exposed observation post himself on 2nd October and brought punishing fire to bear on the enemy crossing the river to reinforce the bridgehead, and on the 3rd and 4th he led "A" Company against the enemy positions with great skill and dash.

The Battalion was relieved on the evening of 4th October after four days' violent fighting against the German bridgehead, in which it lost one hundred and fifty all ranks. Among those killed were, as well as Captain Anaka, Captain Ward, and Lieutenants A. E. Hope and W. Jenkins. In addition, Captain O. D. Quy and three other officers were wounded.

The Battalion then moved south to the Gromsbeek–Mook area on the Dutch–German border facing the Reichswald Forest for a month, being relieved and relieving other battalions in the Division as brigade sectors were changed over. There was much patrolling, and snipers with the forward companies often sent back valuable information by patrolling forward alone and getting to within a few yards of the enemy. Throughout this whole period, of course, the Battalion suffered much shelling, and there was always the added discomfort of the very bad weather.

The Battalion moved out of the area on 9th November and had a week's rest and training near Maastricht, after which it returned with the Division and was moved from position to position, carrying out a number of different roles, though the pattern throughout was much the same. For the forward companies there was always night patrolling, and there was the usual spasmodic shelling and mortaring by the enemy, invariably returned in good measure. Often the enemy were very close and the battalion snipers came into their own.

In one of the positions held by the Battalion in the Gilrath area, the enemy opposite occupied a line of villages on the reverse slope of a ridge so that their positions could not be observed. The forward companies "A," "D," and "C," held a strip of wood about half-way up on our slope of the ridge. During the night of 21st November a fighting patrol from "D" Company got into an enemy "S" minefield and lost five killed and four wounded, including its leader, a most excellent soldier, Sergeant Cozens, M.M. The next night the Company Commander, Major Braithwaite, took out a party to bring in the bodies of those killed. Two were recovered successfully, but the third set off a mine, wounding Major Braithwaite and Captain C. B. Clarke and two men, one of whom was Sergeant Mussell, M.M.

During this period, in which both the 1st and 7th Battalions were in the same area, 21st Army Group was holding a line from the island north of Nijmegen to the Geilenkirchen area, where it linked with the Americans. All the while the Allies were building up in preparation for the final operations, to cross the Rhine and thrust into Germany itself.

The 43rd Division was about to move back to a rest area on 19th December to prepare for the projected large-scale operations to advance to the Rhine, when the Ardennes offensive forced a change of plan. Accordingly 130th Brigade was directed to an area north of Liége to protect the bridges over the Meuse, and the 7th Hampshire moved to Hasselt and then to Celles (Liége), to secure the bridges at Huy and Seraing. They were also to deal with any enemy paratroopers that might be dropped in that area. Fortunately, no enemy appeared and, thanks to the considerable good will and friendliness of the local inhabitants, the Battalion was able to enjoy a most satisfactory Christmas.

PUTT AND WALDENRATH

From Boxing Day until 12th January the Battalion was stationed near Aachen, engaged in digging second-line defences, and then it moved to Teveren and became a reserve battalion in the line. On 15th January Major D. B. Rooke, in temporary command while Colonel Talbot was commanding the Brigade, and the Company Commanders were briefed for an attack on Waldenrath, as part of XII Corps' operation to clear the enemy from the Sittard–Heinsburg–Geilenkirchen triangle.

The Battalion moved to the concentration area at Gangelt on the 22nd, and at five o'clock in the morning went to the forming-up positions in Kangaroos, all ranks wearing white "snow suits." The roads were covered with frozen snow and ice, but there was no delay, and at zero hour "C" and "D" Companies, supported by two squadrons of Coldstream Guards in Churchills, passed the start line and in less than half an hour were on their objectives in Putt. The enemy, seeing the determination with which the attack went in and the weight of the supporting guns, showed little determination to fight, and Putt was captured by eight o'clock with some fifty prisoners.

Next the Battalion attacked Waldenrath from the north-east. "A" Company led, with the object of seizing the north of the village, and it had to cross six hundred yards of open ground. The start of the attack was delayed for three-quarters of an hour while a minefield was cleared so that the artillery smoke programme had finished by the time "A" Company could move off, and both flanks were exposed to heavy fire from mortar, artillery and small arms. But Major Viner led the company across the open stretch with great dash, got in among the enemy posts hidden in haystacks and in the trench system, and very quickly mopped them up and captured the north end of the village.

With "A" Company holding the north of the village, "B" and "D" passed through and set about clearing the village itself and the extensive trench system round it. More than two hundred prisoners were taken, and to cap a most successful day a German soldier drove into the village in the evening with a horse and cart full of canteen rations.

For the manner in which Major Viner led his company on Waldenrath he was awarded a bar to the M.C., and a bar to the M.C. was also awarded to Major D. B. Rooke, who commanded the Battalion with great drive and enthusiasm. Sergeant A. Lane and Corporal Peirce, both of "B" Company, won well-deserved M.Ms. in this action. The Battalion lost Major Dewar, who was wounded, and twenty-eight other ranks.

The Battalion remained in Putt and Waldenrath for the next two days and then, on 25th January, occupied Dremmen and Porselen with no opposition. except from mines. Lieutenant A. Bevan, the very efficient and popular Battalion Signals Officer, was killed when his carrier was blown up on a mine. During the two days they were here several very good patrols were carried out across the River Roer into the enemy's defensive positions on the far bank, positions which were an extension of the Siegfried Line. Sergeant-Major W. Greenyer, M.M. won the D.C.M. for his courage and coolness leading two of these patrols.

THE REICHSWALD

The Battalion moved back from Dremmen on 29th January to Turnhout, and on 7th February it moved to Helmond to prepare for the Reichswald battle. Here the plans for the great offensive to destroy the German army west of the Rhine were made known, and the Battalion moved to an assembly area in Nijmegen on 9th February, where it was joined by the supporting arms allocated to it for the coming battle. These included "A" Squadron, 13th/18th Hussars, one platoon of medium machine guns and two troops of light anti-aircraft guns. The Battalion moved before dawn on 12th February in transport for the Reichswald Forest, and then on to Cleves. The divisional plan was to advance south-east from Cleves to clear the main road to Goch, and the Battalion's task was to attack from the positions held by the 4th Wiltshire near Bedburg to clear the area between the main road and a large wood. As Colonel Talbot had temporarily taken over command of the 129th Brigade, Major Rooke was again in command of the Battalion.

The Battalion began its advance from Bedburg at half-past one in the afternoon of 15th February, with "B" Company under Major F. de R. Morgan leading. The leading company at once ran into the heaviest shelling and mortaring encountered by the Battalion during the campaign, but in spite of this reached its objective at Berkhofel. The next move was for Major Mumford to lead "D" Company through "B" to secure the important cross-roads to the west. When the company was held up, Major Mumford switched the direction of his attack and after furious fighting captured his objective, though not without serious casualties.

Meanwhile "A" Company, supported by tanks, had attacked and captured its section of the main road, and "C," commanded by Major Nayler, moved up to reinforce "B" Company. "B" and "C" together beat off a very determined counter-attack, and the position at dawn on 17th February was that all the battalion objectives were held, with three companies consolidated forward near Berkhofel, with "A" Company in reserve. The Battalion had captured all its first objectives and the next morning "A" and "C" Companies advanced on their second and final objective some thousand yards ahead, which was to be the start-line for 214th Brigade to continue the assault. But owing to very heavy and accurate shelling both companies were pinned down on the forward slopes of the ridge overlooking their objective.

The battle fought by the 7th Battalion on 15th and 16th February at Berkhofel was long and furious, costing the Battalion seventy casualties including Major Viner who was wounded. The enemy were well aware of the significance of this great assault on their main fortifications, and the advance through very intense shell fire called for the greatest resolution.

There was the occasion when "C" Company under Major L. S. Nayler deployed from Berkhofel to advance to a second objective a thousand yards to the south. As soon as the company reached the exposed forward slope from the position it came under very intense fire from artillery, mortars and machine guns, and became somewhat disorganized and scattered. Any movement at once came under observed artillery fire from many self-propelled guns on the flanks. Nevertheless Major Nayler collected and reorganized his company and led them forward to capture the high ground to his front.

In the evening of the 15th Major Mumford led "D" Company forward to capture a small hamlet eight hundred yards ahead, but the company came under such heavy fire that it was obvious that it could not possibly advance farther. Major Mumford thereupon moved his company farther west, seeking a gap through which he could advance. But it was not until darkness had fallen and visibility was down to some twenty yards that a gap was forced. When about a quarter of a mile from its objective the company, by now only thirty-five strong, was halted by close fire from the enemy trench system round the hamlet, but the strong-points were assaulted at once and cleared. The enemy at once switched heavy defensive fire on to the trenches, but Major Mumford led the remnants of his company into the hamlet with great determination, and after a final burst of house and trench fighting captured the hamlet, taking sixty prisoners. For their part in the battle of Berkhofel, Majors C. J. G. Mumford and L. S. Nayler were awarded the M.C., and Private J. E. Letford won the M.M. for his gallant part in dealing with a counter-attack.

Once during the night of the 15th, the 5th Dorset, who were moving up the main road, reached Berkhofel just after a German counter-attack had penetrated into the village, in the rear of the three Hampshire companies who were holding it. In the morning the Dorsets advanced most gallantly, got through and cleared the left of the Brigade start-line, in spite of the enemy's most desperate resistance.

ON THE RHINE

The 7th Battalion was relieved at Berkhofel on 18th February and moved back via Cleves and Nijmegen to take over a stretch along the south bank of the Rhine, north of the Reichswald Forest. It remained in this position until 1st March, and it was probably the most peculiar assignment that the Battalion had ever had. In their withdrawal across the Rhine the Germans had blown up the dam which kept the river out of this low-lying area, with the result that it was completely flooded, leaving only a few houses and trees sticking out of the water. The only dry land was the high river bund itself which ran along the south bank, and consequently the Battalion had to hold an extended line along the bund for some ten thousand yards. All movement to and from the "mainland," was made in boats. It was a comparatively peaceful period, though a very damp one.

The Battalion moved to another position on the river, until 12th March the Battalion pulled back for a well-deserved rest, and it was soon able to get itself into shape again. On the 19th orders were received for the forthcoming operations to cross the Rhine, the operation to which they had looked forward so long, to fight their way into Germany itself.

The Battalion moved up from Marienbaum on 24th March, crossed the Rhine in assault craft and consolidated on the far bank. On 26th it began a series of small but successful advances, crossing the Ijssel Canal after a hard fight and extending the bridgehead to include Millingen. The Carrier Platoon under Lieutenant F. C. Wilson did some very good work patrolling and rounding up enemy pockets. One of the bridges over the Ijssel, which "C" Company captured after a stiff battle, was later named "Hampshire Bridge." Captain J. J. S. Green and Lieutenant R. J. Hingston both won the M.C. in this fighting on the Rhine.

HENGELO AND CLOPPENBURG

The German defences for their fatherland were now well and truly broken, and with the rest of 21st Army Group the Battalion was to be almost continually on the move until the final surrender. On 1st April the Battalion moved forward to secure a bridgehead over the Twente Canal at Delden, but the brigade plan was changed and it was decided to outflank the enemy position by crossing the canal at Enschede to seize Hengelo. The Battalion was taken across country over a poor track in heavy rain during the night of 2nd April and was then directed to capture the northern part of Hengelo while the 5th Dorsets captured the southern half. The Battalion advanced in transport through woods, covered by a screen of carriers. When they came out of the woods, opposition was encountered from enemy posts covering the main road into the town.

"C" Company, supported by tanks and a section of flame-throwers, soon disposed of the opposition, and thereupon "B" and "D" Companies advanced into the town itself, but there was no further opposition. In fact the movement of the Battalion was seriously hampered by the jubilant crowds of civilians who poured exulting out of their houses. The Battalion stayed at Hengelo until 9th April, when it moved in the 130th Brigade column over the frontier and at last entered Germany itself. It went some forty miles north-east to Bawinkel, and spent the night of 9th April in mopping-up operations near Meerdof.

It was magnificent to be within the borders of the enemy's own country, and spirits were wonderfully high as the army swept triumphantly deeper into Germany; the operation itself was called "Forrard on!" and that was the mood of everyone. The 43rd Division was advancing rapidly along a series of parallel roads, striking north-east towards Bremen and Hamburg, with the 130th Brigade on the left.

Preceded by an advance guard of one company 12 K.R.R.C. (Mortar Battalion), and one squadron S.R.Y., battalions took it in turn to lead each day, with the leading two companies of the battalion carried in "Kangaroos" while the remainder followed in T.C.Vs. and unit transport. The 7th Hampshire were leading on 13th April as the column approached the town of Cloppenburg, which the Battalion was ordered to clear and to secure crossings over the river flowing through it. Thus it was that Cloppenburg was the scene of the Battalion's last battle in the war, and it turned out to be as hard a battle as any it had fought; as the Battalion started in Normandy, so it finished in Germany—fighting hard.

There were two bridges over the river in the town, and the plan was to capture both of these and then clear the rest of the town on the far bank. As the Battalion approached two heavy explosions were heard, which indicated that the enemy were still there and had probably blown up the two bridges. Both the leading companies, "B" and "D," were fired on by infantry as they came upon the outskirts of the town, and they promptly left their vehicles and formed up to stage attacks.

"B" Company on the right, commanded by Major Morgan, quickly overcame the enemy strong-point covering the main road, and advanced into the ruined town towards the main bridge, only to find that it had been demolished. Major Morgan made a rapid reconnaissance of the situation and determined to force a way over the river and into the buildings beyond. He tried to get across with one platoon, but it was pinned down by heavy small-arms fire and bazookas used as mortars. The second platoon was then quickly worked round to the left flank, and it infiltrated over the river under cover of smoke and supported by covering fire from tanks. The third platoon followed, and the bridgehead was established. For his determination and personal gallantry in forcing this vital crossing, Major Morgan was awarded the M.C.

On the left, meanwhile, "D" Company, commanded by Major Mumford, found on coming to the river that it had some two hundred yards of open ground to cross to get to the other bridge, which was still standing despite the obvious attempt the enemy had made to demolish it. Beyond the river there was a further two hundred yards of open ground, rising to the gardens and buildings beyond. The leading platoon was pinned down at once astride the road by heavy machine-gun fire from the enemy positions across the river. A second platoon, trying to move round to the left flank, was also trapped by heavy fire. The supporting tanks could not get up to the company because of the boggy ground on the left and the houses on the right.

A fire plan was worked out and eventually the third platoon crossed under a smoke screen and established itself on the left of the bridge. Another platoon followed later and, by clearing a hospital and other buildings, secured the company bridgehead. In clearing the hospital and buildings Corporal Alan Carter won the M.M. by his cool gallantry. He led his section into the garden of a building in which the enemy had a strong-post and overcame it. Then with his section covering him he went into the building alone to search it. When inside he saw that the enemy were preparing to go into it again. So he took up a good position and calmly picked them off one by one as they approached, killing seven and wounding three more, whom he took prisoner by himself.

While "D" Company were establishing their bridgehead, "A" Company, led by Major G. M. Game, had been passed through "B" on the right and it immediately plunged into a confused close-quarter battle among the houses. The Germans holding Cloppenburg fought with a despairing fanaticism. Our supporting tanks could not get across, of course, as the main bridge was blown, and two enemy self-propelled guns firing at point-blank range down the main road hampered "A" Company considerably. It was a difficult situation and no headway seemed to be made; as soon as gardens and houses were cleared of Germans and the platoons moved on, the enemy began to filter back behind them.

The leading platoon of "A" Company was commanded by Lieutenant R. A. Daniels, who led his men against enemy positions one after the other in the most resolute and determined manner, until he was seriously wounded in the face and head. He refused to leave his platoon, however, until he had reorganized it and handed it over to his sergeant. Lieutenant Daniels' splendid fighting at Cloppenburg, and indeed right through the campaign, was recognized by the award of the M.C.

"A" Company's battle in the streets went on desperately. A troop of tanks and a platoon of "B" Company was sent out to the right to try to get round, but one of the tanks was knocked out, and no progress could be made. But succour did at last come through the "D" Company position. Here "C" Company, Major J. J. S. Green, passed through "D" Company while it was still fighting for its bridgehead, losing C.S.M. Greenyer, D.C.M., M.M., who was wounded as they crossed the bridge under heavy fire. He later died of his wounds. The company, like "A," threw itself into the close and desperate street and house-to-house fighting. But unlike "A" it did not have to fight without support, for it was found that one of the bridges, though partially demolished, could bear tanks, and an A.V.R.E. at once crossed to support "C" Company. Under its gallant Sapper commander, Lieutenant Wilton, R.E., who gained a richly deserved M.C., the A.V.R.E. engaged enemy posts in rapid succession, demolishing the buildings with its violent and noisy petard.

With "C" Company's success, "A" Company's supporting arms were able to cross the damaged bridge, pass through "D" and "C" Companies, and join "B," so that the position in their part of the town was made easier. But strong parties of the enemy still continued to appear amid the rabbit warren of the ruins, and about midnight a party of thirty overran one of the Battalion's anti-tank guns which was getting into position. But a quick counter-attack restored the position.

At first light the advance was continued by other battalions passing through the Battalion's hard-won positions, and the advance towards Bremen went on. This last battle of the 7th Battalion had been hard and fierce, and there was a great deal of individual gallantry in the close fighting. One example was Corporal S. W. Brooks, who won the M.M. leading his own section and another through the gardens and houses against desperate defenders, and overcoming every obstacle.

The Battalion lost many men in its last battle, but it took a heavy toll of the enemy, including more than a hundred prisoners of good quality. It remained in Cloppenburg until 19th April, when it joined the rest of 130th Brigade at Bahlum, where the Brigade came under command 52nd Division for operations against Bremen. But there were to be no more battles for the Battalion. It moved forward, first to Bremen and then northwards towards Bremerhaven. On 23rd April there was a wood-clearing operation against some opposition which resulted in a bag of two hundred and thirty-six prisoners for five casualties to the Battalion. Mopping-up continued and on 24th April a further fifty-nine prisoners were taken, and on the 25th, when the Battalion entered battered and defeated Bremen without opposition, it took seven officers and five hundred and twenty men, a military hospital with three hundred patients and sixteen anti-aircraft guns with abundant ammunition. The enemy the Battalion had fought against so hard was broken, and the victors had their reward indeed.

Advancing along roads which were badly cratered and heavily mined, the Battalion made for Bremerhaven, taking the villages of Breddorf and Hanstedt against slight opposition and losing some carriers on mines. There was a temporary flare-up of the old fighting when a patrol fought a sharp and successful engagement at Glinstedt, and then the Battalion took Karlshofen and Barkhausen on 3rd May.

In the early hours of 4th May a strange quiet fell upon the whole area, for at Luneburg Heath a simple but dramatic ceremony had been enacted. Five high-ranking German officers had stood at attention under the Union Jack and had saluted Field-Marshal Montgomery as he came out of his tent. They had come to offer to surrender. Dunkirk was finally avenged. When a patrol of the Hampshires reached the banks of the canal at Gnarrenburg, the burgomaster surrendered the town and it was at once occupied. Late that night it was announced on the radio that the German armies in North-West Germany, Holland and Denmark had surrendered unconditionally to the 21st Army Group. Brigadier B. A. Coad, commanding 130th Brigade, at once ordered a firework display and the sky was joyously alight with Very lights and mortar flares; there was, alas, no beer available for issue on that great occasion. To many the tremendous change in their purpose seemed unreal.

The 7th Hampshire had travelled far since they had landed in Normandy, and parts of that journey had been very hard going; through the bocage country, in Holland, and at last within the frontiers of Germany. When the Battalion held a Thanksgiving Service in Gnarrenburg church on 5th May a great number of the officers and men who had left England with the 7th were no longer there ; for the Battalion had paid a heavy price in dead and wounded.

Lieutenant-Colonel D. E. B. Talbot was still in command when the war in Europe ended, with Major D. B. Rooke Second-in-Command. The rifle companies were commanded by Majors C. G. T. Viner, F. de R. Morgan, J. S. Green and C. J. G. Mumford, with Captains R. W. H. Raikes and F. K. Boschetti-Birch commanding Headquarters and Support Companies respectively. Colonel Talbot's Headquarters at the end was Captain E. G. Dunckley, Adjutant, Lieutenants P. Y. Bowen and H. Shulman, Assistant Adjutant and Intelligence Officer respectively, and R.S.M. A. E. Ware.

Colonel Talbot had taken over the 7th Battalion at a most critical time in June, 1944. Newly arrived in Normandy, the Battalion had been cruelly mauled in its first days, and two Commanding Officers had been killed. The Battalion was sore and a little bewildered by its ill-fortune, but Colonel Talbot swiftly restored its old confidence and Hampshire spirit. His leadership and faith in the Battalion's ability was exactly the tonic it needed, and under him it fought its hard and brilliant campaign with admirable *elan*. Colonel Talbot won a very well-deserved D.S.O. for the splendid way in which he commanded the 7th Hampshire.

In the campaign the Battalion had been awarded one D.S.O., one M.C. and bar, one bar to the M.C., nine M.Cs., one D.C.M., and thirteen M.Ms. It had shown yet again what sterling and splendid fighting qualities the Territorial Army possesses.

At the end of a campaign every infantry battalion has ample reason to be grateful to its good friends the supporting Gunners, and the 7th Battalion was no exception. The officers and men of 217 Battery shared the vicissitudes of the campaign with the 7th Battalion from the Normandy beaches and into Germany, and warm friendship was engendered between Infantry and Gunners. 217 Battery suffered many casualties in the campaign, including five officers killed and four wounded, and won four M.Cs.

CHAPTER XXI

147 REGIMENT, R.A.C.

(THE 10TH BATTALION THE HAMPSHIRE REGIMENT)

(*See maps on pages* 220 *and* 240)

THIS book tells the story of The Royal Hampshire Regiment and is concerned therefore with infantry. It is fitting, however, to include a brief account of 147 Regiment, R.A.C., as it was formed from the 10th Battalion The Hampshire Regiment in November, 1941, and included many Hampshire men in its ranks during its successful campaign in North-West Europe. Moreover the Regiment was eventually designated 147 (Hampshire) Regiment, R.A.C.

The Regiment crossed to the Normandy beaches on 2nd July, 1944, as part of the 34th Armoured Brigade, commanded by Lieutenant-Colonel A. W. Brown, M.C., until September, when Lieutenant-Colonel W. B. Blain took over. The Second-in-Command was Major G. M. Hawtrey, and the Adjutant Captain J. M. M. Yeo until he was killed in action in October, when Captain G. A. Shepherd became Adjutant. The 34th Armoured Brigade was commanded by Brigadier W. S. Clarke, and included 147, 107 and 153 Regiments, R.A.C., and 7 and 9 R.T.R.

147 Regiment first saw action on 17th July at Evrècy, when the Brigade was under command of the 15th (Scottish) Division. It was part of a very bitter battle preceding the Allied break-through east of Caen, and 147 Regiment's task was to support the infantry in breaking through the strong and well-manned enemy positions to capture the village of Evrècy. The attack entailed a long advance down a forward slope leading to Evrècy through murderous fire, and this first battle of the Regiment came very near to disaster; it was, in fact, a very gallant failure.

The tank squadrons pressed forward steadily through accurate fire and overran the enemy positions, so that scores of bewildered Germans were running about in the standing corn amongst the tanks, but there was no infantry to take them prisoner. The infantry, of 158th Infantry Brigade, had already been savagely mauled; they were desperately weak from casualties and too tired to keep up with the tanks. Colonel Brown personally led the attack in his tank and controlled the very confusing battle brilliantly. When as light was failing he saw that no infantry could get forward to consolidate the ground he had won, he extricated his tanks and withdrew.

On one occasion during the battle tank crews dismounted to round up the prisoners, exposing themselves to the mortar and Spandau fire of the more determined of the enemy who were still hanging on to their fox-holes. The Germans were quite impartial as to whom they shot, friend and foe falling alike to their fire. This angered one troop leader so much that, as the range was too close to bring fire to bear, he ran over two such teams with his tank.

Thus 147 Regiment suffered their baptism of fire, and a grim and deadly ordeal it was. Casualties were nine officers and thirty-six other ranks, of whom four officers and twelve other ranks were killed, and eleven tanks. But these heavy losses were by no means in vain, for the Regiment had accounted for a great number of the enemy killed, and took more than two hundred and fifty prisoners.

From 18th July onwards the Regiment settled down to a more or less static life on the perimeter of the Odon bridgehead, in close support of the 53rd (Welsh) Division. It saw action again after the break-out from the bridgehead on 5th August, fighting a brisk and notable battle on 12th August in support of the 2nd Gloucesters at Thury Harcourt. When the break-out was made the Regiment forged ahead steadily, at first slowly against strong enemy resistance, which lessened as the break-through developed and became a triumphant progress to the Seine and beyond. There was a stiff battle on 16th August when "C" Squadron, with the 1st East Lancs, punched its way through the enemy positions near Leffard as an advance guard to 158th Brigade. The battle was fierce, but went beautifully to plan, and at the end positions were taken with a loss of three tanks and seven casualties, the enemy losing some two hundred killed and a further two hundred taken prisoner.

From 23rd to 30th August the Regiment, under command 15th (Scottish) Division again, moved up to and across the River Seine below Les Andelys, where it liberated the village of Fresne Archevècque. The Regiment was left here for a month while the rest of the Brigade moved to assist in the capture of Le Havre. On 29th September the Regiment began a long journey with the rest of the Brigade towards Holland, travelling on their tracks for four days until they were lifted across western Belgium and up to the Eindhoven area on transporters. For two weeks the Regiment supported The Royals between Best and Poppel, occupying itself with a certain amount of offensive prodding. On 14th October the 34th Armoured Brigade moved to an area between Antwerp and Turnhout while 147 Regiment spent a few days employed on aerodrome defence duties at Eindhoven.

When the operations for the clearance of Holland from the north of Antwerp to the River Maas began, 147 Regiment fought a vigorous and successful battle between 21st and 23rd October. It advanced with the 147th Infantry Brigade from Brecht to establish a firm base at Wuestwezel, and to keep clear a line of communication forward to "Clarkeforce," which was punching a hole through the enemy positions. The operation began early in the morning of 20th October, and the long battle was so well fought and was so successful that the morale of the Regiment rose to a very high level. The enemy counter-attacked violently from the west to try to break the thin lifeline forward to "Clarkeforce," but he was driven off every time. Both infantry support and artillery co-operation were well-nigh perfect, and the supply line was kept open. Fifteen self-propelled guns were destroyed, and very heavy casualties were inflicted on the enemy. The Regiment lost three tanks destroyed and five damaged, one officer and eight other ranks killed, and one and three other ranks wounded. The officer killed was Captain J. M. M. Yeo, the Adjutant, whose death was a grievous loss to the Regiment.

On 24th November 34th Armoured Brigade came under command XXX Corps for operations in Germany east of Maastricht, so that 147 Regiment was serving in the same formation as the 7th Hampshire Battalion. Early in December the Regiment was in the line in close support of the 43rd Division, and with them moved south through ice and snow to deal with the German threat of a break-through in the Ardennes. Travelling south through Namur, 147 Regiment went to Celles (Dinant), and by the 2nd January was in contact with the enemy in the line at Rochefort. The Regiment left the Ardennes on 22nd January and made the long and very tiring journey back to Eindhoven. A move of fifty-three miles north-east took the Regiment to a concentration area south of Nijmegen for Operation "Veritable"; the major offensive by XXX Corps to clear the area between the River Maas and the Rhine—"The Battle for Germany."

147 Regiment and 9 R.T.R. were given a vital and a most unusual task, to support infantry right through the heart of the Reichswald Forest, part of the vaunted Siegfried Line. The Forest had always been regarded as a complete tank obstacle; our plan was to disregard that belief and to fight the tanks through it; to attempt the impossible. A German colonel who was captured in the forest was indignant: "Who but the British," he said, "would think of using tanks in this forest? It's not fair!"

The battle lasted for nine days, six of them within the permanent soggy gloom of the forest. It was indeed almost "impossible" country for tanks, but the stalwart Churchills kept going. The prelude was a tremendous five-hour barrage from more than a thousand guns on a narrow front, and at ten minutes past ten in the morning of 8th February "A" Squadron of 147 Regiment led the advance towards the forest with the 4th Royal Welch Fusiliers.

To start with there was some four thousand yards of atrocious going to be crossed, boggy ground sown with mines and under heavy defensive fire. A.V.R.Es., "Flail tanks" and Crocodiles got bogged down or mined, but the ordinary Churchills managed to get across and 147 Regiment led their infantry right up to the edge of the forest, whose area is eight miles long, varying from three to five miles in depth. Then a squadron of 9 R.T.R. passed through with infantry and entered the forest on the night of 8th February, and the next day both Regiments went in and fought through for six days. Neither Regiment had any relief day or night, and squadrons shrank steadily in numbers. There was torrential rain, and for part of the time a high wind approaching gale force. Drinking water was acutely short, and all supply was a most difficult problem. Some tanks were bogged down to turret-top level, others had their traverses wrecked by guns hitting trees.

As well as these natural causes in what was after all unnatural country for tanks, the enemy was in a fanatical and desperate mood, for his own territory was being violently invaded. They who had so haughtily invaded so many countries were at last being rudely awakened from their dreams of conquest. The forest was most suitable for snipers and for camouflaged S.P. guns, and when the tank crews slept for brief spells in the tanks, with the infantry curled up around them, there was the constant danger of counter-attacks. It was "impossible" country for tanks; yet the Churchills of 147 Regiment, R.A.C., and of 9 R.T.R. broke into the forest, smashed their way through it, and the survivors burst out on the other side for two more days' fighting. The impossible was achieved.

The Regiment, with its supporting infantry, accounted for more than a thousand enemy casualties and took a thousand prisoners. It also "slew" a "Jagdpanther" tank, destroyed seven guns and captured four 105-mm. guns intact. The Regiment's losses were remarkably light; one other rank killed and five officers and fifteen other ranks wounded, with eight tanks lost through enemy action and thirty from other causes. The nine-day battle of the Reichswald Forest was the last 147 Regiment, R.A.C., was to fight in the war. It was a great achievement, and the Hampshire Regiment can well be proud that its 10th Battalion, changed from infantrymen into troopers, fought like Tigers indeed.

147 Regiment served in the role of line-holding reserve on 19th February and then, on 2nd March, it began a gallop forward with the 1st S.S. Brigade (of Commandos) as far as Twisteden. A few days later it took over from the Sherwood Rangers Yeomanry on the perimeter of the bridgehead, which enemy paratroops were holding to cover the Wesel bridge over the Rhine, and on 11th March it advanced again to Menzelen, two miles from the Rhine. But the enemy were pulling back fast and surrendering in large blocks, so that the west bank of the Rhine was reached without opposition.

The 34th Armoured Brigade was withdrawn on 12th March and went back into Holland over the Maas, to lick its wounds and do something to recover from the grievous effects of its unorthodox but successful efforts in "knocking out the Reichswald plug." Moving forward again over the Rhine on 3rd April, the Brigade sat down in a large parish of many square miles. Here its task was to keep order, to guard the lines of communication to the triumphant British Second Army, advancing into Germany, and to clear up the more attractive and dangerous stores left behind by the Germans. The Brigade continued with these duties, moving deeper into Germany, until it reached Burgsteinfurt, taking over Munster from the Americans. 147 Regiment was in that area when VE Day came, and it was over.

147 Regiment served as Occupation Forces in Germany for a further five months, and then in October, 1945, it was disbanded, a number of its officers and men having been posted to 107 Regiment, R.A.C., to form a squadron for service in the Far East. VJ Day came, however, before the newly formed Brigade left. 147 Regiment had fought intermittently from the Normandy bridgehead to the Rhine crossings for a period of eight months, doing stalwart service with their Churchill tanks. Both Lieutenant-Colonel A. W. Brown, M.C., and Lieutenant-Colonel W. B. Blain were awarded the D.S.O., Major R. Granthan a bar to his M.C., Captain C. H. Deakin the M.C. and bar, and eight other officers won the M.C. Awards also included one D.C.M., five M.Ms. and the B.E.M.

CHAPTER XXII

THE ROYAL HAMPSHIRE REGIMENT

1945–1948

THE Hampshire Regiment had put six infantry battalions in the field in the war, and the Roll of Honour contains the names of two thousand and ninety-four officers and men of the Regiment killed in action or died of wounds. The battalions had fully maintained the high reputation won by their predecessors, and the quality of their fighting had added lustre to the name of the Regiment. This was recognized for all time by Army Order No. 167 of 28th November, 1946, in which the name of the Regiment appeared in a short list headed: "Regimental Honours." The Order read: "In recognition of past services His Majesty The King has been graciously pleased to approve that the following Regiments shall in future enjoy the distinction of 'Royal'."

The Regiment had already been honoured in its own county when it received the Freedom in turn of Aldershot, on 11th September, 1945, of Bournemouth on the 13th, and of Winchester on the 15th of that month, and of Southampton on 25th April, 1946. The four ceremonies were most impressive, the Colonel of the Regiment, General Sir George Jeffreys, receiving the Freedoms from the Mayors on beautifully illuminated scrolls. These granted the Regiment the "Privilege, Honour and Distinction of marching through the streets with Colours flying, drums beating and bayonets fixed."

At the ceremonies the Regiment was represented by a detachment made up of contingents from all the battalions, including, of course, those still overseas, commanded by Lieutenant-Colonel J. M. Lee. Enthusiastic crowds cheered their county Regiment as it marched to the ceremony with Colours draped; and again as it returned, with Colours flying, drums beating and bayonets fixed. The ceremonies were conducted with all the appropriate pomp and ceremony, and each time there was a formal speech in which the achievements of the Regiment during its long history were recounted. A large number of past and present officers and men of the Regiment watched, and the solemn significance of the presentation, and the sincerity of the tribute, were deeply appreciated.

The parades were immaculate, of course, and what must surely have been a unique feature was the presence of the King's and Regimental Colours of seven battalions at the same time. Some part of the admiration of the crowds was bestowed on the Regimental mascot, Fritz, who headed the marching column, led by the Dog-Major. Fritz was a magnificent Pyrenean mountain dog who had been captured with his master, a German officer, by the 1st Battalion on the Normandy beaches. He arrived in England with a batch of prisoners, and was saved from destruction under the quarantine regulations by Leading Wren Elgar, who undertook to pay the quarantine fees and so save his life. Captain Thomas, who had commanded the platoon which captured

Fritz, heard about Miss Elgar's action while he was in hospital, and got in touch with Major Jeffery, who persuaded her to release the dog so that he could become the Regimental Mascot. The cost of the quarantine fees was raised by subscriptions of men of the Regiment, and when his quarantine period ended Fritz reported for duty at the Regimental Depot.

Fritz had not been an easy prisoner when he first went into quarantine. To quote a letter from the veterinary surgeon who was in charge of him, "as a matter of fact he did about £5 worth of damage to the premises here in the first week, trying to get out. He went straight through a stout corrugated iron fence by chewing and tearing, and he gnawed through the zinc-lined kennel doors. However, he is now a reformed character and very obedient. I do not speak German, but he knows what I mean even to attacking and holding a person against a wall. I should imagine he has been very well trained."

Fritz was posted to Depot in charge of Major Jeffery, who appointed two men to look after him. Fritz weighed 122 pounds and had obviously been trained for service in the field by the German army, as he could clear a six-foot barbed-wire fence with the greatest of ease and was very obedient to orders and calls. He tended to be a "one man" dog and had no vice at all. His sense of guardianship was strong and he would have made short work of an intruder if instructed so to do. He was taken on the strength of the Regiment in the orthodox manner and the appropriate army forms were made out for him. Army Form H1157 showed that he was issued with "Jackets 2, Brushes Hair Dog 1, Combs Hair Dog 1, Badge 1, Collars Dog 1, Harnesses Dog 2, Leads Dog 2, and Containers Food 1."

Fritz's jackets were very beautifully made, of black velvet with an amber fringe ; in the centre was the Regimental badge and above and below it were the names of the countries in which the Regiment served during the Second World War. Groomed and dressed for parade and led by the Dog-Major wearing white gauntlets, the dog's dignity and beauty impressed everyone. On the Royal visit to Winchester on 17th May, 1946, Their Majesties The King and Queen were very interested in Fritz's story and they were photographed with Her Majesty fondling him. He died in 1949, having served the Regiment as its mascot for five years.

* * * * *

The Regiment learned with very real regret, on 5th January, 1945, that its much-loved Colonel, General Sir Richard C. L. Haking, had to resign the appointment through ill health. General Haking had carried out the duties of Colonel of the Hampshire Regiment for twenty-one years with the utmost devotion. Gazetted Second-Lieutenant in the 67th Foot on 22nd January, 1881, he remained with the Regiment until he left it as Major in 1903 to take up an appointment on the General Staff. In the 1914-1918 war General Haking commanded the 5th Brigade in 1914, the 1st Division in 1915, and XI Corps in 1915 to 1918. From 1923 to 1927 he was G.O.C., British troops in Egypt. The General served in the Burma campaign in 1885-1887, being mentioned in despatches and gaining the medal with clasp; in South Africa he was again mentioned in despatches and had the Queen's medal with three clasps.

General Haking was promoted Major-General for distinguished conduct in the field in 1914, was awarded the K.C.B. in 1916 and the K.C.M.G. in 1918. He was mentioned in despatches on eight occasions, was promoted Lieutenant-General in 1915, and was awarded the G.B.E. in 1921 and promoted General in 1925. Sir Richard's reputation among the men who fought under him was tremendous; his bluff, hearty manner and his great personal interest in the British soldier as an individual endeared him to all. He was indeed the ideal officer, a man for whom his men gave of their best and a soldier of high intellectual quality.

General Sir Richard Haking never spared himself in carrying out his duties as Colonel of the Hampshire Regiment. The interest he took was essentially a personal one, and he took every opportunity of visiting his battalions during the war and was present on every appropriate occasion, and he never missed wishing the battalions God-speed when they went overseas. General Haking died in May, 1945, at his home in Bulford, and it is in tribute to the memory of a very great soldier of the Regiment that this History is dedicated.

The new Colonel of the Regiment was another great soldier, General Sir George D. Jeffreys. General Jeffreys served with the Grenadier Guards in the Nile expedition of 1888 and fought in the battle of Khartoum. In the South African War he was awarded the Queen's and King's medals with five clasps, commanded the 2nd Battalion the Grenadier Guards in 1915, the 58th, 57th and 1st Guards Brigades in 1916 to 1917, and the 19th Division from 1917 to 1918, when he was severely wounded. He was mentioned in despatches nine times and created a baronet. His later commands included the 8th Division in the Army of the Rhine in 1919, the London District from 1920 to 1924, the Wessex area and the 43rd (Wessex) Division, T.A., 1926-1930. He was G.O.C.-in-C., Southern Command, India, 1932-1936; A.D.C. General to the King, 1936-1938; and was promoted Lieutenant-General in 1930 and General in 1935. He was M.P. for the Petersfield division of Hampshire. General Sir George Jeffreys was subsequently appointed Colonel of the Grenadier Guards on 8th April, 1952, and was raised to the peerage in 1952.

* * * * *

After hostilities ceased, two years were to pass before the Regiment, which had become remarkably enlarged during the war, could return to its peace-time establishment. As has already been related in Chapter VII, the battalions still serving at home in 1945 were disbanded. It is convenient now to recount the post-war service and the disbandment or return of the battalions which had served overseas in the war.

The 1st Battalion

The 1st Battalion came back from Holland in December, 1944, commanded by Lieutenant-Colonel A. J. D. Turner, and became a training battalion at

Helmsley in Yorkshire. Their task was to train Gunners and other specialist troops as infantrymen, and the enthusiasm of these men made them most apt pupils. In January, 1945, Lieutenant-Colonel J. M. Lee took over the command of the Battalion until August, when Lieutenant-Colonel R. G. F. Frisby succeeded him. The Battalion was warned for service in the Far East, and moved to Louth in Lincolnshire to re-form and re-equip as a fighting unit.

With the news of the surrender of Japan, the Battalion was ordered to remain at full establishment, and on 21st November it sailed from Liverpool for the Middle East. Its destination was Benghazi, where it arrived on 19th December, 1945, to be quartered in some dilapidated Turkish barracks. These were soon made habitable and the Battalion settled down to interesting training and a lot of sport and games, including excellent swimming and sailing.

The nine months the 1st Battalion spent at Benghazi were uneventful. It was a peaceful spell of duty which ended with orders to move to Palestine. The Battalion arrived in Haifa on 2nd October to take its place in the 1st Division (*see map on page* 32). Palestine was in a dangerous condition of unrest, but for the first two months the Battalion had a fairly quiet time. They were busy with guards and road-blocks and all aspects of "internal security," but there was time for a certain amount of training and sport. During November the Battalion moved to Transjordan for a month's brigade training, and returned to a camp at Pardess Hanna near Hadera. The Battalion, now in the 2nd Infantry Brigade, was glad to find itself in an operational formation after a year of comparative independence. Early in January, 1947, Lieutenant-Colonel Frisby was posted to G.H.Q., Middle East Land Forces, and Lieutenant-Colonel R. Chandler went to Hadera to take over the command.

The anti-British outrages committed by the Jews were on the increase and it was a delicate and difficult time. The Battalion was confined to camp for four months, emerging only for operational purposes. Constant patrols of roads and railways had to be maintained as well as an alert guard of the camp itself. When the Jewish Terrorist Dov Gruener was hanged, the whole Battalion was out in a complete operational role for nearly three weeks, and there was an important search of Peta Tikva to release Judge Wyndham, who had been kidnapped by the Terrorists. When Tel Aviv was put under martial law, Colonel Chandler was made magistrate of Peta Tikva, dispensing summary justice to civilian malefactors twice a week.

On 20th March the Commanding Officer broke to the Battalion the melancholy and almost incredible news that the 37th, after two hundred and forty-five years of unbroken and distinguished service, was to be placed in suspended animation. The feelings of all ranks of the Battalion when they first heard this startling news can well be imagined.

In mid-April the Battalion moved south to a dusty and barren camp north of Gaza, and was at once turned out to control an area about half the size of Hampshire. For seven consecutive nights six platoons were out on patrol.

After two weeks of this, however, the Battalion had a peaceful fortnight and then went north again to Jerusalem to guard Zone B of the city, where most of the military and Government headquarters were situated. The work was very arduous; sometimes men did three consecutive nights on guard, and there were innumerable day patrols and searches. Outbreaks of violence were a common occurrence, but the Terrorists misjudged the situation badly when they decided to attack the Battalion's camp during the Minden Day celebrations.

The "IZL" staged the raid to take place at lunch time on Minden Day, to blow up some of the buildings. Consequently while the Battalion was sitting down at the special Minden Day dinner, and while the officers were enjoying a drink in the Sergeants' Mess, there was a series of explosions and an outburst of small-arms fire. The Terrorists did not realize, however, that it is unwise to disturb Tigers when they are eating, particularly so with Hampshire Tigers on 1st August. The Battalion dealt with the situation with great zest, just as though it had been arranged as part of the celebration. Two sentries held the Terrorists at bay while a party from "C" Company, led by Lieutenant Arden, raced round behind them. Everyone turned out in high good humour to see the fun. The Terrorists, realizing their error, tried to withdraw. One was shot dead as he was running away and others were driven into houses and captured. With great presence of mind, Captain J. E. Dunning removed the fuses from two 50-lb. bombs which had been left on the wire. The Battalion then continued its Minden Day celebrations.

In July Colonel Chandler left the Battalion to take up an appointment in the Malta Command, and the Second-in-Command of the Battalion, Major J. S. S. Gratton, took over command, with the rank of Lieutenant-Colonel. The Battalion left Jerusalem in September, and three weeks later sailed for home in the *Otranto*. They arrived at Southampton on 5th November, where the Colonel of the Regiment, the Mayors of Winchester, Southampton and Aldershot, and a large gathering of officers were at the quayside to welcome them home.

The Battalion was already much reduced through postings in the Middle East, and at Purfleet more men left on release from the Army. There were more postings out until, after a Farewell Parade, at which the Colours were trooped for the last time, the Battalion was reduced to a representative cadre. On 17th February, 1948, this cadre of six officers and eighteen men went to Winchester. One of the last to leave the 1st Battalion was Captain (Q.M.) F. Stone. He joined the 1st Battalion in Istanbul in 1922 and served in the Battalion continuously for twenty-five years in Egypt, India, Palestine, and throughout the war and after.

128th Brigade

(*See map inside front cover*)

The Hampshire Brigade had celebrated VE Day near Forli in northern Italy, and on 15th May the three battalions went up into Austria, where they were stationed along the Jugoslav frontier. The 2nd Battalion had its headquarters and two companies at St. Andra, two companies at St. Paul and one at Geogen ; the 1/4th was at Bleiburg, and the 5th at Lavermund, a town on the Jugoslav border.

Austria presented a surprising contrast to the ruin and desolation in Italy and the poverty in Greece. There was wonderful scenery—neat and tidy little towns, "cuckoo clock" houses, and none of the more obvious scars of war. The Battalion received a strange welcome considering that only two weeks before the Austrians had been enemies. There were crowds cheering and waving, and children showered flowers on the vehicles.

The Brigade was engaged on occupational duty, patrolling the frontier, keeping the peace, and rounding up Nazis who were in the area. At first the roads were crowded with bands of forced labour, marching behind Red banners in the general direction of the Red Army ; French slave workers trudging dourly in the opposite direction, and always Jugoslav patriots, armed to the teeth, were liable to pop up in unexpected places. There was also the heart-rending task of returning the Croats to their own country. Some of them tried to commit suicide before they could be handed over, and often there was an ominous burst of small-arms fire soon after they had passed into Jugoslav hands. The fate of Cossacks being returned to the Russians in the north was the same.

This ruthlessly cruel behaviour by their allies was quite incomprehensible to the British soldiers, and the Hampshire men, proud victors after so many battles, carried out their orders in this confusing political atmosphere and, by their tolerance, good discipline and splendid appearance, won the confidence of the people among whom they were now living.

Bleiburg, where the 1/4th were stationed, was a typically quaint and picturesque country town. Battalion Headquarters was set up in the ancient baronial mansion on a hill which dominated both the town and the surrounding countryside. The owner, an old Austrian aristocrat, who was much put out by the occupation of his castle, tried to establish his dignity by asking the R.S.M. of the 1/4th to turn out the Regimental Quarter Guard for him. The R.S.M. was not able to accede to this request and was somewhat emphatic about it. The 1/4th were very happy at Bleiburg, with its old-world architecture, its trout-filled streams and its friendly and gaily attired populace, in which the women outnumbered the men ten to one. Stray horses were found, and saddles to go with them, and many officers and other ranks had their own horses and went riding in the pine-scented hills. To add to the sweets of victory there was a brewery, and a fine sparkling lager became a regular issue in dining-halls. Unfortunately, Brigade Headquarters found out and the other two battalions of the Brigade turned up to share the lager beer. This was tolerated by the 1/4th, but all was spoiled when Division stepped in, organized things and issued the beer on a strict rationing system among its many thirsty thousands.

One duty which fell to the battalions was ensuring that all Austrian adults saw the documentary film on German concentration camps, to convince them that it was not merely Allied propaganda. A few who protested were taken back for a second or even a third time.

For the first few months after the war the battalions retained the same appearance, but then early release began to remove familiar and important figures. Two of the earliest to go from the 5th Battalion were Captain (Q.M.) S. A. Osgood, M.B.E., and R.S.M. Tom "Bismarck" Barnett, M.B.E. No one realizes more than soldiers that no one is indispensable, but when men of the calibre of these two leave it seems it will never be the same again. Captain Osgood had spent his entire army career with the Regiment, serving in every rank up to Captain. He was an all-round sportsman, and a keen boxer who was never knocked out in a hundred boxing matches ; he only lost on points to the All-India champion in the biggest fight of his career. He had played for the Battalion at both rugby and association football and hockey. He was also an athletic champion, and a Bisley champion pistol and Lewis gun shot. Like all true quartermasters, Captain Osgood had the uncanny ability of getting supplies in the most impossible circumstances.

It may have been his facial resemblance to the great man which earned for R.S.M. Barnett the nickname "Bismarck," but certainly his word of command on the parade ground won him a reputation throughout the Division. He had been in the Coldstream Guards for eighteen years when he transferred to the Hampshire Regiment in 1940, although he had served as a Staff Instructor with the 5/7th Battalion from 1936. He had in his time instructed in drill at the Guards Depot, Caterham, he was a C.S.M. at Sandhurst, and he had served with the 5th Battalion from its formation.

The three battalions made great preparations to celebrate the first Minden Day in peace time, and a race meeting was arranged for the Brigade just outside Bleiburg ; but all had to be cancelled when orders were received for a move a hundred miles or more east to the Austro-Hungarian border. So the three battalions packed up and spent Minden Day, 1945, travelling. The move was made to follow up the Russian army of occupation, which was drawing back to an agreed line farther east.

The battalions had a great send-off from the Austrians among whom they had been living. At Bleiburg the townspeople turned out at six o'clock in the morning to see the 1/4th Battalion set off. They cheered, they waved, and many of them wept. Throughout the journey it was the same ; cheering crowds, showers of flowers, and signs hung across the road with the legend "Welcome to our Liberators." It was rather difficult for the British soldier to understand quite why these former enemies were so profoundly and sincerely sad to see him go and pleased to see him come. This move took the 2nd Battalion first to Freidburg and then, in early September, to Bad Gleikenburg, the 1/4th to Furstenfeldt and the 5th to Hartberg.

The duties of the Brigade consisted of manning the frontier and check points. At first the sentries found their Russian opposite numbers friendly in a reserved way, and sometimes cigarettes were exchanged, but gradually this cordiality of our strange allies fell away and they remained austerely aloof.

Lieutenant-Colonel T. A. Rotherham left the 2nd Battalion on release in early August, and Major W. Spencer commanded until Lieutenant-Colonel J. P. Fowler-Esson went out to Austria to take command in October. Lieutenant-Colonel A. Boyce left the 5th Battalion at the end of September, and his Second-in-Command, Major P. R. Sawyer, took his place and commanded the Battalion until on 7th January, 1946, the order came for the Battalion to be disbanded. Owing to an outbreak of typhoid fever at Hartberg, the remnants of the 5th Battalion moved back to Pollau for the melancholy business of posting away remaining men, holding audit boards, and bringing to an end the very distinguished war-time career of the 5th Battalion The Hampshire Regiment. The 5th Battalion had left England over a thousand strong ; when it went to Austria only six officers and one hundred and seventy-four of those still remained. Many of these original members had been wounded, some twice or more, and one N.C.O., Sergeant Samson, four times. While the Battalion was overseas one hundred and sixty-eight officers had served in it. The unhappy condition of "suspended animation" was not, however, to last long, for the 5th Battalion was resuscitated in 1947 as the 14th Parachute Regiment, T.A.

The 2nd Battalion moved to Vienna for five weeks at the end of November, to provide guards for the British zone. With French, American and Russian troops present in the famous and somewhat desolated capital of Austria, great attention was paid to drill and turn-out to do justice to the reputation of the British Army. The guard at the Schonbrunn Palace, which bristled with senior officers and important political personages, had ample opportunity to show what the Hampshire Regiment could do. Christmas was celebrated exuberantly in Vienna, the main feature being a party at which over two thousand Viennese children were entertained by the Battalion. This party was a great success, particularly as the children had lived through such very lean times for most of their lives.

The 2nd Battalion went back to Bad Gleinkenburg in the middle of January, and on 29th January the 1/4th went to Vienna in their turn. Having been warned in good time, R.S.M. Bugden had already begun work to prepare for the guards of honour in Vienna. Men were drilled and re-drilled on the market square of the sleepy country town of Furstenfeldt, which resounded to the crash of arms drill. Arrived in Vienna, the first guard upon the Schonbrunn Palace was praised by the Commander-in-Chief, and the Battalion determined to achieve something really special in the way of guards and guards of honour, and in a riding-school the drill team strove to produce a guard better than any other.

When it was known that the C.I.G.S., Field-Marshal Lord Alanbrooke, was coming to Vienna, the Commander-in-Chief ordered that the finest guard yet known was to be produced for the occasion. The Battalion set about the task eagerly. Captain L. N. Smith, who was to command the guard of honour, had his battledress pressed, re-made, and pressed again. Every possible preparation was made to produce a guard of honour that would be truly impressive. At that time the Battalion was mounting one hundred and ten all ranks daily on guards, and a reinforcement of two hundred and fifty from the disbanded 5th Battalion was most gladly welcomed.

The day came. Every battledress, every chevron and every rifle of the guard of honour was correct; cap badges were polished as never before, and the brass cap of the cover of the Regimental Colours winked in the Vienna sun. The guard arrived at the Schonbrunn Palace at four o'clock in the afternoon and the sky immediately became overcast, two large snow clouds looming up over the Vienna woods. At a quarter past four, just as the C.I.G.S.'s plane was heard approaching, it began to snow. Lord Alanbrooke arrived in a thin fall of snow, but the guard was ready. A small squad of attendants had dusted the snow from the caps, shoulders and boots of the guard, which stood resplendent amid the falling snow as the general salute was sounded. The Field-Marshal inspected the guard and expressed himself as being highly satisfied.

The 1/4th maintained their very high standard of drill and won a fine reputation in Vienna, so much so that they were selected to provide a detachment for the Military Tattoo to be held in June. Their first tour in Vienna ended in March and they returned to Furstenfeldt, but before they left there was one very magnificent ceremony when a guard of honour of a hundred men of the Battalion marched with bayonets fixed and Regimental Colours flying to the Palace of Justice to hand over the guard duties of the Allied control buildings to the French, who were represented by the 6th Chasseurs Alpines. The ceremony was watched by a big crowd, including soldiers of many nationalities—Russian, Belgian, American, French and Jugoslav. The whole impressive ceremony was carried out faultlessly; the National Anthem rang out through the great square, played by an Anglo-French military band, and then the Union Jack was hauled down and the Tricolour broken at the masthead. The march past was taken by Brigadier-General G. L. Verney, commander Vienna area, and a French General.

Back in Furstenfeldt the Battalion settled down once more to its peaceful routine, while parties of men continued to go home on release. Lieutenant-Colonel A. G. Ryshworth-Hill left the Battalion on 14th May to take over the command of a mountain warfare school, and Lieutenant-Colonel J. M. Lee, who had gone out to Austria the week before, took over the command.

The Battalion was back in Vienna on 3rd June and at once began to practise for the drill display in the Vienna Tattoo; they also took up the same very heavy guard duty commitments as before. The Tattoo was a most successful and impressive affair, in which one hundred and fifty warrant officers, N.C.Os. and men of the 1/4th entered the arena to the march of the 1st Battalion played by the band of the Coldstream Guards. The drill was done without any word of command, essential signals being given by flashlight by Major De Broe Ferguson from a control tower. At the end of the Tattoo all the performers marched from the arena, led off by the Hampshire guard of honour.

The 1/4th Battalion left Vienna on 16th July and returned to Furstenfeldt for the melancholy task of disbandment. There were the appropriate farewell parties and dances, and men were posted away—many of them to the 2nd

Battalion. Finally there remained only Colonel Lee, Captain Drake and Sergeant Shears to take the Colours back to the Depot. So, on 1st September, 1946, ended the brilliant career of the 1/4th Battalion The Hampshire Regiment.

The 2nd Battalion, deprived of its old comrades the 1/4th and the 5th, remained on army-of-occupation duties in Austria for a further eighteen months. In that time there were changes in the composition of the Battalion as men were posted out on release and others, many of them from the other two battalions of what had been the Hampshire Brigade, took their place. With the disbandment of other units the occupational responsibility of those remaining was considerably increased. Thus it was that the 2nd Battalion found itself dispersed over a wide area, first on the Austro-Hungarian frontier and later on the Austro-Jugoslav frontier. Units lived a detached existence in pretty little frontier towns and villages with the duties of manning frontier posts, patrolling the frontier itself and from time to time keeping the civilian population from shooting each other. It was a pleasant, civilized existence and the Battalion maintained a very high standard of training and turn-out.

In the periods when the Battalion was relieved from frontier duties it was stationed together and training and exercises were carried out. In the first week of October, 1946, the Battalion team distinguished itself at the British Troops in Austria Small Arms Meeting, winning the Steele Cup Championship in most convincing style.

As with every unit, the constant drain of men going home and of new intake soon changed the Battalion altogether from that which had seen the end of the war. In November, 1946, Lieutenant-Colonel J. P. Fowler-Esson left and Lieutenant-Colonel J. H. H. Robinson took over command of the Battalion. Colonel and Mrs. Fowler-Esson were entertained by the officers to a farewell dance in Graz, which was a memorable occasion for all who were there. Colonel Fowler-Esson will long be remembered with gratitude by the Battalion, both as Second-in-Command in 1939-1940, and as Commanding Officer, 1945-1946, during the difficult period of transition from war to peace in Austria.

On the few occasions when the Battalion was concentrated in one place, usually at Tessendorf, training schemes were undertaken, and during the winter months a battalion ski school was organized and officers and men quickly became proficient at this sport. The Battalion had a second spell of duty in Vienna in April and May, 1947, and great preparations were made to ensure that the many guards and guards of honour which would have to be mounted should attain the high standard necessary in the capital.

From Vienna the Battalion went to Klagenfurt at the end of May, 1947, and was soon scattered on frontier patrols until October, when it concentrated again at Tessendorf and went back to Vienna again on 18th November, leaving one company in camp at Tessendorf. This camp was finally closed at the end of February, 1948, and the whole Battalion was in Vienna, where the by now familiar routine of guard mounting of a very high standard was continually carried out. The normal tour of duty in Vienna had been extended for two months at the beginning of the year, and as the Battalion was under warning orders to go home it was the final post of their three years of occupation duty in Austria. On 1st March the Battalion provided the guard for the ceremonial changing of the guard at the Headquarters, Vienna Inter-Allied Control. As when the 1/4th carried out this interesting and picturesque ceremony, there was a large crowd of spectators, and music was played by the band of the Regiment and of the Chasseurs Alpines. The contrast in uniforms and drill procedure added much to the interest of the impressive ceremony.

During the first fortnight of March officers and men were posted away from the Battalion in large numbers, and it was only a very depleted battalion of one hundred and seventy-five all ranks which boarded the special train on the evening of 15th March for England, via the Hook of Holland. After an uncomfortable night in London, where the Battalion arrived after midnight unexpectedly and had to sleep in an air raid shelter in Goodge Street, the Battalion completed its journey to Salisbury. Here it was welcomed home by the Colonel of the Regiment and made the final lap of a long and tiring journey to Bulford.

The 2nd Battalion soon took up its new duties as the Wessex Brigade Training Battalion at Bulford. In July, 1948, Colonel Robinson retired, to be succeeded by Lieutenant-Colonel R. Chandler. Colonel Robinson had joined the 2nd Battalion at Bordon from Sandhurst in October, 1923, and thus had served twenty-five years with the Regiment. In 1936 he was appointed Adjutant to the 2nd Battalion, and it was largely due to his unremitting efforts that the high reputation of the Battalion for smartness and efficiency was considerably enhanced. He was then Adjutant to the 5/7th Battalion, Second-in-Command to the 5th Battalion at the outbreak of war, and then Second-in-Command to the 2/4th. In 1942 Colonel Robinson was appointed to command the 2/4th Battalion and sailed with them to North Africa. His brilliant leadership in the battle for Hunts Gap was recognized by the award of the D.S.O. Colonel Robinson was wounded in Sicily, and on recovering he was appointed to command the 5th Battalion in October, 1943, leading this Battalion throughout the long and brilliant campaign of the 128th Brigade in Italy. For his part in the many actions that his Battalion fought he was awarded a bar to his D.S.O. and the O.B.E.

THE 2/4TH BATTALION

(*See map on page* 204)

VE Day found the 2/4th Battalion in Crete, supervising the evacuation of German prisoners, and they were there for three months. In August, 1945, the Battalion went back to Greece and settled for two months at Yannina, where they had no operational role, but were occupied to some extent restoring order and keeping the peace when trouble blew up over Albanian-Greek frontier incidents. On 16th September Lieutenant-Colonel J. L. Spencer took over the command of the Battalion in place of Lieutenant-Colonel F. Mitchell. The Battalion moved south to Patras on 22nd October, occupying a pleasant camp on an estate about a mile north of the town and only a hundred yards from the sea. Here they stayed for five months, during which time there was another change in command, Lieutenant-Colonel P. H. Man becoming Commanding Officer on 3rd January, 1946, in the place of Lieutenant-Colonel Spencer.

The next and final move of the Battalion in Greece was on 6th March to billets four miles out of Athens, where they were to stay for the next ten months. The Battalion was comfortably quartered in houses, most of them with sun balconies, and when they first arrived their duty was to stand by in case the Greek elections should cause civil disturbance. Fortunately all went off smoothly, and the Battalion settled down to a peaceful existence, though suffering in common with all other units a constant drain of men through release. There was a further change in command on 29th October when Colonel Man left and the Second-in-Command, Major H. T. Roberts, became Commanding Officer, being promoted to the rank of Lieutenant-Colonel. One incident worthy of note was the mounting of a guard of honour on 1st December at the Hassani airfield for Field-Marshal Viscount Montgomery, who was extremely pleased with the guard and commented on their turn-out, bearing and drill.

Over Christmas those who remained with the Battalion attended a round of farewell parties and functions, and on 3rd January, 1947, the entire Battalion formed up for its last ceremonial parade. This was inspected by Lieutenant-General K. N. Crawford, who spoke stirringly of the record of the 2/4th Hampshire in the war. It was a dismal day with a fine drizzle, in keeping with everyone's feelings. The parade over, men were posted away to other units and everything was wound up.

Among the few officers with the Battalion at the end were two whose service to the 2/4th was notable: Major V. A. Blake, the Quartermaster, and Major G. D. Knight. Both had served with the Battalion with outstanding conscientiousness from 1940 through to the end. Major Blake's services were recognized by the award of the M.B.E., and Major Knight was awarded the M.C. for gallantry.

So the 2/4th Hampshire was put into "suspended animation." But already authority had been given by the War Office for the resuscitation of the 4th (T.A.) Battalion, so the continuity of a very fine Territorial battalion was unbroken.

The 2/4th Battalion had certainly played a great part in the war—in the Mediterranean theatre: in North Africa, Italy and Greece. The Battalion's total casualties were 21 officers and 232 other ranks killed, 32 and 581 wounded, and 9 and 243 missing, a total of 1,118 all ranks. The awards included one Victoria Cross, five D.S.Os., one M.B.E., thirteen M.Cs., four D.C.Ms., sixteen M.Ms. and thirty-five Mentions in Despatches.

The 7th Battalion

The 7th Battalion was at Gnarrenburg when the Germans surrendered, leading the 43rd Division in its advance towards Bremerhaven ; the Battalion was in fact the nearest to the enemy of the whole British Second Army. It fell to the Battalion, with the other two in the Brigade, to go forward to receive the surrender of the 15th Panzer Grenadier Division, against whom the Brigade had fought many a tough battle since landing in Normandy. At first the Panzer Division refused to accept the surrender terms, and it seemed as if the Brigade would have to continue the war on its own for a while, but eventually the Germans surrendered.

On 14th May a party of six officers and two hundred and twenty-four men represented the Battalion in the XXX Corps Victory Parade in Bremerhaven, and on the 20th the Battalion moved to a permanent occupation area at Winsen, a town half-way between Luneburg and Hamburg. Here there were comfortable billets and an unreal feeling of peace. The Battalion's operational activities were confined to routine patrols and the manning of check points to make sure that the Germans behaved themselves. They gave no trouble, but other nationals in the Battalion area seemed to delight in disturbing the peace; there were also nomadic groups of displaced persons, who rather naturally took every opportunity of robbing the Germans.

Colonel Talbot left the Battalion in June, to take command of a battalion in his own regiment, and the Second-in-Command, Major D. B. Rooke, M.C., who was promoted to Lieutenant-Colonel, took his place. Lieutenant-Colonel D. E. B. Talbot had commanded the 7th Battalion from the first days in Normandy and he had led his Battalion with great skill, efficiency and spirit. During the period of his command fifty-six officers and over a thousand other ranks had passed through the Battalion, and a great proportion of them had been killed or wounded in the battles the Battalion had fought.

After five months at Winsen the Battalion moved to Soltau, near Hamburg, which was to be its home for the next five months. Here it was quartered in a German cavalry barracks which had been used by displaced persons. However, it was soon cleaned up, grass was sown, floors were scrubbed, whitewash brushes were wielded and "Bournemouth" Barracks, Soltau, became worthy of their name. The duties of the Battalion were still preserving the peace, and here it was Poles who caused the trouble. But a "flying squad" patrol always standing by soon discouraged the Poles, and peace reigned. "Bournemouth" Barracks developed a Hampshire Farm, and the peaceful life of an army of occupation proceeded calmly. There were constant departures of many of the oldest members of the Battalion, and with men going and others coming in, it soon began to change its personnel if not its character.

The Battalion left Soltau on 10th March, 1946, and finished the journey they began when they landed in Normandy by going to Berlin, to excellent barracks in the Spandau suburbs of the city. The Battalion's responsibility was an important one—the Tiergarten area, where the four Allied zones met. One company group was permanently detached there, to deal as a flying squad with black-marketeers, thugs and trouble-makers whose actions throve best in that region. The speed and efficiency of the Hampshire patrols when there was trouble soon won the respect of the malefactors and the situation was always kept under control.

There were ample facilities for sport in Berlin, and the Olympic Sports Stadium was at the Battalion's disposal ; there was football of both codes, hockey, indoor swimming, badminton, fencing, boxing and table-tennis. The Battalion began to acquire horses, and entered for the Gymkhana. Berlin also offered a wealth of clubs, cinemas and theatres. "Journey's End" turned out to be most satisfactory. It was while the Battalion was in Berlin that it lost its Second-in-Command, Major C. G. T. Viner, M.C., who went to Brigade Headquarters. Major Viner had joined the Battalion as a private soldier in March, 1939, was commissioned in July, and had commanded "A" Company when the Battalion went to Normandy. He had been Second-in-Command since June, 1945.

VE Day, 1946, was a notable occasion, for the Colours of the 7th Battalion were carried in Berlin's famous Charlottenburg Chaussee. This was in the great parade of contingents of the British, French, American and Russian armies, past the four Allied Generals. The British contingent—the Hampshire unit, Marines and R.A.F., was commanded by Colonel Rooke, whose two orderlies attracted much attention from the crowds when they slow marched in front of the Generals, resplendent with white pouches. The Battalion showed its Colours again on Gatow airfield on 24th May with a guard of honour to welcome Field-Marshal Smuts.

In the second week of June the Battalion left Berlin for Luneburg, to be disbanded. This was done quickly, and by the end of June there remained only some of the officers and a few key men to finish winding up the Battalion. On 17th August the final disbandment order was signed. Officially the 7th Battalion The Hampshire Regiment had ceased to exist ; but to the men who had served in the Battalion, the 7th still lived, and indeed it was to rise again as 524 L.A.A./S.L. Regiment, R.A. (T.A.).

When the Territorial Battalions were disbanded, the story of the Royal Hampshire Regiment came to the end of a long and a splendid chapter. The stern fighting, the dour and humorous acceptance of discomfort and danger, the flash of gallantry—all that was past. It was rapidly becoming history, merging magically into the store of honour accumulated through the Regiment's long life. There remained to individuals the friendships forged in service, and the memory of men who had been killed.

CHAPTER XXIII

THE ROYAL HAMPSHIRE REGIMENT
1948–1954

At the end of 1947 General Sir George Jeffreys retired after three years as Colonel of the Regiment. Throughout his tour of duty he had ably helped his Regiment to weather the storms of the post-war period. In spite of the many calls on his time and energy, Sir George had rendered invaluable service and had made many friends amongst all ranks of the Regiment. On the occasions of the presentations of the Freedoms, Sir George proved to be the perfect representative of the Regiment, and at these and many other functions he was invariably a real inspiration as a public speaker.

General Sir George Jeffreys was succeeded as Colonel on 1st January, 1948, by Brigadier P. H. Cadoux-Hudson. Brigadier Cadoux-Hudson had retired from the Regiment after thirty-three years' service in 1947. He saw active service in Gallipoli and France in the 1914-1918 war and was awarded the M.C. As is related in an earlier chapter, Brigadier Cadoux-Hudson commanded the 2nd Battalion in France, and it was due to his forethought and brilliant leadership that the Battalion achieved so disciplined a retreat and evacuation from Dunkirk in 1940.

The 1st Battalion (37th/67th Foot)

The amalgamation of the 1st and 2nd Battalions took place on 11th August, 1949, bringing into being the 1st Battalion (37th/67th Foot) The Royal Hampshire Regiment. The Colours of both Battalions remained in the custody of the new Battalion. This was, in all but name, the old 2nd Battalion and at first there was some confusion as the new 1st looked exactly like the old 2nd. It remained at Bulford as the Wessex Division Training Battalion, dealing with the intake of National Service men.

High-lights of the period at Bulford were the inspections of the Battalion by the C.I.G.S., Field-Marshal Sir William Slim, and the achievement of considerable success in shooting and cross-country running. During 1948 and 1949 the Battalion won numerous trophies for shooting, at one time being in the unique position of holding the Queen Victoria Trophy for units abroad, which had been won by the 2nd Battalion in Austria, and the Queen Victoria Trophy for units at home as well. In 1949 the Battalion won most of the prizes in the Salisbury Plain District Rifle Meeting. In cross-country running the Battalion came fourth in the Army Championship in 1948, and it won both the Salisbury Plain District and the Southern Command Championships. The Battalion also won the District Boxing Championships.

There was a change in command of the 1st Battalion on 31st October, 1949, when Lieutenant-Colonel R. Chandler was posted away; and on 3rd January, 1950, Lieutenant-Colonel R. H. Batten took over from Major C. A. T.

Halliday. Colonel Chandler had joined the 1st Battalion in Cairo twenty-five years before and had served with it in India until 1927. He joined the 2nd Battalion in 1933 at Parkhurst, and in November, 1942, he was posted to the 2/4th Battalion and went with it to North Africa. Brigadier Chandler, as he later became, served throughout the campaign in North Africa and Italy with the 128th (Hampshire) Brigade, with the 2/4th, the 5th and then with the 1/4th. He took over command of the 1/4th after the battle of Bou Arada in April, 1943, when Colonel Smythe was wounded, and he commanded that Battalion throughout its long and successful campaign right up to and through the Gothic Line. In January, 1947, Brigadier Chandler became Commanding Officer of the 1st Battalion in Palestine and finally of the 2nd Battalion at Bulford. Thus he had the distinction of being the last Commanding Officer of the 2nd and the first of the new 1st Battalion.

The 1st Battalion remained at Bulford until 21st February, 1951, when it went to Germany. At the final parade General Sir Ouvry Roberts took the salute and the Battalion marched to the station with Band and Drums, where the Colonel of the Regiment bade the Battalion God-speed. The destination was Clifton Barracks, Minden, and the Order of Battle was : Lieutenant-Colonel R. H. Batten ; Major T. G. Tucker, Second-in-Command ; Captain D. J. Warren, Adjutant ; and Majors T. H. N. Keene, G. R. Young, G. J. A. Dewar, C. L. Speers and Captain H. E. Wingfield commanding the companies.

The Battalion had the privilege of providing the guard of honour for Field-Marshal Lord Montgomery on 17th April, 1951, on the occasion of his visit as Deputy Supreme Commander, Allied Forces in Europe, to Headquarters, B.A.O.R. The Guard, commanded by Captain D. J. Warren, was drawn up in line with Band and Drums in the rear. The Field-Marshal inspected the guard very thoroughly, and complimented it on its turn-out.

The Battalion was very happily stationed at Minden, where the barracks were on the site of the French camp before the great battle two centuries before. It was a novel experience to be able to celebrate Minden Day, 1951, at Minden itself. The main feature in the day's arrangements was the Trooping of the Colour, which was watched by a large crowd ; among the visitors were the Corps, Division and Brigade Commanders. The salute was taken by Brigadier Cadoux-Hudson, Colonel of the Regiment, and the steadiness of the Battalion and the perfection of the drill won high praise. In the evening there was a dinner and a most successful all ranks' dance.

The Battalion suffered throughout its two and a half years in Germany from constant change in the personnel ; officers and rank and file were coming and going, and only a small nucleus remained constant. In spite of this the Battalion won a high reputation, both at work and at play. The climax of each year's training was a period of formation training and a large-scale exercise on the training ground at Soltau.

In October, 1951, the Battalion was moved from Minden to Luneburg, where it shared a barracks with its good friends the Royal Scots Greys. In

October, too, Lieutenant-Colonel Batten left the Battalion to take up another appointment, and on 23rd November Lieutenant-Colonel R. G. F. Frisby became Commanding Officer. He had commanded the 1st Battalion five years before in Cyrenaica, and his father, Lieutenant-Colonel H. G. F. Frisby, had completed his tour of command of the 1st Battalion at Nowshera in 1932.

In its final few months in Germany the Battalion began training for its next role, operational duty in Malaya. It did what it could to learn as much as possible about jungle fighting, and endeavoured in every way to prepare itself for its next task. The Battalion left Germany on 29th October, 1953, and arrived at Fowler Barracks, Perham Down, the next day. Preparations were at once begun for the Battalion to leave for Malaya within six weeks.

There was another change in command of the 1st Battalion before it left England for Malaya on 18th December, 1953. Colonel Frisby relinquished command on that day, to take up another appointment with promotion to Colonel, and Lieutenant-Colonel P. H. Man succeeded him, to command the Battalion in Malaya. Colonel Man's senior officers were Major J. S. S. Gratton, Second-in-Command; Captain J. R. Buckmaster, Adjutant; and commanding the companies, Majors T. H. N. Keene, G. J. A. Dewar, F. M. Shaw, C. J. G. Mumford, P. A. T. Halliday and G. W. Stilwell.

The Battalion was inspected by the Colonel of the Regiment on 11th December, and in his farewell speech Brigadier Cadoux-Hudson pointed out that no battalion of the Regiment had been to Malaya before. At Southampton on 18th December the Band played the Battalion away from an open deck, and a large number of relations and friends were on the quayside. The Colonel of the Regiment went on board to bid farewell to the Battalion, and with him were the Duke of Wellington, the G.O.C., Aldershot Command, and the Mayor of Southampton. The troopship *Dunera* sailed in the afternoon and the 1st Battalion (37th/67th Foot) The Royal Hampshire Regiment sailed away once again on active service, to join the 18th Infantry Brigade, commanded by Brigadier D. E. B. Talbot, in Malaya.

The Territorial Battalions

The authorization to form the 4th Territorial Battalion was given in January, 1947, as has already been stated, and as this was before the 2/4th Battalion was disbanded the continuity of the long-established 4th Battalion was maintained. The Battalion began its new existence on 1st March, 1947, with Lieutenant-Colonel F. Mitchell in command and Major P. R. Sawyer Second-in-Command. The Colours of the old 4th Battalion were handed over to Colonel Mitchell on 20th June at a ceremonial parade, and they were installed in the Battalion Headquarters at Newburgh in Winchester in the presence of many distinguished spectators, including the Colonel of the Regiment and the Mayor of Winchester.

Nine officers and forty-three other ranks were on parade on 20th November,

1947, for the first Commanding Officer's parade, and from the start the Battalion steadily grew in numbers. The enthusiastic few were determined to get the Battalion back to its old high standard of efficiency and *esprit de corps*. The normal domestic life of a Territorial unit went on, with the parades, camps, the social life and, from time to time, the contribution of a detachment to represent the Battalion at Regimental functions. One such occasion was the King's Review of the Territorial Army in Hyde Park on 31st October, 1948, when four officers and twenty-one other ranks were on parade.

The whole tempo of the Battalion's activities was changed in June, 1950, when, under a new War Office scheme, National Service men were attached for a period. This was the first time that the Battalion had had non-volunteers on its strength and everything was done to make the newcomers welcome, and to show them the comradeship and good spirit of the Territorial Army, so that they too would become volunteers.

Lieutenant-Colonel C. A. T. Halliday succeeded Colonel Mitchell in command of the 4th Battalion on 1st April, 1950. Colonel Mitchell had, of course, served with distinction in the 2/4th Battalion throughout the war, winning both the D.S.O. and the M.C. He had thrown himself into the organizing of the new 4th Battalion with his characteristic zest and he had succeeded in making it efficient and happy. Colonel Halliday carried on in the same spirit throughout his three years of command, and he in turn handed it over to Lieutenant-Colonel T. G. Tucker as a flourishing and virile unit.

The old 5th Battalion came into being again in a new guise on 17th October, 1948, when the Colonel of the Regiment entrusted the Colours of the old 5th Battalion to Lieutenant-Colonel A. G. F. Monro, commanding the 14th Battalion The Parachute Regiment. This ceremony joined the "Fighting Fifth" of the Royal Hampshire Regiment with the Parachute Regiment, with the new title—14th Battalion The Parachute Regiment (5th Battalion The Royal Hampshire Regiment) (T.A.).

The ceremony was held in the forecourt of the Southampton Civic Centre, and there were two guards of honour and two Colour parties, one from the 1st Battalion of the Regiment, the other from the 14th Parachute Battalion. A large crowd watched the ceremony and listened to the speeches of the Mayor of Southampton and the Colonel of the Regiment. Brigadier Cadoux-Hudson reminded the parade of the history of the 5th Battalion, and showed how the original Loyal Southampton Volunteers had in turn become The Southampton Volunteer Rifles, the 2nd Battalion The Hampshire Volunteers, and then the 5th Battalion The Hampshire Regiment.

Thus the old 5th Battalion began a new existence, though still the direct heir of its eminent predecessors. The old enthusiasm of Southampton's Territorial Battalion was at once rekindled, and the men began to learn the new technique of soldiering as parachutists. Within a few months the Battalion could boast that it was the strongest Territorial Battalion in the Southern Command. In October, 1949, Lieutenant-Colonel R. G. F. Frisby succeeded Colonel Monro in command, which he held until he left to take command of the

1st Battalion in November, 1951, being succeeded by Lieutenant-Colonel H. D. Nelson Smith.

Three other Territorial Battalions were revived, all of them in a new guise as Gunners. These were the old 7th Battalion, which became 524 L.A.A./S.L. Regiment, R.A. (7th Battalion The Royal Hampshire Regiment) (T.A.); 383 (Duke of Connaught's Own Hampshire) Light Regiment, R.A. (T.A.); and 428 (M.) H.A.A. Regiment, R.A. (Princess Beatrice's Isle of Wight Rifles) (T.A.).

The Regimental Depot

It will be remembered that within two weeks of the outbreak of war the Regimental Depot became the Hampshire Infantry Training Centre and moved to the Isle of Wight, commanded by Lieutenant-Colonel B. B. im Thurn, with Major Smythe commanding the Headquarters Wing. A Depot Party was formed in 1942, when the I.T.C. amalgamated with the Oxfordshire and Buckinghamshire Light Infantry I.T.C. at Oxford, and this was commanded by Major C. D. Fawkes, with Major H. J. Jeffery as Quartermaster. When the Depot Party returned to Winchester in November, 1942, Major Jeffery was in command, and he was appointed to command the Regimental Depot when it was re-established in November, 1946.

Major Jeffery had enlisted in the 3rd (Militia) Battalion at Winchester in June, 1905, became a Regular soldier in September, and joined the 1st Battalion at Portsmouth in March, 1906. He was posted to the 2nd Battalion in Bermuda and served with the Battalion in South Africa and Mauritius, being promoted to lance-corporal and corporal. In 1914 he joined the 1st Battalion with the rank of sergeant, and went to France with the British Expeditionary Force in 1914. He was taken prisoner at Le Cateau.

Joining the 3rd Battalion at Catterick in March, 1919, Sergeant Jeffery was promoted Regimental Sergeant-Major in August and went to Constantinople in March, 1920, and on to Egypt with the Battalion. He was posted as R.S.M. to the 2nd Battalion in January, 1924, where he remained until he was commissioned Lieutenant (Q.M.) in 1926 and joined the 1st Battalion at Jubbulpore. He served with the 1st Battalion in India until he was posted to the 2nd Battalion in 1935, and served with them in Palestine in 1936 and 1937 until appointed Quartermaster to the Regimental Depot in March, 1937.

During the war Major Jeffrey worked hard at raising funds for the Regimental Prisoner-of-War Fund, and the total amount collected was over £25,000. The enormous amount of work connected with the presentation of the Freedoms fell to Major Jeffery, and he undertook it all with enthusiasm and efficiency; after the war the immaculate manner in which the functions went through was proof of his energy and skill. He is gifted with great powers of perseverance and persuasion, and remarkable organizing ability, and just as the splendid ceremonials were faultlessly done, so was all the unknown work of organization behind the scenes.

Retiring from the Army after forty-two years' service in September, 1947,

Major Jeffery took up the appointment of Secretary to the Regimental Committee, and here again the splendid arrangements for the War Memorial ceremonies were mainly due to his efficiency and energy. His enthusiasm and determination in the realm of sport contributed largely to the Regiment's successes in revolver shooting, boxing, and in football, cross-country running and athletics. As Secretary to the Regimental Committee he helped to organize all the post-war functions, as well as editing the Regimental Journal and supervising the writing and publication of the three volumes of the Regimental History.

When Major Jeffery retired in September, 1947, the Regimental Depot was commanded in turn by Major E. R. S. Westropp until 1948, Major C. A. T. Halliday until 1950, and Major H. D. Nelson Smith, M.C., until 1951, when Major D. J. Warren took over and commanded the Depot until 1954.

The Regimental War Memorial

Saturday, 6th May, 1950, was a great day in the history of the Regiment, for at two very impressive ceremonies the Regimental Roll of Honour was dedicated in Winchester Cathedral and the Memorial Garden at Serles House was formally opened. It was an afternoon of splendidly organized functions, faultlessly arranged and carried out. The day was a fitting tribute to the memory of the two thousand men of the Regiment who gave their lives in the war.

The first ceremony was the re-dedication of the County and City War Memorial outside the Cathedral by the Dean of Winchester. On this memorial the inscription had previously read : "To the Glory of God and in proud and grateful memory of 460 citizens of Winchester who upheld, under King George V, the tradition of service and sacrifice handed down from the days of King Alfred." To this was now added : "Remember also their sons and daughters who died 1939-45 and all those who freely gave their life."

For this first ceremony Colour parties of the 1st, 4th, and 14th Parachute Battalions took post round the Memorial, with a guard of honour found by the 1st Battalion. The Mayor and Corporation of Winchester arrived in state, followed by the Colonel of the Regiment and the Duke of Wellington. Wreaths were laid and the Dean re-dedicated the memorial.

The Mayor and Corporation, the Colonel of the Regiment, the Duke of Wellington and the other representatives then moved in procession into the Cathedral itself, which was filled with a congregation of two thousand persons. On a table standing on a dais was the Book of Remembrance, which contains the names of the 2,094 officers and men who died serving in the Regiment. It consists of forty pages, beautifully inscribed, and the title page reads :

"The men of all ranks, to the number of 2,094, whose names are recorded in this book, served their King and Country in the Royal Hampshire Regiment in the Great War in the years 1939-45 A.D., enduring hardship and danger in all parts of the world and on the seas, and gave their lives that posterity might live in freedom and peace. Let those who come after see to it that their unselfish sacrifice was not in vain, and their names be not forgotten. To the Glory of God and in memory of these brave men this book is dedicated."

At the appropriate part of the very beautiful service the Book of Remembrance was unveiled by the Duke of Wellington, who addressed the Bishop of Winchester with these words: "Right Reverend Father in God, on behalf of the Officers, Warrant Officers, Non-Commissioned Officers and Men of The Royal Hampshire Regiment, I beg you to dedicate this book to the Glory of God and for the perpetual remembrance of those whose names are inscribed therein."

The Bishop's reply was: "To the Glory of God and to the sacred and perpetual memory of those who in the wars laid down their lives in our country's cause, we dedicate this Book of Remembrance, in the Name of the Father, and of the Son, and of the Holy Ghost. Amen."

At the conclusion of the service the National Anthem followed the Bishop's Blessing, and then Brigadier Cadoux-Hudson went forward and took the Book of Remembrance and bore it to its permanent resting-place near the west door in procession comprising the Bishop, the Dean and other clergy, the Lord-Lieutenant, the Chief Constable and other dignitaries. The Band of the 1st Battalion played the march "Scipio," and a representative Regimental party of all ranks grouped themselves by the marble stand on which is the bronze framed case which contains the Book. The Colonel of the Regiment placed the Book of Remembrance in its case, locked it and presented the key to the Cathedral Custos, Mr. G. E. Bryant, a former Regimental Sergeant-Major of the Regiment.

The second ceremony of the day took place at half past five when Major P. R. Sawyer, who had designed the Memorial Garden at Serles House, handed the key of the gate to the Duke of Wellington, who unlocked it. Inside the Garden the Colonel of the Regiment presented the Duke with a silver key, saying: "Your Grace, to you, the Lord-Lieutenant of Hampshire, we offer this key of our Garden of Remembrance. May it be a token of our desire to give to yourself, to the County, and to all who wish it, access to one of the most cherished possessions of the Regiment."

The Garden was dedicated by the Bishop; and the setting for the ceremony was splendid. There were the three Colour parties, the twelve standards of the branches of the Comrades Association, the guard of honour and the Band of the 1st Battalion. There were the civic dignitaries of the county and the distinguished guests. Short passages from the New Testament were read by Major H. J. Jeffery, for the Comrades Association, and by Corporal C. Smith, Sergeant C. F. Bechelet and Major H. W. Le Patourel, V.C. After the dedication the "Last Post" and the "Reveille" were sounded, the Colours and Standards dipping in salute. The Regimental Flag was broken at the new flagstaff for the first time, and wreaths were laid at the foot of the flagstaff by a Chelsea Pensioner of the Regiment, Colour-Sergeant D. Prior, aged seventy-eight, and Captain F. H. Waldren for the Comrades Association.

The Garden of Remembrance is in the forecourt of Serles House, and has the flagstaff as its centre-piece. There are rose trees from Minden and a tree from Ploegsteert. The Regiment's War Memorial will be complete with the Book of Remembrance in the Cathedral, the Garden at Serles House, and the publication of the three volumes of the Regimental History. The ceremonies on 6th May, 1950, were indeed an effective and a moving manifestation of the Regiment's recognition of the brave men who made the ultimate sacrifice.

There was another ceremony at Portsmouth when the Regiment received the Freedom of the City. This was on 20th May, 1950, and a detachment of 450 all ranks marched through the city headed by the Regimental Band. The detachment consisted of parties from the 1st Battalion, the 4th and 14th Parachute Battalions and the 642 Light A.A. Searchlight Regiment (the 7th Battalion of the Regiment). There were also representatives of the Comrades Association, and on each side of the dais from which the scroll was presented stood two men of the Regiment in the uniform as worn at the battle of Minden.

As in the earlier Freedom ceremonies, there was the traditional civic ceremony, the immaculate bearing and drill of the parade, the splendid words of the formal speeches and the references to the Regiment's long history. At the end the parade marched off, swinging proudly through the ancient city, and exercising the new privilege of marching with drums beating, Colours flying and bayonets fixed. As the troops marched past, guns fired in salute.

The history of the Regiment was recalled once more on 16th August, 1952, in the ceremonies which marked the two hundred and fiftieth anniversary of the Regiment's formation. The first ceremony was the unveiling by General Lord Jeffreys of the porch and doorway added to Serles House. Detachments of the 1st Battalion and of the 4th and 14th Parachute Battalions were on parade, and there was a composite guard of honour. There was the Regimental Colour of the 4th Battalion, and the standards of ten branches of the Comrades Association.

There was a representative gathering of civic dignitaries and guests. Brigadier Cadoux-Hudson invited General Lord Jeffreys to unveil the Memorial Porch, which was then dedicated by the Assistant Chaplain-General. Later in the afternoon the parade marched to the Guildhall, with a strong detachment of Old Comrades, and there the Colonel of the Regiment presented to the Mayor of Winchester a silver tiger, which was engraved: "Presented to the Mayor, Aldermen and Councillors of the City of Winchester by the Royal Hampshire Regiment to commemorate the 250th anniversary of the raising of the Regiment on 13th February, 1702, and as an appreciation of their long and happy association with the City. 16th August, 1952."

* * * * *

Brigadier Cadoux-Hudson relinquished his appointment as Colonel of The Royal Hampshire Regiment on 19th March, 1954, and he was succeeded by Brigadier G. D. Browne, O.B.E. Brigadier Browne was posted to the 1st Battalion from Sandhurst on 6th February, 1926, and served with the

Battalion for thirteen years, becoming in turn Regimental Signal Officer and then Adjutant in India; the only break in this period of service being seven months as Staff Captain at Rawalpindi in 1935. Nine months at the Staff College, Camberley, was followed by a series of staff appointments, with twelve months as G.S.O.1, 43rd Division, in 1941 and 1942. Between 30th September, 1942, and 30th August, 1943, Brigadier Browne commanded the 7th Hampshire, and then he was appointed G.S.O.1, 3rd Division, 21st Army Group.

Brigadier Browne commanded in turn the 9th, the 158th and the 56th Infantry Brigades in the British Army of the Rhine, and after the war the staff appointments he held included Brigadier in charge of Administration, Headquarters, British Military Mission to Greece, and then Deputy Commander of the Mission. In March, 1952, he took over the command of 130th Infantry Brigade, T.A. Besides the O.B.E., Brigadier Browne's decorations include the Legion of Honour and the Croix de Guerre with Palm.

* * * * *

This history has told something of the story of the Royal Hampshire Regiment through two hundred and fifty years of continuous service to the Crown. This volume has been mainly concerned with recounting the splendid achievements of the Regiment in the war of 1939-1945. A regiment's story is not, however, all of battle. In times of peace the Royal Hampshire Regiment has served all over the world, careful of its good name, always trained and ready both to keep the Queen's peace and to fight the Queen's enemies.

A regiment is ever changing, yet it is ever the same. Generation succeeds generation, yet the men of the Royal Hampshire Regiment of 1954 have kinship with the men of Meredith's Regiment of Foot of 1702. The spirit of a regiment which is symbolized by the Colours cannot be defined, but it is an inspiration at all times; and in moments of stress in battle, a magic source of strength.

The proud and famous record of The Royal Hampshire Regiment is aptly summed up in the words of Shakespeare's *King Henry V*:

> "*In peace there's nothing so becomes a man*
> *As modest stillness and humility:*
> *But when the blast of war blows in our ears,*
> *Then imitate the actions of the tiger . . .*"

HONOURS AND AWARDS

This list contains the names of honours and awards won by officers and men of The Royal Hampshire Regiment in the War of 1939-1945. The officers given are only those, with certain exceptions, who were commissioned into the Regiment. All names given in the narrative, therefore, as winning awards are not necessarily in this list. The rank given is usually that held at the time the award was made.

Victoria Cross

Major H. W. Le Patourel	Tebourba	9.3.43
Capt. R. Wakeford	Cassino	13.5.44
Lieut. G. R. Norton, M.M. (U.D.F., att. R. Hants) ...	Gothic Line	31.8.44

Companion of the Order of the Bath

Major-General W. H. C. Ramsden, C.B.E., D.S.O., M.C.

Commander of the Order of the British Empire

Brigadier C. C. Oxborrow

Major-General W. H. C. Ramsden, D.S.O., M.C.

Bar to Distinguished Service Order

Colonel J. H. H. Robinson, O.B.E.

Distinguished Service Order

Brigadier R. H. Batten, O.B.E.
Lieut.-Colonel A. Boyce
Lieut.-Colonel R. Chandler
Lieut.-Colonel R. G. F. Frisby, M.C.
Lieut.-Colonel J. P. Fowler-Esson, M.C.
Lieut.-Colonel J. M. Lee
Lieut.-Colonel F. Mitchell, M.C.
Lieut.-Colonel H. C. C. Newnham, M.C.
Lieut.-Colonel J. H. H. Robinson, O.B.E.
Lieut.-Colonel T. A. Rotherham, M.C.
Lieut.-Colonel J. L. Spencer, O.B.E., M.C.
Major C. L. Thomas

Officer of the Order of the British Empire

Brigadier R. H. Batten, D.S.O.
Brigadier G. D. Browne
Major W. J. Eldridge
Colonel C. A. T. Halliday
Brigadier A. C. F. Jackson
Colonel W. G. Mason
Lieut.-Colonel A. L. Scaife, M.C.
Lieut.-Colonel J. H. H. Robinson, D.S.O.
Lieut.-Colonel C. C. Smythe, M.C.
Lieut.-Colonel J. L. Spencer, M.C.

Member of the Order of the British Empire

R.S.M. T. A. Barnett
Major (Q.M.) V. A. Blake
Major E. S. W. Cattley
Lieut. (Q.M.) F. P. Edwards
Major R. L. T. Elwin
Major (Q.M.) G. A. Greenway
Major T. G. Harrison
Capt. R. F. M. Humphrey
Major R. King
Capt. B. H. Leader
Major I. Methven
W.O.II F. L. Minter
Lieut. (Q.M.) C. A. Northmore
Capt. (Q.M.) S. A. Osgood
Lieut. (Q.M.) R. T. Slater
Capt. (Q.M.) F. Stone
Major P. G. Street
Lieut. A. J. Truran
Lieut.-Colonel C. E. E. Wells
Major K. Winckles

Bar to Military Cross

Major J. W. Brehaut
Major M. H. Hutchinson
Major C. G. T. Viner
Major E. G. Wright

Military Cross

Lieut. J. B. Alliban
Capt. M. J. Barton
Capt. D. P. Bichard
Major G. B. Blaker
Capt. A. R. D. Bolton
Capt. A. P. Boyd
Capt. J. L. Braithwaite
Major J. W. Brehaut
Lieut. B. P. Brooke
Capt. R. Carver
Lieut. P. B. Chambers
Capt. A. H. C. Cock
Lieut. S. Cockburn
Lieut. Conder
Lieut. F. T. R. Cooper
Major E. S. Corbett
Lieut. D. P. Cunningham
Lieut. C. A. Cutress
Major H. R. A. Dartnall
Major A. Du Pre Denning
Lieut. C. S. Dupre
Lieut. C. J. Elcoate
Lieut. B. D. Fick
Capt. E. B. Foster-Moore
Major A. G. Fry
Major G. E. Gower
Major A. A. Grubb
Capt. A. K. Guest
Capt. T. C. M. Hodges
Major M. H. Hutchinson
Capt. W. H. Hyde
Lieut. S. W. Jary
Major D. Jenkins
Major R. King, M.B.E.
Major G. D. Knight
Lieut. C. W. W. Lake
Major J. L. G. Littlejohns
Lieut.-Colonel P. H. Man
Capt. W. R. B. May
Major F. Mitchell, D.S.O.
Major C. J. G. Mumford
Lieut.-Colonel H. D. Nelson Smith
W.O.I F. G. Newsom
Lieut. H. F. Nicolle
Lieut. A. G. Oakley
Capt. R. F. D. Pemberton
Capt. J. P. Power
Major D. J. Pullen
Major T. A. Rotherham, D.S.O.
Major P. R. Sawyer
Major R. H. Stevens
2/Lieut. R. R. Stolworthy
Lieut. J. M. Symes
Major J. W. Tinniswood
Major T. G. Tucker
Major M. D. Van Lessen
Major C. G. T. Viner
Major A. N. E. Waldron
Major F. H. Waters
Major J. M. C. Wicks
Lieut. C. Y. Williamson
Major H. E. Wingfield
Major E. G. Wright

Distinguished Conduct Medal

W.O.II B. R. Bell
L./Sergt. J. E. Blackwell
W.O.II W. F. J. Brown, M.M.
Sergt. E. R. Carter
W.O.II T. H. Cooke, M.M.
Sergt. R. F. Curley
Sergt. A. Fry
W.O.II W. E. Greenyer, M.M.
Sergt. A. R. Hopgood
W.O.II W. A. Mayne
W.O.II A. A. McAlister
Sergt. G. Minnigin, M.M.
Pte. F. C. Page
Sergt. L. J. Rawlins
Sergt. J. Savage
Pte. H. Towler
Sergt. N. S. Wynn
Sergt. P. S. York

Military Medal

Pte. J. A. Abramides
Pte. J. Anderson
Pte. N. H. Alexander
Sergt. H. Bailey
Pte. W. A. Baldwin
Cpl. R. E. Banff
Pte. A. J. Barnes
Pte. H. C. Barrett
Pte. J. C. Baxter
Sergt. A. D. Bennigsen
Sergt. C. F. Bisson
Sergt. H. W. Bowers
L./Sergt. A. R. Bremner
Cpl. S. W. Brooks
L./Sergt. W. F. J. Brown
L./Cpl. R. H. Bryant
L./Cpl. W. R. Butt
L./Sergt. A. W. Carter
Sergt. D. A. Carter
Pte. R. F. Chalmers
L./Cpl. A. Churchill
Sergt. C. R. E. G. Cockram
Sergt. J. H. Connolly
Sergt. T. H. Cooke, D.C.M.

Military Medal—contd.

Pte. D. J. Couzens
L./Sergt. J. E. Cozens
L./Cpl. C. P. Croucher
Cpl. J. C. A. Cull
Pte. A. C. Dean
Pte. L. Deleysin
L./Cpl. A. G. Dunford
Pte. R. V. Earl
Sergt. B. J. Edmonds
Pte. P. Ellis
Pte. A. W. Epps
Cpl. L. W. Etheridge
Pte. H. P. Evans
Pte. G. P. Fox
Cpl. J. J. Franks
Sergt. A. Fry, D.C.M.
L./Cpl. R. J. Fryer
Sergt. E. W. Godfrey
Sergt. T. R. Grant
Pte. A. Hall
Pte. R. E. Hall
Cpl. M. Harman
L./Cpl. J. E. Harris
Cpl. T. Harrison
L./Cpl. G. Haseley
Cpl. A. H. Hawes
Cpl. H. C. Hayball
L./Cpl. E. G. Henry
Cpl. A. J. Higgins
Cpl. A. T. Holloway
L./Cpl. H. Hooper
Sergt. F. T. J. Hughes
Sergt. N. Johnson
L./Cpl. C. Jones
L./Cpl. R. Kingswell
Pte. F. R. Kneebone
Sergt. A. E. Lane
Pte. H. C. Lee
L./Cpl. J. E. Letford
Pte. H. W. Levy
Pte. W. A. Lias
Sergt. A. T. Light
Pte. H. Mackay
W.O.II R. Maclean
Pte. K. H. V. Magson
Sergt. S. D. Medway
Pte. G. Minnigin
L./Cpl. L. Money
Sergt. P. Murfitt
Sergt. S. Mussell
Sergt. M. Nolan
Sergt. A. E. Norman
Pte. C. T. Nunn
Sergt. W. G. Olive
Pte. E. R. Osborne
Sergt. C. A. Parris
L./Cpl. D. E. Peirce
Pte. E. J. Peters
Pte. R. J. Playford
Pte. M. Pook
L./Sergt. A. R. Powell
L./Sergt. F. Price
W.O.II W. F. Pullinger
Sergt. W. Reddall
Pte. J. L. Roberts
Pte. D. R. Robins
L./Sergt. B. W. J. Roe
Sergt. E. G. Savage
Sergt. G. Scott
Cpl. J. W. Scott
L./Sergt. M. J. Shannon
Pte. L. J. Shepherd
Sergt. A. E. C. Sippets
Sergt. G. J. B. Slade
Pte. E. J. Smith
Pte. K. A. Smith
Pte. R. G. Spencer
Cpl. A. Soles
L./Sergt. R. J. Stevens
L./Cpl. A. A. Stoner
Sergt. C. H. Taylor
Pte. A. G. F. Thorne
Cpl. W. A. Touzel
Cpl. J. G. Vine
L./Cpl. V. L. Waller
L./Cpl. L. J. Webb
L./Cpl. W. Weedy
Sergt. J. D. H. White
L./Sergt. K. M. Wiggins
Pte. V. E. Willmott
Sergt. D. H. Wilton
Pte. W. T. Winter
Sergt. W. G. Wise
Pte. F. A. Woodward
Sergt. R. F. Woodward
Pte. S. P. Wynn
L./Sergt. B. Wynne
L./Cpl. G. E. Yates

British Empire Medal

Sergt. A. S. E. Crockford
Pte. H. W. Grainger
Sergt. J. W. Hare
Pte. J. E. Matkin
Sergt. J. E. Maclaren
W.O.II A. J. Rutherford
Pte. F. Smith

Mentioned in Despatches

Pte. F. H. Abel
L./Cpl. A. Adams
Lieut. R. F. Algie
Pte. C. A. Allen
Pte. M. R. Allo
Pte. P. F. Archer
Lieut. V. K. Astafiev
Capt. P. Ayles
Capt. J. F. Baddeley
Major W. Bagnall
Sergt. A. F. Bailey
Pte. P. Ballard
Major J. Barker
Brigadier R. H. Batten, D.S.O.
Major G. W. Becquet
W.O.II W. G. W. Bennett
Sergt. C. F. Bisson
Lieut. L. M. Blackmore
Major (Q.M.) V. A. Blake
L./Cpl. D. Bostock
2/Lieut. G. Bowell
W.O.II H. W. Bowers, M.M.
Pte. W. C. Boxall
Brigadier A. Boyce
W.O.II H. C. Bray
Pte. R. Briant
Cpl. A. W. Bright
Pte. A. Brooks
Brigadier G. D. Browne, O.B.E.
W.O.I G. I. Bugden
L./Cpl. J. R. Byng
L./Cpl. A. V. Carolan
L./Cpl. I. A. B. Carter
Major H. F. L. Castle
W.O.II J. Charnock
L./Sergt. C. Clayton
Pte. R. F. Cliffe
Sergt. C. E. A. Collins
Pte. P. Connally
Lieut.-Colonel F. H. Cotton, M.B.E.
Pte. E. Courthold
Cpl. H. P. Cox
L./Cpl. R. S. Crowe
Cpl. J. Daniels
Major H. R. A. Dartnall, M.C.
Capt. A. T. Davis
Sergt. M. Davis
Sergt. D. Dicks
Pte. R. T. Dight
Lieut. H. V. Dive
Cpl. R. L. Dixon
W.O.I A. E. Dorrell
Sergt. L. G. Drake
Pte. B. G. Drouet
Pte. E. J. Dunn
L./Cpl. G. Dunn
Capt. K. L. Edwards
Sergt. L. Edwards
C.Q.M.S. J. H. Ellis
Pte. W. J. Ellis
Capt. R. L. T. Elwin
L./Cpl. R. C. W. Evans
Capt. W. A. T. Fairbairn
Cpl. J. Farrar
W.O.II S. A. Findlay
Pte. J. E. Fitler
Cpl. A. J. Fitzgerald
L./Sergt. J. J. Flood
Lieut.-Colonel J. P. Fowler-Esson, D.S.O., M.C.
Lieut. A. W. Freemantle
Pte. J. A. E. French
Lieut. J. W. Gardner
Pte. H. Gaskell
Capt. C. B. Gilbert
Pte. A. H. Glass
Lieut. W. R. Golder
Capt. J. E. Gower
Pte. T. W. Graham
Pte. H. W. Grainger, B.E.M.
W.O.II C. E. Gransden
Major B. W. H. Green
L./Cpl. P. Grimes
Major A. A. Grubb, M.C.
Sergt. H. W. Hall
W.O.II E. D. Hankin
L./Cpl. R. Hardy
Major J. M. Harris
Sergt. J. W. Harris
Lieut. J. R. Hart
Pte. W. Harvey
W.O.II J. A. Hawkewell
W.O.II F. M. Haycocks
W.O.II M. A. J. Hayter
Pte. D. Hayward
C.S.M. R. R. H. Heighes
Sergt. H. R. Hills
Lieut. I. R. Hoar
W.O.II K. Hoare
L./Sergt. A. S. Hogben
Pte. W. J. E. Holton
L./Cpl. A. H. Horne
L./Cpl. A. L. Horner
L./Cpl. T. A. Horton
W.O.II J. P. Hosty
Sergt. E. Howe
L./Sergt. R. L. Howell
C.Q.M.S. J. H. A. Hughes
Lieut. P. A. E. Hughes
Pte. C. J. Hurley
W.O.II W. F. Hutchings
Capt. M. H. Hutchinson
Brigadier A. C. F. Jackson, O.B.E.
Major D. Jenkins
L./Cpl. A. H. Johnson
Major H. G. Jointer

Mentioned in Despatches—contd.
C.Q.M.S. A. Jones
L./Cpl. C. Jones, M.M.
Lieut. G. J. Jones
S./Sergt. D. S. Kelly
Pte. M. Kelly
L./Cpl. T. Kenneally
Cpl. G. Kiernan
Major R. King, M.B.E., M.C.
Sergt. L. Klein
Sergt. E. Knight
L./Cpl. G. Knight
Lieut. G. D. Knight
Major T. F. Knott
Pte. J. Lamb
Major R. C. G. Langrishe
Pte. R. W. Leadbitter
Capt. B. H. Leader
Lieut. J. D. Le Brecht
Lieut.-Colonel J. M. Lee, D.S.O.
L./Cpl. R. W. J. Leggett
Lieut. V. T. G. Liles
Lieut. B. N. P. Lister
Pte. P. A. Lombardi
Capt. C. Q. Loveless
Cpl. A. W. J. Lovelock
C./Sergt. A. P. Lyon
Capt. J. H. Lytle
Capt. F. M. McFarland
Pte. W. McIntosh
Cpl. H. J. MacLachlan
Sergt. J. E. Maclaren
L./Sergt. F. W. Mansfield
L./Cpl. J. Marshall
L./Cpl. G. C. Martin
Pte. S. Martin
Pte. E. Mathews
Sergt. A. V. Meech
Pte. E. F. Millard
Lieut. K. J. Milroy
L./Cpl. K. Mitchell
Lieut.-Colonel F. Mitchell, M.C.
W.O.II C. J. Moore
Sergt. W. R. Moysey
W.O.I F. G. Newsom
Capt. (Q.M.) C. A. Northmore
Lieut. A. G. Oakley
Brigadier C. C. Oxborrow, C.B.E., M.C.
Sergt. A. L. Page
Capt. B. P. Page
Cpl. G. Paige
Sergt. R. V. Paine
C.Q.M.S. A. W. Pamment
Pte. E. T. Parker
Lieut. R. C. Parkin
Sergt. S. J. Patten
W.O.I D. W. Payne
Major R. D. Pead
Capt. H. W. Pedrick
Major M. L. G. Pennington
Capt. R. J. Pennington
Cpl. A. G. Phillips
Pte. D. Phillips
Pte. W. L. Phillips
Pte. G. J. Pinsard
Major H. B. Portsmouth
Pte. C. E. Powell
L./Sergt. C. L. Prangle
Lieut. G. A. Pritchard
W.O.II W. F. Pullinger, M.M.
L./Cpl. A. J. Pyke
Sergt. E. F. Queripel
Major H. N. Raisin
Lieut. G. A. F. Ramsden
Major-General W. H. C. Ramsden, C.B.E., D.S.O., M.C.
Pte. F. Richards
L./Cpl. L. A. Riddle
Cpl. C. R. Robinson
Lieut. M. P. L. Roche
Sergt. F. H. Rolls
Lieut.-Colonel T. A. Rotherham, D.S.O., M.C.
Sergt. A. Ryder
Cpl. E. T. Salter
Pte. A. S. F. Sankey
Major P. R. Sawyer
Pte. H. Searle
Lieut. L. N. Smith
Sergt. N. Smith
Lieut.-Colonel C. C. Smythe, O.B.E., M.C.
Sergt. E. W. J. Snook
Cpl. A. Soles
Brigadier J. L. Spencer, D.S.O., O.B.E., M.C.
Pte. C. P. Spiers
W.O.I A. B. Stevens
Major R. H. Stevens, M.C.
Capt. (Q.M.) A. B. Stone, M.B.E.
Major P. G. Street, M.B.E.
Sergt. G. W. Strugnell
Major A. S. T. Swan
Pte. W. Swancott
Major F. J. S. Symes
W.O.II L. R. Symes
C.Q.M.S. E. Tasker
L./Cpl. F. H. Taylor
Sergt. D. Tesch
2/Lieut. C. H. Thomas
Major C. L. Thomas
Pte. A. Tilley
Pte. D. Tindale
L./Cpl. F. J. Tocock
W.O.II E. G. A. Turner
Capt. V. Vibert
Cpl. F. C. Vinson
Sergt. L. J. H. Vining
Capt. R. Wakeford
Major A. N. E. Waldron
Pte. P. L. Walker

Mentioned in Despatches—contd.

W.O.I A. E. Ware
Lieut. R. T. Warner
L./Cpl. W. J. Waters
Pte. J. J. Watt
Sergt. K. H. Watts
W.O.II H. W. Watts
Capt. W. C. T. N. Way
L./Sergt. A. R. Weeks
Lieut.-Colonel E. C. C. Wells
C.Q.M.S. C. Wheeler
Capt. K. M. White
Lieut.-Colonel J. M. C. Wicks
Lieut. J. M. Williams
Pte. G. A. W. Wilson
Pte. R. Wilson
Pte. L. Wingham
Sergt. W. W. Wood
Sergt. R. Woodling
W.O.II W. T. Woodward
Major E. G. Wright, M.C.
Lieut.-Colonel E. C. Yeldham
Cpl. C. S. T. Young

INDEX

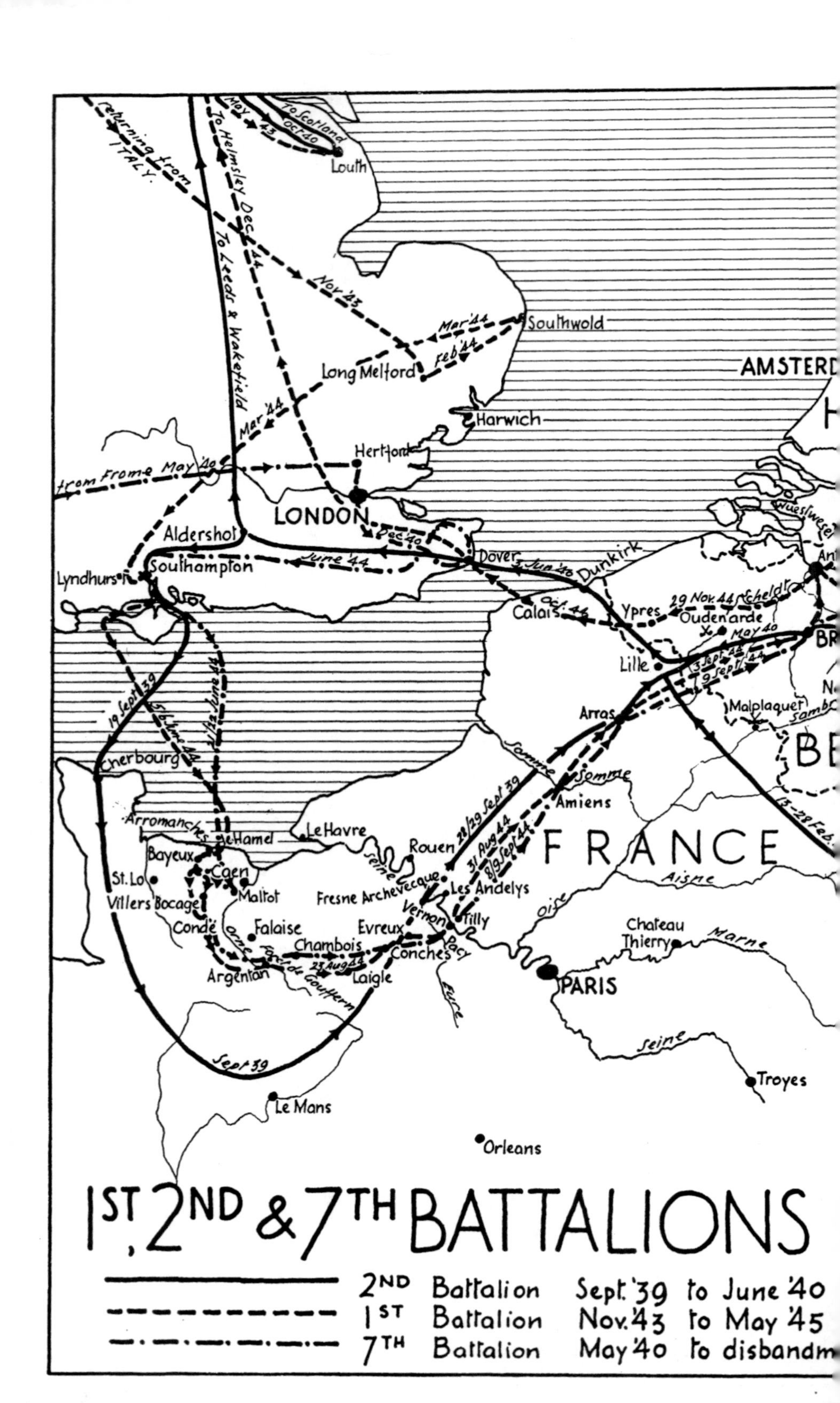

Returning from ITALY
To Helmsley Dec '44
May 43
To Scotland Oct 40
Louth
To Leeds & Wakefield
Nov '43
Southwold
Mar '44
Feb '44
Long Melford
Mar '44
AMSTERD
Harwich
Hertford
from Frome May '40
LONDON
Aldershot
Dec '40
Dover
3 Jun '40
Dunkirk
June '44
Lyndhurst
Southampton
Calais
Oct 44
Ypres
29 Nov. 44
Scheldt
Oudenarde
May 40
Lille
13 Sept 44
9 Sept 44
Malplaquet
Sambre
Arras
19 Sept 39
5/6 June 44
7/12 June 44
Cherbourg
Somme
Amiens
28/29 Sept 39
31 Aug 44
8/9 Sept 44
13-28 Feb.
Arromanches
Le Hamel
Le Havre
Rouen
FRANCE
Bayeux
Caen
St. Lo
Maltot
Villers Bocage
Fresne Archevecque
Les Andelys
Seine
Aisne
Oise
Vernon
Tilly
Condé
Falaise
Evreux
Chateau Thierry
Marne
Chambois
Conches
Pacy
Argentan
Forêt de Gouffern
23 Aug 44
Laigle
PARIS
Eure
Orne
Sept 39
Seine
Le Mans
Troyes
Orleans
1ST, 2ND & 7TH BATTALIONS
2ND Battalion Sept. '39 to June '40
1ST Battalion Nov. '43 to May '45
7TH Battalion May '40 to disbandm

HAMBURG
Bremerhaven
Gnarrenburg
Elbe
Winsen
Luneburg
Glinstedt
Bremen
14 May 45
25 Apr 45
13 Apr 45
Cloppenburg
Bawinkel
BERLIN
GERMANY
Hengelo
Enschede
Minden
Hannover
Weser
Mar. - Jun.46
Magdeburg
Burgsteinfurt
Ems
Munster
Wesel
Ruhr
THE RUHR
Leipzig
Bonn
Rhine
Dettingen
Main
Halstroff
Saarbrucken
Blenheim
Danube
Ulm
Munich
ORTH-WEST EUROPE
SCALE MILES
50 40 30 20 10 0 50 100 150 200

Printed in the United Kingdom
by Lightning Source UK Ltd.
127366UK00002B/49-99/A